God's Peace on the Glory Road

Other Books about Bill's Journey

Yes, God! Volume 1

Daily Devotionals

Our Walk of Faith: The Journey to Bill's Healing
God's Grace on the Winding Road: The Journey to Bill's Healing

Miracle Man Trilogy

#1 Musings of the Miracle Man: Words of Wisdom Words of Hope
#2 Adventures of the Miracle Man: Dreams, Visions & Miracles
#3 Lessons of the Miracle Man: Wit, Wisdom & Wonder (Coming February 2022)

God's Peace on the Glory Road: Our Journey to Healing

Barbara Hollace

Published by Hollace House Publishing Spokane Valley, Washington

For more information or to contact the author: barbara@barbarahollace.com
Website: www.barbarahollace.com

Book layout/Cover design: Ann Mathews
Book editing: Barbara Hollace, www.barbarahollace.com
Book Cover photograph: Azores, Portugal iStock.com Line Drawings:
Couple: Illustration 135760384 © Ahmad Safarudin Dreamstime.com
Praying Woman: Shuttercock.com

ISBN: 978-1-7345159-8-5

Printed in the United States of America

Dedication

This book is dedicated to my mom, Judy J. Knudsen, and my husband, Bill Hollace, who God called home to heaven in 2020. And to all of you who had to say good-bye to friends, family, and loved ones too soon.

Acknowledgments

First and foremost, God deserves all the praise, honor, and glory for guiding us through this life adventure. Bill and I wouldn't have made it without Him.

Thanks to my family for all your love and support, not only through this book, but all my life adventures, which have been many, with more yet to come.

To the countless prayer warriors that stood with us through Bill's health challenges ~our family, church family, friends, and worldwide prayer team, your prayers and words of encouragement kept us afloat.

To Ann Mathews, thank you for your willingness to work with me on this devotional series. Not only for the book layout but for this book's cover design. You are a treasure from the Lord.

To Pastors Dave and Alice Darroch, thank you for your prayers and teaching us to believe in miracles.

God has blessed me with several women who have walked closely by my side through my own health adventure, Andrea, Cherelle, Kelly, and Mary, and so many more who have become my weekly prayer partners. We are better together.

Special thanks to my dear husband, Mr. Bill, my forever love. I am blessed to be your wife and to be given the honor of sharing our story for God's glory. Thank you, Bill, for showing us how to live above the circumstances of our lives as we walk hand in hand with God. He will never leave us or forsake us.

Introduction

"We are a team, we are in this together."

Journeys have a beginning and an end. This book is about both endings and new beginnings.

If you have just discovered this devotional series, let me introduce you to the main characters. We are Bill and Barb Hollace – ordinary people that God called to walk an extraordinary path.

My husband, Bill, walked through an intense storm of health issues that began on January 10, 2018. From the moment the curtain opened, Bill was diagnosed with pneumonia and his heart was in afib (atrial fibrillation.) Three days later, he was diagnosed with Influenza A, and the next morning had a brain bleed.

That brought us to the second hospital where Bill had surgery to remove the pool of blood in his brain. There are too many details to explain here, but our initial journey covered five and a half months, in five hospitals and a skilled care facility in two states. Several surgeries including brain surgery, a pacemaker, heart stents, and an aortic valve replacement. And more than one life and death moment where God intervened with a miracle, which earned Bill the title, "Miracle Man." Our journey had a greater purpose than the health issues that Bill overcame through God's miraculous healing.

The morning Bill entered the hospital God started me on another path that would give even greater meaning to this adventure. Every morning God knew that I needed heavenly manna to sustain me. He would direct me to a specific Bible passage and then "feed" me with new revelation and how it pertained to our journey. Every day I posted them on Facebook, because my blessings were for others too.

Our friend, Evelyne Ello-Hart, months into our journey shared that I should bring these devotions together into a book. I was surprised by her suggestion, but later understood it was exactly what God had in mind.

In the early days of 2020, two years after we started this journey, the first daily devotional was born, "Our Walk of Faith." December 2020, the second book, "God's Grace on the Winding Road" was released. And now you hold my third "book baby" in this series in your hands, "God's Peace on the Glory Road."

What you will find in the pages ahead include a daily anchor verse from the Bible, and a teaching about the passage, along with a personal note about our journey in those moments. The entries in this book follow the actual days of our journey through 2020, the year that God called Bill home to heaven on

April 19, 2020. In the days that followed, God put my feet on a new path, the Glory Road, where God's glory illuminates my way.

2020 was an eventful year as my mom died in February, my husband died in April, and I was diagnosed with breast cancer in July. That's a lot for a family to process, but God has been faithful through every circumstance.

In the first book of the Miracle Man trilogy, "Musings of the Miracle Man" where I shared Bill's words describing this journey, there were many great gems that typified Bill's wisdom and sense of humor.

Bill's great attitude throughout his challenges inspired many, beginning with me, his wife, who walked by his side. "Let's do it!" was Bill's daily battle cry. He showed us what it meant to "live life each day."

This book is in your hands because of Bill's love for me, and most of all, God's love for us. Bill's words below illustrate what can happen when two people put God in the center of their marriage and choose to follow Him wherever He leads.

I've turned the corner. We, as a couple, can do anything. I'm not to do it alone but we'll share it together.

This is our "together" gift for you.

Blessings,
Barb

P.S. Just a note that the butterfly on the front cover has some significance to our story. Our lives were forever changed on this journey – transformed by His love. God used a butterfly to illustrate this transformation. In fact, one day while Bill was in the hospital in 2018, God brought a unique butterfly to the window. God showed me this was Bill and that one day Bill's transformation – body, mind, and spirit would be complete. Today Bill is healed and whole in heaven.

January 2020

Taste and see that the Lord is good.
~ Psalm 34:8

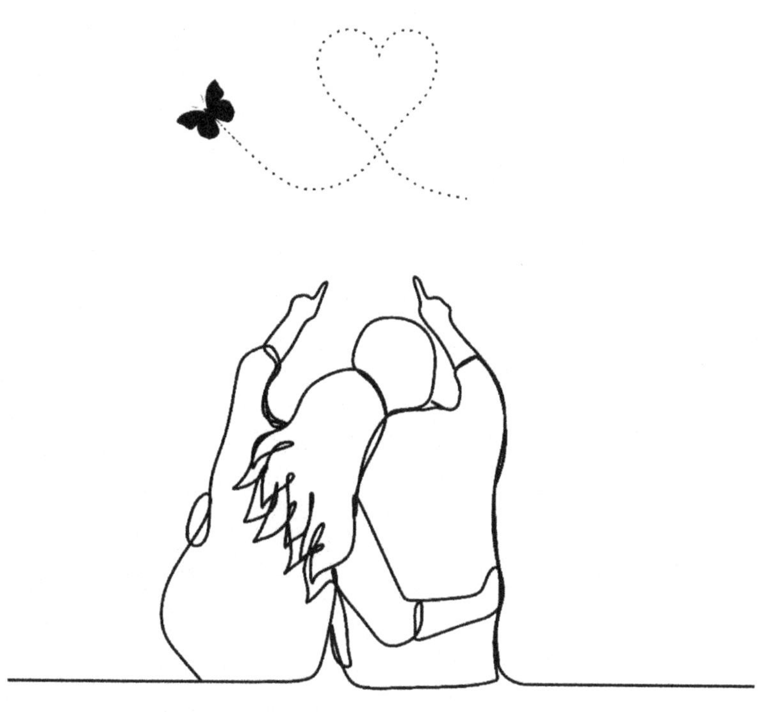

Day #722 January 1

Anchor Verse: Genesis 1:3
And God said, "Let there be light," and there was light. (NIV)

A brand new year lies before us, untainted, untouched, filled with hope and God's good plans for us.

"In the beginning, God created the heavens and the earth." The story may be so familiar to us that we rush through it, not pausing to relish and savor the awe and wonder that surrounds creation.

Every year we see many new products and services. Have we become "numb" to the outstanding achievement that comes with creation?

Today as I began my yearly reading journey through the Bible, I asked the Lord to show me in my "mind's eye" what creation looked like as it unfolded, day after day for those six days.

In the beginning was darkness. I could feel the darkness touch my soul. We all have been in places where it was dark, no street lights, no shopping centers or houses, only dark. Darkness is even greater when it is void of life.

"And God said, 'Let there be light!' and there was light." The very first action of creation was to bring light into the world.

We are carriers of His light as we walk in fellowship and obedience with God. There is no greater light than the light of His love. Its brightness not only extinguishes the darkness but it ignites the flame in others.

On this journey to Bill's healing, we have walked through some dark places, but God's light, the light of His love, the light of life, Jesus, has shone brightly to lead us on our path to victory. We are called to be that light. God's light in us has lit up many hospital rooms and brought hope to others. It is not because of our goodness, but because of God's grace and His resurrection power at work in us.

2020 lies before us. 365 days for God to do the miraculous in our lives as we trust Him and walk in obedience to His commands and plans for our lives.

Thank you for your faithful prayers. Thank you for believing in miracles. May the Lord bless you richly in 2020. #Godisfaithful #pray4bill

Day #723 January 2

Anchor Verse: Acts 4:4

But many who heard the message believed; so the number of men who believed grew to about five thousand. (NIV)

As we start this new year of 2020, the topic of growth is on my mind. As little children, we grow almost automatically.

When God created us, He had a plan of how this helpless child who enters the world will learn how to walk and run, feed themselves, learn right from wrong, and grow into all that God has for them.

Obedience is key for our growth, both as children and adults. We can get distracted or diverted from our path if we follow the wrong people and the wrong advice.

Growth comes when the "good seed" that is planted in us is nurtured and grows. In fact, even as we see the growth of the seeds that are planted in the spring that grow up to be beautiful flowers, or fruits and vegetables, our growth as children of God is like that too.

In the book of Acts, we read about the early church and how it began to grow from a handful of believers to a church that would impact the world of its time, and influence our world today.

This passage in Acts 4 tells us how Peter and John were sharing with the people about the resurrection of Jesus from the dead. The people were moved by what they heard, and five thousand men joined them that day as new believers in Christ.

As God leads us and we walk in obedience, growth will follow. If you are called to a leadership position in your business, church, or home, we must grow ourselves, if we expect our business, church or household to grow.

On this journey to Bill's healing, we have learned about growth, and rebuilding our lives. With God in first place, in every area, we have seen growth in Bill's life and mine too. We look forward to 2020 and God's plan of healing and new direction in our lives.

Thank you for helping us meet our challenges. #Godisfaithful #pray4bill

January 2020

Taste and see that the Lord is good.
~ Psalm 34:8

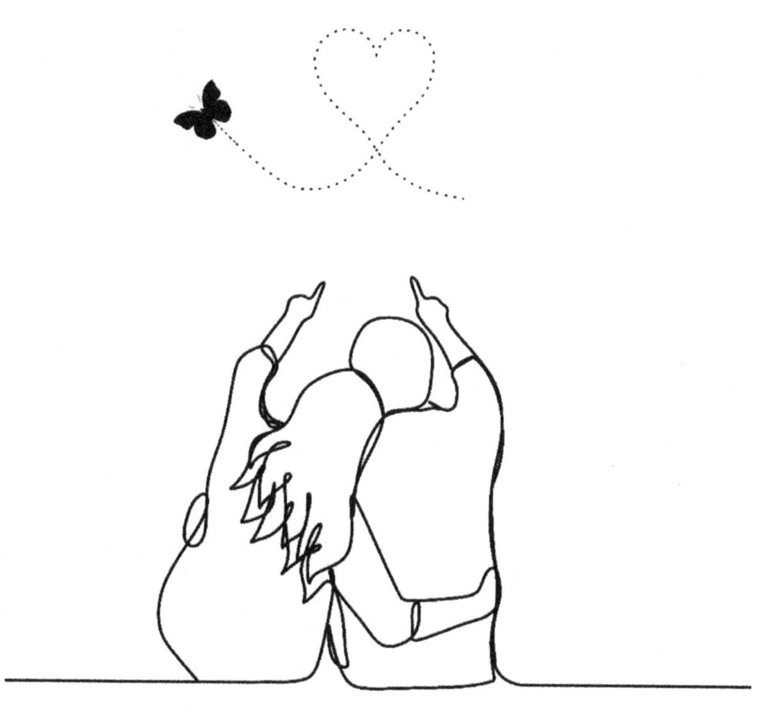

Day #722 January 1

Anchor Verse: Genesis 1:3
And God said, "Let there be light," and there was light. (NIV)

A brand new year lies before us, untainted, untouched, filled with hope and God's good plans for us.

"In the beginning, God created the heavens and the earth." The story may be so familiar to us that we rush through it, not pausing to relish and savor the awe and wonder that surrounds creation.

Every year we see many new products and services. Have we become "numb" to the outstanding achievement that comes with creation?

Today as I began my yearly reading journey through the Bible, I asked the Lord to show me in my "mind's eye" what creation looked like as it unfolded, day after day for those six days.

In the beginning was darkness. I could feel the darkness touch my soul. We all have been in places where it was dark, no street lights, no shopping centers or houses, only dark. Darkness is even greater when it is void of life.

"And God said, 'Let there be light!' and there was light." The very first action of creation was to bring light into the world.

We are carriers of His light as we walk in fellowship and obedience with God. There is no greater light than the light of His love. Its brightness not only extinguishes the darkness but it ignites the flame in others.

On this journey to Bill's healing, we have walked through some dark places, but God's light, the light of His love, the light of life, Jesus, has shone brightly to lead us on our path to victory. We are called to be that light. God's light in us has lit up many hospital rooms and brought hope to others. It is not because of our goodness, but because of God's grace and His resurrection power at work in us.

2020 lies before us. 365 days for God to do the miraculous in our lives as we trust Him and walk in obedience to His commands and plans for our lives.

Thank you for your faithful prayers. Thank you for believing in miracles. May the Lord bless you richly in 2020. #Godisfaithful #pray4bill

Day #723 January 2

Anchor Verse: Acts 4:4

But many who heard the message believed; so the number of men who believed grew to about five thousand. (NIV)

As we start this new year of 2020, the topic of growth is on my mind. As little children, we grow almost automatically.

When God created us, He had a plan of how this helpless child who enters the world will learn how to walk and run, feed themselves, learn right from wrong, and grow into all that God has for them.

Obedience is key for our growth, both as children and adults. We can get distracted or diverted from our path if we follow the wrong people and the wrong advice.

Growth comes when the "good seed" that is planted in us is nurtured and grows. In fact, even as we see the growth of the seeds that are planted in the spring that grow up to be beautiful flowers, or fruits and vegetables, our growth as children of God is like that too.

In the book of Acts, we read about the early church and how it began to grow from a handful of believers to a church that would impact the world of its time, and influence our world today.

This passage in Acts 4 tells us how Peter and John were sharing with the people about the resurrection of Jesus from the dead. The people were moved by what they heard, and five thousand men joined them that day as new believers in Christ.

As God leads us and we walk in obedience, growth will follow. If you are called to a leadership position in your business, church, or home, we must grow ourselves, if we expect our business, church or household to grow.

On this journey to Bill's healing, we have learned about growth, and rebuilding our lives. With God in first place, in every area, we have seen growth in Bill's life and mine too. We look forward to 2020 and God's plan of healing and new direction in our lives.

Thank you for helping us meet our challenges. #Godisfaithful #pray4bill

Day #724 January 3

Anchor Verse: 2 Corinthians 1:13
We are not writing to you in anything resembling codes or riddles; we only write those lessons you are ready to read and understand. I hope you will study them, value them, and truly understand them until the end. (VOICE)

Words are amazing tools that God has given us to convey what we want to say about how we feel, what we think, or even silly things that make us happy. Communication, when it is done well, changes people's lives for the good.

Education has been the foundation for the advancement of civilization from the beginning of time.

When I read this verse from 2 Corinthians 1:13, my author/editor self perked up as I read these words, "We are not writing to you in anything resembling codes or riddles; we only write those lessons you are ready to read and understand. I hope you will study them, value them, and truly understand them until the end."

Writing lessons that people are ready to read and understand brings the greatest value to our writing. Writing in codes and riddles might be "fun" but not everyone's reading ability or interest is at the level of codes and riddles.

As God brought this verse to my attention, I finally "got it." This is the reason why God asked me to write these "Hubby Health Updates" for the last 724 days. It is for the very reason stated in 2 Corinthians 1:13.

On our journey to Bill's healing, God prepared lessons not only for Bill and me to learn, but for you. That's why they are easy to read and understand. And the last portion of this verse is for all of us, God's point: "I hope you will study them, value them, and truly understand them."

What Bill and I have learned on this journey about faith and love and trusting God, and holding on to hope, even when things are tough are God's lessons about life and how to be victorious in Jesus' name. We all are students in God's university where His lessons help us become the men and women of God He knows we can be.

Thank you for never giving up on us. #Godisfaithful #pray4bill

Day #725 January 4

 **Anchor Verse: Deuteronomy 6:13a**
You shall fear [only] the Lord your God; and you shall serve Him [with awe-filled reverence and profound respect]. (AMP)

God is a God of order and not chaos. He created the world and honor is due Him and His holy name.

When we get "out of order", when people say what is "wrong" is "right", and what is "right" is "wrong", things go haywire really fast in your society and your nation.

God knew that mankind needed some parameters to keep them on the straight and narrow path, because our sinful nature is prone to wander. God started with the Ten Commandments, and then in the Old Testament, we read how those commandments were more clearly defined.

As Jesus was tempted in the wilderness by Satan, He used scripture to counter the attacks of the enemy. "It is written…" Jesus gave us a pattern to follow in our own lives.

One of the ways in which the devil "tested" Jesus was when he brought Jesus to a high mountain and showed Him all the kingdoms of the world and their splendor. Matthew 4:9 says, "All this I will give you," he said, "if you will bow down and worship me." Jesus replied, "Away from me, Satan! For it is written, 'Worship the Lord your God and serve him only.'" (verse 10)

When we are in right alignment with the Lord, then our lives are in harmony. The circumstances we face may not always be easy, but we know that with God's help – all things are possible. Yes, ALL things.

Even after walking with the Lord for so many years, I continue to stand in awe and wonder of who He is, what He has done for me and others, and the high calling He has on our lives to do His work here on earth.

On this journey to Bill's healing, we have faced trials and temptations, but through it all, God's way has always been the best way. He will keep you in perfect peace when your mind is focused on Him. (Isaiah 26:3)

As we continue to prepare for Bill's surgery on January 29, we are resting in the Lord, spending time together, and watching Bill's health improve.

Thank you for your words of encouragement. #Godisfaithful #pray4bill

Day #726 January 5

Anchor Verse: Matthew 5:7
Blessed [content, sheltered by God's promises] are the merciful, for they will receive mercy. (AMP)

We all will encounter times in our lives when we need others to be merciful to us. What does it mean to be merciful? The dictionary defines it as compassion or forbearance shown especially to an offender or to one subject to one's power or a blessing that is an act of divine favor or compassion. The second definition refers to when we ask God to have mercy on us.

Matthew 5 is commonly referred to as the Sermon on the Mount and these first few verses are the "Beatitudes." These are the blessings that come when we follow Christ's instructions. As the Amplified version says, we will be blessed, content, and sheltered by God's promises when we follow them.

When I think about a person who is compassionate, full of compassion, it brings to mind those who draw near to us as we go through difficult circumstances. Their source of compassion is the Lord and their hearts are sensitive to the pain and distress that others are walking through.

They are not indifferent to the pain and suffering of others, but instead are drawn to them like a moth to the light. A compassionate heart beats with the love of God but has also learned boundaries so they are not overwhelmed by the sorrow and problems of others.

Jesus promises that those who are merciful (filled with compassion) will themselves receive mercy. It's the law of sowing and reaping that Jesus talks about throughout His teachings.

What we give, we will receive in return. If we are judgmental, prickly, give no mercy, legalistic, that is the same measure we will receive when we ourselves encounter troubles in our own lives.

On this journey to Bill's healing, we have encountered people, both inside and outside of the medical community, who have acted with hearts filled with compassion. When your world comes crashing down around you, these are the moments you need an extra measure of mercy and grace. Because of God's mercy, I am able to extend mercy to others.

Thank you for your compassion. #Godisfaithful #pray4bill

Day #727 January 6

Anchor Verse: John 13:4-5
So he [Jesus] got up from the meal, took off his outer clothing, and wrapped a towel around his waist. After that, he poured water into a basin and began to wash his disciples' feet, drying them with the towel that was wrapped around him. (NIV)

Jesus came to serve not to be served, and He set an example that we should follow in His steps. In Matthew 20:28, the Bible says, "The Son of Man did not come to be served, but to serve, and to give his life as a ransom for many."

Do you find it easy to serve others or do you want to be served?

As a leader, Jesus showed us how to put others first. Not only to His disciples, but to the crowds that came to see Him, Jesus showed them the most excellent way to live. Whether He was in the "front of the room" giving the message that would change lives or healing the sick or restoring people to a right relationship with God or walking on a dusty road to their next destination, Jesus' heart was always to put others first.

Jesus wasn't afraid to get His hands dirty. There was no task too big or too small for Him. Whether that was making sure the people had food to eat to feed their flesh or to serve them spiritual food to nourish their souls, Jesus was willing to meet that need and show others how they could be of service.

His message is the same for us. We are called to be servant leaders. We are called to "wash each other's feet." This doesn't necessarily mean "literally" washing their feet, but we can serve each other in so many ways.

On this journey to Bill's healing, I have learned the blessing of being a caregiver to my husband. God can stretch you and provide all that you need to do what you have never done previously or may seem outside your skillset. God has blessed us greatly in the process and our love for each other has grown exponentially. There is no greater love than to serve others and be Jesus' hands and feet.

Wherever God is calling you to serve, serve with compassion and humility. Blessings will blossom in the most difficult circumstances.

Thank you for the many ways you have "served" us.

Thank you for loving us from around the world. We are so blessed.
#Godisfaithful #pray4bill

Day #728 January 7

Anchor Verse: Genesis 19:17
...Don't look back! (NIV)

There are times in our lives when God specifically directs our path. Often these are times of crisis where action is imperative and questioning the directions is not an option.

As human beings, adults or children, if we are told "not" to do something, it seems all our attention is turned toward doing it. Maybe it started with Eve in the Garden of Eden and not eating from the forbidden tree.

In Genesis 19, we read the story of Lot and his family who were living in bad surroundings. Sodom and Gomorrah were slated for destruction. But God in His mercy was willing to save Lot and his family. Lot had a difficult time convincing his family that they needed to leave "NOW!" In fact, the angels the Lord sent had to grab Lot and his wife and daughters by the hand to get them out of the city before God's destruction came.

Once they were outside the city, this is what the angels told Lot and his family, "Flee for your lives… And don't look back. Escape to the mountains. Don't stay down here on the plain or you will die."

The instructions were simple and clear. Yet, as they were fleeing the city, Lot's wife looked back. And in verse 26, we read the consequences of her actions, "She became a pillar of salt."

On this journey to Bill's healing, God has asked us to leave the past behind. Some of the things that used to be part of our lives won't be in the future. We are often reminded by others of the "new normal" that comes after a catastrophic event in our lives.

Our best days are still ahead of us. We need to keep our eyes on the Lord and "don't' look back." May you have the courage to do the same.

Thank you for holding up our arms. #Godisfaithful #pray4bill

Day #729 January 8

Anchor Verse: Matthew 6:27
Can any one of you by worrying add a single hour to your life? (NIV)

Worrying is a fruitless endeavor. What have any of us gained by worrying about life? The medical professionals would tell you that many of our illnesses and chronic diseases have worry and stress at their roots.

Jesus put it very simply, "Can any one of you by worrying add a single hour to your life?" The New King James version puts it even more bluntly, "… can you add a cubit to your stature?" Can you make yourself taller? There would be some really tall people if that were true.

God gave a friend of mine the creative idea to "burn off" some of her anxiety by doing bead work and then selling her products to boost her income.

Philippians 4:6 says, "Do not be anxious or worried about anything, but in everything [every circumstance and situation] by prayer and petition with thanksgiving, continue to make your [specific] requests known to God." (AMP) Talk to God about everything and thank Him when He answers your prayers.

The result is peace that passes ALL understanding.

On this journey to Bill's healing, we have encountered many difficult circumstances. There have been many times that "worry" seemed to be the best reflex action. As a believer in God and knowing God's track record, instead of worrying, I have chosen to trust God with every circumstance, every need, every moment.

When the load seemed more than I could handle, first, I would turn to God, and second, I called in reinforcements to pray with me for Bill. In the earliest moments of Bill's illness, my first phone call was to our pastors to enlist their prayer support. Through this journey, I have learned that bold prayers are the key to opening the blessings of heaven.

Thank you for carrying our burdens to the Lord. #Godisfaithful #pray4bill

Day #730 January 9

Anchor Verse: Psalm 25:20-21
Guard my life and rescue me; do not let me be put to shame, for I take refuge in you. May integrity and uprightness protect me, because my hope, Lord, is in you. (NIV)

When we are in the middle of life's battles, there is only one place to run and that is into the arms of our heavenly Father. There is no power on earth that can stand against Lord God Almighty and be successful.

In Psalm 25, King David is crying out to the Lord to protect him from his enemies. As we read about David's journey in the Bible, we know that King David was all too familiar with people coming against him. Whether that was King Saul before David even ascended to his leadership position or the armies of other people that fought against the Israelites under David's command.

Let's look at what David says. "Guard my life and rescue me." This prayer is our prayer as I ask the Lord to send His angels to guard, guide, and protect us on our journey to Bill's healing. And rescue you when you are in trouble, and not be put to shame, because you have taken refuge in the Lord.

As part of the family of God, God tells us to run to Him in our day of trouble. That is the first place we should go. Crying out to my heavenly Father, whether in the hospital, at home while waiting for the ambulance to arrive, or in the darkness of the night, has always been my best move. The Lord will move on your behalf the moment you cry out to Him. Your heavenly Father is moved with compassion when His children are in distress.

Living our life with integrity builds a solid foundation on which to stand in our day of trouble. I would echo David's words, "My hope is in you, Lord."

On this journey to Bill's healing, we have faced storms and "enemies" and through it all, God has protected us, our unwavering hope has been in God alone. As we walk in integrity and honesty, the light of the love of God radiates from us and others can see Him at work in our lives.

Thank you for your faithfulness in prayer.

Thank you for joining us on this journey of faith. #Godisfaithful #pray4bill

Day #731 January 10

Anchor Verse: Matthew 8:13

Then Jesus said to the centurion, "Go! Let it be done just as you believed it would." And his servant was healed at that moment. (NIV)

Today is an important day in our lives. Two years, January 10, 2018, at this very hour, Bill was on his way to the hospital because he could hardly breathe. It was the "opening act" in this two-year journey to his healing.

For those of you who have been with us on this whole journey, the litany of troubles included pneumonia (3 times), heart attack, influenza A, brain bleed, and more.

My focus this morning is not about the "bad things" that happened, but instead praising the Lord for the miracles and where we stand today. How much Bill's lungs have improved, and with his latest heart surgery and improved blood flow, that for the last two days while Bill was awake, he didn't need any extra oxygen assistance. That, my friends, is a miracle.

The centurion had that same kind of faith regarding his servant. In fact, Jesus was amazed at this man's faith. The centurion "believed" that Jesus could heal his servant; there was no doubt in his mind.

"And Jesus said to the man, 'Go! Let it be done just as you believed it would.' And his servant was healed at that moment."

We rejoice over this healing miracle but what do we learn from it?

Our faith, our belief in God, our Healer, is what moves the hand of God

God called me to stand in the gap for my husband, to fight for his very life. To believe God's word that Bill would live and not die, even wrestling with a spirit of death, and by the authority and power we have as God's children, speaking life, and hope, and healing over my husband. It has transformed my life and Bill's life.

The story doesn't end with the healing miracle; the miracle is only the beginning of a new life in Christ. Once you have been healed by the hand of God, God will use your life as a testimony to draw others to Him.

Thank you for walking with us. #Godisfaithful #pray4bill

Day #732 January 11

Anchor Verse: Colossians 3:17
Whatever you do [no matter what it is] in word or deed, do everything in the name of the Lord Jesus [and in dependence on Him], giving thanks to God the Father through Him. (AMP)

"Whatever you do in word or deed"... God wants "all" of us – every part of us to walk in obedience to Him. Are you willing to live that way? Are you "all in" in your Christian walk?

As we live our lives, there is a driving force behind what we do. Our lives are built on the foundation of our values, we operate according to our priorities, and the results speak for themselves. As believers in Christ, this verse in Colossians 3:17 reminds us how we should live.

Not only are we to do everything in the name of the Lord Jesus, doing what Jesus would do and how He loves others, but in dependence on Him. We cannot survive on our own in this world without divine help.

The Lord has made me so aware of my need for Him on this journey to Bill's healing. We are limited in our humanity by what we can do and how we do it. When Jesus becomes our Savior, we have a new lease on life, the promise of eternal life with Him. The Bible is filled with instruction about how to live life, as we learn from the examples of others.

In the last part of the verse, our hearts and lives are to be filled with thankfulness, gratitude to God our Father. Living each day with gratitude changes our outlook. It allows us to rise above our circumstances and see our lives from God's perspective.

When we are going through life's challenges, be they physical, mental, emotional, or spiritual, we have heavenly help to guide us. The Holy Spirit is our Comforter and directs us step by step. Our heavenly Father who loves us unconditionally is always available for us to seek wisdom and counsel, and run into His arms of love to be comforted. And Jesus has shown us the way to navigate our lives on earth, even when trouble comes, for He has overcome the world.

Thank you for your faithful prayers. With winter weather keeping us inside, Bill and I are tucked into God's arms of love. #Godisfaithful #pray4bill

Day #733 January 12

Anchor Verse: Psalm 37:7
Quiet your heart in his presence and wait patiently for Yahweh. (TPT)

Being quiet, being still can be challenging for most people; it's been that way since we were babies. Even in their mother's womb, children are in motion.

If you notice, many times in the Bible God talks about quieting our hearts, coming into His presence and resting in Him. "In quietness and confidence shall be your strength." (Isaiah 30:15 NKJV)

Many years ago I learned the necessity of spending time with God as soon as I get up in the morning, reading His Word, praying, and listening for His voice. While our home is still quiet, and so is the neighborhood, there is a sense of holiness. It is a sacred time, a sacred space with the Creator of the universe, who is my heavenly Father. I can almost reach out and touch the power of His presence around me. It's beautiful.

God is with us in the noise of life, but it's more difficult to hear that still small voice when you are trying to cross the street in downtown Manhattan at rush hour than it is to hear His voice beside a babbling brook on a sunny day on a mountain peak.

We can't always quiet the world around us, but with the Lord we can delve deep into our soul and "drop down" into His presence and feel His peace.

On this journey to Bill's healing, I have learned the importance of spending time with the Lord in quietness, not only when I am wound up. It's like the breathing technique they taught Bill. Breathe in deeply through your nose (like you are smelling roses) and then blow out through your mouth (like you are blowing out birthday candles.) This helps increase the oxygen saturation levels in your blood and also calms your breathing. It helps to do it before you go to sleep, too. Three times and often you are fast asleep.

We have entered into our second year on this journey to Bill's healing. It has been a long trek. Our terrain has ranged from sheer cliffs to green pastures and still waters. We have been on the mountaintop of victory and walked through the valley of the shadow of death. Through it all, our hope has been kept alive as we trusted in God knowing that He would come through for us and complete Bill's healing.

Thank you for keeping hope alive in your hearts. #Godisfaithful #pray4bill

Day #734 January 13

Anchor Verse: Matthew 9:21
If I only touch his cloak, I will be healed. (NIV)

Desperate for their healing, people through the ages have gone to great lengths to find help.

In Matthew 9, we read of the woman who had been bleeding for twelve years, who didn't want to "bother" Jesus but knew this was her chance to be healed. She must have been exhausted and weary. Yes, she was desperate for her healing. "If I only touch his [Jesus'] cloak, I will be healed."

As Jesus had started to walk away, she saw her chance. It may have been a desperate lunge as she tried to push her way through the crowd. Then Jesus turned, and His eyes of compassion met hers. Her healer was standing before her, He knew it and so did she.

"Take heart, daughter, your faith has healed you." In that moment, the woman was healed. Not hours later or take this medicine and you will be well, but in that moment, her twelve years of pain and agony were gone.

Her life was forever changed. Jesus had touched and healed her from the inside out. Forever, she would see Jesus' eyes of compassion.

On this journey to Bill's healing, we have faced many moments when life and death were a breath apart. I have been like this woman – one touch from His hand and Bill's body would be restored, reclaimed from the jaws of death. God heard my prayer, your prayers, and spared Bill's life.

There are still parts that need to be mended to complete Bill's healing. In sixteen days, Bill will have heart valve surgery, one step closer. We wait in anticipation for the completion of Bill's healing, and praise the Lord for the gift of life and God's hand of protection over us.

Thank you for your prayers of faith. #Godisfaithful #pray4bill

Day #735 January 14

Anchor Verse: Philippians 1:9

My prayer for you is that you will overflow more and more with love for others, and at the same time keep on growing in spiritual knowledge and insight. (TLB)

God's desire for us is that we would grow both internally and externally in our relationship with Him. That His love for us would overflow into more and more love for others. At the same time, we continue to grow in spiritual knowledge and insight – being fed by God's Word.

As children grow, we make sure that every area receives the needed resources so they mature physically, mentally, emotionally, and spiritually. We need to provide the "fuel" for growth, but thankfully God has put systems in place that help us grow.

More and more I stand in awe of the God who created us. His ways are higher than our ways. God knew exactly which systems needed to be put on auto-pilot or otherwise we would be in big trouble.

We often forget "little" things in our life, I'm so glad God didn't put us in charge of making sure that our heart's beat on schedule or that our lungs are filled with oxygen. Thank you, Lord, that you are our Creator.

How do we show our love for others? There are many ways, not only words but through our deeds. Sometimes a listening ear is needed or to hold a person in your arms when they are going through a tough time, being Jesus with "skin" on. Most of all that the love of Jesus would flow through our words and our lives would reflect not only His love, but integrity and honor.

Our own spiritual growth is very important. We can't give from an empty well. We must be rooted and grounded in the Lord and that comes from spending time in the Bible and in fellowship with other believers. Proverbs 27:17 says, "As iron sharpens iron, so one person sharpens another." What a blessing as believers to help each other in our Christian walk as we learn and grow together.

On this journey to Bill's healing, we have had the opportunity to share God's love with others and also grow in the knowledge of the Lord and His ways. Our walk with the Lord has become deeper and wider. Our love for others has increased as God has so freely poured His love into us.

Thank you for your fervent prayers. #Godisfaithful #pray4bill

Day #736 January 15

Anchor Verse: Psalm 73:26b
God is…my portion forever. (NIV)

Coming out of the starting gate in the morning, we often have a plan, a list, a whole bunch of things we want to accomplish. Unfortunately, that's not always the way it works. Well, often that's not what happens.

We have good intentions but one small misstep and everything is thrown off-kilter. Maybe you overslept or the dog ran away or one of your children can't find their homework. What was supposed to be a peaceful, orderly entrance into the day turns into a whirlwind, sometimes more like a tornado.

About mid-morning you try for a reset, but then your computer isn't cooperating, the internet is down, and the phone is busy when you call customer support or you are #45 in the queue.

Are you totally frustrated by this time? Your peace has been stolen and the grumbling has started to rumble.

When your plans are spinning out of control, stop for a moment. Take a deep breath and thank the Lord that He is control of our lives. You can thank God that the character quality of self-control or patience or peace is being sharpened in your life. Our attitude is half the battle.

On this journey to Bill's healing, there have been many days when my plans were not God's plans. Through these last 736 days, I have learned to make tentative plans and hold them in my open hand offering them as a sacrifice of praise to the Lord every morning. There are days His plans are to accomplish far more than I could ever imagine. Other days spending time with Bill in quietness and rest are exactly what the Great Physician orders.

How about you? Have you learned to trust God with your day? Have you learned to praise Him when things don't go "your way?" This morning let us praise the Lord that He is in control of our lives. There is no safer place.

Two years ago, Bill had a brain bleed. God reminds me that the past does not dictate the future. That is history, God continues to write our future and it is good.

Thank you for your faithfulness. Your prayers have moved the hand of God. #Godisfaithful #pray4bill

Day #737 January 16

Anchor Verse: Genesis 39:5
The Lord blessed the household of the Egyptian because of Joseph. The blessing of the Lord was on everything Potiphar had, both in the house and in the field. (NIV)

When the blessing of the Lord is on our lives, as believers, it spills out to those who surround us. It's like His glory, His radiance, His love; we can't hide the light of the love of Jesus Christ.

The story of Joseph in the Old Testament is one of my favorites. It is such a great reminder that even in times of adversity the Lord is with us. When others have "done us wrong" or the enemy has come against us, we can be assured that the God of justice will balance the scales in our favor.

In the beginning of chapter 39, it says that when Joseph was taken down to Egypt, Potiphar, captain of the guard, bought Joseph. "The Lord was with Joseph so that he prospered, and he lived in the house of his Egyptian master." (Genesis 39:2)

What a great reminder for us today that even when the enemy means our circumstances, our troubles for evil that God will use them for the good. Joseph had been betrayed by his brothers, yet God was with him in this foreign land. Not only did Joseph prosper, but so did Potiphar. The Passion translation says, "All his household affairs began to run smoothly, his crops flourished and his flocks multiplied."

Joseph was not removed from his difficult circumstances immediately. God didn't return him to his family, but instead God used Joseph to accomplish God's will, God's plan so that many lives would be saved.

Maybe you find yourself in a difficult situation that is not of your choosing. You are feeling rejected and betrayed. It is definitely not your "happy place." Even in the midst of this adversity, God is with you and will prosper you. The end will be better than the beginning.

On this journey to Bill's healing, even when we found ourselves in the most desperate circumstances, the Lord was there. His mercy and grace paved the way for favor with men and God. His light points the way to His blessings.

Thank you for praying. Thank you for sacrificing your sleep. May the favor of the Lord rest upon you this day. #Godisfaithful #pray4bill

Day #738 January 17

Anchor Verse: Zechariah 13:9
I will refine them like silver and test them like gold. They will call on my name and I will answer them; I will say, 'They are my people,' and they will say, 'The LORD is our God.' (NIV)

God's refining fire is not a place of punishment; it is an honor and privilege to find yourself there. An object or person is only refined if potential is seen in them.

Gold and silver are refined to improve their purity, their quality. They are "precious" metals. We don't throw just any "rock" in the refining fire. The refining process has a purpose, as God has a purpose for refining us.

We often equate our trials and tribulations with the refining fire. It is in those difficult circumstances of life that we test our foundation, the rock on which we stand. As believers, our foundation is Jesus Christ, who has overcome the world. We can hold on to His hand as we go through the deep valleys and as we stand on the truth of God and His promises in the Bible.

This verse in Zechariah 13:9 tells us, "I will refine them like silver and test them like gold. They will call on my name and I will answer them; I will say, 'They are my people,' and they will say, 'The Lord is our God.'"

Look at God's promises. Yes, He will refine His people like silver and test us like gold, but when we call on His name, He will answer us. God answers you when you call on His name. Not only when you are going through the refining fire, but daily, hourly, day or night, God hears you and answers.

He will say, "They are my people." You belong to God. He will carry you through your trials and God will fight for you. God has all the resources of heaven and earth at His command, and by His word, they are dispatched. You will find no better protection.

And with our lives – through our actions and our words, we will say, "The Lord is our God." Yes, we will.

On this journey to Bill's healing, we have had many opportunities to share what God has done for us. The fact that Bill has survived all his many medical conditions and episodes is a testimony to God's lovingkindness and His ability to heal. He is the God of miracles.

Thank you for staying through the storm. #pray4bill #Godisfaithful

Day #739 January 18

Anchor Verse: Genesis 45:8
...it was not you who sent me here, but God. (NIV)

Do you ever find yourself in circumstances, in places that are not of your own choosing? In that moment, it may not seem like the change is better.

Often we are quick to put the blame on someone else, in fact, you might even be angry at God for allowing it to happen. It might not feel good or profitable – it just plain hurts.

How do you react? Do you lash out or implode or retreat? Or do you praise God in the storm and choose to see things from a heavenly perspective?

In Genesis 45 and the preceding chapters, we read the story of Joseph and the desperate circumstances he endured. From being attacked by his brothers, sold into slavery, put in prison, and now we find Joseph elevated to the second highest position in Egypt, just below the pharaoh. Only God could have orchestrated a comeback like this.

"...it was not you who sent me here, but God," Joseph said to them. God sent Joseph before them so that many lives could be saved, including Joseph's own family. The brothers then returned home to their father and all of them moved to live in the area with Joseph.

On this journey to Bill's healing, God has graciously given me Joseph's perspective. I rejoice, we both do, that God has called us to walk this road ultimately not only for Bill's good – better health – but for God's glory.

We are two ordinary people that God has used to touch your lives in a way we couldn't have done except for Bill's illness. In one of Bill's eloquent moments he said, "God created my body, I messed it up, and now God is recreating me."

God can use the messes of our lives and turn them into a message. He takes the tests of our lives and turns them into testimonies.

If you find yourself in a "foreign land" or unfortunate circumstances, ask God to show you how it can be for your good and His glory.

Thank you for your persistent prayers. With eleven days until Bill's surgery, we are resting in God's arms of love. #Godisfaithful #pray4bill

Day #740 January 19

Anchor Verse: Matthew 13:23
But he who received seed on the good ground is he who hears the word and understands it, who indeed bears fruit and produces: some a hundredfold, some sixty, some thirty. (NKJV)

Jesus used parables to share lessons with the crowds that followed Him. In order to convey His message regarding the Kingdom of God and right living, Jesus would use something familiar to get their attention. Once they could relate the principle to everyday living, the "seed" that Jesus was sowing found its way into their heart. As with all seed, Jesus' prayer was that it would take root and bear much fruit.

This passage from Matthew 23 is from the familiar parable about the sower and the seed. In the first part of the parable, Jesus shared with the crowd and told the story of the sower and the seed that fell along the path, on rocky places, among the thorns, and finally, good soil. Jesus shared with them the fate of the seed that was sown in each of those places.

His disciples questioned Jesus about why He spoke to the people in parables. Jesus responded, "Because the knowledge of the secrets of the kingdom of heaven has been given to you, but not to them." Jesus wanted them to understand that as His disciples He was teaching them Kingdom principles so they would carry on this message after He was gone.

He then retells the parable showing them that the "seed" is the message about the kingdom of God. This message is very relevant for us today.

I pray that we are the people who receive the "seed" – the message of the Kingdom of God and it falls on good soil – we hear the Word of God, and receive it, and understand it, and then we bear much fruit. Verse 23 also tells us that the harvest will differ from one person to another – some a hundredfold, some sixty, some thirty.

The Living Bible is even more specific: "…understands it and goes out and brings thirty, sixty, or even a hundred others into the Kingdom."

On this journey to Bill's healing, we have not hidden the fact that we are believers, citizens of the Kingdom of God. I pray that the fruit that is seen in our lives, the light of the love of Jesus and the miracles of God will bring others into the Kingdom. This journey is not only about us, it's about you and what God wants to do in your life.

Thank you for planting good seed in our lives. #Godisfaithful #pray4bill

Day #741 January 20

Anchor Verse: Genesis 50:25
...God will surely visit you and take care of you... (AMP)

"God will surely visit you and take care of you." This was Joseph's promise to his brothers and family as he came to the end of his life.

What a great reminder that Joseph had forgiven his brothers completely. There was no bitterness or last words of revenge or ugliness on his deathbed. Joseph was confident that the Lord would look after them as God had watched over Joseph when he was brought to Egypt as a young man.

In the preceding verses, we see that his brothers might not have been as confident about Joseph's forgiveness or maybe it was an issue in their own hearts. In Genesis 50:15-17 it says, "When Joseph's brothers saw that their father was dead, they said, 'What if Joseph holds a grudge against us and pays us back for all the wrongs we did to him?' So they sent word to Joseph, saying, 'Your father left these instructions before he died: 'This is what you are to say to Joseph: I ask you to forgive your brothers the sins and the wrongs they committed in treating you so badly.' Now please forgive the sins of the servants of the God of your father.' When their message came to him, Joseph wept."

The brothers even offered to be Joseph's slaves. And in verse 20, we read the famous passage, "You intended to harm me, but God intended it for good to accomplish what is now being done, the saving of many lives." Joseph had seen what God had done over all these years. Many lives were saved from the extensive famine because Joseph was in the "right place at the right time." There was no bitterness in Joseph's heart toward his brothers. In fact, Joseph took care of his brothers and their children for the rest of his life.

What a beautiful example of forgiveness and how a restored relationship can result after a fracture in a family.

On this journey to Bill's healing, we have been so blessed by the way God visited us and helped us every step of the way. What the enemy meant for evil... all the health challenges...God used for the good that many lives would be touched in the process. We have seen the mighty miracles that came from the hands and heart of God.

Thank you for your faithful prayers. #Godisfaithful #pray4bill

Day #742 January 21

Anchor Verse: Matthew 14:17

They answered, "But all we have is five barley loaves and two fish." (TPT)

Have you ever wondered what it was like to be one of Jesus' disciples? His disciples were hand-picked. They didn't apply for the job. Jesus chose them at their current workplace. Jesus didn't only recruit them, He said, "Come with me today, now."

Jesus and His disciples were always on the move. Often they had no place to lay their head but their needs were always met.

The disciples had private training sessions with Jesus and the miracles often were beyond their comprehension. Jesus could heal the sick by speaking. He had authority like none other they had ever seen.

He wanted them to be part of the miracle. The crowd of over 5000 had gathered to hear Jesus speak and teach. They were hungry. The disciples wanted to send them away to the neighboring villages to get food to eat, Jesus had a different plan.

"They don't need to leave," Jesus responded. "You can give them something to eat."

What? I can see the shocked look on the disciples' faces. They didn't have the supplies or money to feed more than 5000 people. Going through the crowd, the disciples had gathered only five loaves and two fish.

Everyone sat down on the grass and Jesus took the five loaves and two fish and looking up to heaven, Jesus gave thanks and broke the loaves and gave them to the disciples to distribute. The food multiplied… with leftovers.

We will be faced with what seems to be an impossible situation. There won't be enough resources – time, money, supplies to meet the need before us. People waiting for us to fulfill a need, and all we see is our lack.

On this journey to Bill's healing, we have seen the miracles of Jesus. Many times what we had was "not enough" to meet the need. But when we put what we had, sometimes that was only our faith and trust, in Jesus' hands, the miracles sprang forth like water in a dry parched land.

Thank you for your prayers of faith.#pray4bill #Godisfaithful

Day #743 January 22

Anchor Verse: Exodus 4:12
Now go; I will help you speak and will teach you what to say. (NIV)

Have you ever been assigned a task, a mission, a project that you felt unprepared to complete? Like you didn't have the right skills or you weren't brave enough to finish? In fact, you felt overwhelmed.

God directed Moses to return to Egypt to free the Israelites from bondage. The Lord told Moses that He would help him, equip Moses for the task. Moses wasn't so sure.

"I can't speak very well, won't you send someone else? They won't listen to me."

Maybe you have said something similar when God called upon you with an assignment.

These are God's words to Moses, "Now go; I will help you speak and will teach you what to say." These are God's words to us today.

It is in the "going" that God equips us. As we walk in obedience, God will give us the words to speak and teach us what to say and even what to do. Often God does not give us everything we need before we start the race, but as we walk, with each step God will provide.

When we started our journey to Bill's healing on January 10, 2018, we felt ill-equipped as Bill was taken by ambulance to the hospital that morning. Of course, we had no idea that this would be the 743rd day of our journey to Bill's healing, but God did.

God sees the end from the beginning. God knows what He wants to accomplish on the path to completing your assignment for Him. It's not always about the destination; it's often about what we learn on the journey.

Every time we choose to obey the Lord and walk in obedience to His commands we become more like Him. The transformation continues as we say "yes" to God and "no" to the lesser things of this world.

What is God calling you to do? Put your hand in His hand and enjoy the journey. With God all things are possible, ALL things.

Thank you for saying "yes" to God. Thank you for your prayers and your faithfulness. You are loved. #Godisfaithful #pray4bill

Day #744 January 23

Anchor Verse: Matthew 15:16
"Are you still so dull?" Jesus asked them. (NIV)

Teaching others and learning lessons a portion of our life pursuit, whether officially as a "teacher" or as part of life as a parent or grandparent.

Adults teach children, children teach children, even children teach adults – it's the cycle of life. God has given each one of us gifts and talents to share, and then we are encouraged, even commanded, by the Lord to share our wisdom with others.

Sometimes our independent spirit, deaf ears, and gung-ho attitude get us in trouble. It may have caused trouble in school with your teachers as you were growing up, but greater still is the trouble as adults when we stray away from the Lord and His ways.

Today's passage from Matthew 15 is Jesus' responding to Peter's question. Jesus had been teaching the crowd with His disciples present. After the crowd left, His disciples drew closer to ask Jesus some questions. And then Peter said, "Explain the parable to us." It was the proverbial straw that broke the camel's back.

Jesus said, "Even after all that I've taught you, you still remain clueless? (TPT)

He was frustrated, maybe even a little sad, that after all this time His disciples still didn't get it. Every day they saw miracles and heard Jesus teach the crowd. His disciples even had private tutoring sessions with Jesus as He explained things that He shared with no other.

By God's grace, may we seek to understand His teachings and walk in obedience to His word and His ways.

On this journey to Bill's healing, there have been times when the way ahead wasn't clear. Especially in the early days, I fumbled around a bit, and asked the Lord to repeat a lesson. But as we have progressed on this path, I know that God is faithful and I am able to trust Him implicitly, in every circumstance. Trusting Him even when I can't see beyond this moment, I choose to walk in obedience with my hand in His hand.

Thank you for letting your light shine for God. Thank you for your countless prayers, they move mountains in our lives. #Godisfaithful #pray4bill

Day #745 January 24

Anchor Verse: Matthew 15:31
What a spectacle it was! Those who hadn't been able to say a word before were talking excitedly, and those with missing arms and legs had new ones; the crippled were walking and jumping around, and those who had been blind were gazing about them! The crowds just marveled [were amazed] and praised the God of Israel. (TLB)

What happens when God does a miracle? What do people see? How does the crowd respond?

In the New Testament, we have many accounts of Jesus healing people – the lame, blind, deaf, even people raised from the dead. The Bible states the facts about Jesus healing people and then moves on. Matthew 15:31 in the Living Bible translation gives us a more graphic picture.

"What a spectacle it was! Those who hadn't been able to say a word before were talking excitedly, and those with missing arms and legs had new ones; the crippled were walking and jumping around, and those who had been blind were gazing about them!"

Tears of joy fill my eyes as I think of lives that were forever changed, hope that was restored. And for the men and women who had seen darkness for years, their eyes were opened to the breathtaking sight of God's creation with its brilliant colors.

On this journey to Bill's healing, we have been blessed to be the recipients of God's mighty miracles on more than one occasion. In places, God has moved through the hands of doctors and taken the healing to a higher level. At other times, it was the hand of God alone that took Bill from the gates of death and brought him back to life. Forever we will praise His holy name.

What I realized not only here in Matthew but in our own lives, God performed His miracles not only for those who were sick and needed to be healed, but for the crowd, for those of us watching on. God wanted to do a work in our lives too.

But it's not only about what we "receive" when a miracle is done in our lives, in our view, but what we give. We need to make sure that we give praise to God, and all glory and honor to Him.

Thank you for being part of the crowd of witnesses that has seen the miracles God has done in our lives. #Godisfaithful #pray4bill

Day #746 January 25

Anchor Verse: Psalm 32:11
So rejoice in the LORD and be glad, all you who obey him! Shout for joy, all you whose hearts are pure! (NLT)

What does it mean to rejoice? The definition is to feel or show great joy or delight. When was the last time that you "rejoiced" because of something that God did for you?

Rejoicing goes beyond being happy about something. "Great joy" fills your whole mind, body, and spirit. It's like when you ask the one you love to marry you and she says "yes", or the birth of a new baby, or an achievement, or honor you have been seeking for a long time, finally comes to fruition.

On this journey to Bill's healing, it reminds me of the times Bill reached a new milestone. For example, for a man who was sedated for several weeks without much of any movement, for Bill to be awake and able to roll over on his own or when he was able to eat "real food" for the first time, or when Bill could speak again after being intubated and having a trach for so long. The sound of his voice moved me to tears, the voice of the man I love.

Even today, recounting these "miracles", tears of joy fill my eyes and I rejoice in the Lord.

When we walk in obedience to the Lord and His ways, our spirit is filled with joy. Why? Because obedience brings life. When our hearts are pure and we desire God's best for us and others, and we walk uprightly before Him, joy and rejoicing flood our souls.

It's important to stop and remember what God has done for you. We must never forget the goodness of the Lord. When we enter the desert season in our lives, when we go through the wilderness and the storms of life threaten to overcome us, there, too, we must rejoice in the Lord for His love for us.

It might be easier to rejoice and praise the Lord in the good times but the greater joy comes when we still praise Him in the storm.

Thank you for standing with us in both the calm and the storm. Thank you for rejoicing in the God of our salvation for He has done great things for us.

We sing praises to His name this morning. #Godisfaithful #pray4bill

Day #747 January 26

Anchor Verse: 1 Corinthians 12:22
In fact, some parts of the body that seem weakest and least important are actually the most necessary. (NLT)

Our bodies are one of the most amazing aspects of all creation. God, the Creator of the universe, created us in His image that we might reflect His glory. We rarely give it a second thought that our hearts will continue beating, our legs will support us, our lungs will provide the oxygen we need to breathe.

Even our skin, our largest organ, was designed to protect us from germs and the elements and regulates our body temperature. Through our skin, we experience hot and cold and the sensation of touch. Our skin accounts for 16% of our body weight and has different thicknesses from our eyelids to the soles of our feet. Isn't God amazing?

Just like our bodies, people are uniquely created for a purpose.

Many years ago, my husband and I managed a homeless shelter for a time and then a low-income apartment building. We encountered people from all walks of life who had different experiences than ours. Some had mental health challenges or were trying to walk away from drug or alcohol addiction. Others had relationship issues or physical health issues, some caused by their choices or the choices of others.

God taught us so much during those years about how people are people. In so many ways, we are the same. We all have hopes and dreams. We all have challenges and we all have something to contribute. You may have to dig a little deeper in some to find the "treasure" but it's there to be found.

In God's eyes, we are precious in His sight – every single one of us. There are no mistakes. Each one of us has a story to tell, a purpose to accomplish on this earth.

On this journey to Bill's healing, we have learned so much about the human body. We have stood in awe of the God who created us. God has repaired and even "re-created" parts of Bill's body that were damaged. Bill is stronger than ever because of God's grace and God's power.

Thank you for your powerful, persistent prayers. #pray4bill #Godisfaithful

Day #748 January 27

Anchor Verse: Exodus 17:12
Moses' arms finally became too tired to hold up the rod any longer; so Aaron and Hur rolled a stone for him to sit on, and they stood on each side, holding up his hands until sunset. (TLB)

There will be times in our lives when we cannot carry out our assignment, the task the Lord has given us, alone. We will need to ask for help. We must humble ourselves and admit that we will not succeed except someone "holds up our hands."

It is only by God's grace and wisdom that a leader can successfully accomplish this task with God by his side and others to support him. It is too great a task to handle on your own.

This passage from Exodus 17 tells us that the Amalekites attacked the Israelites. Moses told Joshua to take some of his men and go fight the Amalekites. Moses would stand on top of the hill with the staff of God in his hands to assure their victory.

Joshua and his men went into battle and Moses, Aaron, and Hur went to the top of the hill. As long as Moses held up his hands, the Israelites were winning. Whenever his hands were lowered, the Amakelites were winning.

Aaron and Hur found a rock for Moses to sit on and then as his hands grew tired, they held up his hands until sunset. Joshua and his men were victorious and won the battle.

Moses knew what was needed to win the battle – the staff of God in his hands would assure their victory. His human strength, even combined with his willpower – a strong mind – was not enough to keep the rod in the air for the length of the battle. Aaron and Hur needed to help their friend and leader, or the Israelites would be defeated.

On this journey to Bill's healing, we have been so blessed to have others come alongside of us to lift up our hands as the battle raged. Your prayers have lifted our hands – emotionally, mentally, and spiritually. And through the course of this journey, others have helped with physical needs like cooking, cleaning, shopping, transportation, and more. We are winning this battle for Bill's complete healing because of your gifts and sacrifice.

Thank you for holding up our arms on days when we were weary.
#Godisfaithful #pray4bill

Day #749 January 28

Anchor Verse: Psalm 139:17-18

How precious it is, Lord, to realize that you are thinking about me constantly! I can't even count how many times a day your thoughts turn toward me. And when I waken in the morning, you are still thinking of me. (TLB)

When you fall in love, you can't stop thinking about that person. You long to be in their presence and see their face and hear their voice. Whether you are awake or asleep, thoughts of the one you love are always with you.

On this journey to Bill's healing, my love for my husband has multiplied. Like when I first fell in love with him, even now I can't stop thinking about him. I love to see Bill's face and to hear his voice, to listen to his wisdom and to laugh with him. Even when I cry, whether I am overcome with joy or overwhelmed, Bill is there to comfort me and dry my tears.

But as great as my love is for Bill, God's love for me is greater still. God wrote a book about my life before I was born. God has a unique plan for your life and for my life too. God loves me unconditionally with an everlasting love.

We cannot understand God and His ways, but Psalm 139 tells us that God thinks about you and me constantly. The Lord rejoices when we take a leap of faith knowing that He will catch us. Our heavenly Father holds us close to comfort us when a loved one dies too soon. God cheers us on as we continue to grow and become the man or woman of God He created us to be. He also delights in every moment that we rest in His presence and experience the fullness of His joy.

When you woke up this morning, God was still thinking of you. Isn't that good news? God who created the whole universe loves you so much that He was hopeful you would spend time with Him this morning.

Walk in that truth. Dare to take that next step of faith because God loves you and He is with you and will empower you.

On this journey to Bill's healing, we have not only been blessed by God's love for us and our love for each other, but your love and encouragement. We thank the Lord for each one of you and pray that God would multiply His blessings in your life.

Thank you for your faithfulness in prayer. #Godisfaithful #pray4bill

Day #750 January 29

Anchor Verse: Matthew 19:6
From then on, they are no longer two, but united as one. So what God unites let no one divide! (TPT)

"Whom God has joined together, let no man separate." (paraphrase Mark 10:9)

When Bill and I got married, I designed a counted cross stitch picture that included these words. Little did I know at the time how important it was that God had joined us together in the future battles we would face.

These words are often spoken during a marriage ceremony. Two individuals come together and now as "one flesh" they walk together through life. They are still two unique individuals, but as they move forward their thoughts are not what is best for "me" but what is best for "us."

There is the power of being "one" when you face life's trials as a married couple. I praise the Lord this morning for the gift of our marriage and how God has strengthened it as we have walked through these last two years.

So many times on this journey, it was just Bill, me, and God… that's all. But that's all we needed as we fought for Bill's life and our future together.

Is it easy? No. Nothing that is worth fighting for in this life is easy. But, oh, the blessings that come when you stay committed to each other and trust God to bring you through the deep waters, rivers, and refining fires of life.

Practically, it means dying to self… to your desires, your wants, your way, and embracing God's way. When your spouse is going through deep waters, it's an opportunity to be Jesus' hands and feet.

Bill and I have alongside each other to save his life. Even during the days when Bill was sedated and wasn't communicating with anyone (but God), I prayed for him. I was also his advocate with the medical staff. My question always was, "What's best for Bill?" Not, "What's best for me?"

Listening without interrupting, being a safe place for your spouse to express their true feelings and together asking God for victory, that is how we fight out battles triumphantly. How can you be your spouse's advocate – with God and man? Be a praying spouse. It's the greatest gift you can give.

Thank you for walking this path to victory. #Godisfaithful #pray4bill

Day #751 January 30

Anchor Verse: Exodus 23:20
Behold, I am going to send an Angel before you to keep and guard you on the way and to bring you to the place I have prepared. (AMP)

Can you imagine going on a 40-year journey and not knowing your destination? That's what the Israelites faced as they left Egypt on their way to the Promised Land. The other "surprise" – they didn't know it would take 40 years to get there.

Sometimes God's plans take a short time to accomplish, and other times, it's a long journey. It's not always about our destination but what God wants to teach on us on the way.

This morning as I was reading Exodus 23 this verse popped off the page – "Behold, I am going to send an Angel before you to keep and guard you on the way and to bring you to the place I have prepared."

It was as if I heard God whisper that this promise was also for Bill and me. This is true for all His children. God does not leave us alone to wander through this life. Before Jesus left this world, He promises that the Holy Spirit would come to be our guide and our Comforter. I also believe there are angels assigned to us to guard us and guide us on this pathway to the place God has prepared for us.

The angel's task is to keep us and guard us on the way. He will help maintain some control and keep the people on the right path.

What was their destination? "To bring you to the place I have prepared." God wasn't sending them on a wild goose chase – He already had a place prepared for them 40 years before they arrived.

These trials will not last forever. God has prepared a place for you and He is polishing and refining you to receive His best for you.

A change of perspective can help us weather the storms of life. Our circumstances are not out of control. All things work together for good to those who love Him and are called according to His purpose – all things. (Romans 8:28) It won't always feel good, but ultimately it's for our good.

On this journey to Bill's healing, we have encountered many storms and what seemed like unnecessary delays… but from God's viewpoint, our journey was right on schedule.

Thank you for your countless prayers. #Godisfaithful #pray4bill

Day #752 January 31

Anchor Verse: Exodus 18:19
Listen now to my voice; I will give you counsel, and God will be with you. (NKJV)

Listening… it's one of the most important skills that we must develop in this life. At an early age once our "mouth is engaged", it seems that it is much easier to "speak" than it is to "listen." When we forget the importance of listening, we miss out on so much – too much.

We don't know it all. We might "think" we do, but we don't. When I think of "good listeners" and the wisdom that comes from listening, I think of my paternal grandfather who lived to be 93 years old.

Grandpa spent a lot of time listening to others, but when he spoke, wisdom flowed from his lips. Keeping life simple and getting wiser involves speaking less and listening more. God gave us two ears and one mouth for a good reason.

From whom do you seek counsel? When you have a decision to make, or you are embarking on a new journey, where do you turn for help? Who is part of your team of advisors?

A wise person will first run to the Lord and God's Word, the Bible, to find good advice. Prayer is not a one-way street, where we do all the talking. It is important that we sit and listen to the Lord and hear His words, "This is the way, walk in it."

On this journey to Bill's healing, I have learned priceless information by listening. The first place I listen is to the Lord in my quiet time as I start my day. He speaks to me throughout the day and night; I must be attentive to the sound of His voice.

Most of all, I learned to listen to Bill. Even when he couldn't communicate with words, I would "listen" to his body language. As his communication skills returned, I listened closely to Bill's words to know what was on his heart and mind. Bill has great wisdom to share after all he has been through.

Thank you for walking this path with us. #pray4bill #Godisfaithful

February 2020

There is no fear in love.
~ 1 John 4:18

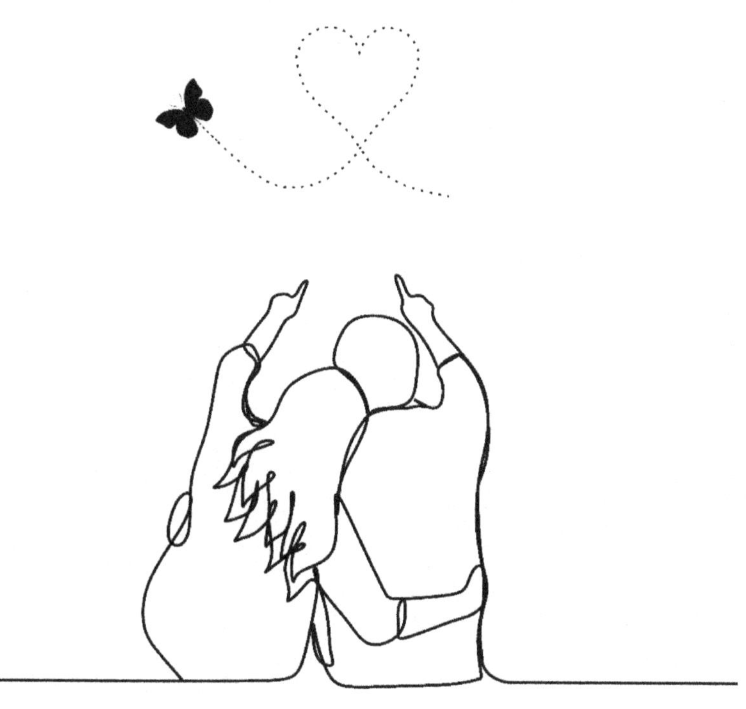

Day #753 February 1

Anchor Verse: Matthew 21:6
So the two disciples went on ahead and did as Jesus had instructed them. (TPT)

"Doing what you are told" – is a lesson we learn as children.

From the moment we enter this world, we enter a place where there are actions and consequences. There is right and wrong, better and best, reward and punishment.

As believers, God has given us an instruction manual about how to live – the Bible. The Bible not only shares "rules and regulations" but stories of those who made good choices and those who did not. The New Testament tells us the story of Jesus and His great love for us that bridged the gap between life and death. We have a bright future because Jesus lives.

Matthew 21:6 says, "The disciples went and did as Jesus commanded them."

Jesus gave His disciples specific instructions about where to find the donkey and its colt in the city of Jerusalem. Jesus stayed outside the city as they went to fulfill His request. The disciples were part of His preparation plan.

There are times in our lives where Jesus will ask us to be part of His preparation team. We may not understand the reason behind what we are asked to do, but we trust Him without question and obey.

Our "blind" obedience often prepares the "soil" of our lives for the miracle God wants to do there. We may be called to carry out that task without knowing the "why" – Jesus sends us "ahead" of Him.

On this journey to Bill's healing, there have been many times when God instructed me through the Holy Spirit to do something – complete a task, ask a question, make a phone call. Later as I looked back, I could see that action set in motion the change in circumstances we needed for Bill's health and healing. It was the first domino to fall in a chain reaction that would impact our lives forever.

Thank you for praying without ceasing. #Godisfaithful #pray4bill

Day #754 February 2

Anchor Verse: Philippians 2:5
Your attitude should be the kind that was shown us by Jesus Christ. (TLB)

Did you know that your attitude can determine the course of your day, the course of your life? It does. I see evidence of it every day in my own life and in the lives of others.

We call it different things: positive or negative outlook, cup half-full or cup half-empty, a good or a bad attitude.

Whatever you call it, you know the difference. There is so much of life beyond our control. Good things happen to bad people and bad things happen to good people, it's a fact of life.

There will be days when your life feels out of control. Wherever you look, the opposite is happening of what you wanted or even prayed for. You might be frustrated or even angry at God.

When things are going wrong, we tend to put the blame on someone else, because it's not our fault, right?

Jesus even told us that "in the world you will have tribulation, but be of good cheer (have a good attitude) I have overcome the world. (John 16:33 NKJV)

Stuff is going to happen, bad stuff, stuff that will frustrate you, and make you cry, and maybe even stomp your feet. In that moment ask, what would Jesus do? Philippians 2:5 says, "Your attitude should be the kind that was shown us by Jesus Christ."

What will you choose? Even in this very moment.

On this journey to Bill's healing, choosing our attitude not only about our circumstances but about the final outcome has been a moment by moment choice. I like what Bill often says to others, "Stay positive." That is how Bill personally has made it through the daily battles he has faced.

As we prepare for Bill's heart valve surgery in a few days, we both are choosing a positive attitude, an attitude of expectation about the miracle that is about to take place. Please join us at the foot of the cross as we sing praises to the Lord for what He has done in our lives and yours.

Thank you for your prevailing, persistent prayers. #Godisfaithful #pray4bill

Day #755 February 3

Anchor Verse: Exodus 33:14
The LORD replied, "My Presence will go with you, and I will give you rest." (NIV)

Rest is often elusive. In this "modern" society in which we live, life runs at a frantic pace, both day and night. There is always something to do, somewhere to go. It can be overwhelming at times.

Before some of our "modern" inventions, people got up with the sun and retired when the sun went down. Life was simple, definitely more rugged, but it is a level of simplicity that we have lost.

The key to this passage is this strong foundational truth, "My Presence will go with you." It is only when the Lord goes with us that we will find rest, that we find peace.

Other translations talk about God personally going with us.

Our heavenly Father is a God of relationships. He loves to be involved in our lives. We were created to have intimacy with Him – to hear His voice and walk in the way He sets before us.

The good news: You don't have to do life alone.

You may not be called to lead a nation of people to the Promised Land, but God has specific tasks for you. He has a plan and a purpose for your life. And you will need His help, His presence to go with you to accomplish your mission.

On this journey to Bill's healing, I am so grateful for God's presence with me day and night, in the hospital or in our home. It is comforting to know that I do not travel this path alone. Wherever I am, I can abide in His peace.

His rest is not only for our bodies as we sleep at night, but mentally, emotionally, and spiritually.

God's rest and peace are what Bill needs right now with surgery a couple of days away. Anxiety tries to reclaim "old" territory that God has claimed as His own and filled with peace.

Thank you for your faithful prayers. #pray4bill #Godisfaithful

Day #756 February 4

Anchor Verse: Exodus 34:6
"The LORD, the LORD, the compassionate and gracious God, slow to anger, abounding in love and faithfulness." (NIV)

God is compassionate and gracious, slow to anger, abounding in love, and faithfulness.

Without these qualities, surely we would perish. But because this is the truth, we are blessed beyond our understanding.

In Exodus 33, Moses asked God to "show me your glory." God told Moses that wasn't possible, "You cannot see my face, for no one may see me and live." God came down to Moses in a cloud and stood with him, and proclaimed His name, "The Lord, the Lord, the compassionate and gracious God, slow to anger, abounding in love and faithfulness." When Moses left God's presence, his face was radiant.

The Lord is "compassionate and gracious": There are many people whose lives are marked with compassion. Mother Teresa comes to mind and her work with the poor, especially in India. Because of God's compassion, He sent Jesus into the world to die for our sins.

Slow to anger: The Bible says the Lord is "slow to anger" but there is a tipping point where His heart of justice must respond to injustice. May we be quick to obey so we do not test the limits of His mercy.

Abounding in love and faithfulness: What does it mean to "abound"? To be present in large amounts – to overflow. Yes, I would testify to the fact that God's love and faithfulness overflow to His children.

On this journey to Bill's healing, we have experienced all of these attributes, but His love and faithfulness have exceeded all method of measurement. When the answers were evident, His love and faithfulness celebrated with us. When the trials were difficult and the night seasons were filled with tension, His love and faithfulness wrapped us in His loving embrace.

Even today on the eve of Bill's heart valve surgery (2.4.20), God is here. As Bill battles anxiety and his sleep is restless, God's presence is with us.

Thank you for standing with us as we approach Bill's surgery tomorrow. We know that God is faithful and this will be another testimony of God's hand of restoration at work in Bill's life and body. #pray4bill #Godisfaithful

Day #757 February 5

Anchor Verse: Matthew 26:39

Then he walked a short distance away, and overcome with grief, he threw himself face down on the ground and prayed, "My Father, if there is any way you can deliver me from this suffering, please take it from me. Yet what I want is not important, for I only desire to fulfill your plan for me." Then an angel from heaven appeared to strengthen him. (TPT)

On the night Jesus was betrayed, He entered the Garden of Gethsemane alone in many ways. Alone with His thoughts, alone with the overwhelming burden of grief, not only because of what He was about to endure, but Jesus was leaving behind those He loved.

Even in the Garden, as Jesus went alone to pray, He left a couple of trusted disciples to watch and pray. But they fell asleep… more than once.

In spite of the heaviness of the load, Jesus was willing to submit to God's will and fulfill God's plan for Him – no matter the cost. In the Passion translation, it says that an angel appeared to strengthen Him. Thank God for the angels that come to strengthen us today in our own hour of need.

Today (2.5.20) as we face Bill's heart valve replacement surgery, I am reminded that there are circumstances in our lives that we face alone. I can't be in the operating room. I must put Bill in God's hands, knowing that the Great Physician will be there performing the operation.

Even in these last days as we have prepared for this moment, Bill has been "alone" with his thoughts, as I have been alone with mine. We share the same viewpoint when it comes to God's hand in all of this. We submit to His will, His path. There wasn't an instantaneous healing when a new aortic valve appeared. This is the path that will give God the greatest glory.

It has strengthened our faith and yours. We have seen the mighty miracles God has performed in Bill's body, mind, and spirit.

Early in this journey, Bill told me "prophetically, "Just as God raised Jesus from the dead, God will do the same for me." Yes, Bill has been delivered from death's door many times. Many hospitals know Bill as the "Miracle Man." Today God will do another miracle through the hands of man.

Thank you for your faithfulness, day and night. #Godisfaithful #pray4bill

Day #758 February 6

Anchor Verse: Revelation 21:4

He will wipe away every tear from their eyes and eliminate death entirely. No one will mourn or weep any longer. The pain of wounds will no longer exist, for the old order has ceased. (TPT)

Pain – many of you live with it every day... all day and night. When you go through a surgery, pain is often the result because your body has been invaded – assaulted.

Yes, Mr. Bill's body was the site of an assault by one of the finest tactical assault teams. We had a great team of doctors – Wallace and Montero. Excellent men at their craft, vessels in the Great Physician's hands to do His will, His way. Thank you, Lord.

Pain is pain. It keeps you awake at night when sleep is what you need to heal. Figuring out appropriate pain management that will help the immediate problem and not cause more problems. It's a fine line to walk. But we walked it last night.

Having your own pain is tough but watching your loved one in pain is even worse – that's my opinion.

This verse from Revelation reminds us that there will be no pain in the world to come. Our tears will be gone and so will our pain.

In the meantime, pain is one of our "light and momentary troubles" that comes with the package deal called "life." It makes us appreciate the good days and pain-free days – the days filled with hope and healing.

It's early but the entourage of medical support have already been through here – EKG, chest X-ray, vital signs, and a blood draw all before 5 a.m. A hospital – this is the place of help and healing.... but not much sleep. But it's okay, sleep is what home is for…right?

We continue to sing praises to the Lord for the process of healing. We will see what lies ahead of us this day. We know it will be a good gift from God.

On this journey to Bill's healing, we have encountered storms, turbulence, pain, and on the flip side, joy, peace, and healing. We are grateful for the hand of God at work in our lives.

Thank you for bearing our burdens. #Godisfaithful #pray4bill

Day #759 February 7

Anchor Verse: Psalm 84:5-7

How enriched are they who find their strength in the Lord; within their hearts are the highways of holiness! Even when their paths wind through the dark valley of tears, they dig deep to find a pleasant pool where others find only pain. He gives to them a brook of blessing filled from the rain of an outpouring. They grow stronger and stronger with every step forward, and the God of all gods will appear before them in Zion. (TPT)

There will be seasons in our lives when we go through deep valleys and our only strength can be found in God. Our weakness is exchanged for His strength, our ashes for the oil of joy, and His blessings for the rubbish the world has forced into our hands.

It is in this place that we will praise His holy name. It is in this place that sorrow and mourning will flee. It is in this place where we exchange our plans for His best dreams for us.

This section from Psalm 84 contains powerful imagery. There will be journeys in our lives that follow a path not of our choosing to a place we never expected, and frankly, never wanted. But it is the path to God's best for us. It is the path of blessing, not of cursing. It is there that we will dig deeply and find a pleasant pool where others only find pain.

I know that place. I know those places... all too well. But it is a place of blessing. I am beside that brook of blessing this morning and I declare I am growing stronger and stronger with each step.

Our current circumstances, only a couple days after Bill's aortic valve replacement, I find myself there...again. The simple path is not always simple. The path requires courage and strength that only God can provide. His promises are true. He will never leave you or forsake you.

Bill's isn't in his 20s but his 70s.... his body is a little weaker than we anticipated. But we move forward in anticipation of God's plan, God's path for Bill's good and God's glory.

We are surrounded by your prayers and uplifted by God's power. Today we walk in victory in Jesus' mighty name. His resurrection power will continue to be manifested in Bill's body in Jesus' name.

Thank you for your prayers of faith. #Godisfaithful #pray4bill

Day #760 February 8

Anchor Verse: Psalm 56:4

With God on my side I will not be afraid of what comes. The roaring praises of God fill my heart, and I will always triumph as I trust his promises. (TPT)

Even on the darkest night, His promises are true. The light of the presence of the Lord fills the place where we stand and the rays of light from His manifest presence are a comfort to the weary traveler.

We cannot do this life alone. I declare the truth of God with the psalmist this morning, "With God on my side I will not be afraid of what comes."

Often our fear blossoms in the void of knowledge. What we don't know... what we create in the absence of truth – that is what keeps us awake at night. It is often in our isolation, not in the midst of dialogue and debate that we grow weary to the point of giving up.

This week I have experienced that in a new way at the hospital. I am immersed not only in Bill's surgery and the aftermath of healing, but feeling and observing its effects on others.

Storms are fierce. The time to do battle is in the middle of the storm. It is not the time for recess or sunbathing. Sometimes we fight the battle alone or with an army of others, from both heaven and earth. In every case, the Lord is with us. He will fight for us, and we will always win the war.

As believers, this is the difference in our battle, "the roaring praises of God fill my heart, and I will always triumph as I trust his promises." We fight our battles by praising the Lord and declaring His promises are true. We fight even when we cannot see the way ahead or the person fighting at our side. We fight from a place of victory in Jesus' name.

Last night was a tough night here at the hospital. This close to a full moon, the atmosphere was charged. Even in Bill's room with the door closed, the tension was tangible in the air. Yet... the cross of Christ is still standing this morning. Our hope comes in the name of the Lord.

On this journey to Bill's healing, we have stood on mountaintops and we have slugged our way through the swamps. Through it all, we have followed His path of righteousness and we have found comfort in His arms of love. Even though there is fog on the path ahead, one thing is clear, Jesus loves me, this I know.

Thank you for your continued prayers. #Godisfaithful #pray4bill

Day #761 February 9

Anchor Verse: Isaiah 40:28

Don't you know? Haven't you been listening? Yahweh is the one and only everlasting God, the Creator of all you can see and imagine! He never gets weary or worn out. His intelligence is unlimited; he is never puzzled over what to do! (TPT)

God never gets weary or worn out...isn't that good news? Yes, it is.

The truth is that as human beings we do get worn out. We grow weary in the battle of life but when God is our source, then weariness is never a permanent condition.

His intelligence is unlimited... ours is not. God is never puzzled about what to do but how many times a day do we hit a roadblock and don't know which way to turn?

God is our source. He is our strength. When we are weary, He infuses us with new life, new love, and new hope. God is my ever-present help in trouble. (Psalm 46:1)

This passage is not only about the qualities of God and what He will do for us but also about our part.

"Don't you know? Haven't you been listening?"

How many times a day does God says that as He watches us from heaven?

Often in our lives it's not that God hasn't given us the answer to our problems, it's that we haven't been listening.

Listening can be more important than talking. There have been days in the past when Bill was unusually quiet, not saying much, and I would ask if he was okay. And his response, "Today is a listening day - to listen more than I speak." Oh, the wisdom that lies in those words.

Maybe today should be a listening day for all of us... Listening to God, to others, our own heartbeat, our own bodies. We learn so much by listening.

On this journey to Bill's healing, we find ourselves in a place we didn't expect to be. It is where we need to be to give Bill the tools to increase his strength.

Thank you for your prayers for Bill's surgery and now his rehab time to help his body reclaim his strength. #Godisfaithful #pray4bill

Day #762 February 10

Anchor Verse: Psalm 115:1
Not to us, O Lord, not to us, but to your name goes all the glory for your unfailing love and faithfulness. (NLT)

Whatever we do in word and deed, let it be done to the glory of God. It's not about us, but all about God and His glory.

Life's greatest accomplishments come when we allow God to have His way in us. As we surrender our gifts and talents, even our trials and challenges, so that He might receive all the glory.

What does that mean, so that He would be glorified? It means that others would see the qualities of God exemplified in our lives, in our circumstances. That God's faithfulness, love, truth, and righteousness would shine brightly. That our lives and testimonies point others to Him.

On this journey to Bill's healing, God has done many miraculous things. We have had the honor and privilege to see them played out in our lives and in your lives. We chose to submit and obey. We chose to surrender our way for His ways. We chose to say "yes, Lord" You can have ALL of me and not only lip service or Sunday morning service. We must be "all in" so that His pure and holy light might be reflected in us.

Lord, have Your way in me. Use me until all of the gifts, talents, and resources You have given me are gone and all that remains is a testimony to Your faithfulness.

Think about it in the decisions you make, in the path you choose, is God being honored and glorified because of my choices? May we reflect His glory.

Thank you for holding up our arms on days when we are weary. Your prayers move the hand of God. #Godisfaithful #pray4bill

Day #763 February 11

Anchor Verse: Isaiah 26:3

You will keep in perfect peace all who trust in you, all whose thoughts are fixed on you! (NLT)

Perfect peace...it's a peace that can only be found in the Lord's presence. Our physical circumstances can contribute to the peace we find in our environment but God's peace can overpower even the most stormy sea.

The Amplified version expands our understanding of this peace: "You will keep in perfect and constant peace the one whose mind is steadfast [that is, committed and focused on You—in both inclination and character], Because he trusts and takes refuge in You [with hope and confident expectation]."

Is your mind committed and focused on God this morning? As you can see, it's a two-part process. We must be committed to finding the Lord, to seeing His face. It's not a willy-nilly process. Without commitment, like anything else in our lives, we will miss the target and get dragged off the path because of distractions.

Throughout the day our minds lose focus. Daydreaming can be a good mental break but not a good place to camp permanently.

We have perfect peace because we trust and take refuge in the Lord. Trusting God is the only way to live. If we can't trust God, who can we trust? Even our currency in the United States says, "In God we trust."

When you trust someone, you are willing to walk with them through life. You can believe they are speaking the truth. Trust is powerful. It can magnify the depth of a relationship, like the lack of trust can destroy it.

We take refuge in the Lord – a place to be called apart, a place of protection from the storm, from the fight. It's where God's presence permeates the air even as the storm rages. In our soul, we have found His perfect peace.

On this journey to Bill's healing, I am so grateful for God's perfect peace. It is a place I seek when life abruptly changes. It is a place I choose to abide as God fights for me. I can rest in God alone as Bill resides there with me. And sometimes I am the one who can usher in His peace and Bill can bask in it until he is strong enough to seek it himself.

Thank you for abiding with us. #Godisfaithful #pray4bill

Day #764 February 12

Anchor Verse: Exodus 20:19
Then they said to Moses, "You speak to us and we will listen, but do not let God speak to us or we will die." (AMP)

Are we afraid to hear the voice of God speaking to us? Do we prefer to hear His voice second-hand? Would you rather have the Goodwill/Value Village version rather than the pure truth and message that comes from the River of life?

Too often we are willing to settle for less than the best even when it comes to hearing the truth of God. The children of Israel in the wilderness had seen the presence of the Lord descend on the mountain when Moses met with God. Frankly, it terrified them.

Was it God's power and majesty or His glory and holiness that made them tremble in terror? Was it their sin and shortcomings and grumbling that made them want to hide as Adam and Eve hid from God in the Garden of Eden?

Our heavenly Father loves us so much that He beckons us to come to Him even when we are tired and dirty and seemingly unlovable to others. We may judge ourselves to be unworthy, but the truth is, our worthiness comes from God.

When we confess our sins and shortcomings, He strips us of our dirty rags and clothes us in robes of righteousness and places His mantle of peace upon our shoulders.

On this journey to Bill's healing, I have met God on the mountaintop, in the wilderness, in ICU units, walking through the valley of the shadow of death, and beside still waters. I have knelt at His feet and I have stood and fought against the darkness that sought to consume me and the one I love.

I'm not willing to settle for watered-down porridge, instead I choose to take my place at the seat reserved for me at the Lord's banqueting table. Please join me there.

Thank you for running into the Lord's presence on our behalf. Your prayers have moved the hand of God. #Godisfaithful #pray4bill

Day #765 February 13

Anchor Verse: John 11:41
So they took away the stone. And Jesus raised His eyes [toward heaven] and said, "Father, I thank You that You have heard Me." (AMP)

When you pray do you have the same certainty that Jesus had when He looked toward heaven and said, " Father, I thank You that You have heard Me."?

Lazarus died before Jesus arrived. His death became the stage for a greater miracle.

Jesus asked for the stone to be rolled away. Then He prayed and took action. With confidence, Jesus spoke to Lazarus, "Lazarus, come forth." Lazarus emerged from the tomb with linen strips around him, his burial clothes... but Lazarus was very much alive.

We are at another bump in the road on Bill's healing journey. Last night (2.12.20) he had the chills and then a fever. With Tylenol, the fever went down... a couple of hours later it started to go up again. More Tylenol, more prayer. His blood pressure was up too... more prayer. Within two hours, even his blood pressure went down. Another sign of God's healing touch.

Ruling out possibilities... they drew blood and will do a urine test. Pray for answers. Pray for healing. His incision sites look great. Praying that all things related to Bill's heart come into perfect alignment.

I learned a valuable lesson this morning from Jesus at Lazarus's tomb. As I pray, I stand on God's promises, on His reputation, not mine. My job is to proceed in faith. To stand and believe and not be moved by doubt or fear. "Thank you, Lord, that you have heard me."

At the name of Jesus, God moves. He comforts. He empowers. He gives new life. He is the God of second chances. He is Bill's healer and yours too.

Thank you for standing with us in faith that God would complete the miracle. Calling down His power to heal. #Godisfaithful #pray4bill

Day #766 February 14

 **Anchor Verse: Matthew 10:27**
What I tell you now in the darkness, shout abroad when daybreak comes. What I whisper in your ear, shout from the housetops for all to hear! (NLT)

The dark seasons of our lives are often where God teaches us the most profound lessons. It is there in the darkness where we cannot see the path ahead that we must hold God's hand and trust Him who knows the way.

In the darkness, there is also silence. It is often the place where there are no other travelers that you can see. Many may be going through that dark season but each path is custom-designed by the Master's hand for our good and His glory.

There is a gentleness and tenderness in that place because it is there we hear and feel God's heartbeat. We press in to Him because no other can understand the depth of the experience like God who designed it.

We have often heard that the night is always the darkest before dawn, so, too, it is in the night season of our soul.

Let us not focus only on the darkness but rather the lesson, the message that comes from the heart of God. For the message that was delivered in the crucible of our pain and suffering is a life lesson we will never forget. But greater still is the glory, the light, the bright flame that is destined to be shared with others.

This suffering is not only for you but that the glory of God, the message of God would be trumpeted from the housetops by you as you have been transformed in the dark. What was birthed in that dark place will now shine brightly as a testimony to God's love and faithfulness.

On this journey to Bill's healing, this has been our story. This was the Lord's message to me on the first steps back in January 2018. God called me to share what we have learned in this dark season, in the silence, in the pain, in the place where all we had was God and His love for us.

Your pain is never wasted. Your trials are a foretaste of His glorious plan for your life.

Thank you for your faithfulness. Thank you for sharing your lessons with us. We are in this battle called life together. #Godisfaithful #pray4bill

Day #767 February 15

Anchor Verse: Romans 14:7
For none of us lives for ourselves alone... (NIV)

No man is an island... even the "world" knows that we don't exist for ourselves alone. When we choose to live for Christ and Christ alone, our ability to touch the lives of others expands exponentially.

Why? Because we have turned the reins over to Jesus. He is not only our Savior but He is our Lord. There is freedom in that place, not bondage. There is hope, not despair. There is power, not weakness.

It is in our own lives where we see God at work as His light in us shines brightly to light the way for others. We are the blackboard on which God writes His message of love for others to read.

We have a responsibility to walk in faith, to trust Him when our eyes can't see, and to hasten to obey His commands. It is there that life begins. It is there where He can touch your life with hope and love. If I fail to remember that I live not only to myself, then your life is impacted too. I have cheated you of the opportunity to know God, to see God in a new way.

On this journey to Bill's healing, what if I had ignored, declined God's request to share Bill's health adventure on Facebook? We all would have been impacted by my disobedience. Multiple miracles have happened in our lives and yours because we said "yes" to God.

Many of you have been inspired to share your story, your walk with God because of Bill's courageous walk as I have shared our lives with you. It's not only on the mountaintops but the valleys, the wilderness, and the refining fire where God's love, power, grace, and presence have been seen.

Then you have shared His light and love with others. You have chosen to live not for yourselves alone. Thank you for your faithfulness.

Since God is for us, we ultimately win every time. There will be moments when in the thick of the battle, the devil will sow seeds of doubt and fear.

Thank you for standing with us. Thank you for believing even when your eyes couldn't see the end. Your prayers have reached heaven's throne room.

As the battle with Bill's infection and claiming his ultimate healing continues, we praise God that you have chosen not to live for yourself alone but to join us on this path to victory. #Godisfaithful #pray4bill

Day #768 February 16

Anchor Verse: Ephesians 5:14
Arise from the dead... (AMP)

There are seasons when our hopes and dreams feel like they have died. It is a barren wasteland in our soul. The desert is dry and dusty, and daily survival is all we can consider.

But that is not who God created us to be. God created us to live and love and enjoy life to the fullest. He created you and me with gifts and talents to impact the world and bring Him glory.

This verse in Ephesians is a call to rise up. Rise up from that desert place. Strip off the grave clothes and be clothed in the radiance of resurrection life. Even as Christ rose from the grave and death had no hold on Him, we are called to do the same.

Awake, you who slumber! Waking up is a choice. Some people are quick to rise in the morning and are full of instant energy with a song in their heart and praises on their lips. Others wake up a little more slowly.

Whatever your style, God is calling you to arise from the dead. It is a choice. You can stay mired in that pit of despair or you can choose life. You can choose to say my dreams are dead or someone stole my dreams but the truth is Jesus died that you might live – now!

On this journey to Bill's healing, Bill and I have both heard these words from the Lord. In Bill's case, literally, he was at death's door and the Lord called him to arise from the dead and choose life because God had plans for him. Bill said "yes" and continues to say "yes" even on the difficult days when the path ahead is foggy and where he is now is not where he wants to be.

For me, God has called me many times to take a stand and step away from fear, plant my feet on God's truth, declare life over Bill, and choose to walk in His resurrection power. In the midst of this storm, God has brought new life. There is revival, redemption, reassurance, and rest.

We have seen His power and felt His peace. We have new hope and joy. We know that our heavenly Father loves us with an everlasting love and will never leave us or forsake us.

Thank you for your persevering prayers. #Godisfaithful #pray4bill

Day #769 February 17

Anchor Verse: Jeremiah 17:7
But blessed are those who trust in the Lord and have made the Lord their hope and confidence. (NLT)

What does it mean to be blessed? The word "blessed" in Greek means to be fully satisfied. The word is associated with happiness. It is a place of joy...a place where we abide with the Lord, where His blessings transcend any temporary pleasure we might find in the world.

Our blessings are not associated with our bank account, our possessions, the number of friends we have, or even those who follow us on social media. We are blessed because we know that God can be trusted in the valleys and on the mountaintops. He may be silent in the desert or the wilderness but this is where our trust grows even stronger.

When you are with someone you love, words are not always necessary. There is unspeakable joy by being near the one you love.

Bill and I have found this to be true on our journey to his healing. We take "our world" with us wherever we go. Bill and me and God are an unstoppable force as we move forward on the path He has for us.

This verse tells us it's not only about trusting God; we make God our "hope and confidence." Hope and confidence are not something we conjure up through our own efforts. When we have hope and confidence in the Lord, the clouds part and the sunshine of His love shines upon us.

When my hope and confidence are firmly secured on the solid rock of Jesus Christ, on the character of God, on the abundance of His provision, and His vigilance as He executes His "best" for my life, I need not doubt or fear.

I'm not sure I can put into words the peace I have found in the middle of this storm that we have walked through in these last two plus years. When I keep my eyes on the Lord, not on the stormy sea. When I obey His commands and choose the narrow path that leads to life rather than wandering off the path in search of the world's answers or temporary pleasures. When I run into my heavenly Father's arms when the load is too heavy for me to carry alone, He restores my strength to take the next step on this path to Bill's healing.

Thank you for standing with us. #Godisfaithful #pray4bill

Day #770 February 18

Anchor Verse: Matthew 6:25
Do not worry about your life. (NIV)

Worrying consumes energy we really don't have to give. It's not like we have an extra 10% or 15% energy reserve that is devoted to worrying. In fact, worry not only drains us of our energy, it contaminates everything.

Think about it. When we worry, our mind rehearses all the horrible things that have happened, are happening, and might happen in our lifetime and beyond. It affects our appetite, our attitude, and even our appearance.

It's like too much salt in the soup that spoils the whole kettle. (NOTE: We don't use salt anymore.)

Worry turns a sunny day to gray skies. When we are worried, we tend to lash out at others because the pot of negativity is full and overflowing.

It's time to stop that madness.

Jesus tells us here in Matthew 6, do not worry about your life, don't worry about tomorrow. I know the words sound "easy" but let's see how we can put that into practice.

God doesn't leave us alone to "figure it out." It's not like a math test in school where you are on your own to find the answers. Invite the Lord into every circumstance, every situation, and see what He will do.

Do not worry... I have heard Him say this over and over again to me on this journey.

On our journey to Bill's healing, I have had the opportunity to say "yes" to God and "no" to worry, doubt, and fear. Many times, challenges have jumped into my lifeboat and threatened to capsize it. I could have succumbed to the wind and waves but instead I got out my bucket and started bailing water.

The Word of God has sustained me. His promises have been the strong foundation on which I have chosen to stand. Nothing will separate me from the love of God.

Thank you for your faithfulness. Your prayers are moving the mountains in our lives. Bill continues to improve. Praying that soon we will be able to go home. #Godisfaithful #pray4bill

Day #771 February 19

Anchor Verse: John 13:14
If I then, your Lord and Teacher, have washed your feet, you also ought to wash one another's feet. (NKJV)

There are tasks in our lives that are not pleasant. We might call them "dirty work." In our homes, we do them every day. Taking out the garbage, taking care of unexpected messes that come with children or those who are ill – or life stuff. I don't have to describe them – you know what I mean.

Even now as Bill has been in the hospital since February 5 (2020), the 15th day, I continue to give thanks for nurses, CNAs, therapists, housekeepers, and all those who tend to patient care and make sure that a facility stays clean and sanitized.

Many of them have the attitude that they treat their patients like they would treat their own family member. They serve with a heart of compassion. They are Jesus' hands and feet. It is a beautiful symphony of service when carried out with a heart of love.

This is what Jesus was trying to show His disciples. That service – putting love in action, should be a way of life.

It is not only the action of what Jesus did but the attitude with which He did it. Jesus, the Savior of the world, humbled himself when He came to earth to die for our sins. His heart, His hands, His feet, His words were filled with love and compassion.

Today we are called to do the same thing. Whether it be a family member, a friend, a stranger or a member of the body of Christ, let us serve one another with love, joy, and grace.

On this journey to Bill's healing, I have the honor and privilege of serving my husband with love, joy, and compassion. We have gone through some deep valleys, but we have also stood on the mountaintop of victory. We are climbing another mountain again, but as Bill told me the other day, "I can see the top of the mountain." We are making progress.

Lord, fill us with new joy. May we be Your hands and feet. Thank you for Your example that we might follow in Your steps.

Thank you for your faithfulness. #Godisfaithful #pray4bill

Day #772 February 20

Anchor Verse: Psalm 40:8
I delight to fulfill your will, my God, for your living words are written upon the pages of my heart. (TPT)

Too often we fall into the trap of believing that doing God's will, following His way is the path of drudgery. Far from it. When we choose to follow God, listen to His still small voice over the noise of the world, we discover that walking with God is an amazing adventure.

It is not without risk but great is the reward. It is not always easy but the Lord promises to never leave your side, He will never leave you or forsake you.

The Passion translation describes God's will for you with beautiful words, "Your living words are written upon the pages of my heart." Isn't that beautiful?

God's living words are written on the pages of your heart and my heart. That inspires me. That gives me confidence that I can walk in His way and do His will because His plan is already written in my heart. Now that's good news!

We need only to listen to His voice and follow Him, God's plan is already in place. Does that inspire you?

In light of that truth, we cannot say we don't know what to do because the plan is already in us, it's part of us. Our problem is that we want to go our own way rather than God's way.

If you have been wandering aimlessly, lost, hopeless, today is a new day. God has a plan and purpose for your life and His living words are written on the pages of your heart. He is calling you to walk with Him and experience the fullness of His joy.

On this path to Bill's healing, we have found great joy in walking in His way. In the scary places, God has always provided a safety net – His hands of love. We have seen Him at work in the sunshine and in the storm. As we put our trust in Him, He has never let us go. For seasons He has carried us, God never left our side, and countless times, He has fought for us.

Thank you for your prayers. We are headed home from the rehab hospital in a few days. #Godisfaithful #pray4bill

Day #773 February 21

Anchor Verse: Matthew 4:19
Come, follow me, Jesus said. (NIV)

Following another calls for self-discipline and self-control. If we are really following, we must lay down our independence. We give up a certain amount of control and the ability to wander at will.

When Jesus called each man to become His disciple, they were asked to walk away from the life they once knew and trade it for an unknown future.

In that moment, they had no idea what they would experience on the path that lay ahead of them, but they were willing to surrender all to Jesus.

Are we willing to do the same?

Americans pride themselves in their independence. There are many who don't want anyone to tell them what to do and when to do it.

The Christian life is filled with God's blessings but they follow our obedience. It is in our trials that God gives us multiplied peace as we follow Him though the storm. Our light shines the brightest when we reflect His light and love as we sow good seed into the lives of others. It is when we die to self and become alive in Christ that we experience our greatest joy.

Following Jesus will also have its own set of trials and tribulations. But we also have victory over them. Jesus told us that in this world we would encounter trials and tribulations but to be of good cheer for He has overcome the world.

On this journey to Bill's healing, we have learned so much about the joys of following Jesus. On the rough seas, He has spoken peace to the storm. In the blizzards where the ice of adversity was thick, Jesus cut a path through it. In the refining fire, Jesus has been our cool breeze as He purified us to be of greater service to Him. We couldn't have made it this far without Him.

As we prepare to go home in a few days, I hear the voice of Jesus saying, "Come, follow Me." He will lead us through this next season. Jesus will be our calm in the storm. He will give us rest. He will challenge us to grow with Him and claim new territory. Jesus will lead Bill to victory as Bill puts his hand in the hand of Jesus and "walks" in his healing.

Thank you for walking with us. #Godisfaithful #pray4bill

Day #774 February 22

Anchor Verse: Matthew 5:4
Blessed are those who mourn, For they shall be comforted. (NIV)

Life is filled with both joys and challenges. There are moments of ecstasy and valleys of disappointment. But the greatest comfort is that we don't have to face life alone.

Jesus walks by our side. He carries us through the difficult places. He is our shelter in the storm. He rejoices in our victories. Jesus is our all in all.

The longer we live, the more opportunities we have to experience the length and depth and breadth of life. And with each wave of life we face, there is a lesson to be learned. There is a rough edge to be polished. There is a next step to take. There is a gift that God will uncover.

Our verse this morning about the comfort that comes even as we mourn. There are multiple facets to it. It refers not only to the mourning that comes with physical death but the loss of other things.

On this journey to Bill's healing, I have been aware of the "machete" that has carved away so much in our lives. But greater still are the things that God has replaced them with in the form of spiritual blessings.

Bill and I have always been close but "our world" is now locked in tight. The Lord's presence is powerfully with us wherever we are. Even this last week, someone entered Bill's room and commented about how peaceful it was.

Life changed suddenly yesterday. My mom has been sick since 2014. She had been cared for at home and surrounded by the home she loves and family that love her so much. Yesterday morning my dad called to let me know that Mom was not doing well. In fact, that she could be in heaven before the weekend was over.

It was a shock as she had been quite stable. Thanks to technology I was able to have a video call with my folks and siblings last night. In less than an hour after we concluded our call, Mom passed from earth into the arms of Jesus. No more suffering, only joy in the presence of the Lord.

Thank you for walking with us on our path to victory. Bill is more than a conqueror; he is an overcomer in Jesus' name. #Godisfaithful #pray4bill

Day #775 February 23

Anchor Verse: Psalm 46:10
Be still, and know that I am God! (NIV)

Being still and resting, not moving, not going, is one of the hardest things we need to do as human beings. Sometimes I think we should be called "human doings."

In the stillness, God wants us to have fellowship with Him, to trust Him, to lean on Him. God created us to be in relationship with Him. We need Him. Our soul longs for Him. We need God like we need water for our bodies.

This verse goes on to tell us the rest of the story. Let me share a couple of translations with you. The New Living translation says "I will be honored by every nation. I will be honored throughout the world."

The Passion version says, "Surrender your anxiety. Be silent and stop your striving and you will see that I am God. I am the God above all the nations, and I will be exalted throughout the whole earth."

On this journey to Bill's healing, that is what you have seen happen in our lives. When we have faced storms, God was there. When we walked through the desert places, over mountains, through the wilderness, and walked on dry ground through the Red Sea, He was the one who received all the glory. Bill's success has been because of God's faithfulness. My ability to keep my head above water is because God was carrying me.

Now with the added dimension of my mom's death, I need my Lord all the more. But He will be honored and glorified through it all.

Today we are scheduled to take Bill home and begin the next leg of his recovery. It will be more new territory. Home health will return with nursing and a complement of therapists. Add to that cardiac rehab and follow-up doctor appointments, and we will be busy people.

Most importantly will be the rest, resting in our own bed. As you know, hospital beds are designed to be easy to keep sanitized rather than for comfort. The plastic surface usually finds Bill slid to the end of the bed by the middle of the night. I have been sleeping on a cot with an air mattress. It's better than the chair. But I am not a camping kind of girl.... so we are both looking forward to sleeping in our own bed tonight.

Thank you for holding up our arms. #Godisfaithful #pray4bill

Day #776 February 24

Anchor Verse: Mark 4:39

When Jesus woke up, he rebuked the wind and said to the waves, "Silence! Be still!" Suddenly the wind stopped, and there was a great calm. (NLT)

The storms of life, everyone has them. They are a part of nature. They are a part of life.

Jesus had spent the day teaching the crowd that followed Him and His disciples. By evening, Jesus was exhausted. He told His disciples to get in the boat and go to the other side. The voyage was from Capernaum from the west to the east side of the lake. While they were crossing the lake a storm came up that was so fierce, it even frightened these seasoned fishermen. That must have been quite a storm.. Finally Jesus woke up from his exhausted sleep (you know the kind of sleep that is). Even though His human flesh was weary, Jesus' divine power rose up and calmed the storm, and solved the problem. At His command, nature responded and all was calm.

In your mind's eye, you can picture the disciples. They are drenched from the storm. They are exhausted from the sheer human strength they exerted to keep the boat from capsizing and all of them being drowned. At the same time, I can sense them thinking, "What happened?"

Even though they had been with Jesus and even had private time with Him, as Jesus revealed more of His teachings, they still didn't always understand. They stood in awe and wonder that at Jesus' command, the wind and the waves responded.

Lord, I pray that I would remember the times You have moved in a mighty way and the next time I face the storm, I stand courageously and in Your power and authority, rebuke the wind and tell the waves to be calm.

On this journey to Bill's healing, we have experienced many squalls – storms that came out of nowhere. We have faced the unexpected. But as we cry out to Jesus, we know that He is able to calm any storm. Even this month, we have been hit by a couple of unexpected storms. After Bill's heart valve replacement, the body weakness that followed resulting in two weeks in the rehab hospital and then the unexpected death of my mom in the midst of fighting the first storm.

God never promised that it would be easy, but He did promise to be faithful.

Thank you for standing through the storm. #Godisfaithful #pray4bill

Day #777 February 25

Anchor Verse: Numbers 11:23
Is the LORD'S arm too short? (NIV)

Do you ever doubt God's ability to take care of you? To answer your requests? To protect your loved ones? To provide for you financially? To keep you out of danger?

The children of Israel were prone to complaining. Often they complained to Moses about their hardships (Why didn't we stay in Egypt?), even though what they left behind was not a good situation.

This time they complained where the Lord heard them and in Numbers 11:1, it says that "his anger was aroused." It's not a good idea to have God mad at you. God's wrath can be lethal. The fire of the Lord came down and consumed some of the outskirts of the camp. The people cried out to Moses who prayed to the Lord and the fire died down.

Then they started complaining about the food. Moses was growing weary of leading these ungrateful people, so the Lord had Moses choose 70 of Israel's elders to help Moses lead them.

God promised to provide meat that the people had requested. Moses couldn't understand how God would provide meat for 600,000 men plus all the women and children.

The Lord replied to Moses, "Is the Lord's arm too short? Is the Lord's power limited? Is my arm too weak? Do you think I'm weak? So, you don't think I can take care of you?"

"Now you will see whether or not what I say will come true for you," is what God said. Let me show you, My power, My mercy, My grace, My provision.

On this journey to Bill's healing, we have seen the impossible become possible. I will testify over and over again that God's hand IS NOT too short.

Even today, as we are in this transition period after surgery to the next phase of Bill's healing and grieving my mom's death, we celebrate the goodness of the Lord. We know in our spirits that God is for us and not against us. That God will lead us forward by His powerful hand.

Thank you for your continuous prayers.. #pray4bill #Godisfaithful

Day #778 February 26

Anchor Verse: Numbers 14:9
The LORD is with us. Do not be afraid... (NIV)

No matter what you face in your life, if you know that the Lord is with you, you can conquer anything. We must not count on our own resources, our own strength, our own finances, but instead, put our trust in God and He will lead us to victory.

When the Israelites were nearing their destination, God told Moses to send scouts into the land of Canaan to do some "intel" work. Moses chose one leader from each of the tribes of Israel, twelve men with a mission for forty days to explore the land and bring back their report.

They returned with fruit from the land – grapes, pomegranates, and figs along with a report about the people who lived there.

Ten of the men described the people who lived there as more powerful than the Israelites and spread a bad report throughout the camp. Caleb encouraged the people by saying, "We should go up and take possession of the land, for we can certainly do it." Joshua also joined Caleb.

The Israelites had seen God do the impossible many times on their journey from Egypt, but they were quick to believe the negative report, and doubt the truth, that God was with them and the Promised Land was theirs.

Grumbling has a high price. God is willing to forgive us when we sin, but is there a limit to His mercy? I don't want to find out. My choice is to believe the truth of God. I choose to believe that His promises are true. My eyes of faith are wide open to see what He would have me see and my feet want to walk in obedience to His commands.

Repeat these words, "The Lord is with me. I will not be afraid." Every day faith is a better choice than fear.

On this journey to Bill's healing, there have been many crossroads. We have entered a "foreign land," and yes, there were times that our problems looked like "giants" standing in our way. Instead of bowing to our fears, we have chosen to be brave and courageous. Even as Caleb and Joshua believed that God would give them victory, we believe God will give us victory and deliver the "Promised Land" of Bill's restored health into our hands.

Thank you for walking in faith. #Godisfaithful #pray4bill

Day #779 February 27

Anchor Verse: Proverbs 19:21
You can make many plans, but the LORD's purpose will prevail. (NLT)

Making plans, setting goals, using planners and technology, and reminders on our phones, we are creatures who are driven by doing things. Not only doing something, but having a plan and a purpose.

God must shake His head sometimes as we run in circles spending more time on "the plan" than living our lives and being surprised by the divine appointments God arranges.

Are you are planner? Does everything in life have to fall "within the lines?"

I used to make lists and check off the things that I accomplished. These days, I don't have time to make a list. I ask the Holy Spirit to lead me on the path God has for me.

On this journey to Bill's healing, we have seen the Lord's purpose prevail. What modern medicine said was the outcome at times turned out not to be true because God had a different plan.

We have heard testimonies of how Bill's journey to healing has touched your lives. The Lord has used our commitment to each other and to Him to cause you to stop and reflect about your life and relationships. It's a good thing to stop and assess where your life is going and whether it is pleasing to the Lord.

As we prepare for my mom's memorial service this weekend (2.29.20), my dad shared how so many people have reached out in love to our family and shared with Dad how Mom touched their lives. What a beautiful legacy of love to leave behind as she has passed through heaven's gates.

Erma Bombeck once talked about standing before God at the end of her life, and declaring that she had used every single talent God gave her. May that be our prayer, our goal too.

Thank you for touching our lives through your prayers and acts of kindness. #pray4bill #Godisfaithful

Day #780 February 28

Anchor Verse: Mark 6:46
He [Jesus] went up on a mountainside to pray. (NIV)

Prayer is one of the most powerful weapons we have as Christians to fight life's battles. We can pray anytime and anyplace. You may not be able to pray out loud, but the prayers of your heart nothing on earth can stop.

After Jesus had been teaching the crowds and speaking with His disciples, He sends His disciples ahead in a boat and climbs a mountain to pray.

Likely Jesus was exhausted. After feeding the 5,000 with five loaves and two fish, with all the noise and energy of the crowd. There are people who wanted to be healed, those who were curious about who Jesus was, and those who may have come even for a free meal.

Many people were healed. Healing power flowed from Jesus to heal them. Yes, He was Jesus the son of God, yet He lived in a human body. There must have been a personal price to pay for all of the activity that day.

Jesus knew that time alone with His heavenly Father, having a conversation with God, restored Him. It wasn't that Jesus had to go to a mountaintop to speak to God, but it teaches us that in the silence and the solitude, our peace is restored and our minds and bodies are rejuvenated.

Do you have a place where you can go away and pray? I have a friend who spends several hours in the middle of the night praying even after a busy day. It is there she meets the Lord. It is there that her prayers are answered and revelation given. It is in the quietness of the night when the world is silent that we can hear the heartbeat of God.

On this journey to Bill's healing, I have been reminded so many times of the necessity of spending time in prayer with the Lord. There is power in unified prayer when we get together to pray with others, but the sweet fellowship we encounter with the Lord when we are in the garden or the mountaintop or the hills or the valleys with Him is nothing that the world can duplicate.

Thank you for your continued prayers, day and night. They have filled us with hope on our challenging days. #Godisfaithful #pray4bill

Day #781 February 29

Anchor Verse: Matthew 25:40
And the King will answer them, "Don't you know? When you cared for one of the least important of these my little ones, my true brothers and sisters, you demonstrated love for me." (TPT)

There will come a day when we will be accountable for the things we did here on earth, and also those we did not do.

Every day we have opportunities to serve the Lord with gladness, to love as Jesus loved, and to serve without counting the cost. How many times do we let them pass us by? How often are we "too busy" to speak up for those who have no voice? How often is our focus only on ourselves as we pass by someone who needs our help?

"Then the King will say to those on his right, 'Come, you who are blessed by my Father; take your inheritance, the kingdom prepared for you since the creation of the world. For I was hungry and you gave me something to eat, I was thirsty and you gave me something to drink, I was a stranger and you invited me in, I needed clothes and you clothed me, I was sick and you looked after me, I was in prison and you came to visit me.'"

Today is my mom's funeral service (2.29.20) – a day to celebrate her life and her legacy. My mom understood what it meant to be Jesus' hands and feet. She loved to help others – my parents both demonstrated that to us.

We often had "strangers" stay in our home – whether pastors, missionaries, foreign exchange students, or others. There was always room at the table for one more person to enjoy my mom's cooking. If there was a need, Mom asked how she could help. Often our whole family was mobilized to help meet that need. I am blessed with a rich heritage of service to others.

My blessings continue as I am married to a man who understands this concept. Bill and I have been blessed with many opportunities to sow into the lives of others who could not repay our kindness. We serve not for the reward but to honor the Lord.

Even on this journey to Bill's healing, the Lord has made a way to sow into your lives even during our greatest challenges. He is a good, good Father.

Thank you for your kindness. #Godisfaithful #pray4bill

March 2020

Be still and know that I am God.
~ Psalm 46:10

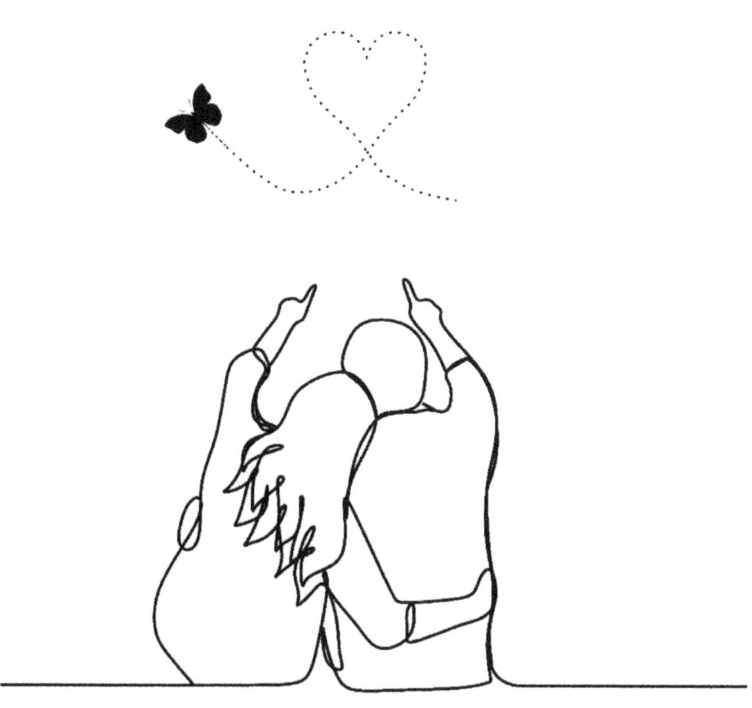

Day #782 March 1

Anchor Verse: Numbers 22:28
Then the Lord opened the mouth of the donkey. (NJKV)

God will do whatever it takes to deliver His message to us. We may be "deaf" to His cries when we are walking in sin, but that will not stop Him. God loves us so much, He will even use a donkey.

In Numbers 22, we read that Balak, the king of Moab, saw what the Israelites had done to the Amorites and he was terrified. So Balak summoned Balaam, a non-Israelite prophet, a diviner, to come and put a curse on the Israelites because they were too powerful for the Moabites to defeat. The king said, "For I know that whoever you bless is blessed, and whoever you curse is cursed."

During the night God visited Baalam and told him not to go with them. "Don't put a curse on them because [the Israelites] are blessed." Balaam told them no, the Lord had refused to let him go with them.

The Lord finally agreed to let Balaam go but only if he did what God told him. The next morning Balaam gets on his donkey and off he goes.

It doesn't go well. God gets angry and opens the mouth of the donkey to deliver His message. Balaam has this conversation with his donkey and THEN God opened Balaam's eyes so he could see the angel of the Lord in the road with his sword drawn. Balaam fell facedown before him. Then God has him continue to carry out His plans.

When God has a plan and a purpose for us, He will use any means to keep us on the right path. The angel of the Lord would have killed Balaam except his donkey had more sense than he did. God spared his life thanks to his donkey.

On this journey to Bill's healing, we haven't encountered any "speaking donkeys" but the Lord has definitely directed our path in ways we didn't understand. We have often been told to step out in faith even when it seemed "crazy" from a common sense standpoint.

Thank you for your continued prayers. We see progress on Bill's path to healing, but the fatigue is a foe that still needs to be beaten. The Lord will prevail! He is Bill's healer. #pray4bill #Godisfaithful

Day #783 March 2

Anchor Verse: Psalm 121:1b-2
Where does my help come from?
My help comes from the LORD, the Maker of heaven and earth. (NIV)

Often in our lives, we need help. Asking for help is called wisdom.

When we are at the end of our rope, life is throwing things at us that we cannot cope with, where do we turn for help? The psalmist recommends that we look heavenward, to the Lord, the Maker (Creator) of heaven and earth.

God made you. He breathed life into you. Surely your heavenly Father can help you in your time of trouble. He will never leave us or forsake us.

Because He is God, all of us can have our needs met, even at the same time. God is not a man, who can only do one thing at a time.

Where does my help come from when my husband is recovering from surgery, I am grieving the loss of my mother, my office looks like a bomb hit it, and my physical body needs rest? My help comes in the name of the Lord, Maker of heaven and earth.

There is NOTHING too hard for God. And if nothing is too hard for God, then nothing is too hard for me. With every breath I take in, and breathe out, I know He is with me. When I lie down to sleep, I sleep in peace for He is with me.

On this journey to Bill's healing, God has ALWAYS been my helper. He has provided for us even when I didn't know what to ask for to meet our needs. God has never let me down. Even when I didn't understand the "why", I knew I could trust God to bring something good out of it.

Today, I choose to put my hand in God's hand, and ask Him to lead me on the path ahead. I ask the Lord to fill both Bill and me with His strength, to make a way when the way ahead is not clear. Lord, please carve out a path through the wilderness and lead us to the Promised Land, direct us to our destination.

Every day we trust Him. Daily, we see Bill improving and new light, new hope in his eyes. We are more than conquerors through Him who loves us.

Thank you for your persistent prayers. Thank you for speaking words of life to us and over us. #Godisfaithful #pray4bill

Day #784 March 3

Anchor Verse: Mark 8:2
I have compassion for these people. (NIV)

What does it mean to have compassion for others? Merriam Webster's dictionary defines it as sympathetic consciousness of others' distress together with a desire to alleviate it. What a great definition!

Often we recognize the distress of others and have the desire to alleviate it, but we don't know how to take action.

In Mark 8, Jesus has been speaking to the crowd of over 4000 people for several days. The food is all gone and the people are hungry. Jesus says to His disciples, "I have compassion for these people, they have already been with me for three days and have nothing to eat." Jesus knew if He sent them home without feeding them they would collapse on the way because some had come a long distance.

Jesus asked a practical question, "How many loaves do you have? They replied, seven loaves. Jesus directed the crowd to sit down. Jesus took the loaves gave thanks, broke them, and asked the disciples to distribute them to the crowd. He did the same with some small fish. Everyone ate and was satisfied and there were seven basketsful of leftovers.

Without Jesus' compassion, the crowd would not have been fed. Other orators or teachers might have told the people to fend for themselves, and sent them on their way. Speakers focused on their message and schedule rather than the audience who had come to hear them speak.

Jesus not only saw the crowd's souls that were hungry for His living word and also needed to be healed, but Jesus saw their physical hunger. Without food, the heavenly bread He offered would not be received.

On this journey to Bill's healing, so many times my plea has been to stop Bill's distress and heal him. Yet the healing process continues. Often I still cry out to the Lord in tears, asking for Bill's suffering and discomfort to end that he might walk in all God has for him.

Yet, I know that on this path to healing, it is not only about the end result. God's miracles – God's healing touch is not only for Bill; God is moved by compassion for you.

Thank you for being compassionate people. #Godisfaithful #pray4bill

Day #785 March 4

Anchor Verse: Mark 9:22b
But if You can do anything, take pity on us and help us! [AMP]

The battles in our life may bring us to a place of desperation. We have tried everything – been to every doctor, tried home remedies, cried, expressed our frustration, done everything we could think of, and yet there is no solution.

In this story in Mark 9, a father comes to Jesus whose son is possessed by a spirit who keeps the boy from speaking and tries to harm him.

When they bring the boy to Jesus, the demon throws him to the ground in a convulsion. This has been happening since the boy's childhood. The demon has thrown him into the fire and water trying to kill him.

Then the father pleads with Jesus, "But if You can do anything, take pity on us and help us!" The man is desperate, yet in his heart, he believes that Jesus can do something. The boy's father has heard the stories of Jesus' many miracles, maybe their family, too, will be granted this gift.

Jesus responds, "'If You can?' All things are possible for the one who believes and trusts [in Me]!" The father senses Jesus' rebuke, and responds, "I do believe, help [me overcome] my unbelief."

Many of you who have been facing what seems like impossible health situations. The battle is relentless, day after day, week after week, year after year. You are weary. You may even be discouraged and frustrated.

Your desperation overrides your pride. Please, Lord, save my child, my spouse, my parent, my friend. Take pity on us. I have nothing more to give. I have exhausted all my resources and still the enemy of my soul harasses me, taunts me, and hurts the one I love. Lord Jesus, help me now.

On this journey to Bill's healing, we have faced situations that only our loving heavenly Father could remedy. In our most desperate hour when Bill was hanging between life and death, God in His infinite mercy responded, "All things are possible for those who believe and trust in Me."

Bill is very much alive and on the path to his complete healing. Praise the Lord for His amazing grace.

Thank you for your prayers of faith. #Godisfaithful #pray4bill

Day #786 March 5

Anchor Verse: Philippians 1:6
Being confident of this very thing, that He who has begun a good work in you will complete it. (NKJV)

"Being confident"… is that how you describe yourself as you wait for the Lord to finish His work in you?

When we are confident in God's work in us, it means that we believe God's promises are true for us. We trust God even when the path is long and there are "scary" things that happen on the way. We believe even when there are detours, or we get stuck in a mud pit or fall into a puddle of self-pity, or the road is blocked by a distraction from the enemy.

God's good work was planned out before your birth. We are on a path that is filled with God's promises, God's purpose for you. There may be long stretches of the road before we hit a "gem" that we can decipher as a "big gift" from the Lord. The truth is that every day God is providing encouragement on this path to the completion of His good work in us.

On this journey to Bill's healing, often I have prayed and spoken over Bill about the completion of his healing that God has purposed for him. I must choose to see God's fingerprints in our lives.

The day after his last surgery (2.6.20) when his body was consumed by weakness after what was a less intrusive method to complete his aortic valve replacement, I had to choose to thank God for every breath Bill took, every beat of his heart, every bite of food he ate, and liquid that he drank.

What I was seeing with my eyes was not "planned" but it was what we faced. Instead of "freaking out", I chose to run to my heavenly Father, pour out my heart, and then stand on the truth of His promises. "Being confident of this" – Lord, You started this healing work in Bill and You promised to complete it. (Philippians 1:6) I am holding You to Your promise.

Bill continues to improve daily on this path to healing. God's ways are not always our ways, or our thoughts, His thoughts.

Although it was not the path we planned, there were many bonuses including oversight of the healing of his incisions and making sure the valve was working properly, starting to exercise Bill's heart and body with people who are trained to do it right.

Thank you for cheering Bill on to victory. #Godisfaithful #pray4bill

Day #787 March 6

Anchor Verse: Deuteronomy 28:2
And all these blessings shall come upon you and overtake you, because you obey the voice of the Lord your God. (AMP)

From the time we are little children, most of us are taught right from wrong. We are taught to obey the voice of authority whether that is our parents, our employers, law enforcement officers, or the rules of living we find in the Bible.

Obedience brings life. Making good choices will reap many good rewards while breaking the law will result in a hard life.

In Deuteronomy 28: 3:13, there is a long list of how the Lord will reward His people as they follow the voice of the Lord.

What are some of the blessings that will come to them if they obey the voice of the Lord?

You will be blessed in the city and blessed in the country. Their crops, livestock, food and children will be blessed. Your enemies will be defeated. Everything you put your hand to will be blessed. You will be a holy people and people of all nations will know you as My people and they will fear you. The Lord will open the storehouses of heaven and send rain on your land in season and bless all the work of your hands. You will be the head and not the tail as long as you follow My commands.

What an amazing list of blessings that come to those who obey the voice of the Lord. God still rewards our obedience. His blessings flow to us and through us as we walk the path of holiness.

On this journey to Bill's healing, we have seen God bless us in so many ways. Not only in the physical realm, but the peace that passes all understanding has guarded our hearts and our minds as we have walked this path to Bill's healing.

Your prayers have lifted us up when times were tough and you celebrated with us on our days of rejoicing. Thank you for your faithfulness. #Godisfaithful #pray4bill

Day #788 March 7

Anchor Verse: Deuteronomy 3:22
You must not fear them, for the Lord your God Himself fights for you. (NKJV)

"The Lord your God Himself fights for you." This is God's promise to you today just as it was to the Israelites.

There are battles that we face in our lives that on our own, we would fail. Without God's help, you would be exhausted and overrun by the "enemy" in the first 24 hours. The truth is that God is fighting for you. Hold on to that truth. It is more valuable than silver or gold or precious stones or millions of dollars in a bank account.

The enemy of our souls would cause us to doubt the presence of the Lord. When we are struggling through a difficult time, the enemy would have us believe we are not worthy of God's help or that we are beyond God's reach. All of those are lies to trick us into believing we are helpless and hopeless.

On this journey to Bill's healing, God has fought for us, and He still fights for us. It has been a "stormy" week in our world. As we have held on to God, He has given us hope and help that comes in the name of the Lord.

Yesterday (3.6.20) Bill's hernia was in full rebellion all day… it was a long day. But as Bill rested in God's arms of love, by the end of the day, we finally had the breakthrough we had been seeking. God followed that with a restful night's sleep.

One other revelation came from the occupational therapist. Bill is doing these exercises to strengthen his body, not focusing on his body that is weak from the past surgery, but to prepare his body to be strong for the hernia surgery yet to come to minimize his recovery time. Isn't that a great perspective?

Lord, thank you for fighting for us. You don't send someone else to do Your bidding, even though You could. You love us so much that You, Yourself, are willing to fight for us. You will hold us when we are weak. You speak words of life and encouragement when we are weary. You have bought us with a price, and You delight in the fellowship we share with You.

Thank you for your persistent prayers. They have moved the hand of God. #Godisfaithful #pray4bill

Day #789 March 8

Anchor Verse: Psalm 84:11
For the Lord God is brighter than the brilliance of a sunrise! Wrapping himself around me like a shield, he is so generous with his gifts of grace and glory. Those who walk along his paths with integrity will never lack one thing they need, for he provides it all! (TPT)

Let us celebrate the goodness of the Lord, this day and every day that He gives us breath to breathe. He is great and greatly to be praised!

He is our Provider – Jehovah Jireh. He is our Savior and Lord.

Psalm 84 reminds us that He is brighter than the brilliance of a sunrise. When the first rays of light break through the darkness, Lord God Almighty is there with the promise of a new day of His grace. The darkness flees at the brilliance of His glory – the Lord sets our enemies to flight.

God wraps himself around you and me like a shield. It reminds me of that verse from Psalm 91:7, "A thousand may fall at my side and ten thousand at my right hand but it won't come near me."

Your heavenly Father delights in you – just as you are. When you get out of bed in the morning, with your hair uncombed, no makeup, half awake, happy or grumpy, God loves you as much then as when you have yourself "all together." His love is not dependent on your appearance; He loves you on the good days and the challenging ones.

We have a responsibility. In the second half of the verse, we are reminded that "those who walk along His paths with integrity will never lack one thing they need, for He provides it all!"

What does it mean to walk in integrity? The definition of integrity is the quality of being honest and having strong moral principles that you refuse to change. What we say and what we do are in alignment with God's Word as we follow His commandments.

On this journey to Bill's healing, we have been blessed by those who have walked in integrity as they cared for Bill and the reward of God's goodness has been a blessing to many. Bill and I have had the opportunity to hold fast to the Lord and follow His path to life without compromise. What a blessing it has been to have people of integrity, like yourselves, join us on this path to Bill's healing.

Thank you for your continued prayers. #Godisfaithful #pray4bill

Day #790 March 9

Anchor Verse: Proverbs 18:21
Death and life are in the power of the tongue. (AMP)

The words we speak are so powerful that they can cut deeper than a knife and build a person up faster than any self-help course.

Much has been written about the power of the tongue – both for good and for evil. James 3 expands more on this topic about the tongue and the power of such a small piece of our anatomy. In verses 7-8 it says, "All kinds of animals, birds, reptiles and sea creatures are being tamed and have been tamed by mankind, but no human being can tame the tongue. It is a restless evil, full of deadly poison." (NIV) We need God's help to tame our tongues.

This morning the Lord had me focusing not on how our tongues are used to speak "death or life" about others, but about how the words I speak about myself influence my life.

There are times in our lives where we are our own greatest enemy. When the devil sows seeds of doubt, fear, and anxiety into our lives and we choose to believe those lies rather than the truth of God – "I am a child of the King of kings and the Lord of lords", we can quickly fall into the pit of despair.

Have we been defeated, or never left the starting blocks, because our "self-talk" was negative and we talked ourselves out of even trying?

How many inventions, new ideas, new businesses or financial turnarounds have "died on the vine" because we let someone talk us out of what was possible? What God wanted to do in our lives?

My husband has often shared this little anecdote with me. We wake up in the morning with a million dollar idea and by the end of the day we have talked ourselves out of it. Likely all of us have dreamed of a great opportunity, but not many have taken it to completion.

On this journey to Bill's healing, I have had the opportunity to use my tongue to speak life, not only to myself, but to Bill. Especially in those early days when Bill was sedated and not able to respond, I was very vigilant about the words that were spoken around him and to him. Our words are like seeds that are sown into the garden of our soul, our heart, and our mind. Choose to plant good seed and watch what happens.

Thank you for your encouraging words that feed the flame of hope in our hearts and minds. #pray4bill #Godisfaithful

Day #791 March 10

Anchor Verse: Numbers 6:24-26
May the Lord bless and protect you; may the Lord's face radiate with joy because of you; may he be gracious to you, show you his favor, and give you his peace. (TLB)

Our days are not always filled with words of blessing. In fact, some days our days are filled with negativity. Latch on to these words of blessing as you head out the door this morning.

Today the Lord is blessing you and protecting you. His hedge of protection surrounds you. "A thousand may fall at your side and ten thousand at your right hand but it won't come near you." (Psalm 91:7) We have no idea how often we are saved from the devil's snares. If God is for you, who can be against you? No one will prevail with God on your side.

May the Lord's face radiate with joy because of you: When we walk in obedience to the Lord's commands and to His word, the Lord is like a proud parent. As children, many of us were blessed with those moments when our parents stood with us during an achievement and smiled and rejoiced with us.

May He be gracious to you: Without God's amazing grace, we cannot take our next breath. We would have no hope for our sins. God's grace not only follows us but it precedes us anywhere we go. Eternity awaits.

May He show you His favor: God's favor – we pray for it. We need it every hour. It is God's favor that turns a curse into a blessing. It is God's favor that creates financial turnarounds. It is God's favor that turns our mourning into dancing.

May He give you His peace: God's peace quiets the storms in our lives. God's peace can keep you calm even when the storm is still raging. His peace helps you sleep when your mind is trying to solve the mysteries of life.

On this journey to Bill's healing, we have been blessed by so many of you, not only in word but in deed. Keep God's blessing at the forefront of your mind and write it on your heart. You are loved. You are appreciated. See the Lord smiling upon you. Accept His grace. May His peace quiet your heart.

Thank you for your faithful prayers. We could not make it through the day without your intercession for us. Bill's sinuses are clogged this morning (3.10.20) – please pray for God's healing touch and good nose breathing. God is able! #pray4bill #Godisfaithful

Day #792 March 11

Anchor Verse: Mark 12:44
For they all put in out of their abundance, but she [the poor widow] out of her poverty put in all that she had, her whole livelihood. (NKJV)

What are you willing to give to the Lord? Do you give out of your excess – your leftovers or do you give your first, your best, and maybe even your last?

In Mark 12, Jesus found a place to sit and watch the crowd putting their money into the temple treasury – where the offering plates were available to receive their contributions.

Many rich people threw in large sums of money. When the poor widow came, she put in two very small copper coins, worth only a few cents. It is also referred to as the widow's mite. A mite (Greek lepta) was a copper coin worth a quadrans, the smallest Roman coin. In our monetary system, we might think of it like pennies, something of small worth.

Jesus gathered His disciples, and pointed out that what this poor widow had given, a few cents, was a better gift than the large offerings given by those who were wealthy. It wasn't the amount of the gift that mattered it was what it represented. The widow gave her whole livelihood trusting that the Lord would provide for her needs while the others gave from their abundance – what they had to spare. It wasn't a sacrifice for them.

Today is a great opportunity to look at our lives and examine our contribution to the Lord. It is not only our finances where God wants us to give our all but our time and talents. There are seasons in our life where we might not have much to contribute financially but we go a little deeper and offer our time to the Lord. It may include doing some work at our church or an outreach ministry, visiting the sick, helping a young family who needs help with their children. The list is endless.

You may be a talented craftsman – woodwork, even the trades – electrician, plumber, etc. there are opportunities to help neighbors, friends, those in other countries who could use a helping hand.

On this journey to Bill's healing, we have walked through seasons where we relied heavily on God and the kindness of others to meet our needs. But we always gave back to Him first out of what God gave to us. Always our needs were met. Life was simplified.

Thank you for serving the Lord through your actions. #Godisfaithful #pray4bill

Day #793 March 12

Anchor Verse: Psalm 51:12
Let my passion for life be restored, tasting joy in every breakthrough you bring to me. Hold me close to you with a willing spirit that obeys whatever you say. (TPT)

There are times in our lives when we are broken by what life sends our way.

Psalm 51 is a psalm of repentance by King David after he had sinned by sleeping with Bathsheba, another man's wife, and then conspired to have her husband killed in battle.

These words help us learn about the path of brokenness. After the time of mourning has passed and we ask God to restore the broken places, it's time for us to resume living.

In verse 12 we are reminded of this path, "Let my passion for life be restored, tasting joy in every breakthrough you bring to me. Hold me close to you with a willing spirit that obeys whatever you say."

Lord, this is my prayer. Let my passion for life be restored. The month of February was a difficult month with Bill's surgery and extended time in rehab and then my mom's unexpected death while Bill was in the hospital. It took me by surprise. There are some things in life we can plan for and anticipate, and others that knock the wind out of us when they come storming into our lives.

The time for being "knocked out" and "knocked down" is over. There will still be moments when grief sneaks up on me, but it's time for my passion for life to be restored. It's time to live. It's time to love. Like King David, I am committing myself anew to the Lord and asking God to fill me up with His resurrection power and "tasting joy in every breakthrough you [God] bring to me."

Spring is right around the corner and like nature that is starting to spring to life, my soul also desires new life.

Lord, I can't make it without Your help. "Hold me close to You with a willing spirit that obeys whatever You say."

On this journey to Bill's healing, we have experienced highs and lows. However, through it all, God's faithfulness has always carried us. This morning a new flame of hope, love, and joy has been rekindled as we walk forward into ALL that God has for us. Will you join us there? Thank you for persevering with us through prayer. #Godisfaithful #pray4bill

Day #794 March 13

Anchor Verse: 3 John 2
Dear friend, I am praying that all is well with you and that your body is as healthy as I know your soul is. (TLB)

How is your spiritual health this morning? Yes, I'm talking about your soul and your faith in God. Are you healthy? Would the Great Physician give you a clean bill of health this morning?

In this fallen world in which we live, there is sin and sickness. People of all ages are touched by infections, viruses, and accidents. It is a world that is filled with great joy and also grief.

Our physical bodies are temporary but our souls are eternal. We are spiritual beings and God has given us the opportunity through the sacrifice of His son, Jesus, and His resurrection, to live with God forever for eternity.

Currently, in the world, we are facing two problems that are dominating the headlines: the coronavirus and the fear that is being generated alongside of it.

At this point, it's difficult to discern which is the greater problem – the virus or the fear. Many people have entered panic mode and are behaving irrationally. Similar to the children of Israel after they left Egypt and didn't know where they would get enough food to eat. God told Moses He would provide manna from heaven. Gather what you need for the day, don't hoard it. Some listened, other did not. What was kept overnight was filled with maggots the next day.

We are to be wise like the story of the virgins who were waiting for the bridegroom to come, half had enough oil, the others did not. We must be prepared but not to the point of hoarding.

This morning, if you are a believer, we need your prayers, not your panic. Together we need to stand in faith, not falter in our fear. This is the hour when our faith is being tested. This is the hour when God's people are asked to put their trust in God, act wisely, and pray for God's help in our time of trouble.

On this journey to Bill's healing, we have encountered what seemed like impossible situations. Many times we faced life and death crossroads, but instead of responding in fear, I chose to stand in faith and believe, and declare that God's promises were true.

Thank you for praying without ceasing. #Godisfaithful #pray4bill

Day #795 March 14

Anchor Verse: Galatians 6:9

Let us not grow weary or become discouraged in doing good, for at the proper time we will reap, if we do not give in [up]. (AMP)

If you do the right thing, keep a positive attitude even when you are surrounded by negativity, and trust in God when those around you are throwing up their hands in despair, God will reward your faithfulness.

When the Chicken Little mentality ("the sky is falling") is running rampant, don't jump on the bandwagon. Stand on the promises of God. Take one step forward at a time and do so with confidence.

This verse from Galatians 6:9 seems very fitting for our world. The coronavirus has center stage in the media and everywhere we go, we are impacted by the fallout. The fear, panic, and anxiety that have been stirred up in the process may be of greater danger than the virus itself. It's time to take a step back and breathe.

The apostle Paul in his letter to the church in Galatia tells them to not grow weary or become discouraged in doing good. In his own personal experience, Paul knows that hard times come but they also pass. God in His faithfulness will sustain you. You may be stretched in the process, but God will not leave your side. He is only a prayer away.

Do you ever grow weary and discouraged by doing good? What action do you take? Do you quit doing good? Give up? Hold on. Ask for help – whether that is God or someone else. Finish the race. Great will be your reward if you don't give up.

The last part of the verse reminds us why we shouldn't give up – because at the proper time, in due season, we will reap a harvest, claim the reward.

On this journey to Bill's healing, we have been so blessed to experience God's faithfulness. Because we have chosen to not grow weary in doing good, to not get so discouraged that we gave up, God has been faithful and continued to heal Bill. Thank you, Lord. And we are still reaping the harvest, daily we see Bill's improvement and we will hold on until the completion of Bill's healing.

Thank you for your faithfulness in prayer. On this wintry morning (3.14.20) (9 degrees with the wind chill), we are bundled up and staying where it's warm. #Godisfaithful #pray4bill

Day #796 March 15

Anchor Verse: 2 Chronicles 7:14
If my people, who are called by my name, will humble themselves and pray… (NIV)

Humble yourself and pray…does that mean we are a "proud" people who believe that with enough determination or grit that we can solve any problem? Have we taken God out of the equation?

2 Chronicles 7:14 is not aimed at the unbeliever, the one who is still lost in the darkness of sin, but to God's people, the believers who know that God holds the answer to any problem we face. Those of us who are called to stand in faith and not jump on the "fear" train.

"Will humble themselves and pray" – this part of the verse tells us what to do. We are to humble ourselves. What does it mean to be "humble?" Humble as a verb succinctly means to "make less proud." We are not proud or haughty, not arrogant or assertive.

As I picture it in my mind, I see a person on their knees before the Lord, maybe even laying prostrate before Him – totally laid out on the floor worshiping Him as King of kings and Lord of lords. As we humble ourselves and pray, we admit that we don't have the answers, but He does.

After we humble ourselves, we "pray." We pray without ceasing. We are constantly in an attitude of prayer. Words may not always be flowing from your mouth, but a humble spirit is your posture and your heart is turned toward the Lord as you seek His face.

I liken it to a mother and child or a loved one who is caring for someone who is ill. There is always a part of you that is vigilant and listening for their cry or sensing a change in their condition. Often it cannot be seen with your eyes, but it is felt in your heart. That is how our relationship with God should be.

On our journey to Bill's healing, when we have faced what seemed like impossible situations, when fear demanded that we follow its path of chaos, we chose to stand on our faith in God. That is where we choose to stand. God knows the way. Let us put our hand in His hand and follow this path to heal our land.

Thank you for your faithfulness in prayer. Thank you for believing even when your eyes couldn't see the outcome. #Godisfaithful #pray4bill

Day #797 March 16

Anchor Verse: Mark 14:72
Then Peter remembered the words Jesus had spoken to him… (NIV)

Remembering… it's one of God's greatest gifts. Reliving memories can bring us great joy. How many times has your family experienced renewed laughter recounting past escapades from your youth? I know our family has. However, remembering our mistakes can bring great sorrow.

When Jesus was alone with His disciples in his final hours on earth, Mark 14:27-28 tells us, "'You will all fall away,' Jesus told them, 'for it is written: 'I will strike the shepherd, and the sheep will be scattered.'"

As you can imagine, His disciples were shocked by Jesus' words. They had followed him without failing, leaving everything behind to follow Jesus – careers, family, the comforts of home. Walk away from Jesus – never!

Peter who was known for speaking his mind said, "Even if all fall away, I will not." Jesus turned to Peter, and with compassion in His eyes spoke these words, "Truly I tell you, today – yes, tonight – before the rooster crows twice you yourself will disown me three times."

I can feel those words pierce Peter's heart. But Peter insisted emphatically, "Even if I have to die with you, I will never disown you." But as we know the story, Peter did disown Jesus three times. It is easy to read this account and condemn Peter for denying he knew Jesus, not once or twice, but three times. In our pride, we may boldly say, "I wouldn't have done that. I would have followed Jesus all the way to the cross."

The truth is we all have blown it at some point in our lives. Through our actions, or even our thoughts, we have failed. We have chosen the path of sin rather than obedience to God.

There is a good ending to this story. After Jesus died and rose again from the dead, Jesus restored Peter. Peter was forgiven and went on to serve the Lord for the rest of his life.

On our journey to Bill's healing, we have seen that Jesus is still in the restoration business. He not only restores our bodies but our mind and spirit. All we have to do is run to Him. Jesus will restore us, like He did for Peter. None of us is perfect. We all need Jesus, as our Savior.

Thank you for getting up when you have fallen. #Godisfaithful #pray4bill

Day #798 March 17

Anchor Verse: Deuteronomy 30:20

Love the Lord your God, listen to His voice, and hold fast to Him. (NIV)

When we walk through seasons of hardship, quickly we simplify our lives.

In that moment when something shifts – in our own personal life, the world economy or health arena, like our current circumstances, it feels like we have been shaken like in an earthquake. Everything feels off-kilter.

The result is we have to make adjustments to find "normal" in our lives. On our journey to Bill's healing, we have often found ourselves in circumstances that called for "adjustments" to what we call our "new normal."

In Deuteronomy 30 and the preceding text, Moses is speaking to the children of Israel whom he has led out of Egypt and through the wilderness for 40 years – talk about adjustment! Because of Moses' disobedience, he will not be entering the Promised Land. However, in his final moments as their leader, Moses is imparting his final words of wisdom to them.

We read these three short phrases in verse 20, "Love the Lord your God, listen to His voice, and hold fast to Him."

<u>Love the Lord your God.</u> God loved us before the creation of the world. He loved you so much that God sent His son to die for you that you might have eternal life. Your choice today, and every day, is to love Him with all your heart, soul, mind, and strength. And then love your neighbor as yourself.

<u>Listen to His voice.</u> Do you listen to God or is it a one-way conversation? You do all the talking and expect God to do the listening? The Bible is a good place to start to learn about God and how to live a life that pleases Him. God wants us to learn to listen for His still small voice as He speaks personally to us. The first step is to be willing to listen. As Samuel did, may we say, "Speak, Lord, your servant is listening." (1 Samuel 3:10)

<u>Cling to Him</u>. God invites us to cling to Him, just like a little child holds tightly to their parent when they are frightened. "Come to me all you who are weary and heavy laden and I will give you rest." (Matthew 11:28) In these times of uncertainty, the safest place to run is into God's arms of love. God longs to comfort you. He will make a way for you.

Thank you for staying as we faced giants. #Godisfaithful #pray4bill

Day #799 March 18

Anchor Verse: Deuteronomy 34:9
Now Joshua son of Nun was filled with the spirit of wisdom. (NIV)

Are we willing to pay the price to receive wisdom? The dictionary defines "wisdom" as the quality of having experience, knowledge, and good judgment; the quality of being wise.

Wisdom often is learned in the "school of hard knocks." Our pastor uses this example. Experience is what we learn by making our own mistakes. Wisdom is what we learn from the mistakes of others.

In this last chapter of Deuteronomy, we read of Moses' final days. Moses climbs up Mount Nebo and God shows Moses all of the Promised Land. In verse 4 it says, "Then the LORD said to him, 'This is the land I promised on oath to Abraham, Isaac and Jacob when I said, 'I will give it to your descendants.' I have let you see it with your eyes, but you will not cross over into it.'"

Because of Moses' disobedience, he will not enter the Promised Land. After 40 years, he falls short of his destination. However, there is no other man that God buried after his death, Moses' grave has never been found. Moses went to be in the presence of the Lord.

Joshua is Moses' successor. Joshua was "filled" with the spirit of wisdom. God poured the spirit of wisdom into Joshua until he was filled up. Now Joshua was ready to lead God's people after Moses laid his hands on him. Solomon asked for wisdom to lead God's people, Joshua also needed that wisdom.

In Deuteronomy 34:9, we read that God filled Joshua with the spirit of wisdom to lead His people into the Promised Land. Wisdom from God is essential to make good choices and to walk the path that pleases the Lord. Wisdom is a necessary quality for a good leader.

On this journey to Bill's healing, a spirit of wisdom has been essential to make the best choices for Bill, and for me. God's wisdom and peace have been my faithful companions on this journey.

Thank you for giving us a helping hand when life was overwhelming. We continue to shelter in place to keep Bill safe as he rests in the hollow of God's hands. Yesterday (3.17.20) the physical therapist was here and Bill practiced walking and getting stronger even in the midst of this storm. #Godisfaithful #pray4bill

Day #800 March 19

Anchor Verse: Joshua 1:9
This is my command – be strong and courageous! Do not be afraid or discouraged. For the LORD your God is with you wherever you go. (NLT)

When we face challenges in our lives, where do we turn for comfort? As a child, when we were frightened, it may have been grandma's lap that brought comfort or a stuffed animal or a special hiding place. As an adult, we may turn to God in prayer, spend time with a loved one, or go to a specific place, like a park, or listen to praise music when life gets overwhelming.

It's Joshua's first day on the job and God is giving him instructions – a pep talk. God says, "This is My command – be strong and courageous." Other translations use this wording, "Have I not commanded you?" There is no room for doubt. If God said it, He means it.

Strength and courage is what we need when we face any challenge or crisis in our lives. It speaks not only to our physical strength and fortitude, but also to our mental and emotional strength – be courageous. The only way we can be strong and courageous is if our faith and trust is secure in God alone.

"Do not be afraid or discouraged." The Lord is saying to Joshua not to be afraid of what he will see, or what he will face in the days ahead. God tells us not to be afraid. God is still in control of the world, not a virus.

Joshua is also told not to be discouraged. Discouragement can come when you have traveled a long road and it seems that the problem you are facing is still a problem. You are getting weary of the battle and when fatigue hits, discouragement often follows.

On our journey to Bill's healing, we have heard these words from the Lord many times. Be strong and courageous – do not be afraid or discouraged. We have chosen to believe God's words are true.

During our most difficult days and darkest nights, these words rang through the chaos and crisis, and lit up the sky with hope and God's truth. That is why I have stood boldly and fought for Bill. I trust God to bring all of this that we have faced and are facing, in our lives and in the greater world, to be for our good and for His glory.

Thank you for remembering us even when you face your own trials. For the next couple of weeks, we are "on our own" as Bill's caregivers and other support staff are staying away to minimize our exposure. For 800 days God has been faithful and that won't change now. #Godisfaithful #pray4bill

Day #801 March 20

Anchor Verse: Luke 1:18
Zechariah asked the angel, "How do you expect me to believe this? (TPT)

Doubt has killed many dreams and often makes us falter. Doubt caused Peter to sink while walking on the water to meet Jesus. Thomas, one of Jesus' disciples, refused to believe that Jesus was alive until he felt the nail prints in Jesus' hands. That's how he got the name "Doubting Thomas."

When we doubt God's promises, we are robbed of His blessings. Doubting is one of our enemy's favorite tools.

In Luke 1, we read the story of Zechariah, a priest, and his wife Elizabeth. The Bible says they walked blamelessly before the Lord but they were old and childless.

One day while Zechariah was in the temple, an angel of the Lord appeared to him. Zechariah was gripped with fear. The angel told him to not be afraid because his prayer had been heard. "Your wife will bear you a son and you are to call him John." The angel described in detail how God would use their son to "make ready a people prepared for the Lord."

Zechariah is overwhelmed by what has happened. "How do you expect me to believe this?" The Living Bible says, "But that's impossible!"

Because of his unbelief, Zechariah couldn't speak until after his son was born. When God chooses to make His plan and presence known, we must embrace it as truth and not doubt.

Esther, an orphan, was chosen to save a nation as the wife of the king. Moses, a shepherd with a history of mistakes, was chosen to lead the children of Israel out of Egypt. Mary, a young virgin, was chosen to become the mother of Jesus. And the list goes on…

They were chosen by God for a task that seemed to be greater than what they could accomplish on their own, but with a "mustard seed" of faith, they stepped out in faith. All God asks for is our willingness. If we would "only believe" that God can do the impossible.

On this journey to Bill's healing, God has done the impossible, time and time again. We have walked in partnership with God surrendering our lives to Him, allowing Him to write His story, to show His wonders in our lives. Thank you for walking with us. Every day we are one step closer to Bill's complete healing. #Godisfaithful #pray4bill

Day #802 March 21

Anchor Verse: Luke 1:38
Not one promise from God is empty of power, for nothing is impossible with God! (TPT)

Standing on the truth of God we will not be moved, we will not be shaken. God's promises are true. They have been for thousands of years and there is nothing we face that will change that fact. He is the same – yesterday, today, and forever.

Luke 1 shares Mary's encounter with the angel Gabriel when he came to tell her she would give birth to the Son of God. Mary was troubled at his words and wondered what kind of greeting this might be ("Greetings, you who are highly favored! The Lord is with you.").

Then the angel proceeded to tell Mary in detail what was going to happen – she would conceive and her son would be called Jesus, the Son of God. Gabriel also told her that her cousin Elizabeth in her old age was pregnant, in her sixth month. The angel then delivered this message, "Not one promise from God is empty of power, for nothing is impossible with God!"

This is God's word to us – not one promise from God…not even one… is empty of power. Read that again. Not one promise from God… not even one… is empty of power!

Whatever you are facing – health issues (you or a family member), financial issues (your workplace is closed), spiritual issues (a lack of faith), or emotional issues (you are afraid and anxious) – none of them are too big for you to handle with God's help.

God has always made a way for His people to come through a crisis. Even in this portion of scripture, Mary is told she will give birth to the Son of God. She is a young virgin girl. You know that many tongues "wagged" when she became pregnant, even Joseph, her fiancé, wanted to quietly go away. Instead of responding in fear or doubt, Mary responded, "I am the Lord's servant. May your word to me be fulfilled." There were no more questions. Mary walked forward trusting God to work out the details.

On this journey to Bill's healing, there have been places where God asked us to trust Him when it didn't make sense. God asked us to do what seemed to be counterintuitive. It didn't make sense to other people, yet if God said it, we believed it and obeyed.

Thank you for your faithful prayers. #Godisfaithful #pray4bill

Day #803 March 22

Anchor Verse: Luke 1:45
Blessed is she who has believed that the Lord would fulfill his promises to her. (NIV)

Faith is believing when you cannot "see" what lies ahead. Hebrews 11:1 defines "faith" like this: "Now faith is the substance of things hoped for, the evidence of things not seen." (NKJV)

As a believer, every day we walk by faith. We must believe the truth of God that we find in the Bible, and what God is speaking to us.

Yesterday we studied Gabriel's appearance to Mary that God had chosen her to give birth to Jesus, the Son of God. Mary chose to believe and said, "I am the Lord's servant. May your word to me be fulfilled."

Mary's cousin, Elizabeth, comes to visit her and declares, "Blessed is she who has believed that the Lord would fulfill His promises to her."

Elizabeth knew that God could do the impossible, she was pregnant herself in her old age. Her voice of praise ascends to the throne room of heaven. Two women that God has chosen to accomplish His purpose on earth. Two unlikely women – one who is too old to have children in the natural order of things, and the other, a young unmarried woman, engaged to be married, whose season to have a child in the natural had not yet come.

God's plans supersede their plans. He wanted to bring the sinful world back into fellowship with Him. The creation of the world was unique and supernatural, so would be this event to restore His people.

His methods have not changed. God still colors outside the lines. God knows the end result and He will move heaven and earth to accomplish it. He has "best plans" for you and for me. The question is, are we willing to receive them? Do we believe God can and will fulfill His promises to us?

On this journey to Bill's healing, God has made promises to me about Bill's recovery. God said it and I believe it. It is from this foundation of truth that I stand firm and hold my ground. I "fight" for Bill – not only in the natural as his advocate and caregiver, but in the supernatural/spiritual realm where the battle between God and the enemy rages over Bill's life and future.

Thank you for believing even when your eyes couldn't see. May the blessings of the Lord be multiplied in your life. #Godisfaithful #pray4bill

Day #804 March 23

Anchor Verse: Joshua 14:8

But my fellow Israelites who went up with me made the hearts of the people melt in fear. I, however, followed the LORD my God wholeheartedly. (NIV)

Do you follow the crowd like a sheep or are you willing to stand on your godly convictions? Are you like Caleb who saw the good in the Promised Land (along with Joshua) or are you like the other ten spies who made the people tremble in fear?

At this time in history, as the world and its people are battling a world-wide illness, we have the choice to follow the Lord our God wholeheartedly or to melt in fear and bring others along with us.

This is an hour when we, as believers, can walk forward in faith and be Jesus' hands and feet. As we stay tucked in with God, literally in our homes, we can pray, we can encourage others through phone calls, and what we post on social media. Are you good at sewing? There is a shortage of masks in our hospitals and other places where those on the frontlines need protection.

Let's take a look for a moment at Caleb, whose is the subject of this verse in Joshua 14:8. When he was 40 years old, Caleb was one of twelve spies that Moses sent into the Promised Land to scout it out. When they returned, ten of the men brought back a doom and gloom report while Caleb and Joshua told Moses with God's help they could take the land.

Forty-five years have passed and Caleb at the age of 85 is as strong and vigorous as the day God sent him out. The Lord has been good to Caleb because of his faithfulness. Caleb could truthfully declare, " I followed the Lord my God wholeheartedly."

On this journey to Bill's healing, we have had the opportunity at many crossroads to view the path ahead as one filled with opportunity that with the Lord's help we could overcome our challenges or deliver a "gloom and doom" report. We have chosen to follow Caleb's example and follow the Lord wholeheartedly.

As we continue to face the effects of the coronavirus, my prayer for you and for me is that we face this challenge in faith, believing God will make a way through it. But in the meantime, we have the opportunity to be His hands and feet.

Thank you for your encouraging words and faithful prayers. Even in the midst of the storm, God continues Bill's healing. #Godisfaithful #pray4bill

Day #805 March 24

Anchor Verse: 2 Chronicles 16:9
The eyes of the LORD search the whole earth in order to strengthen those whose hearts are fully committed to him. (NLT)

The eyes of the Lord are searching the whole earth – every continent – places seemingly invisible to the naked eye – for only one purpose – to strengthen those whose hearts are fully committed to Him.

As with many of God's promises, there is something you must do first. Some would call it a "catch" – meaning it's a promise that has a condition attached to it. What is the "condition" or the "catch?"

Your heart, my heart, must be FULLY committed to God. We must be serious about our relationship with God and our desire to follow Him.

We develop close friendships with those who are willing to commit time and effort to a friendship. Your friend must be willing to spend time with you, engage in conversation, be a "safe" place where you can share, and as a believer, the common bond of your relationship with God is also important.

In our commitment with God, He wants the same things. God wants to spend time with you, talk with you, and have you share the concerns of your heart. Your belief in God as your Lord and Savior is the foundation of that friendship, that relationship.

As we read the part about God searching the "whole earth" to find those whose hearts are fully committed to Him, it makes me wonder. Does that mean there are not many of us that are "fully committed" to God? Do we need to examine our own hearts and see how important God is in our life?

My second thought is that God is relentless in His search to find you and me. Of the billions of people that live in this world, you are that important to God. His eyes are searching to find you and your commitment to Him. What you do matters to God.

On this journey to Bill's healing, God has honored our commitment that through all of what we have experienced and walked through our chief goal is that God would be honored and glorified. Without God's miracles in Bill's life, our story would have a different ending. However, because of God's mercy and grace and His resurrection power, we are strengthened as we walk this road to victory in Jesus' name.

Thank you for your perseverance. #Godisfaithful #pray4bill

Day #806 March 25

Anchor Verse: Matthew 6:33

But first and most importantly seek (aim at, strive after) His kingdom and His righteousness [His way of doing and being right—the attitude and character of God], and all these things will be given to you also. (AMP)

When systems and structures and what's "normal" shift around us, God does not. As we face new challenges in the world, the Ten Commandments have not been altered. God is still on His throne and the path to life has not changed. Jesus is the way, the truth, and the life. The Bible says that no man comes to the Father except through Jesus.

As we look at this familiar verse, our call is still to seek the Kingdom of God and His righteousness. The Amplified Version says, "But first and most importantly seek (aim at, strike after) His kingdom and His righteousness [His way of doing and being right – the attitude and character of God]." In a nutshell, God has given us His strategy for living life in this world as we prepare for eternity.

It's not only about what we are seeking but about our attitude in the process of doing it.

We can choose to have a good attitude no matter what is happening around us. Yesterday (3.24.20) in our neighborhood, the battle in the heavenlies was intense. In the sky you could see this dark black cloud that was threatening to overcome the sunshine and puffy white clouds. The sky would grow dark – we even had a rain downpour with some hail… and then it backed off again. The battle raged through the night.

More than what we saw with our physical eyes, in my body and spirit, I could feel the battle of good and evil being played out. It's possible the warring angels were close by fighting the coronavirus and the destructive forces behind it. The best thing to do was to stay inside and trust God's protective covering over us.

On this journey to Bill's healing, there have been many nights, and days, when the battle was intense. My cries to the Lord, my prayers for hope and healing, pounding the gates of heaven day and night were my first priority – sleep and anything else could wait.

Thank you for your prayers, day and night, we couldn't make it without them. #Godisfaithful #pray4bill

Day #807 March 26

Anchor Verse: Proverbs 25:11
Like apples of gold in settings of silver is a word spoken at the right time. (AMP)

Beautiful things, beautiful words have been appreciated for generations.

Proverbs 25:11 reminds us that words spoken at "the right time" can be compared to a work of art – apples of gold in settings of silver. If you study some of the commentaries on this verse, there is a discussion about what "fruit" was being described. Likely it was a "golden-colored" fruit – maybe an apple, orange, citron, or even a pomegranate. It wasn't actually made out of "gold" – it wasn't that kind of treasure. In fact, Solomon could have been describing a gift he received.

More important than the beauty of the item described is the second part of this verse, a word spoken at the right time. From an early age, we learn the power of words. Some of the first words spoken or taught are "Yes" and "No." As we continue to grow up, we learn that words have the power to build up another person, and unfortunately, words that hurt or tear another person down. Life and death are in the power of the tongue.

It is so important to remember the power of our words, both spoken and written. Modern technology allows us to send messages almost instantaneously – maybe too fast at times – via text, instant messaging, or a quick comment in response to a post on social media.

Our words are more powerful than a raging wildfire or hurricane-force winds. Words can get people "whipped up" into a frenzy of fear or calm the raging sea. Words spoken with kindness, gentleness, love, peace, and joy will turn the tide and start a new movement to counter the flood of negativity, anxiety, and fear that has been flowing in the last weeks.

As we "shelter in place" we have an opportunity to create our own atmosphere of peace and positivity in our homes. Get reacquainted and do something fun like share stories of past adventures.

On this journey to Bill's healing, we have had the opportunity to create our "own world" inside the four walls of our home. We have chosen to fill it first with God's presence as we invite Him to guide our lives. Then we add positive things, positive words, and actions that have helped in the rebuilding of our lives and Bill's body.

Thank you for your encouraging words. #Godisfaithful #pray4bill

Day #808 March 27

Anchor Verse: Matthew 11:28
Are you weary, carrying a heavy burden? Then come to me. I will refresh your life, for I am your oasis. (TPT)

Are you weary this morning? Weariness comes when we are carrying heavy burdens. Weariness wears on us, it's a mental fatigue, emotional draining that comes from carrying a burden in our heart, mind, or soul.

Through the days of home quarantine, many are realizing that their "daydream" of staying home instead of going to work, isn't quite what they imagined. Of course, their "daydream" didn't include having the children home from school, and in many cases, businesses closed down and no paycheck coming in. "These are the times that try men's souls." Even as Thomas Paine first spoke these words during the winter of 1776 during the American Revolution, they seem to fit our current situation.

But Jesus in Matthew 11:28 offers us shelter in the storm, a place of peace, a place of rest. He spoke these words, "Come to me all you who are weary and heavy laden and I will give you rest." The Passion translation says, "Are you weary, carrying a heavy burden? Then come to me. I will refresh your life, for I am your oasis."

An oasis in the desert is not a mirage, a figment of a thirsty man's imagination, it offers water to quench his thirst and hope that he will live and complete his journey.

As we came to the end of 2019, many people were excited about 2020 – the year of "perfect vision" – 20/20 vision. 2020 marks the beginning of a new decade. No one predicted that we would be hit with a worldwide pandemic that would cause such havoc.

None of this has taken God by surprise. He has a plan and a purpose for this time in history. It is an opportunity to draw closer to God and improve your prayer life. Look at how God has flooded social media with church services bringing a message of hope to those who are weary and troubled. Hold on to God and don't give up.

On this journey to Bill's healing, there have been days where we have grown weary of the relentless battle, but as He promised, God has been there to carry us through. We have heard the words of Jesus to "come to Him" and it is there we have found rest and His sweet peace.

Thank you for your prayers. #pray4bill #Godisfaithful

Day #809 March 28

Anchor Verse: Judges 6:12
When the angel of the Lord appeared to Gideon, he said, "The Lord is with you, mighty warrior." (NIV)

This morning you need to hear these words and believe them. You are a mighty warrior. You may not feel like it right now, but we must stand on the truth and not our feelings.

Gideon didn't think he had what it took to be mighty leader for God, but God knew better.

God sent an angel to deliver a message to Gideon. "The Lord is with you, mighty warrior." And Gideon's response wasn't very positive. Lord, if You are with us then why are all these bad things happening? The Lord brought us out of Egypt but now He has abandoned us.

Does this sound familiar? In the midst of this battle with the coronavirus as people are quarantined at home, are some people, some of us asking where is God?

It is the enemy's greatest weapon to fill us with doubt and fear. The enemy has come to steal, kill, and destroy but Jesus came to bring us life. That is the truth.

God's response, Go in the strength you have and save Israel out of Midian's hand. Am I not sending you? Gideon says he comes from the weakest tribe of Israel and he is the least in his family.

"I will be with you." This is God's response. This is all Gideon needed because he would have God's strength to empower him... not his own.

The same is true today. God will go with you. If He says go, then "go"... but for right now our command physically is to "stay" to stop the spread of the virus.

On this journey to Bill's healing, I have learned that "staying" is far more difficult than "going." We love to go, go, go. That is our lifestyle in this culture. We are often humans "doing" rather than a human "being."

I was talking to one of my prayer warrior friends the other night and she said that we needed to stand firm and not let the enemy steal ground that we have already taken, that God has promised to us.

Thank you for covering us in prayer. #Godisfaithful #pray4bill

Day #810 March 29

Anchor Verse: Luke 5:5
But Simon answered and said to Him [Jesus], "Master, we have toiled all night and caught nothing; nevertheless at Your word I will let down the net." (NKJV)

Are you willing to obey Jesus even when it doesn't make sense? Do you trust Him enough to do what flies in the face of your past experience?

Simon Peter and his fisherman friends had been fishing all night and caught nothing. They would return home with empty hands and nothing to sell at the market to put any money in their pockets. Tired, dirty, hungry, and maybe even sore from hauling the nets in and out of the boat, they are washing their nets when Jesus gets into Simon's boat and asks him to put out a little from the shore. Simon obeyed.

When Jesus finished speaking, He said, "Put out into the deep water, and let down the nets for a catch." In verse five, Simon says, We haven't caught anything all night, but because "you say so" I will let down the nets.

They caught such a large number of fish that their nets began to break. They had to ask for another boat to come and help them, and both boats were so full they began to sink.

Their obedience brought a double measure of blessing. Simon and all of his companions were astonished at the catch including James and John, the sons of Zebedee, Simon's partners.

Jesus responded, "Don't be afraid, from now on you will fish for people. And they pulled their boats on shore, left everything and followed Jesus."

When the storms of life come, Jesus speaks peace to them. If we choose to trust Him and follow His commands, Jesus will calm the seas and help us walk through these stormy waters.

On this journey to Bill's healing, we have been in that place of exhaustion, but hearing the words of Jesus we have been revived. We have been willing to do what Jesus said even when it didn't necessarily make sense to us. Obedience brings life.

March 29, 2020, we find ourselves in the midst of the coronavirus storm. A call was issued for another National Day of Prayer and Fasting to seek God's face and God's favor to bring this nightmare to an end. Thank you for obeying Jesus when all those around you have been walking the wrong direction. #pray4bill #Godisfaithful

Day #811 March 30

Anchor Verse: Matthew 6:13
Deliver us from evil...(AMP)

Jesus chose twelve men to be His disciples, to learn from Him and prepare them to teach the world and love as Jesus loved. One day the disciples asked Jesus to teach them how to pray. You may be asking this same question, "Lord, how do I pray in the midst of this world crisis?"

He taught them this simple yet all-encompassing and powerful prayer. We often refer to it as the Lord's Prayer.

In the early hours of this morning, when it was yet too early to get up, the Lord asked me to sit with Him for a while in the quietness. I was thanking Him for the gift of a new day as I listened to Bill sleeping beside me.

The Lord led me to this prayer. Word by word I let it seep into my parched soul, as water seeps into the dry earth. As I came near the end of the prayer, "And lead us not into temptation, but deliver us from evil" I stopped.

We spent a few moments there... my heavenly Father and me. In this battle with the coronavirus, it feels like we need to be delivered from evil. Not only the virus itself, but the fear and anxiety that has been whipped up and the actions and attitudes of stressed-out, fearful people.

Balanced against that is kindness and generosity of so many who are looking out for their neighbors, family, and friends. Those who are sharing what they have with others. Words of hope and encouragement that are being spoken to those who have grown weary in this battle.

What we need to remember is that Jesus is our anchor that holds our ship steady through the storms of life. Hold on to hope. Hold on to His hand.

In the darkness and quietness with the light from my alarm clock, in my mind's eye, I pictured the battle over evil being won. The day when the coronavirus is history, not the battle we daily face. When once again, our churches are filled and the playgrounds echo with our children's laughter.

On this journey to Bill's healing, we have faced mountains that were too big for us to conquer alone, but the Lord in His faithfulness delivered us every time by the power of His might. Yes, God will deliver us from evil again this time... He promised that nothing is impossible for Him. Thank you for your faithful prayers. Together we touch the world for good, one kind deed, one prayer at a time. #Godisfaithful #pray4bill

Day #812 March 31

Anchor Verse: Psalm 80:7
Restore us, God Almighty; make Your face shine on us, that we may be saved. (NIV)

Our help comes in the name of the Lord, Maker of heaven and earth. There is none other like Him. God first breathed the breath of life into us and every breath is a gift from God.

It's the last day of March 2020. It has been a long month for each one of us. There have been challenges in our lives the likes of which we have not seen before. It has been by God's grace and His grace alone that we have arrived here safely.

Throughout history there have been times when mankind went through great trials. They tried to figure out the solution on their own but their attempts were fruitless.

Often we try to figure out the solution to our problems in our own strength, our own wisdom when the truth is, our only hope comes from God.

Shouldn't we run to God first instead of last? The answer is yes. The good news is that God because of His great love for us is waiting for us with arms wide open to receive us when we run to Him.

During this month as the coronavirus has been running rampant around the world, we all have been touched by it in some way. Whether through the illness itself, the threat of the illness, or finding ourselves quarantined at home to stop the spread of it, the cry of our hearts is the same as the psalmist in Psalm 80:7, "Restore us, God Almighty; make your face shine on us, that we may be saved."

This is the prayer on our lips as we come to the end of March. Restore us, O Lord. Not because of our goodness, but because of Your grace and mercy. This morning we pray for those who are sick that they may be healed, for their loved ones who cannot be at their bedside that they would be comforted. Lord, we pray that today You would move in Your mighty power and visit us and speak Your words of peace to our weary souls.

On this journey to Bill's healing, there have been portions of the path that passed through uncharted territory where our only hope was God, and He was faithful. That is why I know that God is still faithful today and every day.

Thank you for praying for us. #Godisfaithful #pray4bill

April 2020

Love never fails.
~ 1 Corinthians 13:8

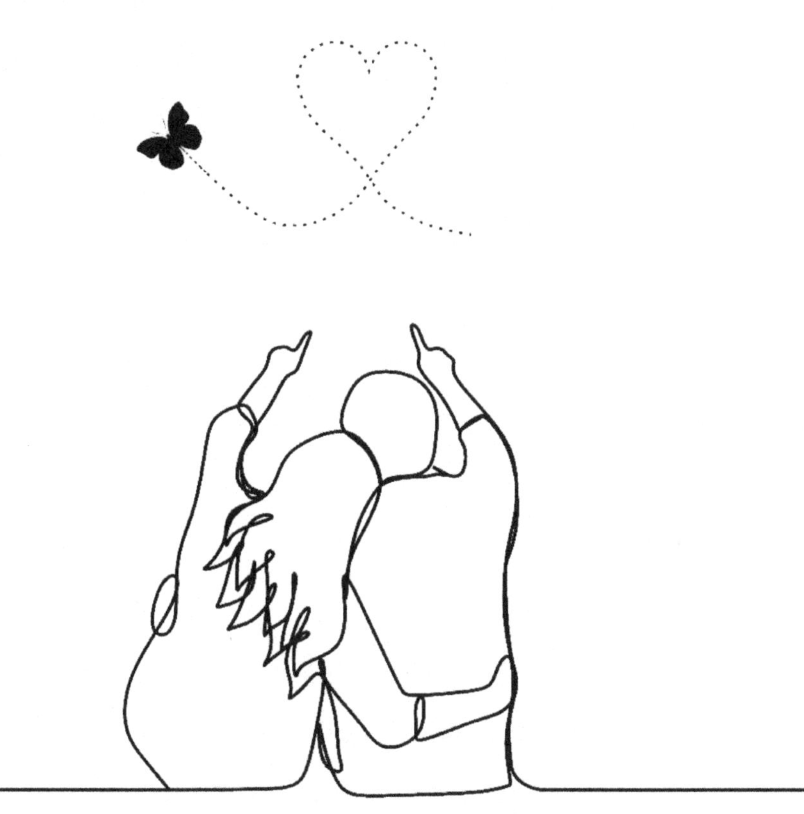

Day #813 April 1

Anchor Verse: Luke 6:31
Treat others as you want them to treat you. (TLB)

The Golden Rule… many of us were trained as children to treat others like we want to be treated.

It is not old-fashioned or out of style. If we all lived by this rule, our headlines would change.

There are many who do live their lives this way. We often see their acts of kindness highlighted. But when Jesus shared this truth, He meant for all people to lead with kindness.

In this challenging time in which we are living, there are many ways to offer comfort and kindness to each other. With the "Stay Home, Stay Safe" guidelines in place across the nation, many families find themselves in unusual circumstances. It probably has been a long time since everyone was under the same roof for 24 hours a day, seven days a week.

Showing kindness to each other is like Mary Poppins' bright idea that "a spoonful of sugar helps the medicine go down." It might help calm some ruffled feathers from being in such close proximity to each other.

Maybe this is a lesson we can re-learn and then when we return to our "normal" routines, it will be with hearts softened by kindness looking for opportunities to do good.

Jesus goes on to say not only to show kindness to those who are good to you, but also to love your enemies. As we are merciful to others, God will be merciful to us. Thank you, Lord.

On this journey to Bill's healing, we have had the opportunity to treat others as we wanted to be treated. As we made our way through the healthcare system, we treated others with respect and kindness, and offered kindness to those who were going through similar circumstances.

We have been so blessed to have you traveling this road with us and we thank God for your faithfulness. Bill and I are grateful for the opportunities to pray for you and speak encouraging words into your life because of God's goodness to us.

Thank you for putting love in action. #Godisfaithful #pray4bill

Day #814 April 2

Anchor Verse: Luke 7:9
When Jesus heard this, He was amazed…"not even in Israel have I found such great faith [as this man's]." (AMP)

When Jesus walked this earth, it wasn't only the Jews that were curious about this Jesus. People from other backgrounds and regions heard of Jesus' healing miracles. Even today, when news of a scientific breakthrough, a new medical procedure or alternative treatment is announced, people are drawn to this new "cure."

Jesus was the source of miracles. The deaf could hear. The blind could see. The lame could walk again. And people were being raised from the dead!

A Roman centurion's servant was ill and about to die. The centurion sent some Jewish elders to Jesus asking Him to come and heal his servant. Later he sent word, that he was not worthy for Jesus to enter his home. "But say the word and my servant will be healed."

This Roman centurion was a man of authority and believed that Jesus had the power to heal this valued servant without coming near his home.

Jesus was "amazed" by this man's faith. "I haven't seen this kind of faith in all of Israel." At that moment, the centurion's servant was healed.

Do you have that kind of faith? Would Jesus be "amazed" at your great faith?

On this journey to Bill's healing, I have cried out to the Lord to heal my husband on many occasions. There have been life and death moments, where God was our only hope, man's medicine did not hold the answer. And God heard me and answered, like He did for this centurion.

Today marks two years ago (4.2.18) that Bill received his pacemaker, a tool to help regulate his heart. God continues to direct Bill's healing and "fine tune" his body as we give God all the glory. Thank you, Lord.

When God has a plan and purpose for your life, nothing can stop Him. We don't always understand the roller coaster ride, or the mountains we face, but God will never leave us or forsake us.

Thank you for your prayers that have moved mountains. Rejoice with us. God is the God of miracles. #Godisfaithful #pray4bill

Day #815 April 3

Anchor Verse: 2 Corinthians 8:7

You people there are leaders in so many ways – you have so much faith, so many good preachers, so much learning, so much enthusiasm, so much love for us. Now I want you to be leaders also in the spirit of cheerful giving. (TLB)

From my childhood I can remember this lesson, "It is more blessed to give than receive." As a child, that's not always the easiest lesson to understand. We love to receive but sharing and giving is a lesson learned that will last for a lifetime.

Once you catch the spirit of giving, there is a thrill that is like none other. It is really fun to give while remaining anonymous. The Bible talks about not letting your left hand know what your right hand is doing. Don't be like the Pharisees who made a big deal about what they gave in the temple but rather like the woman who gave out of her need rather than her excess.

This verse in 2 Corinthians reminds us that we can excel in everything else – you have so much faith, so many good preachers, so much learning, so much enthusiasm, so much love for us but now Paul says, I want you to be leaders also in the spirit of cheerful giving.

Are you a cheerful giver? Is every day like Christmas morning as you seek opportunities to share from the goodness that God has given you?

Mark Batterson's book, *Double Blessing* teaches not only about how God blesses us but how we should "flip the blessing" and bless others.

We can bless others through our time, talent, and treasure. Learn to be a cheerful giver in this season of your life. And then when life turns around, your new habit will have an even greater impact on the world.

On this journey to Bill's healing, we have learned the power of being a cheerful giver. Our financial treasure chest might have been lean at times but throwing three-minute blessing parties for those who helped care for Bill became a way of life. It still is today.

Thank you for blessing us in so many ways. Your prayers have often been our lifeline. May the Lord bless you indeed. #Godisfaithful #pray4bill

Day #816 April 4

Anchor Verse: Ruth 2:12
May the Lord repay you for what you have done. May you be richly rewarded by the Lord, the God of Israel, under whose wings you have come to take refuge. (NIV)

God rewards our faithfulness as we listen to Him and walk in His way. Obedience involves trust... often going places we do not know. In Ruth's case, it involved leaving her homeland, a familiar place, and following her mother-in-law to Naomi's homeland.

Ruth was a young widow. Naomi, her mother-in-law, urged her to stay there in Moab and find a new husband. Ruth would not stay behind but was committed to accompany Naomi without knowing what was ahead of her.

"Where you go, I will go. Where you lodge, I will lodge. Your people will be my people. And your God will be my God." Ruth's words are often used in marriage ceremonies to signify a couple's commitment to each other.

When Ruth arrived in this foreign place, she followed Naomi's instructions and went to work gleaning in the fields so the two women had food to eat.

As the story unfolds, Ruth becomes Boaz's wife and gives birth to a son, Obed. Obed is the grandfather of King David. Ruth because of her obedience is part of the lineage of Jesus.

The truth is that Ruth didn't obey because of the reward. Ruth obeyed because of her love and commitment to her mother-in-law and to God. "Your people will be my people and your God will be my God."

"May the Lord repay you for what you have done. " Because of her kindness, Boaz asked the Lord to repay Ruth for her sacrifice, for the hard work she was doing, for the loneliness she must have felt in a foreign land, and even to help her as she mourned the loss of her husband.

The second part of the blessing, "May you be richly rewarded by the Lord, the God of Israel, under whose wings you have come to take refuge" reminds me of Psalm 91:4. "He will cover you with his feathers, and under his wings you will find refuge."

On this journey to Bill's healing, we have walked into "foreign lands" to follow God and His will. God went before us and has accomplished His purpose in our lives and continues to do so.Thank you for your faithful prayers. #Godisfaithful #pray4bill

Day #817 April 5

Anchor Verse: Luke 19:37
The entire multitude of the disciples [all those who were or claimed to be His followers] began praising God [adoring Him enthusiastically and] joyfully with loud voices for all the miracles and works of power that they had seen. (AMP)

Today is Palm Sunday 2020 – a day that marks the beginning of Jesus' journey to the cross – Christ's triumphal entry into Jerusalem. "Blessed is the King who comes in the name of the Lord." (Luke 9:38 NIV)

Jesus instructed two of his disciples to go into the village and when they found a colt tied there to untie it and bring it to Him. If anyone asks why you are untying it tell them, "The Lord needs it."

They did as he asked and then put their cloaks on the colt and then Jesus. As the colt moved forward, people lay their cloaks on the ground before Him.

For so much of His ministry, it appeared that people came to Jesus only to receive what He had to offer. Relentlessly they pursued Him, wanting to see His miracles, to receive their healing or that of a loved one or friend. It seemed to be a selfish pursuit... "Jesus, what can you do for me?"

On this day, Jesus would receive the praise and honor due Him. Jesus would enter Jerusalem on His terms, not at the hands of man, but by the will of God.

As Jesus entered Jerusalem, He wept over it. So many had missed His true purpose. They missed the day of His visitation. They were blind to His presence. They were deaf to His words of life. Their hearts were not touched by His love because they refused to open their heart to Jesus.

As the world around us seems to be in chaos, where do we stand? Are we part of the crowd cheering enthusiastically as Jesus enters triumphantly? Or are we like so many whose eyes were blind and hearts were cold and refused His gift of life?

On this journey to Bill's healing, we have been blessed by the Lord's presence each day. As we lift our hands and hearts in praise, we thank the Lord for the gift of life and praise Him for His mighty miracles. The Lord is good and His love endures forever.

Thank you for praising the Lord with us. #pray4bill #Godisfaithful

Day #818 April 6

Anchor Verse: 2 Corinthians 8:2
Though they have been going through much trouble and hard times, they have mixed their wonderful joy with their deep poverty, and the result has been an overflow of giving to others. (TLB)

In the midst of the most trying times of our lives, the love of God shines through us. Throughout history, we have seen the light rise above the darkness.

Paul is speaking of the Macedonian churches here in 2 Corinthians 8 and how they gave generously, not out of their abundance, but out of their poverty. In verse three, it says they gave as much as they were able and even beyond their ability.

In 2020, JoAnn Fabrics through their Make a Facemask program have helped meet a need. Customers are able to pick up a facemask kit at any open store, free of charge, to create masks to donate to healthcare systems and organizations in need. In two weeks, donated materials have helped make nearly five million masks.

The response has been incredible, and customers are making even more than what is being donated. They estimate that customers have purchased enough material to make an additional 20 million masks in that same period. That's 25 million masks going to protect healthcare workers, public service employees, and communities in need. It's one example of God's love in action. It also extends to finances and donations to help others. Food and other supplies shared with those who don't have enough. And the power of our prayers can never be underestimated.

Reaching out in love and sharing our blessings, living with a generous heart can become a way of life. It's how Jesus lived. May we follow His example.

Are you a generous giver? Do you give out of your lack rather than your overflow? May the Lord bless you as you give with a generous heart.

On this journey to Bill's healing, we have had the opportunity to be recipients of the generosity of others and to give generously. It is an amazing way to live and to love others. It's not only about your finances. We have time, talent, and treasure that God can use to be of service to others.

Thank you for praying without ceasing. #Godisfaithful #pray4bill

Day #819 April 7

Anchor Verse: Luke 9:18
And He (Jesus) asked them, saying, "Who do the crowds say that I am?"(NKJV)

Jesus often took His disciples to a private place to teach them and reveal His plans. It's similar to the way we live our lives. There is some information we share with the general public, other information we share with our friends, and the most personal information we share with our family.

In this passage in Luke 9, Jesus has performed the miracle of feeding the 5000 people with five loaves and two fish. Jesus and His disciples are in a private place and it says, "Jesus was praying." I am certain Jesus did this a lot. After all, prayer is communicating with God, our heavenly Father.

Jesus and His heavenly Father always had much to discuss. We can learn from Jesus' example to take everything to God in prayer.

But Jesus said to His disciples, "Who do the crowds say I am?" The crowds knew there was something special about Jesus. They knew Jesus had a connection to God but did not recognize who He was.

Then Jesus asked His disciples, "Who do you say that I am?" Peter responded, "God's Messiah."

He knew the truth. Jesus warned them not to tell anyone else. And then Jesus told them of the difficult path He would walk, the suffering and rejection Jesus would endure at the hands of the religious leaders. And ultimately Jesus would be killed and on the third day raised to life.

His resurrection is still our hope. Because Jesus is alive, we can face tomorrow and all our fear is gone.

On this journey to Bill's healing, we have come to know Jesus in a more personal way. It is often in our greatest trials where we receive a greater revelation of who Jesus is. Jesus is all you need.

Thank you for your faithfulness in prayer and holding up our arms when we are weary. Bill is growing stronger in the Lord. Continue to pray for perfect alignment throughout Bill's body. #Godisfaithful #pray4bill

Day #820 April 8

Anchor Verse: Psalm 80:19

Turn us again to Yourself [restore us], O God of the armies of heaven. Look down on us, Your face aglow with joy and love – only then shall we be saved. (TLB)

Praise the Lord with me this morning. He alone is worthy of our praise.

It is through prayer, praise, and worship that God is invited into our lives, our circumstances so that He can reign victoriously. As we step out in faith declaring that not only is God all we want, but all we need.

We are mid-week as we move toward Easter, Resurrection Sunday (2020), Christ's great triumph over death and the grave. It is an opportunity to fully embrace the full power, joy, and love of God's gift to us through Jesus Christ.

In Psalm 80, the psalmist is crying out to the Lord to rescue them out of their dire circumstances. He is reminding the Lord of how He rescued them in the past. Revive us, O Lord.

"Turn us again to yourself, O God of the armies of heaven. Look down on us, your face aglow with joy and love – only then shall we be saved." (TLB)

The God of the armies of heaven is unstoppable. He will not be defeated by any enemy – no man, no sickness will prevail against the will of God.

And the latter part of the verse brings comfort... "Look down on us, Your face aglow with love and joy, only then will we be saved."

For a moment, shut out all the distractions. Turn off the news. Open your Bible. Turn on some praise music and let the Lord minister to your soul.

You are beat up from this relentless attack. You are tired and weary. God wants to restore you. Your hope, my hope comes in the name of the Lord. You only need to be willing to accept the gift.

On this journey to Bill's healing, there have been times when we were weary in the flesh. Even times when the attacks from the enemy threatened our peace and sought to diminish the power of God, but on every occasion, God has been faithful. When we cried out to Him in our distress and desperation, He heard the cries of our heart and answered by restoring us.

We thank God for you every day. #Godisfaithful #pray4bill

Day #821 April 9

Anchor Verse: Luke 22:28
You are those who have remained and have stood by Me in My trials. (AMP)

Our heavenly Father is always looking for those who are willing to walk with Him and obey His commands.

This passage from Luke is part of the story of Jesus' walk to the cross. In Luke 22:7-65, we read what happened on that Thursday, often referred to as Maundy Thursday in the Christian faith, from the Last Supper through Jesus' arrest and what followed to the end of that day.

When I was a child, I can remember our church having Maundy Thursday services. I could feel the heaviness, the weight that must have been on Jesus' shoulders as He would face His betrayal leading to His death on the cross that night. All alone in so many ways.

However, in the midst of this, Jesus celebrates the Passover with His disciples. We often refer to it as the "Last Supper." And Jesus reveals to them what will take place that night. Jesus is the sacrificial Lamb that will take away the sins of the world. His body would be broken. His blood would be shed for our sins.

In the midst of this solemn moment, a dispute breaks out about who is the greatest. Really?? We read this and wonder, what they were thinking? Then we realize that we too have not responded as we should in sacred moments.

Yet Jesus in His patient loving way, even to the end, reminds them that the greatest is the one who serves. "I am among you as one who serves." That is a truth that echoes through time to us.

In verse 28 it says, "You are those who have remained and have stood by Me in My trials." Jesus recognizes their faithfulness and confers on them a kingdom, just as His father conferred on Jesus. There would continue to be a high price to pay for their allegiance.

On our journey to Bill's healing, Jesus has been with us through every test and trial. We have chosen to hold on to His hand and never let go. Our faith remains in God and God alone.

Thank you for abiding with us. #pray4bill #Godisfaithful

Day #822 April 10

Anchor Verse: 1 Samuel 16:7
But the Lord said to Samuel, "Do not consider his appearance or his height, for I have rejected him. The Lord does not look at the things people look at. People look at the outward appearance, but the Lord looks at the heart." (NIV)

We are often quick to judge people and products by what they look like on the outside. Yes, we judge a book by its cover.

God has never been moved by the outward appearance of a man or woman, God looks at our heart, our intentions, and our integrity.

This story from 1 Samuel was when Samuel was sent to anoint the new king of Israel after Saul disobeyed the Lord and the Lord departed from him. Samuel was heart-broken when that happened, but after Samuel had mourned for a time, God told him to get up and go, there was a new man God had chosen. (There are some lessons we can learn from God through this experience.)

As Samuel is sent to Jesse's home, Jesse's sons are brought to Samuel. Eliab came first. Samuel thought, surely the Lord's anointed stands before me. And the Lord responded, "Do not consider his appearance or his height, for I have rejected him. The Lord does not look at the things people look at. People look at the outward appearance, but the Lord looks at the heart."

Saul, the first king of Israel, "looked" like a king, but that didn't turn out so well. Quickly the lesson is driven home to Samuel, and to us, that God uses the unlikely to do His will, often to do the impossible. When that is the case, we know it's all about God, not about "how good we are."

As we celebrate Good Friday, the day Jesus went to the cross to pay the price for our sins, we are reminded that Jesus didn't "look" like a king or the picture of the Messiah that had been promised for generations.

On this journey to Bill's healing, we have seen the miraculous. We have seen God move in circumstances that seemed impossible. We have seen God use the most unlikely people in the most difficult circumstances to be His instruments of hope, help, and healing.

Bill was known as the "Miracle Man" not because of his outward appearance, his wealth, or possessions, but because God chose Bill to show the world what God can do when a heart is fully surrendered to Him.

Thank you for standing with us. #Godisfaithful #pray4bill

Day #823 April 11

Anchor Verse: Psalm 92:4
You thrill me, Lord, with all you have done for me! I sing for joy because of what you have done. (NLT)

Make today a day of praise and thanksgiving. Memories are powerful... sometimes good and sometimes difficult. As we are waiting in anticipation for Resurrection Sunday, let's turn our hearts and hands toward heaven.

Give God a praise offering. Join with the psalmist and say, "You thrill me, Lord, with all you have done for me! I sing for joy because of what you have done."

God has done so much for us throughout our lives...We have so much to be grateful for every day.

In this season of staying home, staying healthy, we have learned to appreciate some of our blessings that we took for granted. The freedom to come and go as we pleased. To visit with friends and family. To go to the grocery store without wondering if what you want is on the shelf. And to go to church and be with the family of God liberally dishing out hugs and love to others.

Sometimes we appreciate what we have only after we lose it. Thank the Lord for the "old" normal and praise Him for His grace in difficult places. His faithfulness has not changed.

His love for you has not changed. God's power has not changed. And His plans for your future have not changed.

Turn on some praise music and let your spirit soar. We know the next chapter of the story... He is risen! He is risen indeed!

On this journey to Bill's healing, God has been so good to us. Even in the most difficult circumstances, His love was always present, His power was never diminished. There were times, and still are, when I must turn my eyes toward heaven and away from the day's trials and thank God for His faithfulness. He is Lord!

Thank you for your faithfulness in prayer. We are navigating through a medication change and Bill's allergies... a fun place...but day and night declaring God's faithfulness #Godisfaithful #pray4bill

Day #824 April 12

Anchor Verse: Matthew 28:6-7
He is not here; he has risen, just as he said...And now, go quickly and tell his disciples that he has risen from the dead. (TLB)

Jesus has risen from the dead! He is alive!

The good news that the women were met with at the empty tomb that morning is still our good news.

Even as the angel directed them to go quickly and share the good news, that is our instruction from the Lord. This news is too good to keep to ourselves.

It means that we have hope. No matter what we face – isolation, illness, coronavirus, unemployment, or limited funds, God is bigger than all of them.

God gave His son, Jesus, to come into the world to pay the price for our sins on the cross. After three days, God raised Jesus from the dead and back to life, and now He is in heaven at the right hand of God. There is no greater story. There is no greater hope.

This morning I am reminded of the many Easter sunrise survives that I participated in in years past and the joy that was present in those early morning hours as we celebrated Jesus' resurrection.

Even though we are not gathered in one building with our church family, we are reminded that the church universal... across the world...is celebrating the resurrection of Jesus. What an opportunity that the Lord is using to remind us how big the kingdom of God is.

Don't let the joy we feel this day disappear as we walk into tomorrow. Jesus Christ is the same – yesterday, today, and forever!

On this journey to Bill's healing, we have experienced that resurrection power of Jesus that heals, delivers, and restores. Each day we celebrate the gift of life because Jesus is alive!

Join us in celebration. Share the good news wherever you go. Let your light shine for Jesus. People need to be directed to the light of His love in this time of darkness. Be that lighthouse of Jesus' love. You are loved.

Thank you for your prayers of faith. Thank you for celebrating the gift of life with us. God is so good. #Godisfaithful #pray4bill

Day #825 April 13

Anchor Verse: Psalm 33:20
The Lord alone is our radiant hope and we trust in Him with all our hearts. His wrap-around presence will strengthen us. (TPT)

It is the day after Easter. We celebrated the risen Christ yesterday. We sang with joy and our hearts were filled with hope.

How is your heart? The coronavirus didn't disappear overnight. The battle still rages on but we have been fortified to run the next leg of the race. Don't be discouraged. Know that we are one day closer to the resolution.

This morning my eyes fell on Psalm 33 and it reminded me that we need to hold on to hope, hold on to God. Verse 20 says, "The Lord alone is our radiant hope and we trust in him with all our hearts. His wrap-around presence will strengthen us."

The Lord alone is our radiant hope... It's the only place we find that abiding hope. We trust in God not just a little bit, but with ALL our hearts. That means we do not doubt God's faithfulness or His ability to deliver us in time of trouble.

And the last part of the verse paints a beautiful picture, "His wrap-around presence will strengthen us." It reminds me of someone completely engulfing you in a hug – a giant bear hug. You feel safe and secure. But God's presence is greater than that because there are no gaps in the armor of God. There is no place that is left unguarded. If we stay tucked in with the Lord, we are safe.

Verse 21-22 say, "In Him our hearts rejoice, for we trust in His holy name. May Your unfailing love be with us, Lord, even as we put our hope in You."

Let us rejoice this morning. He promised to never leave us or forsake us. And His promises are true. It doesn't mean we won't face hard times and challenges. We won't ever have to face them alone.

On this journey to Bill's healing, we have faced mountains and valleys, but we never had to doubt God's presence and power with us. He was, and still is, our constant companion. He is our shield and defender. He is Bill's healer.

Thank you for your continued prayers. Bill is fighting allergies right now and we haven't figured out a solution. Please join us in asking God for a solution. #Godisfaithful #pray4bill

Day #826 April 14

Anchor Verse: 1 Samuel 26:23
The LORD rewards everyone for their righteousness and faithfulness. (NIV)

God always rewards our obedience – always. The reward may not appear instantaneously but choosing to walk the path of righteousness and faithfulness will reap a lifetime of God's blessings.

In the book of 1 Samuel, we have read of King Saul's pursuit of David. King Saul, because of his disobedience, has lost God's favor and the favor of the Lord now rests upon David. Many times King Saul has tried to kill David. David and his men are constantly on the move to stay out of Saul's way.

Even when presented with an opportunity to kill Saul, David responds, "Don't destroy him! Who can lay a hand on the LORD's anointed and be guiltless?"

They did not lay a hand on Saul. Instead they took his spear and water jug to prove how close they had been to King Saul without hurting him.

There will be times when God will put us in situations to test our integrity and our obedience. The stakes may be high. As in David's case, it was an opportunity to get rid of his enemy and stop running for his life. David did not "take the bait" instead he chose to trust the Lord to fight for him rather than taking matters into his own hands.

This is a time of testing for all of us, not only about staying well. There is a supernatural dimension to this whole event. May we be like David and take the path of righteousness and faithfulness as we trust the Lord to protect us and provide for us.

On this journey to Bill's healing, we have seen God reward our faithfulness as we have chosen the path of righteousness trusting God with every step we take. Looking to heaven and surrendering our lives, our hopes, and our dreams to our heavenly Father who always keeps His promises, we know that delay is not denial. God has a way of turning what looks like a side trip off the road into another leg of our journey to make Bill stronger. It's not a timeout, it's another opportunity to build our faith.

Thank you for your persistent prayers. #Godisfaithful #pray4bill

Day #827 April 15

Anchor Verse: Matthew 17:20
If you have [living] faith the size of a mustard seed... (AMP)

Faith – it's something we talk about especially when we or someone we love is going through a tough time.

Today's verse from Matthew reminds us that we don't need a "gigantic" amount of faith in God to see miracles happen, all we need is faith the size of a mustard seed. A mustard seed is not very big, but once it is planted, it grows a lot. It represents that "living" faith that Matthew talks about here.

A plant or tree that has deep roots is not easily moved. As we have seen in many windstorms, if the roots are shallow, a tree can easily be blown over. Not only small trees, but BIG ones. The bigger they are, the harder they fall.

Jesus was trying to make a point when He was speaking to His disciples. A father came to have a demon cast out of his son and the disciples were unsuccessful. They asked Jesus why they failed. It says in verse 20, "He answered, 'Because of your little faith [your lack of trust and confidence in the power of God]; for I assure you and most solemnly say to you, if you have [living] faith the size of a mustard seed, you will say to this mountain, 'Move from here to there,' and [if it is God's will] it will move; and nothing will be impossible for you.'"

Faith is like a muscle that needs to be exercised. The more we believe that all things are possible with God and we trust Him to do the impossible, the more God CAN do the impossible in our lives.

On this journey to Bill's healing, what started out as a mustard seed of faith has become rooted and grounded in the fertile soil of the God of miracles. It has become a large tree as God provides more circumstances for our faith to grow.

One day at the hospital, God had a conversation with me. He said, "For a long time, you and your church have been praying for revival. But are you willing for revival to start in your own life, in your own heart? Revival doesn't come from the outside and wash over you like a tidal wave. It rises up like a fountain inside of you." I was moved to tears.

God was "calling me out" to join Him in a deeper place, a greater faith.

Thank you for your mustard seed of faith as we have seen the manifestation of God's miracles. #Godisfaithful #pray4bill

Day #828 April 16

Anchor Verse: 1 Samuel 30:4,6b
So David and his men wept aloud until they had no strength left to weep...But David found strength in the Lord his God. (NIV)

There will be times in our lives when we are overwhelmed by a wave of grief, a tsunami so great we weep until we have no strength.

In this passage in 1 Samuel, we read that David and his men had been fighting alongside Achish until the Philistine commanders decided that David and his men couldn't be trusted anymore, so they were sent home. Before they returned, the Amalekites attacked Ziklag and had taken captive their women and everyone else, both young and old.

When David and his men returned home, they found Ziklag destroyed by fire, and their wives and sons and daughters captive.

"So David and his men wept aloud until they had no strength left to weep..." These were seasoned warriors who had won battles, seen great carnage and destruction but seeing their homes burned and their families gone was too much. They broke down, and cried until they had no strength left to weep.

Then David's men needed someone to blame. They talked about stoning David. "But David found strength in the Lord his God."

Even though David was grief-stricken, he ran to the Lord and found strength and strategies in God's presence.

It's okay to express your emotions through crying...even if you are a guy. Some of the bravest warriors in biblical history cried out loud until they had no strength because those they held dear were gone. Then they took action. David found strength in God when his strength was gone. David was devastated, just like his men, but after he mourned, as their leader, David needed to have his strength renewed and wisdom for what came next.

On this journey to Bill's healing, I have cried many tears, but like David I found new strength in the Lord. Even in this coronavirus season, as we deal with our own challenges, I can feel the weight of the world's challenges. It brings me to my knees and often tears are the best expression of the emotions we are feeling. But then we move on and take action.

Thank you for praying us through the valleys and rejoicing on the mountaintops with us. #Godisfaithful #pray4bill

Day #829 April 17

Anchor Verse: Romans 8:28
And we know that all things work together for good to those who love God, to those who are the called according to His purpose. (NKJV)

The depth of our love for others springs from the depth of our love for God.

What a joy it is to live in harmony with God… and with others. It's not always that way but even in our discord, God can bring good out of it. In the times in which we are living, we see evidence of both harmony and discord.

After we "survive" this season, we will look back and see how God has worked "all things" together for our good, that we have "thrived." Romans 8:28 doesn't say that "all things" are "good" but somehow God can take difficult things and use them for our good and for His glory.

Today is our 18th wedding anniversary. We will find some creative way to celebrate at home since Bill's doctors agree that home is the best place for us. God has shown us that our home is the shelter He has created for us. "He who dwells in the presence of the Most High will "rest" in the shadow of the Almighty." (Psalm 91:1)

What got my attention this morning was not the "all things" or working together for "our good" but rather called according to "His purpose."

Bill and I have gone through some difficult seasons during the 18 years of our marriage. As I ask God for that heavenly perspective, I know that God has had a plan and purpose in our trials, not only for us, but to impact your lives.

On this journey to Bill's healing, there have been moments of great joy and moments of sorrow and loss. I will testify that God has used "everything" for good as He continues to groom Bill and me to be the man and woman of God He desires us to be. Also how a husband and wife can get through the tough times in life with their faith in God, loving each other, and fighting for each other (not against each other) through life's difficult seasons.

I love Bill today even more than I did on the day I said "I do" and our love continues to bloom and grow. Every day, I thank God for the gift of life, the breath of life, and His hand of protection over us.

Thank you for your love for us. #pray4bill #Godisfaithful

Day #830 April 18

Anchor Verse: Psalm 68:28
Summon your power, God; show us your strength, our God, as you have done before. (NIV)

When you pray, do you ever remind God of the mighty miracles He has previously done in your life? How God's power has come through in other difficult circumstances? I have.

I praise the Lord for how He has cared for us, how He has saved Bill.

Especially in the Old Testament, we see how people remembered what the Lord had done for them. During those 40 years in the wilderness, I think there must have been times when parents shared with their children, and even grandparents with their grandchildren of how God's mighty power rescued them from Pharaoh with the ten plagues and then parting the Red Sea on their way to the Promised Land.

It is because of God's faithfulness in the past that we can count on God's faithfulness today and tomorrow.

During this coronavirus season, as so many are at home with their families for extended periods of time, we are all finding ways to cope. One of the profitable things to do is to spend time with God in prayer and studying the Bible. We learn so much from those who have gone through previous trials, what they did right, and also their mistakes.

But above all, may the Lord hear our voices crying out for His grace and mercy, and yes, His mighty power to save us as He has before.

On this journey to Bill's healing, we have encountered mountains and valleys. Even places like the Red Sea that looked impossible to cross except with God's help. In every instance, God has been faithful. The solution wasn't always what we expected but always what we needed and what brought God the greatest honor and glory.

Thank you for standing with us. Thank you for your prevailing prayers and praying without ceasing. #Godisfaithful #pray4bill

Day #831 April 19

Anchor Verse: Psalm 116:15
Precious in the sight of the Lord is the death of His saints. (NKJV)

A life well lived, a battle well fought ended this morning (4.19.20). Bill fought the good fight. He finished his race. Bill kept the faith. (2 Timothy 4:7)

I write this several days after God called Bill home. Although my heart rejoices that my husband, who loved me so well, is healed and whole, and walking, running, and dancing in heaven, my heart is broken, because the other half of my heart is missing.

Psalm 116:15 best captures my thoughts about Bill's home-going. The Living Bible translation says, "His loved ones are very precious to him, and he does not lightly let them die."

It cost the Lord something to take Bill too. "He does not lightly let them die." Many of you have been witnesses to God's miraculous work in Bill's life over the past 2+ years, Bill's every breath was a testimony to God's faithfulness.

Bill reminded all of us that miracles happen every day. He showed us that the devil doesn't have the final say in our lives, God does. That illness does not define us, God does.

Even when our bodies may not be completely restored, that doesn't mean life is any less precious or less fully lived. In fact, I believe as you have faced life and death and lived, that God's love, grace, mercy, and peace are even more powerful.

We learned that every moment, every day, every hour is a gift from God. It's not always the "big" things in life that define us, it is laughter shared, the words "I love you" that come from the mouth of the one we love, or even tears shed and dried by their loving hands.

In the few quick hours that elapsed from the time the paramedics were called until Bill entered heaven's gates, God held Bill in His arms of love. God held me too.

So many thoughts raced through my head, was this the stage on which God would showcase another resurrection miracle?

As things began to unfold, and it was obvious that Bill's earthly body had finished its race, I put down my sword that had been valiantly used to fight for Bill's life, and opened my hands to allow my heavenly Father to take Bill home.

Even in death, God, and Bill, had something unusual planned. The doctor told me, "Bill did not have a stroke. In fact, the whole body scan shows nothing wrong."

On one hand, that made no sense. It did to God, that's exactly how He had it planned. The grand finale to an adventure that was peppered with the unexplainable, the unpredictable, and the unexpected. That's our God… and that was Mr. Bill.

After Bill left his mortal body behind, I was blessed to spend a little time with him and by God's grace, the hospital even allowed two others to join me – a good friend walking through her own battles and our dear friend and pastor, Pastor Dave.

Thank God for spiritual leaders who love God and their flock so much. Pastor Dave invited me to come and sit in the church sanctuary that morning as they live-streamed the morning service. The best place to be – in the presence of the Lord. Bill was seeing the glory of God in heaven, but I could catch a few glimmers here on earth.

That morning at church, Pastor Alice after hearing of the morning's events said, "Barb, it means that God had the final word, the final victory. It was not the devil through illness that cut Bill's life short. But rather God said, "Bill, it's time to come home." God extended His hand and Bill took it and entered the gates of heaven.

So many miracles, even that morning to be allowed into the ER so I could see the one I loved in his final hours on earth, was definitely a gift from God in the midst of this Covid season.

Today, we raise a hallelujah. On this journey to Bill's healing, there have been many unexpected twists and turns. But the greatest one came this morning, when God chose to complete Bill's healing on his entrance into heaven rather than completing it here on earth.

Thank you for your faithfulness. Your prayers moved mountains. They encouraged us and lifted us up. I know you mourn with me. Thank you for loving Mr. Bill through his final days on earth. I am grateful. #Godisfaithful

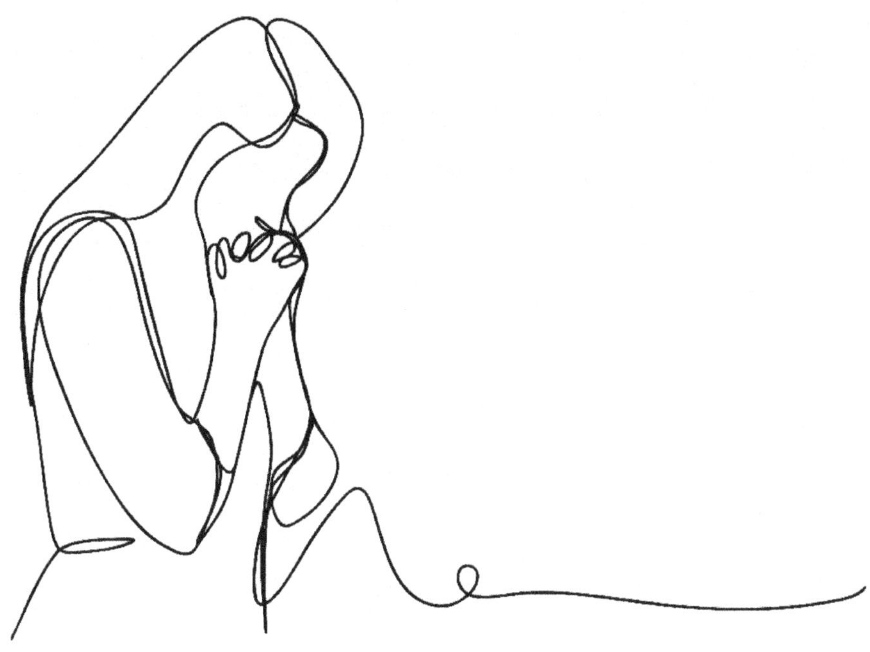

Stepping onto the Glory Road…

"The Glory Road" emerged the day after Bill died. In my grieving over the sudden loss of my husband on April 19, 2020, I didn't know what was ahead. For more than two years, daily, I posted on Facebook my "Hubby Health Update" about what God was doing in Bill's life and how the healing was progressing. Then suddenly Bill was gone. Was I supposed to stop writing?

As I poured out my heart to the Lord, God let me grieve on Sunday (4.19) and Monday morning (4.20), and then Monday afternoon, the Lord spoke to me.

"This is what you are going to do. You will write the final "Hubby Health Update" for April 19, the day I took Bill home. And then you're going to start a new path and call it "The Glory Road." You are going to show others what it looks like to grieve and to walk the path that lies before you with My help. Tomorrow morning, get up and write those three devotionals (Sunday, Monday and Tuesday). I am with you."

Even today, it brings me to tears. Not only as I recount that "suddenly moment" but that even in the midst of this life-changing event, God had a plan, and He had you, my friends, on His heart.

When we started Bill's journey on January 10, 2018, and I asked the Lord about posting on Facebook what was happening in Bill's life, God said, "I want to do a work there." Again on April 20, 2020, the day after Bill died, again, God reiterated His plan to "feed" you and love you through me.

I am called to testify of His faithfulness. Now with the added dimension of my healing from cancer (a journey which began in 7/2020), God is showing all of us what His glory – His healing released in us looks like.

We live for His glory!

Day #1 April 20

Anchor Verse: 2 Samuel 12:20
Then David got up from the ground. After he had washed, put on lotions and changed his clothes, he went into the house of the LORD and worshiped. (NIV)

Today marks a new leg of the journey. For 831 days, you walked with me on the "journey to Bill's healing."

When Bill first entered the hospital on January 10, 2018, I knew that prayer support would be essential. There were many prayer warriors on Facebook who had fought other battles with me.

Once something is posted on Facebook, it's there "forever." So I went to the Lord and asked Him what to do. God's response, "I want to do a work there (on Facebook.)" The door was opened for me to share our journey publicly.

You walked with us through the valleys and mountains. You rejoiced in our victories and you cried and prayed as we went through the deep valleys. Your prayers and your love sustained us. And God did a work in your life too.

This journey to Bill's healing is not only about Bill Hollace and his fight for life. Nor is it "just" about me, his wife, who God called to fight for her husband's life, and take her to a new level of spiritual warfare. God wanted all of you to see His hand at work and to experience it in your own life too.

Many of you have come into a new season with the Lord. You have experienced miracles in your own life. You have danced with joy, you have wept in sorrow, yet none of it was apart from God. Because of your obedience in walking with us, God has blessed you.

As I am wrestling with my grief, I want to continue to honor God and Bill's life journey. I know that in the days ahead, there will be even greater growth as I emerge from this pit of sorrow.

In 2 Samuel 12, David got up from his mourning. I also arose from the ground of my sorrow, got cleaned up, and went into the house of the Lord and worshiped God. The morning Bill died I was also given the opportunity to share a vision/dream that God had given Bill about a month before God took Bill home. God is so good. Even in death, there is life and victory.

Thank you for your prayers as I grieve and wrap up the "old life" and walk onto a new path. #Godisfaithful #TheGloryRoad

Day #2 April 21

Anchor Verse: Luke 16:10
Whoever can be trusted with very little can also be trusted with much. (NIV)

Have you ever considered that when God entrusts you with trials and tests, it's because He trusts you?

In the "natural" world, we don't put heavy items in a box or a bag that cannot hold them. In the "supernatural" realm, God exercises this same principle. Of course, this is where the principle originated.

On Bill's journey to healing, God stretched both of us, not only in the physical realm, but in the spiritual realm.

Our faith was tested and continued to bloom and grow. God learned that we could be trusted with the small things and the big ones too.

It is in surrendering to the Lord and His will, His way, and His power, that we will experience life in a way that is unprecedented. Bill and I experienced the Lord's joy, peace, and power on a "mega" level. Now as Bill has taken his place in heaven, there is still a path for me to walk. Our story is not finished.

"God must trust you a lot" were the words my dear pastor said moments after Bill died. God rewards our faithfulness in many ways. Often not according to the world's reward system. In the world, "death" is seen as a punishment or defeat. In the Lord's eyes, it is but a gateway into the glory of His presence.

During the last few years of Bill's walk here on earth, Bill developed an intimacy with the Lord that was so powerful.

God trusted Bill too. "Whoever can be trusted with very little can also be trusted with much." God must have trusted Bill a lot to help him endure all those medical procedures, glimpses of heaven, and then returning to earth to complete his race. And Bill did it all with a great attitude, a never-ending sense of humor, and lots of laughter.

Bill told me on more than one occasion that God used to come and "visit" with Bill because Bill even made God laugh when He was having a tough day. And God has a loud laugh I have been told.

Thank you for your prayers. As the tears fall, I am grateful for your support and all your love for us. #Godisfaithful #TheGloryRoad

Day #3 April 22

Anchor Verse: Isaiah 25:8
It is the gloom of death! He will swallow it up in victory forever! And God, Lord Yahweh, will wipe away every tear from every face. (TPT)

The gloom of death… that's what it felt like at 1:15 am this morning as I woke up to relive the trauma of Bill's final hours on earth on Sunday morning. There was nothing glamorous about it. It was painful and it hurt… a lot.

My tears flowed. My breathing was jagged as the sorrow rippled through my body. The hole is big this morning… and my swollen eyes are not pretty and my heart is aching.

Yet my spirit knows that Bill is with God in heaven. His body is healed and whole in Jesus' name. That was a prayer I often prayed for him. I praised the Lord for Bill's healing from the top of his head to the soles of his feet.

Morning and night as I "prayed on" the armor of God over both of us, I started with the "belt of truth" – the truth being that Bill was "healed and whole" in Jesus' name. That is still the truth this morning… but I expected that to be the truth here on earth where I could wrap my arms around him, kiss him, and tell him how much I loved him – many, many times during the day and night.

This morning as my grief is raw and my body is fatigued by this whole traumatic process, I turn my eyes toward heaven to have my hope restored. I ask the Lord to hold me and restore me and help me through this hurt. The Passion translation says it well, "It is the gloom of death!" There is nothing pretty about this part.

Bill's "unexpected" death came as a surprise to all of us, but it does not diminish the countless miracles God performed in the last 2+ years. Bill's "final stand" was not a victory for death or disease, but rather the translation of a servant of the Lord into glory in God's perfect timing.

Our journey to Bill's healing was filled with altars of praise to God's faithfulness. The road ahead of me, the Glory Road, will also be filled with altars of praise. Looking forward to the day when I can kiss Bill again in heaven and cash in on that dance he promised me.

Thank you for your faithfulness. I will be leaning on you in the days ahead as God heals my heart. We are each facing our own battles in the world, may the Lord meet our every need. #Godisfaithful #TheGloryRoad

Day #4 April 23

Anchor Verse: Nehemiah 8:10
And do not be worried, for the joy of the LORD is your strength and your stronghold. (AMP)

Strength – emotionally, physically, mentally, and spiritually – is needed on this new path. It's a new kind of strength. I won't find it working out at a gym, walking in nature, or doing exercises at home.

The only lasting source of strength is my Lord and God.

On Sunday morning as my husband's life hung in the balance, my strength was being tested. Quickly I realized that in my own personal frame, I didn't have the resources to make it through those last hours of Bill's life.

The nursing supervisor in the Emergency Room asked me more than once, "Are you going to faint? Do you need to sit down?" She didn't want me to crash on the floor, they were trying to save Bill's life.

Would I faint? No. The spirit of the Lord rose up in me in what turned out to be the final hour of Bill's life. My feet were firmly planted on holy ground. I will not cower around the corner. Devil, you will not have the victory.

When a warrior fights a battle, he doesn't sit. As spiritual warriors, the armor of God is in place and we stand on the promises of God, in the power of God, and we await the Lord's command.

After you have fought with all your strength for your husband to live, when do you know it's time to lay down your sword and let God take him home? I could see that unlike the earlier part of this journey, Bill was not "fighting" to stay; Bill was likely seeing the glory of heaven's gates calling him home.

Bill's legacy is that he found good in the most unlikely people and uncomfortable situations. Even on this final healing journey, his sense of humor, his kindness, his grace, and caring for others was always evident.

His life on earth may have ended, but Bill's legacy will live on.

Joy in the Lord doesn't mean there will be no sorrow. They can be opposite sides of the same coin, a double-edged sword. As I walk forward and deal with the funeral arrangements, it is with Bill's spirit to comfort me and God's power to help me stand.

Thank you for your prayers. Thank you for sharing the joy you have found on this journey with us. #Godisfaithful #TheGloryRoad

Day #5 April 24

Anchor Verse: Luke 18:1
Now Jesus was telling the disciples a parable to make the point that at all times they ought to pray and not give up and lose heart [hope]. (AMP)

Praying is our communication link to God. It's how we bring our praise and petitions before the Lord and ask for His help. Jesus told this parable to His disciples to "make the point that at ALL times they ought to PRAY and NOT GIVE UP and LOSE heart or hope."

Not only are we to keep on praying and not give up, but we're also not to lose hope.

On this journey to Bill's healing, we saw new life erupt out of a broken body. We heard Bill's laughter ring out loudly (I still hear it). We knew the power of Bill's prayers as he interceded for us.

After all his trials and troubles, Bill wasn't distanced from God, instead Bill was drawn into a closer, more intimate relationship with the Lord.

Some of you may be wrestling with the question, why did Bill die? Why didn't God answer our prayers for Bill's complete healing? Did we fail as prayer warriors? Did God fail us?

Don't fall into the doubt trap! God is still on His throne. Our command is to pray and not give up. Pray without ceasing. (1 Thessalonians 5:17)

Our prayers for healing were answered. Bill was healed as he entered heaven's gates. No assistance needed to walk or run. No more hernia. No more weakness or memory gaps – only pure joy in the presence of the Lord.

The first few days I wrestled with the thought that I had failed, that I missed something. But then God in His love quickly reminded me that His timing is perfect. There was nothing we could have done to change the outcome. Our prayers had moved the hand of God on Bill's behalf and he lived more than two years, when he "should have" died more times than we could count.

On this Glory Road, rejoice with me that prayer works. Prayer is still our greatest weapon on this battlefield called life. Pray without ceasing. Pray and do not give up.

Thank you for every prayer you prayed for Bill. Thank you for the gift of life that your prayers produced as God answered them. Bill is now alive forevermore. #Godisfaithful #TheGloryRoad

Day #6 April 25

Anchor Verse: 2 Samuel 22:26
To the faithful you show yourself faithful. (NIV)

"You stick with people who stick with You," is how the Message translation states this verse.

Life is not easy. Triumph and tragedy – they are our companions through life. But God transcends both of them.

When we abide in His presence, He will see us through the storm. When we go through a storm in nature, we look with hope to the horizon watching for the end of the downpour. Our hope comes in the name of the Lord.

What does the Lord require of us? Our faithfulness. We must hold on to His hand no matter what we face. Don't let go when the rains and wind pummel you or the winter storm seeks to overcome you. When you go through the desert places and God seems absent or through the wilderness of uncharted territory, though you may not see any familiar places, He is there.

A week ago, Bill was walking out his last day in this world. We didn't know that and I'm not sure what we would have done differently. Would I have told him, "I love you" more times than the many times I did every day? Would I have had one last cup of tea with him at Panera? Would I have cried my tears in his presence rather than flooding my nights now in his absence?

That's why God doesn't tell us the day or the hour when we will go home. It's too much to bear. God wants us to live every moment of life to the fullest. Let not death's shadow rob us of God's goodness, love, and grace in the light of this day.

Last night before bedtime, I got knocked over by a wave of grief. It can be triggered by a song or a memory or something else. So swiftly, like a riptide, you can be standing on what seems to be solid ground, and suddenly, you've been carried out to sea and you're being pulled under by grief's octopus-like tentacles.

Once you're pulled under, it's hard to fight your way back to that surface of peace. Sometimes the best advice is not to fight back, fruitlessly, but instead cry out to the Lord and let Him ride with you back to that place of peace.

Thank you for your companionship and prayers on the Glory Road in the days ahead. #Godisfaithful #TheGloryRoad

Day #7 April 26

Anchor Verse: Psalm 107:8

So lift your hands and thank God for his marvelous kindness [unfailing love] and for all his miracles of mercy for those he loves. (TPT)

God's unfailing love is what has helped me through this week. This morning, the crater in my heart is still deep, but I lift my hands in praise because of God's unfailing love, mercy, and grace.

His "miracles of mercy" help keep my loss in perspective. God chose Bill's life – our lives to be a "platform" for a beautiful symphony of God's love, power, and grace. Every time God would snatch Bill out of death's bony grip, it was not only a victory for us, but a victory for God.

Over the course of our lives, we often get so wrapped up in "living" that we fail to stop and remember that every breath, every step we take is a gift from God. Every person God brings into your life is a gift of love from the heart of God. Bill and I learned that our muscles grow stronger when they are tried and tested. That applies not only to our physical muscles but also our spiritual, mental, and emotional "muscles."

On this healing road, I saw Bill become stronger in so many ways. His upper body strength was phenomenal. Moving from the recliner to his wheelchair, I had to make sure that he "pushed" himself up using the arms of the recliner, because if he grabbed the arm of the wheelchair, Bill could move it even with the brakes on. God continued to build his strength every day.

Bill also asked God a lot of questions and was taught at the feet of Jesus. As they often walked together at night, Bill was not only strengthened in his physical body, but his "spirit man" was strengthened.

As the spiritual head of our home, God would reveal things to Bill that were meant for both of us. What a blessing to be "fed" God's revelation by my husband, as God designed it to be.

Through this last week, God has offered me glimpses of Bill, and often I have heard Bill's infectious laughter, as he lives in the presence of the Lord. Bill is chatting with all the new people he is meeting and talking to some of the great heroes of the faith, even those God sent to Bill in his dreams.

Our dog, Duke, died in 2004. Bill and Duke are back on "security patrol." Once a Marine, always a Marine. Thank you, Lord, for showing me Bill's joy.

Thank you for being prayer warriors for us. #Godisfaithful #TheGloryRoad

Day #8 April 27

Anchor Verse: Luke 18:8
God will give swift justice to those who don't give up. So be ever praying, ever expecting, just like the widow was with the judge. Yet when the Son of Man comes back, will he find this kind of persistent faithfulness in his people? (TPT)

There was a persistent widow who kept "bothering" a judge to get the justice she needed. Today, the judge would have gotten a restraining order against the woman. She took an extra step in pursuing justice. Some might say she crossed the line – the widow went to the judge's house to get what she wanted – "Grant me justice and protect me against my oppressor!"

He got annoyed with the woman's persistent pleas and decided to "get her off his back" and rule in her favor, then she would leave him alone.

Jesus expanded this illustration to God the true judge. "God will give swift justice to those who don't give up. So be ever praying, ever expecting!"

Mark Batterson in his book, *Draw the Circle*, describes the widow's faith as "crazy faith." The judge quickly learned that there was "no quit" in this woman with crazy faith.

Would others describe you as a person with "crazy faith?" On this 2+ year journey on the path to Bill's healing, likely many said I was a woman with crazy faith, or maybe just a "crazy" woman. I don't mind because I was on a holy mission, a mission to save Bill's life that was ordained by God.

There will be times in our lives when we are called upon to be persistent in prayer until we receive the blessing, the miracle, the answer we need.

You have been faithful on our journey as you prayed for Bill. God answered with unprecedented miracles. The day Bill died we lost a great man. (Bill often called me "prejudiced" but I replied I was only speaking the truth.)

Now that a week has passed, I am reminded that God's timing is always perfect, even when it might not match my timing or expectations. What Jesus said is still true. "God will give swift justice to those who don't give up. So be ever praying, ever expecting."

On this Glory Road moving forward, let us continue to be children of God who have persistent "crazy" faith. Jesus said all it takes is faith the size of a mustard seed, which is very small (you can find it in the pickle jar).

Thank you for your persistent prayers. #Godisfaithful #TheGloryRoad

Day #9 April 28

Anchor Verse: 1 Corinthians 3:9
For we are co-workers in God's service. (NIV)

What an honor and privilege to work together in service to the Lord.

He has given each of us a purpose. God has specifically equipped us to complete it. That's why we are created uniquely and called to serve in a particular place.

Some people are amazing craftsman – those who can build and are gifted in the trades. Others have been gifted as artists and other creative ways. There are those who are created to nurture and encourage while others are great at organization and making sure those "numbers" line up.

It's also about our heart for service. Are you willing to love as Jesus loved? Are you willing to serve rather than be served? Are you willing to serve without counting the cost and to do it without fame or recognition?

On Bill's journey to healing, I learned how to surrender all of my life to the Lord – every area. When Bill got sick and entered the hospital in January 2018, it was my honor and privilege to be with him. This journey has not only been about Bill's healing but God was using it to shape me.

With a giant "machete" God walked through my life and said "This can go and that can go." It might have been a "good" thing but it definitely wasn't in the top two important things. Those were reserved for God and Mr. Bill.

What are you willing to surrender to the Lord? The first sacrifice must be "our will" for "God's will." To be a co-laborer with God, we need to be on the same page with God, not running our own race.

Once we sacrifice our "will" then God has access to all of us – our body, mind, and spirit, and even our finances. No matter what God points to, you are willing to place it in His hands, even the one you love the most. No sacrifice is too great in exchange for God's best for you.

As I begin this new journey on the Glory Road, I am reminded that God is always with me. He will never leave me or forsake me. Bill is working with God in heaven, on the other side of the veil, to accomplish His purposes.

My heart is still tender and fragile, and I can still cry at a moment's notice, but God is my shelter in the midst of this storm called widowhood.

Thank you for holding up my arms. #Godisfaithful #TheGloryRoad

Day #10 April 29

Anchor Verse: Psalm 143:8
Let the dawning day bring me revelation of your tender, unfailing love. Give me light for my path and teach me, for I trust in you. (TPT)

A couple of days after Bill died, a friend shared this verse with me, "Let the morning bring me word of your unfailing love, for I have put my trust in you. Show me the way I should go, for to you I entrust my life." (NLT)

My grief was still so raw there wasn't room for much else inside of me.

I am ready to embrace God's unfailing love because God has been so faithful to me in these last ten days as I walk this new path, the Glory Road.

As it gets light earlier every morning, nature is expanding the depth and breadth of our days. Even in the midst of the coronavirus, God continues to march forward and remind us that He doesn't change.

Most of the time, like God's love, Bill's love gives me strength to do the "hard" things of life – like write his obituary and contact the long list of medical providers, both physicians and others who provided support services. So many people have been part of this 2+ year journey to Bill's healing. They have impacted our lives and we have impacted them.

Spring is sprouting up around us. This year as the earth is blooming with new life, it's different. Without Bill by my side and the "new life" we anticipated – a trip to the ocean and greater progress in his healing, the tears roll down my face.

God did not recklessly call Bill home to be with Him. Although the waves of grief roll over me at times, and threaten to knock me over, I am learning a new song in my heart. It is a song of praise that comes from my deep love of God and my trust in Him. I can sing this new song because Bill loved me with all his heart. My prayer is that others will be loved like this too.

On this path to Bill's healing, we learned so much about life and love. Living in the moment allowed us to love, laugh, and "dance" in the midst of the storm. We "lived" life every day. Each moment was a precious gift.

Now as I walk this new path, the Glory Road, I am choosing to continue to live each day in awe and wonder and look for the Lord's hand at work. Please join me and embrace the gift of today. Thank you for your continued prayers. Every day I make a little bit of progress. #Godisfaithful #TheGloryRoad

Day #11 April 30

Anchor Verse: Psalm 57:1
Have mercy on me, my God, have mercy on me, for in you I take refuge. I will take refuge in the shadow of your wings until the disaster has passed. (NIV)

Taking refuge under the shadow of God's wings – a place of safety, shelter, and peace. There's a similar passage in Psalm 91:1, "He who dwells in the shelter of the Most High will rest in the shadow of the Almighty."

God loves you and He loves me. He knows that there will be storms that come into our lives. They threaten to overwhelm us, even to "sink" our ship. But with our faith in God we can find refuge under the shadow of His wings.

In nature, we think of the eagle and their huge wing span and their beauty as they soar in the sky. An adult eagle's wing span can range from 5.9 feet – 8 feet. Think of how secure the baby eagles must feel tucked under their parent's wings.

God's wings, although they are not physical like the eagle's wings, are able to help us withstand every weapon formed against us. God's "wings" will never grow old or tired. Their warranty will never run out. God's love never waxes or wains.

When grief or confusion or overwhelm rolls over me, it is Lord God Almighty that keeps me on my feet or on my knees before His throne of grace.

"Until this disaster has passed." This verse is heavy with meaning. Bill died in the middle of the coronavirus season. God called Bill home in a time when were are "socially distancing" to prevent the spread of this deadly virus and when large public gatherings are banned. A time when, as believers, we gather via the internet to sing praises to the Lord and to be fed from His Word rather than gathering together where we can comfort each other and be held in each other's embrace.

As my days on this new Glory Road take on a rhythm of their own, they are so different than the structured days when Bill and I were walking on his path to healing and recovery.

In the silence, I can hear the echoes of our conversations. I can hear his laughter ring through our apartment and the sparkle in his beautiful blue eyes as we talked about our next "adventure."

Thank you for your kindness. #Godisfaithful #TheGloryRoad

May 2020

Great is His faithfulness.
~ Lamentations 3:23

Day #12 May 1

Anchor Verse: Luke 21:19
Stand firm, and you will win life. (NIV)

"Stand firm!" Those are powerful words, a powerful command from the heart of God.

When I think about standing firm, it means that I am facing circumstances that are difficult and that in my flesh, I am weak, but God is speaking to my spirit to be strong.

It's interesting to note that God put Bill and me in an advanced training class before He brought the rest of you on board. Beginning in January 2018, there were many days, weeks, even months during the last 2+ years where God had us "standing firm" at home.

I will testify to the blessings that we experienced because we chose to willingly embrace the gift as from the Father's hand. Many of you are experiencing "family time" in a whole new way. Our children and grandchildren are learning "survival skills" that will equip them for a lifetime.

As believers, we have more time to spend with God as we ask Him to open our eyes to see the blessing, the lessons He is teaching us. There is a whole new appreciation for life and for freedom when it is threatened.

Hallelujah for the gift of prayer! We have seen it move mountains. God has provided an amazing opportunity for us to develop a new intimacy with the Lord.

As we "stand firm", what is our reward? We will win life. That would be "eternal life"… thank you, Lord.

Daily, even hourly, I miss Bill so much. But I am still here. God did not take us both home on that Sunday morning, April 19. Instead, the Lord has work for me to do. There are more people that need to hear our story of the Lord's faithfulness and His mighty miracles as I walk down this Glory Road.

On this first day of May, I stand firm on the promises of God and believe I will see the deliverance of the Lord in my life and in yours. Please join me before the throne of grace as we seek help from the Lord in our time of need.

Thank you for your faithfulness. #Godisfaithful #TheGloryRoad

Day #13 May 2

Anchor Verse: Psalm 131:3

O people of God, your time has come to quietly trust [to put your hope in God], waiting upon the Lord now and forever. (TPT)

Your time has come – my time has come to quietly trust in the Lord. We are to put our hope in God, not in our circumstances, not in our possessions, not in the promises of others, but only in God.

I will confess that my picture of life on May 2, 2020, looked nothing like this. An empty apartment missing my husband's laughter and his very heartbeat, is filled with beautiful memories and unfulfilled dreams.

Throughout the Bible, we have read of times when God came and delivered His people from plagues, from wars, from horrible circumstances, why not now? On the flip side, we have also seen that God had a purpose in people's suffering in going through uncomfortable places. There are always lessons to be learned if we are willing to be taught.

Wandering through the wilderness for 40 years with hundreds of thousands of people couldn't have been a very pleasant experience. It was a journey of faith; they had to quietly trust the Lord. Well, the children of Israel weren't so quiet, they grumbled a lot. The landscape isn't exactly quiet here either. Most people are not used to having their movement restricted so much and it's wearing many people out.

A good friend uses the perfect word to describe where many are today… they are getting "cranky" like a little child who needs to sleep but refuses to "give in" and rest. Maybe you are that cranky child.

Psalm 131 reminds us that we are to "wait on the Lord both now and forever." Learning to wait is a gift, it's also a discipline. We are discovering more every day that in our society we are "instant gratification" people… we want it and we want it now.

On the journey to Bill's healing and now on my solo path down the Glory Road, I am learning the high cost of obedience. No matter the price we pay, God's rewards are eternal; everything else will quickly pass away.

I encourage you to "quietly wait" before the Lord. Take some time to be still. Turn off your phone, the internet, Facebook and listen and wait.

Thank you for remembering Bill and mourning with me even as we rejoice that Bill is safe in his heavenly home. #Godisfaithful #TheGloryRoad

Day #14 May 3

Anchor Verse: Revelation 21:4
He will wipe away all tears from their eyes, and there shall be no more death, nor sorrow, nor crying, nor pain. All of that has gone forever. (TLB)

Heaven – I think a lot more about it lately. Two weeks ago(4.19.20), God took Bill home to heaven. Bill is seeing firsthand the glimpses of heaven we read about in the Bible or the books from those who have visited heaven.

Since yesterday, the Lord has been talking to me a lot about Bill's home-going and offered me a different perspective than my initial observations. It's been a quite revelation but it totally makes sense.

Revelation 21:4 captured that message from the heart of God. "He will wipe away ALL tears from their eyes, and there shall be no more death, nor sorrow, nor crying, nor pain. All of that has gone forever."

In the last two weeks, there have been a lot of tears. I came to the conclusion that the depth of my love for Bill is being matched by the depth of my grief.

My night was a little "bumpy" – it's okay. God woke me up a little after 1 a.m. to remind me that the "replay" of Bill's final hours on earth was about to start. The Lord and I talked for a bit and I went back to sleep. I don't remember dreaming, but at exactly "3:54 a.m." the moment that Bill was officially pronounced dead at the hospital that morning, God woke me up.

This time, my reaction was different. Yes, a huge sense of loss, my "other" half, the other half of my heart is in heaven. However, God spoke new revelation to me. When I was growing up, the prefix (the first three numbers) of our home phone number were "354" – wow!

God said it would always be a reminder to me that God took Bill "home" at 3:54 a.m. like the beginning of my home phone number as a child. Isn't God a good, good Father? Yes, He is.

On the journey to Bill's healing, and ultimately his entrance into heaven, we saw the hand of God at work. Many times on Bill's journey God dried our tears when death looked certain, but God said it wasn't time.

As I walk this new Glory Road, Bill's spirit is with me and God is ordering my steps. Sometimes they are herky-jerky steps, and other times they glide more smoothly, but always for my good and His glory.

Thank you for your continued prayers. #Godisfaithful #TheGloryRoad

Day #15 May 4

Anchor Verse: 1 Kings 17:5
So he [Elijah] did what the Lord had told him. (NIV)

It sounds so simple. God told Elijah what to do and Elijah did it.

Obedience keeps us on the straight and narrow path. It keeps us "out of trouble" and walking in harmony with our heavenly Father. Anything else is a mere shadow of the goodness that God wants to do in our lives.

In my youth, there was a hymn we used to sing at church, "Trust and Obey." The first verse tells us that when we walk with the Lord following His directions in the Bible, His glory will shine on us. His glory – there's nothing like it. A glimpse of His glory here on earth is a small foretaste of what heaven will be like.

Trust and Obey – it's that simple. I remember talking with my grandfather about "life" and how it seemed that sometimes we made it "so hard." Grandpa told me to keep life "simple" that was the key. Children keep life simple and often those in their "older" years return to life's simplicity, but in the middle, we get so wrapped up it looks like a plate of spaghetti.

We find ourselves in unusual circumstances in this pandemic season. And now as we "steer the ship" toward coming out of it, there are more questions that arise about the "safe" way to do it.

It's interesting because I find myself faced with a double challenge. Learning how to walk into "freedom" as the threat of the coronavirus diminishes and we "safely" learn how to interact with each other again, but also learning how to navigate life without Bill at my side. It's like a double Whammy (and it's not a hamburger from Dick's Drive-In either).

As I take the next step on the Glory Road, I walk in obedience, not able to see the way ahead of me, but trusting the Lord who saved me. Trusting that God who knew the "best" time to take Bill home to heaven has good plans for all of us, we need to trust Him and walk in obedience.

Thank you for your countless prayers. #Godisfaithful #TheGloryRoad

Day #16 May 5

Anchor Verse: 1 Kings 19:5
Then he [Elijah] lay down and slept under the broom tree. But as he was sleeping, an angel touched him and told him, "Get up and eat!" (TLB)

Sleeping and eating are the two best gifts toward restoring our bodies. One of the lessons Bill taught me was to "listen to your body."

God designed our bodies to send us "messages" about what we need and when we need it. The secret to much of Bill's recovery was that very thing, listening to his body when it needed food and when it needed rest. The rest of Bill's healing was in God's hands.

Here in 1 Kings we read that Ahab told Jezebel everything Elijah had done and how he had killed all the prophets with a sword. Jezebel threatens Elijah, "May the gods deal with me, be it ever so severely, if by this time tomorrow I do not make your life like that of one of them." (1 Kings 19:2)

Yikes! That's quite the death threat from a woman who had the reputation of being ruthless. Elijah was afraid and ran for his life. When he came to Beersheba, Elijah left his servant there and went a day's journey into the wilderness.

Elijah finds a broom tree, sits down under it and prays that he might die. "I have had enough, Lord. I'm done. Take my life." Elijah is exhausted – physically, mentally, emotionally, and spiritually. He wants to quit.

At this point in the story, Elijah falls asleep. Oh yes, the gift of sleep. It's one of the most powerful restoration tools God has given us. Without sleep, we get a little "crazy."

On our journey to Bill's healing, we learned the necessity of good food and good sleep. There were nights when our sleep was disturbed and neither of us slept well, that resulted in a more difficult day.

In those first few days on the Glory Road, nothing really sounded good to eat, but I could "hear" my dear husband reminding me of the need to take care of my body. Three meals a day has been my goal, and listening to what my body needs. And for the record, it's not junk food either. I know if I take care of my body, my body will take care of me.

Sleep has been the greatest challenge, but God is helping me establish some good practices to improve my sleep at night. Thank you for taking care of yourselves. #Godisfaithful #TheGloryRoad

Day #17 May 6

Anchor Verse: Proverbs 3:24
With them [wisdom and understanding] on guard you can sleep without fear; you need not be afraid of disaster or the plots of wicked men, for the Lord is with you; he protects you. (TLB)

The Lord protects us when we are awake or asleep. We need not fear.

As children, I think we can all remember nights when we were afraid to go to sleep because of "monsters" under the bed or something that made us afraid to close our eyes. It could have been something as simple as a tree limb scraping against the roof on the house or a door banging in the wind, or our imagination gone astray.

As adults, we may still face situations that are "scary" to us, because they are unknown and we don't know the answers.

The good news: God has not left us alone to deal with our problems, or even our fears.

Wisdom and understanding accompany us – day and night – and with God's wisdom, we have the mind of Christ to navigate deep waters.

During the daylight hours, it seems that it is easier to "rationally" think through your problems. But during the nighttime hours, when it's dark and you feel alone, it seems that the "enemy" tends to slither into our thoughts and all kinds of crazy scenarios race through our minds.

On our journey to Bill's healing, two very good friends would often repeat this phrase in their Facebook posts – "God is on the night shift." What a great reminder that God neither slumbers nor sleeps and is not taking a "cat nap" when we need Him in those dark hours when fear comes knocking at the door.

One of the best "weapons" that I have used is God's Word – God's promises in scripture to bring light to the darkness.

On this new path, the Glory Road, without Bill next to me in our bed, I have had to choose to trust in the Lord believing that even now wisdom and understanding are with me and I can "sleep without fear." I can sleep without reliving those last hours of Bill's life.

Thank you for your prayers and words of encouragement. They bring light to my path. #Godisfaithful #TheGloryRoad

Day #18 May 7

Anchor Verse: Titus 2:7
Above all, set yourself apart as a model of a life nobly lived. With dignity, demonstrate integrity in all that you teach. (TPT)

It is the National Day of Prayer (2020), a day set aside to be steadfast in prayer. We are called to pray in unity for healing in our land. "One nation under God...indivisible"....we cannot be divided if we choose to stand together.

The enemy of our souls would try and divide us so that we see our differences rather than our similarities. We must focus on what is good and what we can do together, not our constraints.

Many of you have found ways to rise above this unpleasant situation and still love and encourage. You have chosen not to be defined by an illness and the cloud of fear that has followed in its wake.

This verse in Titus 2 reminds us that we don't live life alone. We must remember that others are watching how we live in the good times and those that shake the very foundation of our lives.

When we first entered the "adventure" of Bill's healing journey, God asked me to invite you into our world. By nature and practice, Bill and I are pretty private people. There were times God called us to interact with the world and then retreat to the privacy of our home.

This "adventure" was different. God asked us to allow Him to do a work in us in front of you and invited you to be a part of it.

God wanted us to be transparent. What it looks like to face life and death with God fighting for you. To teach all of us, the power of prayer as you partner with God to change the world, and even your own circumstances.

As we pray for each other and for our nation, the country of our birth, Bill is not standing next to us. But all of heaven, including Bill, is praying for God's will to be done here on earth as it is in heaven.

On this Glory Road, God continues to show me that His hand is with me. Whether in that moment I am strong or find myself in a puddle of tears, God is faithful. Nothing is too hard for Him, and nothing is too hard for me.

Thank you for your prayers #Godisfaithful #TheGloryRoad

Day #19 May 8

Anchor Verse: Luke 24:38
He [Jesus] said to them, "Why are you troubled [frightened], and why do doubts rise in your minds [hearts]?" (NIV)

After Jesus rose from the grave, He appeared to His disciples. In Luke 24, it says that Jesus stood among them and said, "Peace be with you."

His own disciples were frightened and doubted that Jesus stood before them. They were shocked even though Jesus told them what would happen before He died.

There are times in our lives, even when we know the truth of God, we are frightened and doubts arise in our minds.

I hear the voice of the Jesus speaking to us this morning, "Why are you troubled, and why do doubts rise in your minds?"

We must stand on the truth of God, the promises of God. It is the unshakeable foundation of our faith. The winds, rain, and storms may blow in our lives but God has us tucked under the shadow of His wings. It is there that we are filled with peace and the Lord is our fortress and strength.

What can we do to be proactive when the enemy attacks us? How can we protect our mind from doubt and fear?

Through our journey to Bill's healing, it was the Word of God, Bible verses that I had memorized in my youth that were the most powerful weapons. Speaking scripture out loud not only puts the enemy on notice, but with our own ears, we heard God's power in the spoken word.

In this new season as I walk down the Glory Road, I hear the words of Jesus. The other afternoon the spirit of fear tried to sneak into my mind and our home. Immediately, the promises of God rose up in me and I spoke them out loud to send fear running. "For the Lord has not given us a spirit of fear but of power and love and a sound mind." (2 Timothy 1:7)

As I look for a new "rhythm" in my life, my strong foundation is the truth of God. Daily, I choose to trust Him. I do what I can do. I take small steps. I take care of my mind and body as best I can. I cry when I need to cry. Every day there are more moments when I am strong, not weak.

Thank you for your love and kindness. #Godisfaithful #TheGloryRoad

Day #20 May 9

Anchor Verse: John 1:8
The light [His life] shines in the darkness, and the darkness can never extinguish it. (NLT)

Jesus is that light that came into the world. He is the light that is still shining. The light and the love of Jesus shines through the lives of believers as we walk this earth. His light can never be extinguished by the darkness.

Instead of being "overcome" by what is happening around us or the drastic changes that have happened in our lives, this is a time to turn our eyes to the Lord and seek His face and stand in His light.

In March (2020), when Bill and I began our self-quarantine to keep him safe, God tucked us under His wings. Our pattern during the journey to Bill's healing was to abide in God's presence and bathed in His peace.

"He who dwells in the shelter of the Most High will rest in the shadow of the Almighty." (Psalm 91:1) Bill and I learned how to rest in God even when we didn't always understand the path where God was leading us.

There was always peace when we abided with Him – peace in our home, in our minds, and in our hearts.

Because of God's grace, I can go to that place again and abide with Him. In the quietness of our home, I can feel God's presence. I can feel Bill's presence and often I am blessed by words from heaven to remind me that God is still in control, even on the chaotic days.

Now as I walk this Glory Road, I am reminded of those last few hours of Bill's life, when according to my human eyes, things were totally out of control. Then I am reminded of God's peace in the midst of that storm, how the Lord took my hand and led me through those last hours. My heavenly Father carried me during those final moments of Bill's life.

The Lord had me pause and ask for wise spiritual counsel. In His own quiet way, God said, "I've got this. Trust Me, once again, it's for Bill's best and for My glory."

Thank you for your countless prayers. #Godisfaithful #TheGloryRoad

Day #21 May 10

Anchor Verse: John 1:46
"Come and see," said Philip. (NIV)

"Come and see" is the Lord's invitation to us.

Come and see My glory. Come and see My provision. Come and see how I will give you peace. Come and see how much I love you.

There are two actions we must take. First, we must come. We must come into the presence of the Lord. We must step out in faith trusting that the Lord will provide, that the Lord will heal, deliver, and set us free.

Come! Do you see Jesus' arms wide open to you? Jesus will take you as you are. He knows your joy. He knows your struggles. He knows your heartache. He knows...and Jesus loves you all the more.

The second thing we must do is "see." Seeing is an action verb. Seeing means that we take in what is before our eyes and it impacts us at some level. When we see something beautiful, it fills us with joy. When we see someone we love, it fills us with great happiness. When we see injustice, it spurs us to action.

In the gospel of Matthew, chapter 28, verse 6, the angel at the tomb said to the women, "He is not here; he has risen just as he said, 'Come and see the place where he lay.'"

Come and see... Weeping Women, I want you to see with your own eyes so that you can go and tell the disciples that Jesus Christ is no longer dead.

What are the mighty miracles that God wants us to "come and see?" Come and see your heavenly Father waiting to welcome you home. There is provision. There is power. Hope is waiting for us at the foot of the cross.

On the journey to Bill's healing, many times the Lord invited me, invited us to "come and see" what He could do. Come and see and bring your friends and family so they can see I am alive and I have the power to save.

As I walk the unfamiliar steps of the Glory Road, the Lord is beckoning me to "come and see" what He can do. He will bring beauty out of the ashes of broken dreams. He will turn my mourning into dancing. He will turn my tears into testimonies of the Lord's faithfulness.

Thank you for your continued prayers. #Godisfaithful #TheGloryRoad

Day #22 May 11

Anchor Verse: Psalm 96:1

Go ahead – sing your new song to the Lord! Let everyone in every language sing him a new song. (TPT)

Sing a new song! All of us are learning to sing new songs. In this coronavirus season, we are learning to "sing" and live as we never have in our lives.

Some are learning how to sing solo while others are learning what the choir, called their family, sounds like singing from their home stage.

In this season, there are new sounds of birth and sounds of death. There are "near misses" and the sound of joy in overcoming huge challenges.

There is a new song of joy as we are learning more about our heavenly Father and how He provides for us. There are peals of laughter and the rumbling of a deep belly laugh as we have time to appreciate family members in our own home and remember why God made the family in the first place.

New songs are bursting forth on the internet as churches are quickly learning technology to stay in touch with their flock to keep them fed and connected, even at arm's length.

It is a time for new revelation from the Lord. It is a time of wisdom. It is a time for stretching our faith. And for many, it's a time to walk a new path, to sing a new song.

On this journey to Bill's healing, we learned to sing new songs. Bill said he couldn't "carry a tune in a bucket" but his life, his voice through the last 2+ years of this fight for life has been a beautiful melody, a testimony to God's faithfulness. Bill must have a beautiful voice in heaven.

On this Glory Road, I am learning many new songs. Often my song is laced with tears, and there is a pause before I continue. It is raw, authentic, and filled with hope and life. It speaks of God's continued faithfulness as I lean in and ask God to show me the way. My song is a tribute to my husband who taught me how to live each day with grace, strength, love, and determination – the melody Bill learned from his heavenly Father.

Our new song must also be filled with rest. A new song takes time to learn and lots of practice. Know that the Lord is with you, wherever you go.

Thank you for your prayers. #Godisfaithful #TheGloryRoad

Day #23 May 12

Anchor Verse: Psalm 92:1-2
It is good to praise the Lord and make music to your name, O Most High, proclaiming your love in the morning and your faithfulness at night. (NIV)

Life's terrain is filled with mountains and valleys. There are also green pastures and places of celebration. There is swampland and desert. The one constant through it all is God's love and faithfulness.

As a child chooses to be comforted by its mother, so too we have the choice to rest in God's love and faithfulness.

In the alternative, we can remain the fussy baby. Not asking for a show of hands, but adversity can bring out the best or worst in us.

No one gets it right all the time. We should be so grateful that God's grace is sufficient and His power is made perfect in our weakness.

What God does ask of us is to walk in obedience, to follow Him, not run ahead of Him, not make up our own rules, but abide with Him.

As Solomon so wisely put it, "There is nothing new under the sun." We are not the first people in the history of the world to walk through a valley of difficulty or ascend the mountain of joy. We are in good company. God is faithful and He will see us through this season.

One of the keys found in Psalm 92 is praising the Lord – "proclaiming your love in the morning and your faithfulness at night."

Proclaiming is a powerful stance – it is done with power and authority... the power of the king behind you. In our case, we are proclaiming the power of God and declaring to the darkness, to the enemy of our souls that God loves us and that He is faithful and will never leave us or forsake us.

On this journey to Bill's healing, we learned to often speak of God's love and faithfulness. It also planted those seeds in our own hearts and lives. I am a blessed woman to have been loved so well by a man who so loved the Lord. I wish all of you could have experienced the joy of being in Bill's presence the last couple of years as he shared what God shared with him.

On this Glory Road, I am learning how to declare God's love in the morning and His faithfulness at night. It's the best way to start and end the day.

Thank you for being so vigilant. #Godisfaithful #TheGloryRoad

Day #24 May 13

Anchor Verse: Psalm 62:5
I am standing in absolute stillness, silent before the one I love, waiting as long as it takes for him to rescue me. Only God is my Savior, and he will not fail me. (TPT)

Silence...many people cannot stand the "sound" of silence. They want to fill their space with noise – music, television, videos, or voices. Do they feel alone or lonely in the silence?

Personally, I have found that the early morning hours of the day – the quiet hours before neighbors and the rest of the world wake up to be my favorite time of the day. I can hear His voice more clearly when it's not competing with other things.

When you are with the one you love, especially between a husband and wife, silence speaks volumes. The bond of your love sends non-verbal messages that are more beautiful than poetry or a great orator's speech.

I loved the times when Bill and I would hang out together in silence. Often I was the first one who wanted to fill the space with words.

On the journey to Bill's healing, he loved to go for a car ride, with no special destination. As we would ride through neighborhoods, Bill would observe what had changed. It was amazing how God restored Bill's eyesight and his brain. Bill would often see details that I would miss. But in my defense, I was the driver. It was important for me to keep my eyes on the road.

On the Glory Road, I am doing a 40-day television fast. I haven't turned on the T.V. since Bill died.

God often whispers and I don't want to miss my next assignment or His words of comfort. I also want to listen for Bill's voice – either echoes of past conversations or words of assurance and instruction from heaven

The last part of this verse says, "Only God is my Savior, and He will not fail me." That is the truth on which I stand as I move forward. God will not fail me, He will not fail us.

Reach out to the Lord in the silence, He is there waiting for you.

Thank you for your prayers. I had a good night's rest. Looking forward to the blessings of this day. #Godisfaithful #TheGloryRoad

Day #25 May 14

Anchor Verse: Revelation 12:11
They triumphed over him by the blood of the Lamb and by the word of their testimony...(NIV)

The test you are going through right now is creating a beautiful testimony of God's faithfulness. Those hairpin curves and narrow mountain roads where it seems there are no guardrails only steep cliffs is the perfect setting for God's miracles and His deliverance.

"The word of our testimony"... your story is powerful. Your story of what God has done in your life will impact others. We all have a story to tell and by telling it we encourage others.

I wouldn't be sharing this testimony if God was not for us. Our heavenly Father fought for us every day. Often the Lord would say to Bill, daily in fact, "I am here to fight for you."

God carried us. He helped us stand. God gave us the courage to get up every day to face that day's blessings and battles because of His love for us.

This is the hour we must trust the Lord even more. We must rest under the shadow of His wings, as we abide in His presence.

We must not fear but trust the Lord's mercy and grace. It is also a time to come together in prayer and "pound" the gates of heaven like we never have before.

On this journey to Bill's healing, we have witnessed the power of prayer. Prayer moves the hand of God, the heart of God.

As I walk "alone" on this Glory Road, there are only one set of footprints left behind, every day a new chapter is written of God's love and faithfulness.

Lord, we thank you this morning that because of Your love, power, grace, and mercy, we need not fear as You write another chapter in the book of our testimony. We love you. We trust you. We rely on You to bring us out of this season of trials and testing. Great will be our testimony, Lord, for You alone are mighty to save. Amen.

Thank you for your prayers and holding up my arms on days when I am weary. You are appreciated. #Godisfaithful #TheGloryRoad

Day #26 May 15

Anchor Verse: 2 Kings 6:17
Then Elisha prayed, "O Lord, open his eyes and let him see!" The Lord opened the young man's eyes, and when he looked up, he saw that the hillside around Elisha was filled with horses and chariots of fire. (NLT)

When we walk looking down at the ground, we miss a lot. We see the dirt, garbage, cracks and crevices in the sidewalk but we miss the birds in the trees, the clouds, the people that pass by, and most of all the messages God has in store for those who look up.

We are being stretched and challenged on many fronts. The world would have us watch the news and become overwhelmed by what we hear.

But the Lord is speaking the truth through His Word and His still small voice that says, "Look up, and see the deliverance of the Lord."

Elisha's servant could only see all the troops sent from the king of Aram that surrounded the city to capture Elijah. He was afraid. "What shall we do?"

He said, "Don't be afraid. Those who are with us are more than those who are with them."

Sometimes "words" are not enough to take away our fear and anxiety. So Elisha prayed and asked God to open his servant's eyes. The servant "looked up" and saw that the hills were filled with horses and chariots of fire – troops sent from heaven, from the Lord to defeat the enemy.

Those troops are fighting for us.

On the road to Bill's healing, we discovered the secret was "looking up" into God's face, into heaven where our help came from in the name of the Lord. It was there we found comfort, power, and victory.

Now on this Glory Road, the troops of heaven are guiding my steps. Some days when I am weak, weary, and grieving, they stand guard over me to a allow me to heal in safety. Other days, they empower me to ride with them and we conquer the enemy. But it is only when I "look up" that I see the deliverance of the Lord.

Thank you for your prayers. Ask the Lord to open your eyes to see those who are fighting for you. #Godisfaithful #TheGloryRoad

Day #27 May 16

Anchor Verse: Zechariah 4:10
Do not despise these small beginnings, for the Lord rejoices to see the work begin. (TLB)

The first step on a new path often feels awkward. When you make a decision to turn away from an old destructive lifestyle or walk away from an abusive relationship or a toxic work environment, that first step is the most difficult.

Old patterns, old ways are comfortable. It's like trying to step off a merry-go-round when it's moving, you will face resistance. But the end result is worth it.

This morning I am reminded of so many times on Bill's journey to healing when he had to "start over" due to a medical procedure or "attack" on his body. After his stroke, learning how to walk again, talk again, eat again, even learning to breathe again. All of these took a first step of faith and commitment. Bill put his trust in God and asked God to show him how to start over as a man in his mid-70s.

We were surrounded by amazing therapists and doctors who knew when to "push" Bill's body and when he needed to rest. But at the end of the day, Bill's success was in the hands of God.

Bill was willing to humble himself and do what was necessary to recover. I was so blessed to be at his side to encourage him, pray with him and for him, and rejoice as we celebrated victory at every step.

Even today, tears of joy quickly spring to my eyes as I remember watching Bill "walk" from the bed to the chair the first time when days before some doubted he would even live. That's my Bill!

Now as I walk this Glory Road without his physical presence, I must remember to not despise small beginnings. I must exhibit the same courage Bill showed us. There will be days I make good progress forward and other days when treading water will be a challenge. I know that God is faithful. What He did for Bill, God will do for me, and for you.

The time to start is now – take that first step.

My life was changed by my amazing husband and his courage and strength as Bill put his trust in God and walked with Him. Thank you, Mr. Bill.

Thank you for your persistent prayers. #Godisfaithful #TheGloryRoad

Day #28 May 17

Anchor Verse: Philippians 1:21

For to me, to live is Christ [He is my source of joy, my reason to live] and to die is gain [for I will be with Him in eternity]. (AMP)

Life and death, they are the bookends of every human life. There is great anticipation as families await the entrance of a new baby into the world. Great preparation precedes the event and great joy. The cries of a child are "cute" as they signal healthy lungs and a grand entrance into the world.

The baby is likely in "shock" because that quiet place he/she has lived for nine months has been exchanged for quite a noisy, crazy world.

Watching the development of a child into the man or woman of God created them to be is an amazing journey.

In our adult years, our choices indicate whether we have chosen to live for Christ. We may have reached this decision as a child, hallelujah if you did.

As the Amplified version says, when we live for Christ, He is our source of joy and our reason to live.

On the journey to Bill's healing, this is an accurate description of how we lived each day. We found joy in places that others might not have found so joyful but God was there. God was Bill's reason to live. It was the hope Bill found in God that propelled him forward to fight one more battle and to take the next step. There is joy in serving Jesus, in living for God.

The last part of the verse says, "to die is gain." We like the life part but preparing for death isn't met with quite the same enthusiasm as buying cute little outfits for our new granddaughter. Death is only a comma at the end of our story if we follow Jesus. We move from death into eternal life. There is no pain or sorrow in heaven.

Four weeks ago this morning, Bill finished his race here on earth and God took Bill to his heavenly home. For Bill to die was gain.

As I walk these new steps on the Glory Road, I am eager to hear the Lord's voice saying, "This is the way, walk in it." Every day I see His hand of provision. He holds me when I cry and gives me courage to take on another mountain or endurance to finish a task.

Thank you for your prayers. They help me conquer mountains and find peace in the valleys. #Godisfaithful #TheGloryRoad

Day #29 May 18

Anchor Verse: John 6:18
A strong wind was blowing and the waters grew rough. (NIV)

We can read the signs in nature and know a storm is coming.

Jesus sent His disciples out in the boat while He stayed behind to pray, these were seasoned fishermen who were very familiar with storms on the water.

Note that they didn't stop and turn around and head back to the shore when the strong wind was blowing and the waters were getting rough, they kept on going. They didn't cry out to Jesus and ask why He sent them out in the middle of the storm. They didn't complain at all, they kept going.

In fact, the Bible says they had rowed 3-4 miles when something unusual happened. Everything changed when Jesus enters the picture. They are battling the storm, the wind is blowing, they are getting wet from the waves splashing over them, and here comes Jesus walking across the water to their boat. They were scared. Seasoned fishermen who had seen many things in storms were afraid because they had never seen anyone walk on water.

After they were reassured by Jesus, they were "willing" to take Him into the boat and immediately the boat reached the shore where they were heading. The difference was Jesus. Not only did it calm their fears but they made it to their destination safely.

The same is true today. The difference is Jesus. We must be willing to take Jesus into the boat with us. Are you willing to let Jesus help you through this coronavirus storm?

On the journey to Bill's healing, we asked Jesus to pilot our boat. Often we found ourselves in rough waters where the wind was howling. But when Jesus was in the boat, we were at peace as we trusted in His ability to help us through the storm.

As I take faltering steps on this new Glory Road, I have encountered strong winds in this strange land. This time Bill's hand is not here to hold on to, but Jesus is here. As the tears of grief roll over me and even the stormy waters of change, my boat will not sink because I have invited Jesus into my boat.

Thank you for your prayers. Your love and kindness mean so much. God bless you. #Godisfaithful #TheGloryRoad

Day #30 May 19

Anchor Verse: Psalm 23:4
Even though I walk through the [sunless] valley of the shadow of death, I fear no evil, for You are with me; Your rod [to protect] and Your staff [to guide], they comfort and console me. (AMP)

One month ago, I walked into the valley of the shadow of death. It wasn't a place I wanted to go but the Lord walked with me into that place as a friend of ours drove me down the freeway in those early morning hours following the ambulance that was carrying Bill.

The truth is, God was carrying both of us.

We do not enter the valley of the shadow of death alone, the Lord is with us and His ministering angels surround us. There is such a mixture of emotions at work in that valley. For me, I wasn't prepared for it. There were no indications Bill was entering the final lap of his life. Bam! We were there.

What I do know is that the Good Shepherd was there, just as He promised in Psalm 23. "Even though I walk through the [sunless] valley of the shadow of death, I fear no evil, for You are with me; Your rod [to protect] and Your staff [to guide], they comfort and console me."

God took me by the hand in those final hours of Bill's life and led me through it. God made the decisions that I couldn't make. God choreographed Bill's final hours here on earth as He had all the preceding days of his life.

I believe that Bill was so wrapped in God's arms of love that through those final hours all Bill saw was God's glory not what I was seeing with my human eyes. God showed me in the spirit that He was putting a "period" at the end of Bill's life here on earth and then writing the opening sentence of the new book of Bill's life in eternity where I will join Bill one day.

On this journey to Bill's healing, we have walked through some treacherous places, but we were never alone.

Now on this Glory Road, I ask the Lord for an extra measure of His grace and strength. I don't know the path that lies ahead of me, it is virgin territory. But I do know that I trust the Lord to lead me by the hand with His rod and staff at the ready to help me.

Thank you for your faithfulness in prayer. #Godisfaithful #TheGloryRoad

Day #31 May 20

Anchor Verse: Habakkuk 2:1
I will climb up to my watchtower and stand at my guardpost. There I will wait to see what the Lord says. (NLT)

Being a watchman was an important job when cities were surrounded by walls. It was a place where you had the best vantage point to see the enemy coming from afar.

Those who lived within the walls relied on those at that guardposts to stay awake, day and night, so they would be safe and live their lives without fear of the enemy. In the military, those who are on guard duty have a very important job.

You and I have the opportunity to climb our watchtower and stand at our guardposts as prayer warriors. Prayer is our opportunity to stand in the gap for others. We use that phrase "stand in the gap"...what do I mean?

It means I am willing to stand in the place where you are vulnerable from an attack by the enemy. You are doing that for me right now. You did it for Bill, and me, for the last 2+ years.

Sometimes we are the answer to the prayer. That might be a listening ear or a meal or financial support or something else that we might have in our possession that ultimately is the answer to someone else's prayer.

On this journey to Bill's healing, I quickly learned how to climb my watchtower and stand at my guardpost, wherever we were at home or hospital. As Bill's wife, I had assumed that position for many years, since we met back in 1993. I would ask the Lord to protect Bill and shape him into the man of God he was created to be. The prayers intensified as Bill's physical issues multiplied. I was a "mama bear"... don't mess with Mr. Bill.

As I walk this Glory Road, as I heal in every area of my life from my battle wounds. The Lord is asking me to resume my position in my watchtower and my guardpost. My prayers have remained with you in this last month but God had me step back a bit from the intense frontline battle for a moment.

Thank you for fighting for us. #Godisfaithful #TheGloryRoad

Day #32 May 21

Anchor Verse: 1 Chronicles 14:10
So David inquired of God... (NIV)

Do you ask God to direct your path? Specifically ask the Lord, what you should do and where you should go.

King David quickly learned the lesson from his youth about the importance of seeking God's face and asking God to direct His path. As the leader of God's people, it was even more critical that David inquire of the Lord before going into battle or taking a step forward.

"If it seems good to you and it is the will of the Lord our God"... let's move the ark of the Lord back to us. David and the people made a strategic error – they didn't inquire of the Lord.

They move the ark of God on a cart, the oxen stumbled, Uzzah reached out to steady the ark. As he touched the ark, the Lord struck him down. King David was not only angry with God but he was afraid of God for a time.

In chapter 14, we read that the Philistines heard that David was king over all Israel. David went out to meet them. As the Philistines invaded the Valley of Rephaim, verse 10 says, "So David inquired of God: "Shall I go and attack the Philistines? Will you deliver them into my hands?" The Lord answered him, "Go, I will deliver them into your hands." And David and his men defeated the enemy.

What was different? David sought the Lord first. And the Lord answered.

On the journey to Bill's healing, we often inquired of the Lord, the right path to follow. Every day I would start the day in God's presence and ask Him to direct our path. As the day ended, Bill and I would seek God's face as we ended the day asking for His hand of protection over us. Sometimes the decisions needed to be made in a split second, but God never let us down.

As I walk the Glory Road, I find myself stopping often and asking the Lord the way to go. I don't see any familiar landmarks. Even familiar places look different without Bill by my side. But God will never leave me or forsake me.

Thank you for standing with me. #Godisfaithful #TheGloryRoad

Day #33 May 22

Anchor Verse: 1 Chronicles 17:16
Then King David went in and sat before the Lord and prayed, "Who am I, O Lord God, and what is my family, that you have brought me this far?" (NIV)

When David received blessings, he knew they were from the hand of God. It wasn't because of David's mighty exploits, his "stunning" personality, his strength, or his superior knowledge, it was all because of the grace of God.

This morning David's prayer is also the cry of my heart. By human standards, I have lost a lot on the last few months – both my husband and my mom have died. With my husband's death, there went a large chunk of our family's income along with half my heart.

In the flesh, I could be curled into a ball in the corner, but in the spirit, God continues to breathe new life into me.

For all these months and more than two years on this journey to Bill's healing, we have seen God's hand at work as He moved with His mighty power. We have seen God move mountains and also felt the tenderness of His embrace as He held both of us through moments of pain and suffering.

God has been so faithful through the calm and the storm. Though I didn't always understand His methods or the places He guided us, I trusted my heavenly Father that every single thing would be for our good and for His glory, even when it seemed to the contrary. He never failed us – never!

With tears of gratitude this morning, I sing praises to His name and with King David come into the presence of the Lord and say, "Who am I, O Lord God, and what is my family, that you have brought me this far?"

On this new path, the Glory Road, I am reminded to look to the hills where my help comes from, "My help comes in the name of the Lord!" That is where your help comes from too.

Jehovah Jireh moved in a mighty way in my life yesterday. Instead of one handful of blessings, He gave me two. I praise the Lord for His faithfulness this morning. A seed planted about 30 years ago finally bloomed and bore fruit. What a great reminder that what may look like barren ground, a dead end, in the Lord's eyes is the perfect soil for His next miracle.

Thank you for your faithfulness in prayer. #Godisfaithful #TheGloryRoad

Day #34 May 23

Anchor Verse: Ephesians 3:16
I pray that out of His glorious riches He may strengthen you with power through His Spirit in your inner being. (NIV)

It's what's on the inside that matters. Who you are isn't defined by how you look, the list of your possessions or the lack of them, or even the people you associate with, but rather by who you are in your inner being.

To get another perspective, looking at other translations of this verse may be helpful. The Passion version says it this way: "And I pray that he would unveil within you the unlimited riches of his glory and favor until supernatural strength floods your innermost being with his divine might and explosive power."

As I read that verse, the promises of God in the Bible have new power:

"I can do all things through Christ who strengthens me."

"The joy of the Lord is my strength."

"No weapon formed against me will prosper."

If you are feeling less than powerful this morning. If the weather or this difficult season has you feeling weak and weary, ask the Lord to fill you with His divine might and explosive power. The Lord says we are overcomers in Jesus's name, more than conquerors.

My friends, why do we choose to live like "98 lb. weaklings" when we can do all things through Christ? The good news is that can change today. When we say "yes" to God, we are filled with resurrection power and we can rise above our circumstances.

On the journey to Bill's healing, we were blessed by tapping into that source of God's unlimited might and resurrection power. It was Christ living in Bill that gave him the victory. Together we chose to let God lead the way and He never failed us. His love always led us to higher ground.

As I walk this Glory Road, I must remember not to rely on my own strength but instead rest in His arms of love when I am weary. Empowered by His strength I accept my new assignments and carry them out with joy.

Thank you for covering me. #Godisfaithful #TheGloryRoad

Day #35 May 24

Anchor Verse: John 8:32
Then you will know the truth, and the truth will set you free. (NIV)

Freedom – it's what we all long for in some part of our heart and mind.

Living in a country where its citizens have been granted certain freedoms due to the government structure and living environment is one thing but greater still is the freedom we have in Christ.

In John 8, Jesus is talking about the freedom that comes when you know the "truth" because the "truth will set you free."

Verse 8 starts out with the word "then"... which gives us a clue that we need to look at the previous verse. Verse 31 says, "To the Jews who believed him, Jesus said, 'If you hold to my teaching, you are really my disciples.'"

The key is believing Jesus and then holding to His teaching. Then and only then will the truth set you free.

Your mind and your spirit are "free" when you hold on to the truth of Jesus no matter your circumstances in the flesh.

The truth is, one day the warranty on our body will run out, and as a believer, God will take us to heaven to be with Him for eternity.

On this journey to Bill's healing, Bill and I both hung on to the truth of the Word of God. It was a lamp to our feet and a light to our path. Our hope was secure because we knew the truth. Bill is in heaven because he knew the truth and the truth set him free.

As I walk this new path on the Glory Road, it is the truth I find in God's Word that sets me free. The whispers of His love, the love letters the Lord sends me every day as I read the Bible and ask Him to show me the way.

In this world, what we hear is a mixture of truth and lies. We need the Lord's wisdom and discernment to separate the good from the bad. But God is faithful, He delights in helping us if we ask.

We need to be alert so we don't get caught in the spider web of the devil's lies. Because once we swallow the first lie, others seem to more quickly follow. Be careful that you "feast" only in the Word of God.

Thank you for letting your light shine. #Godisfaithful #TheGloryRoad

Day #36 May 25

Anchor Verse: Psalm 25:1
In you, Lord my God, I put my trust. (NIV)

What does it mean to "trust" someone? The dictionary defines "trust" as the firm belief in the reliability, truth, ability, or strength of someone or something. Or other words like: confidence, belief, faith, from suspicion/doubt, certainty, or conviction.

Children learn to trust their parents at an early age and others that they find to be trustworthy.

Here in Psalm 25, David says, "In you, Lord my God, I put my trust."

I echo David's words this morning. I cannot think of a safer place to put my trust. I know that I can rely on God to always have my best interest in mind. God loves me with an everlasting love. He created me. My heavenly Father knows the plans He has for me and they are good.

God knows what makes me happy and the things that weigh me down. If I can't trust God, then I can't trust anyone because the characteristic of trust comes from the heart of God.

We are trustworthy because we learned how to be trustworthy by watching God work in our lives. As children, but even as adults, often we learn new skills, new character qualities by watching others.

My grandfather as he tried to find work during the Great Depression learned how to do a new job by watching others. We often learn good habits, or bad ones, through the influence of others.

On this journey to Bill's healing, every day we put Bill's life in God's hands because we knew God was safe to trust. And we put our faith in the character of God, our loving heavenly Father who only wanted what was best for us. I can't imagine living any other way.

Now as I walk the Glory Road, I continue to put my life in God's hands. I trust Him with today and all my tomorrows. I trust Him because what God does is always for our good and for His glory. Even when I don't always understand His ways, I rely and trust on the character of God.

Thank you for your faithful prayers. On days when the waves of grief knock me down, your thoughts, prayers, and encouraging words lift me up. May the Lord bless you indeed. #Godisfaithful #TheGloryRoad

Day #37 May 26

Anchor Verse: 1 Chronicles 28:20
Then he [David] continued, "Be strong and courageous and get to work. Don't be frightened by the size of the task, for the Lord my God is with you; he will not forsake you. He [God] will see to it that everything is finished correctly." (TLB)

Get to work! How many times have we heard those words in our lifetime from a parent or a boss? Many!

Sometimes those words come from our heavenly Father. God has a plan and purpose for our lives. All He wants is our obedience...that's it. If we take the first step, and the next step, God will provide the increase.

In this passage, it is King David instructing his son, Solomon, about building the temple for the Lord. God told David, the father, that it was not his task to build the temple but God had a special plan for David's son to carry out.

The Living Bible translation describes it in words we can understand. "Then he [David] continued, "Be strong and courageous and get to work. Don't be frightened by the size of the task, for the Lord my God is with you; he will not forsake you. He will see to it that everything is finished correctly."

That is what God is telling each one of us. The work may be difficult. It will require strength and courage but God will not forsake you. God will see to it that everything is "finished correctly."

God is in charge of quality control. He is the building inspector. God is in charge of the workers and the workmanship. Nothing will be less than the best because that's God's standard – excellence. This is good news.

On the journey to Bill's healing, God taught me how to fight those battles, to fight for Bill's life and win. We were blessed by the mighty miracles that came from the hand and heart of God. This blessing continues today.

As I walk this new path on the Glory Road, I understand that I don't know how to navigate this new stretch of road, it's unknown territory. Every day I ask the Lord to show me how to fight these new battles. Yes, how to be strong and courageous and do the work God has planned for me. He is my teacher, my comforter, my peace.

Thank you for courageously taking a stand with us as we fought the good fight for Bill's life. #Godisfaithful #TheGloryRoad

Day #38 May 27

Anchor Verse: John 10:4
...His sheep follow him because they know his voice. (NIV)

A shepherd and his sheep – Jesus loved to tell stories using parables. What's a parable? A simple story that Jesus used to share a moral or spiritual lesson by using something that was familiar to people.

We do it all the time. It's how we teach our children lessons, and sometimes adults too.

Jesus sets up the lesson by describing how a thief comes in to steal the sheep. The thief or robber doesn't come through the gate, he comes in over the fence with the intent of doing harm.

The one who enters by the gate is the shepherd of the sheep. The gatekeeper opens the gate and the sheep listen for his voice. He knows each sheep by name and leads them out to the green pastures to be fed. The sheep will not follow a stranger.

Sheep have a reputation of needing guidance. They don't do well on their own. We have the same problem at times. It's easy to get "lost" in this world.

But in spite of their challenges, sheep know their shepherd's voice and they will follow him. I find that incredible. For an animal that doesn't always practice good judgment, the sheep knows who is safe to trust.

How about you and me? Are we as smart as those sheep? Unfortunately, sometimes we are not. We choose to follow the wrong "shepherd" or hang out with other sheep that lead us on the path of destruction.

On this road to Bill's healing, we were so blessed to have Jesus, our Shepherd, lead us on this treacherous path. He always had Bill's best interest in mind. We were led through some deep valleys and also along high mountains and steep cliffs with only Jesus as our "guardrail" but we had no reason to fear. He was with us.

Now as I walk this Glory Road, I desperately need to hear His voice. Nothing looks familiar and I can't reach out and grab Bill's hand as I walk through those scary places. God reminds me that His hand is always there, day or night. He will never leave me or forsake me.

Thank you for your prayers. This new path still surprises me and some days the "grief monster" ambushes me. Thank you for holding up my arms on days when I am weary. #Godisfaithful #TheGloryRoad

Day #39 May 28

Anchor Verse: Psalm 40:3

He has given me a new song to sing, of praises to our God. Now many will hear of the glorious things he did for me, and stand in awe before the Lord, and put their trust in him.(TLB)

This is the day the Lord has made, let us rejoice and be glad in it.

King David, who wrote many of the psalms, walked through some deep valleys in his life. Not only valleys of sorrow and deep repentance for the times he went his own way rather than God's way, but also physical danger, when Saul was actually trying to kill him.

We may not face that kind of danger in our own lives but often we walk through the valley of the shadow of death with our loved ones.

David had a great perspective, he clothed himself in joy. "He has put a new song in my mouth, a hymn of praise to our God." (NIV)

It wasn't an old familiar song that David repeated the words from memory and without feeling, his mind distracted by other things. This is a new song. It's a hymn of praise to our God. It's filled with passion and David may have even danced before the Lord as he sang this new song.

New songs aren't birthed at "microwave speed" but rather slowly like in a crock pot. The high notes and the low notes speak of the hills and valleys but together they bring forth songs of praise. Far greater than the song itself is God's purpose for the song.

On this journey to Bill's healing, God wanted us to share our journey with you. You have heard the songs we sang in the night seasons and the songs of rejoicing on the mountaintops. Every note of our song has been filled with praise to our God.

On this new path, the Glory Road, God is giving me a new song. These new verses are sung with arms raised high in praise or on my knees worshipping God. Or the notes are mixed with my tears of grief as I recount precious memories and the goodness of our heavenly Father. May every verse of our story cause you to stand in awe of God and draw you closer to Him.

Thank you for singing God's songs of deliverance with me. #Godisfaithful #TheGloryRoad

Day #40 May 29

Anchor Verse: 3 John 2
Beloved, I pray that in every way you may succeed and prosper and be in good health [physically], just as [I know] your soul prospers [spiritually]. (AMP)

As we draw near to the end of May, it's time to check in about your health in every area – physically, mentally, emotionally, and spiritually.

Coming through this coronavirus season, even with some parts of the country opening up to Phase 2 (5/2020), we are still in the process of healing and practicing safety while not walking in fear.

There is so much we have learned about ourselves and each other. We may have discovered strengths and skills we didn't know we had and also our "breaking points" as we have been "tucked in" at home for a long time.

I find it interesting the author of this passage "knows" they are prospering spiritually and his prayer is that physically their health matches that spiritual strength.

Could God say the same of you? Of me?

My prayer for each one of us is that we are in good health physically and spiritually. For those who are sick, we pray for healing in Jesus' name this morning. For those who have lost loved ones during this season, because of the virus or something else, I pray that God would heal your broken heart. That soon life would resume its "normal" course so services can be held and our loved one's remains put to rest. (Their spirit is already rejoicing in heaven.) Each day I am reminded that nothing is impossible with God.

He is writing a new chapter in our lives. God is guiding us to a new place.

On this journey to Bill's healing, we passed through many different places – seasons of healing and seasons of illness but the most important thing we learned is that God is always with us. God is faithful and always we can trust Him with our lives and loved ones...always.

As I walk this Glory Road, I am grateful for God's grace and His faithfulness. As I "recover" from this incredible path where God has led us through mountains and valleys, I believe that I will prosper and be in good health as I am spiritually. There is a price to pay for every leg of our life's journey, some places the cost is greater than others.

Thank you for your love and your prayers. #Godisfaithful #TheGloryRoad

Day #41 May 30

Anchor Verse: Deuteronomy 29:29
The secret things belong to the Lord our God, but the things which are revealed and disclosed belong to us and to our children forever, so that we may do [obey] all of the words of this law. (NIV)

Are you a person who loves to keep secrets or are you the type of person that an unrevealed secret makes you a little bit "crazy?"

God, the Creator of the universe, has chosen to reveal many things to His people but there are some "big" questions/secrets that go unanswered on this side of eternity.

As I write this, I realize that often our questions revolve around "difficult" things that happen in life. When was the last time that you questioned why God did an "amazing" thing for you? Something to think about the next time you can't sleep in the middle of the night. Count your blessings...name them one by one...

There have been many times in these last 2+ years that my heart was so filled with gratitude about what the Lord had done that tears of joy poured like a river down my face as I praised the Lord.

However, there are some things we will not have the answers to in our lifetime, they are beyond what we can handle right now. Our finite minds can't comprehend God's ways which are always higher than our ways.

"The secret things belong to the Lord our God." This morning I can rejoice in that truth.

On the journey to Bill's healing, we encountered both God's secrets and His miraculous revelations. It's like being on a roller coaster ride when you're not sure what will happen next. Through the blessings and the bumps in the road, we learned to trust God's love and hold on to His hand and each other's hand.

On this Glory Road, there are still many secrets that the Lord has not revealed, many. Graciously in those first few hours after God took Bill home, God opened my spiritual eyes to see those final moments from God's perspective. Even with tears streaming down my face, God allowed me to see the "greater glory" that was at work. It was in those moments that I learned not only did I trust God but He trusted me.

Thank you for rejoicing in our victories. #Godisfaithful #TheGloryRoad

Day #42 May 31

Anchor Verse: Acts 1:8

But you will receive power when the Holy Spirit comes on you; and you will be my witnesses in Jerusalem, and in all Judea and Samaria, and to the end of the earth. (NIV)

Today is Pentecost Sunday (2020). Fifty days have passed since Easter, in many ways it seems like yesterday. It's an important day in the Christian faith. God sent the gift of the Holy Spirit to His people.

In Acts 1, it tells us that Jesus appeared to the apostles for a period of 40 days after his resurrection and spoke to them about the kingdom of God. Jesus told them to remain in Jerusalem and wait until they received the gift that God promised them.

Where did they start? Right where they lived. So for us it would be comparable to our hometown, state, United States, and the whole world.

With the advent of technology, we can reach the world almost instantaneously. It's one of the advantages of technology. The key for them, and the key for us, is that we go with God guided by the Holy Spirit. We are commissioned to go and tell the story about what God has done.

In the last 50 days, you are aware about how much my life has changed. Easter Sunday at home, Bill and I celebrated the resurrection of Jesus and we had a magnificent turkey dinner with all the trimmings with our best silver and china at a table set for a "king and queen"... a glorious day. Then one week later, God took Bill to heaven. It was also a day of victory and rejoicing in heaven as Bill entered the gates of glory.

These last 42 days on the Glory Road have been filled with their own challenges. Like Jesus' disciples who were learning to follow a new path without Him, on Pentecost Sunday God gave them a special gift, the Comforter, the gift of the Holy Spirit to guide them in Jesus' absence, God is giving me that renewed power too.

On the journey to Bill's healing, even the day Bill stepped from earth to heaven, the Lord was with us to guide and direct us. As we asked the Lord for help, we were guided by the Holy Spirit's power to stand when in our flesh we were weak and trusting God alone through uncharted waters.

Thank you for walking this path with us. #Godisfaithful #TheGloryRoad

June 2020

Joy comes in the morning.
~ Psalm 30:5

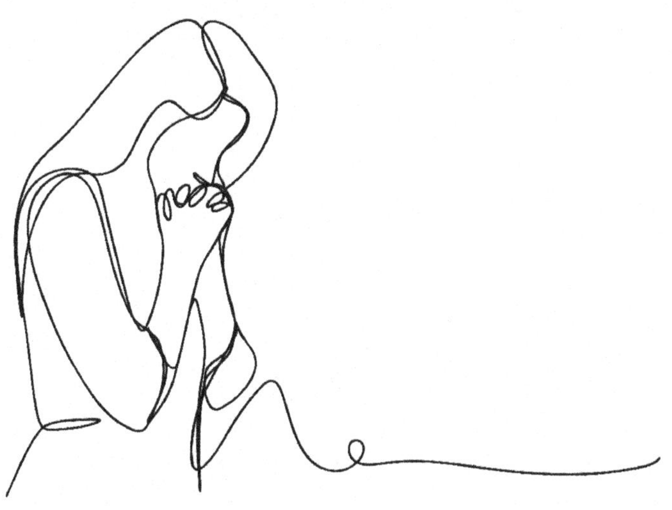

Day #43 June 1

Anchor Verse: 2 Chronicles 15:4
But in their distress they turned to the Lord, the God of Israel, and sought him, and he was found by them. (NIV)

Often things "suddenly" change in our lives. Distress. Trouble. Illness. Natural Disasters. They all can come upon us suddenly and without warning. We are caught off-guard, but God is never taken by surprise.

In Spokane last night (5.31.20), we had one of those "suddenly" moments. Many prayer warriors had been praying over our city as we heard about the protest that would take place on Sunday afternoon. We prayed for peace and in the afternoon hours, cooler heads prevailed and nothing escalated out of control. As we moved into the early evening hours, there was a "shift", and what had been peaceful changed. New players entered the stage.

Gratefully, no lives were lost and no burning in the streets. The damage was contained to small areas. Yes, the National Guard has been called in and a curfew is in place as it is in many other cities across the nation.

We may be shaken, but we are not undone. As prayer warriors, we ask all of you, across this area and around the world, to continue to pray for Spokane and all the cities across the United States that have been rocked over this last week by unrest.

On our journey to Bill's healing, we encountered turmoil many times. I'm sure there were times for Bill that it felt like his body was a "battleground" and that the enemy was "looting" and "pillaging" his body, mind, and peace. But through it all, Bill kept his eyes on the Lord. Bill knew where his help came from, and in his distress, he cried out to the Lord and God answered.

With the beginning of a new month, the Glory Road has taken a new turn. This morning I find that my world has a new landscape. Throughout the night, the Lord woke me up to pray for our city, our nation. I wouldn't be surprised if many of you were boldly approaching the throne room of grace through the night, too. It is on our knees this battle will be won, and then as we walk out peace in the flesh.

Thank you for your prayers for protection. #Godisfaithful #TheGloryRoad

Day #44 June 2

Anchor Verse: Proverbs 11:11a
Through the blessing of the upright a city is exalted… (NIV)

Early in our lives we learn the power of words, blessings or curses – words spoken to us and the words that come out of our own mouths.

Metaphorically, and literally in some cases, "washing our mouths out with soap" is an action meant to cleanse and purify our speech. But more than our speech, but what is in our hearts.

In Matthew 15:17-18 says, "Do you not understand that whatever goes into the mouth passes into the stomach, and is eliminated? But whatever [word] comes out of the mouth comes from the heart, and this is what defiles and dishonors the man." (AMP)

When we speak words that are negative, full of hate and sin, and evil, they defile and dishonor the person who speaks them.

On the same note, when we speak blessings, words that build up, encourage, see the light of the love of Jesus in others, we bring honor to the Lord and each other. Light creates more light. Blessings create more blessings.

Like the mustard seed of faith that becomes a big tree that blesses others and causes us to walk on the path of goodness the Lord has prepared for us, so darkness and "dark" words cut off God's blessings.

Make sure that the garden of your heart is free of weeds. Pull out the negative, the ugly, the profane. Fertilize and water the good seed through prayer, reading the Bible, and speaking blessings over your city.

As Bill and I walked the journey to his healing, we quickly learned the power of our words, speaking blessings over our bodies, our lives, and those we came in contact with each day. It is no coincidence that in speaking blessings Bill was blessed and new life sprang out of him.

Now as the Glory Road unfolds before me, I realize that I have a choice. I can choose to cling to the loss, the grief, the pain of losing the other "half of my heart" or I can speak blessings, I can embrace the plan God has for me because of the seeds that Bill and I sowed in the garden of our lives.

Thank you for your faithfulness in prayer. #Godisfaithful #TheGloryRoad

Day #45 June 3

Anchor Verse: Colossians 4:6
Let every word you speak be drenched with grace and tempered with truth and clarity. For then you will be prepared to give a respectful answer to anyone who asks about your faith. (TPT)

How do people know who we are and what we believe? It is often through our words, words paired with actions.

We have heard the expression "walk the walk, talk the talk" but then it is taken one step further… do you walk your talk?

Does what you say line up with what you do? But more important than that, does what we say and do line up with what God asks us to do, what Jesus did as He walked the earth? Jesus left us an example to walk in His steps.

This passage from Colossians 4:6 reminds us that every word we speak should be drenched in grace and tempered with truth and clarity. We are to give respectful answers to each other.

Our society, our world would be transformed if we acted this way – brought out the best in others in our conversation with them, not put them down or cut them out. It's a goal we should strive for with the help of the Holy Spirit.

As image-bearers of Christ, we act differently, speak differently, we reflect His light and His love. We are not filled with anger, frustration, and hate, but rather the fruit of the spirit is evidenced in our lives: love, joy, peace, patience, kindness, goodness, gentleness, faithfulness, and self-control.

On the journey to Bill's healing, I witnessed a man who chose to rely on God to help him through extremely difficult circumstances. His hope came in the name of the Lord. Bill's strength and recovery were because of Jesus' resurrection power at work in him. "Let's do it!" was his battle cry.

As I walk this Glory Road, I have two great examples – Jesus and my dear husband. As I read the Bible, I marinate my faith, my hope, my life with what is possible with God's help. Then throughout the day, memories of my life with Bill remind me of the power of the impossible that comes through my walk with God. I am a blessed woman. It's my turn to "walk the talk."

Thank you for your comforting prayers. #Godisfaithful #TheGloryRoad

Day #46 June 4

Anchor Verse: Psalm 27:13
I would have despaired had I not believed that I would see the goodness of the Lord in the land of the living. (AMP)

Inviting God's peace into our hearts, minds, and lives is an invitation to rest in Him, in His peace. As we rest in His peace, His resurrection power rises up in us. But it is not a power that destroys; it's a power that brings new life in us and in those around us.

The psalmist's message in Psalm 27 couldn't be more appropriate for our times. "I would have despaired"… many are walking in despair, they are sitting in it, they go to sleep with it, and they wake up with it.

The seeds that are planted in the soil of our minds and our hearts determine what the fruit will be, what the harvest will bring and what is put into our storehouses. The harvest, the fruit is what we "eat", what we consume that gives us power to heal and facilitate healing, or the power to destroy and bring destruction to ourselves and others.

The key is rest. In Matthew 11:28-30, Jesus says come and lay your burdens down and take My yoke upon you… and you will find rest for your soul. We must trust God enough to rest in Him. We need to work, to move from a place of rest, not striving for rest.

On this journey to Bill's healing, I was reminded, we rested in the Lord. We trusted God to direct our path. We believed that the Great Physician knew the way. He was the author of the miracles Bill needed. The Holy Spirit spoke words of comfort and peace every day into our lives. It was in resting that Bill found new life and a river of endless hope.

On the Glory Road this morning, God met me in a place I wasn't expecting. It wasn't His power or His might, or even His love that changed my stance, my stride, my mindset this morning, it was His rest. I continue to hear my heavenly Father say this morning, "Cease striving. Stop worrying about today and all your tomorrows. Rest in Me, trust Me with your life even as you trusted me with Bill's life. My plans for you are good. You are loved, my daughter."

Thank you for being prayer warriors for the Lord and for those who need new strength. #Godisfaithful #TheGloryRoad

Day #47 June 5

Anchor Verse: Psalm 78:2-4

A parable and a proverb are hidden in what I say – an intriguing riddle from the past. We've heard true stories from our fathers about our rich heritage. We will continue to tell our children and not hide from the rising generation the great marvels of our God – his miracles and power that have brought us all this far. (TPT)

How many of you have been blessed by the stories of parents and grandparents about their lives and God's faithfulness?

God's promises are for generations yet to come, for our children, and their children, and their children's children. God is not dead, He is very alive.

In this challenging season, our beliefs are being showcased not only in our homes in front of our family members – young and old, but onto a wider stage of social media and even the streets of our cities. Our children are learning by our actions. We are teaching them not only through our words, but our very thoughts and beliefs permeate our homes.

I was honored to listen to the prayers of some young children this morning that come from the heart of God.

"God, I love that you make people who love others. Where no one would be mean and everyone would be nice."

"That people would control their emotions and not be violent."

On this journey to Bill's healing, we have been surrounded by the prayers of God's people of every age, even the Sunday School children at our church were praying for Bill, prayers of faith.

As my grandfather planted seeds of wisdom in my heart, my grandma taught me how to pray, Bill and I have had the honor and privilege of sharing what the Lord has done. How else will they know except we tell them that God is faithful? May this be our legacy.

On this Glory Road, I am surrounded by a beautiful rainbow of God's people, those who bring Him great pleasure by their unique voices. I look forward to planting more seeds in the generations yet to come.

Thank you for joining me in prayer for future. May we sow blessings instead of discord. #Godisfaithful #TheGloryRoad

Day #48 June 6

Anchor Verse: 2 Corinthians 2:14
But thanks be to God, who always leads us in triumph in Christ [as trophies of Christ's victory], and through us spreads and makes evident everywhere the sweet fragrance of the knowledge of Him. (AMP)

Thanks be to God who ALWAYS leads us in triumph in Christ!

When we are properly aligned, when our vertical relationship with God is intact, then we will also have victory on the horizontal relationships in our lives. It is when God is first in my life that I can love you, understand you, and empathize with you.

We know the scents that are appealing to our olfactory receptor… that's a fancy name for the "human nose." The human nose has roughly 400 types of scent receptors and can detect at least 1 trillion different odors.

Our sense of "smell" goes beyond the ability to detect 1 trillion odors. We can "smell" when something's not quite right.

We are living in a time when things are not quite right on many levels, but we are not without hope because God can make what's wrong, right. He offers hope when all you see is the darkness. God offers peace when your heart and mind are in turmoil. God's promises spoken in the Bible are as true for you as when they were written.

Yesterday a seasoned prayer warrior reminded me that there is no greater power than the power of God's love. When we pray, we need to bind the devil and his cohorts with a spirit of love. It drives them crazy! God's love dissolves hate, division, fear, anxiety, anything that the devil would throw at us – God's love is the answer.

On our journey to Bill's healing, I can remember the sweet fragrance, the aroma of Christ being present in ICU units, where death surrounded us. There is life is Christ, there is hope, there is love – we were surrounded and protected by a bubble of His love.

As I walk one step at a time on this Glory Road, there are steps that are marinated in tears, tears of grief, tears of gratitude, and tears of joy. At times I feel the "spit wads" that are being unleashed by the enemy and sometimes they are rocks that seek to bruise my flesh. On Christ the solid rock I stand – I will not be shaken, I will not be moved. Christ alone is my hope.

Thank you for your faithful prayers. #Godisfaithful #TheGloryRoad

Day #49 June 7

Anchor Verse: Psalm 33:12
Blessed is the nation whose God is the Lord. (TLB)

What does it mean that God is Lord of the nation? One explanation is that God is the boss, the master, the ruler of all of our lives collectively and systemically. We surrender all our potential, our hopes, our dreams, our future into God's hands and ask Him to direct our path.

We often pray and ask God to be our protector, our provider, our refuge and strength but to be willing to let God set the agenda for your nation, your country is taking life to a new level. It is a "new" place. It is a place of infinite possibilities because we break out of our own limitations and step into God's infinite wisdom and creativity.

In the last decade or so, God has directed my thoughts to the difference between good, better, and best. Often you and I are willing to settle for "good enough." Some will push the envelope a little further and strive for what is "better" but the "air is thinner" in that place where we boldly pursue "God's best" for us.

On the journey to Bill's healing, shortly out of the starting gate on that wild wide, we chose "God's best" for Bill and for me. Bill might not have been in a place to verbally express that desire, but as his praying wife, I was settling and pursuing nothing "less" than God's best for Bill.

To do that, I had to surrender to God, every day in every way. I had to surrender my expectations about what that journey would look like and the speed at which it would happen. It was a route that would bring so many of you, and so many others into this arena to see what God wanted to do in a life totally surrendered to Him.

As I walk on this Glory Road, into this new season, I am surrounded by a nation that is in turmoil, a world turned upside down. Honestly, I am grateful that Bill is viewing this from heaven and not immersed in the anxiety, fear, and brokenness that flashes on our television screens and infiltrates our lives day and night.

Seven weeks ago, Bill entered glory. The truth is that "glory" entered Bill long before April19, 2020.

Thank you for your steadfastness. #Godisfaithful #TheGloryRoad

Day #50 June 8

Anchor Verse: Matthew 5:14
You are the light of [Christ to] the world. A city set on a hill cannot be hidden. (AMP)

You are the light of Christ to the world. What an amazing opportunity! What a sacred responsibility!

The good news is that when Jesus lives in you, His light shines from the inside out… you can't help but be a light unless you are engaged in activities that block the light.

It's why we need to stay in close fellowship with Him. Intentionally having quiet time with the Lord – time spent reading God's Word, sitting with the Lord and listening for His voice, and bringing our praise, our prayers, and our petitions to the throne room of grace.

Our relationship with God is the most important relationship we will ever have in our lives. It influences all the rest of our relationships – for the good.

Today is my birthday. And as I woke up this morning, my first thought wasn't that, but rather that I was grateful for the gift of another day of life. I "heard" in my spirit my dear husband say, "Happy Birthday, my love." It warmed my heart. Yes, Bill is as close as my next breath, forever in my heart.

This morning God has given me a new outlook. It's time to shift my perspective from what I have "lost" to what God has on the road before me what I will "gain." The Lord reminded me who I am in Christ. I am the light of Christ to the world. I am a city set on a hill that cannot be hidden.

On this journey to Bill's healing, God invited you in from the very first day. God did amazing things in our lives, amazing miracles because you were part of Bill's journey. Your prayers have moved the hand of God.

As I walk this new path, this Glory Road, God is showing me "new" things. There are new routes to travel, new places to see. And trust me, life looks a lot different to me as a "widow" than it did as a "wife." During the day, I hear something or read something and my first thought is, "I can't wait to share that with Bill." Then I realize that he probably already knows about it… and much more.

Thank you for your faithfulness. #Godisfaithful #TheGloryRoad

Day #51 June 9

Anchor Verse: Galatians 3:3
How foolish can you be? After starting your new lives in the Spirit, why are you now trying to become perfect by your own human effort? (NLT)

You know, sometimes we are not very smart. I'm not talking about our "intelligence"… I am referring to common sense and "God" sense.

The Bible outlines for us the way to live an "abundant" life in Christ. We start down that path and then for whatever reason, we decide we can do it on our own.

And then we fall into the proverbial "ditch." Whether that is an addiction of some kind or hopelessness, fear, aggression, or shame… you fill in the blank, because we all have wandered off the path at some point in our lives.

In this verse from Galatians 3, Paul says to the Galatian believers, "How foolish can you be?" Doesn't this sound like something a parent would say to a child? Or something our heavenly Father would say to us?

As believers, God has given us a "new" life in the Spirit, to walk in harmony and intimacy with the Lord. Then one day we decide to become "perfect" in our own human effort… not a great plan.

Bill was one of the best listeners I know. After he listened to what a person was saying he might ask a question or with his sage wisdom respond, "Look at this situation as if you were a 'third person' what advice would you give another person in this situation?" It opened the door to a new perspective and as Bill continued to listen, often the person would "hear themselves" speaking the answer they needed. It was powerful to watch.

On the journey to Bill's healing, I know that Bill listened a lot to what was being said by all those around him. He may not have responded but he took it all in. And those who were "wise", listened when Bill spoke. Mr. Bill didn't waste his words. He didn't speak for the sake of speaking but rather only when he had something to say.

From the opening moments on this Glory Road, God impressed upon my heart the importance of listening. It is why our home is filled with "silence" so that I can hear God's wisdom, His healing words, His words of instruction, and words of comfort.

Thank you for your faithful prayers. #Godisfaithful #TheGloryRoad

Day #52 June 10

Anchor Verse: Psalm 62:11-12a
God said to me once and for all, "All the strength and power you need flows from me!" And again I heard it clearly said, "All the love you need is found in me!" (TPT)

Our rest is sacrificed as we play a ping-pong match in our heads. We weigh different scenarios trying to figure out the best result when there seems to be no "best" result. Our struggle is not only a personal struggle, but a national struggle, even a worldwide struggle.

The good news is that our heavenly Father has not left us alone to face these trials and tribulations. He is not deaf to the cries of our heart. God hears your whispers. He catches our tears. God hears your shouts of frustration and anger. He feels your anxiety and even the depths of your despair.

It stirs His heart. God loves you so much. He desires to raise us up out of this pit of despair, the trenches of our warfare.

God said "once and for all" – that means no wavering, there is no time limit, the offer doesn't expire. ALL the strength and power and love we need flows from God, it is found in God and God alone.

On our journey to Bill's healing, this is what we saw, what we experienced, and how we could face each day of the battle for Bill's life. We knew beyond a shadow of a doubt that God was able to do "abundantly more than all we could ask or think."

We saw God raise Bill up "from the dead" many times. For those of you who "saw" Bill in person during those weeks and months, you saw the glory of the Lord transform him. Bill "radiated" the light of the love of Jesus and the peace that passes all understanding.

As I take the next steps on the Glory Road, this morning, my steps are not faltering, I think I might even be skipping! Why? Because I get it! ALL the strength and power and love I need in the days ahead flow from God. It is more than enough to supply my needs, to help me conquer the mountains and encourage me through the valleys. I can celebrate God's goodness even in my mourning because I know the "rest of the story" – and it ends well.

Thank you for being the hands and feet of Jesus. Thank you for your encouraging words and bold prayers. May the Lord bless you abundantly this day in Jesus' name. #Godisfaithful #TheGloryRoad

Day #53 June 11

Anchor Verse: Isaiah 58:11

The LORD will guide you continually, And satisfy your soul in drought, And strengthen your bones; You shall be like a watered garden, And like a spring of water, whose waters do not fail. (TPT)

After destruction comes the rebuilding. The rubble is cleared, the sturdiness of the foundation examined, supplies are gathered, and the work begins.

Sometimes in our lives, our cities, even in our world, there is a period of time that elapses before the time of rebuilding begins. You don't begin the reconstruction until after the "war" is over, it would be a fruitless effort.

Your "dream" home was conceived in your mind long before the architect drew up the first blueprints. God has hopes and dreams for your life and they were written long before you were born.

Those who are the "repairers" and "restorers" often are not the "destroyers." There is a different mentality involved to build buildings or people "up" rather than to tear down and destroy cities and people.

In verse 11 it says, "The LORD will guide you continually, and satisfy your soul in drought, and strengthen your bones; You shall be like a watered garden, and like a spring of water, whose waters do not fail." (NKJV)

There are great blessings that flow from God as we walk in obedience. And with it comes the honor and privilege of being known as the "Repairers of the Cities and Restorers of Communities." (Isaiah 58:12)

On this journey to Bill's healing, we learned about restoration and renovation. Bill's body was where God did miraculous work as He "recreated" Bill in so many ways. I remember Bill saying that God created him, Bill contributed to the tearing down process, and that God was recreating Bill – body, mind, and spirit. It was beautiful!

As I follow the winding Glory Road, it is also a path of rebuilding in the world that surrounds me and my own heart. God is in charge of this process. As the Master Architect, He has a blueprint that I am not privy to, but I know the end result will shine with the glory of the Lord.

Thank you for your faithful prayers. As my life boomerangs from the hills to the valleys, I am grateful for the amazing intercessors and encouragers that surround me. #Godisfaithful #TheGloryRoad

Day #54 June 12

Anchor Verse: John 20:15
Jesus said to her, "Woman, why are you weeping?" (NKJV)

Tears express what words cannot, whether that is sorrow, confusion, pain, even a flood of joy. I'm so grateful that "tears are a language God understands."

In this season of grieving and healing, it is not uncommon for tears to be my daily companion. At times, tears are the way my heart and mind deal with a wave of sorrow, or joy, that rushes over it. It's the overflow of my emotions.

Bill once told me that I should be grateful that I could cry because his tears remained unshed on the inside, which made me cry even more.

In John 20:15, we find Mary Magdalene outside the tomb of Jesus. It was the first day of the week and when Mary Magdalene arrived at Jesus' tomb she found the stone rolled away. His body was gone. After she told His disciples, Peter and the other disciples ran to the tomb and verified that Jesus was indeed gone. It says that they saw and believed.

Mary Magdalene remained outside the tomb weeping after they left. Not only was Jesus dead, but now His body was gone. Two angels appeared to her and then Jesus came.

Jesus said to her, "Woman, why are you weeping?" And Mary explained the reason for her sorrow. Then Jesus spoke her name, "Mary." In that moment, Mary recognized His voice and she ran to Him.

This morning, Jesus sees your weeping and He is reaching out to you. Jesus is saying, "Woman, Man, Child, why are you weeping?" You can personalize it even more and put your name in that place, "Alice, Mary, Barbara, Phil, Roger, Bob why are you weeping?"

On our journey to Bill's healing, there are tear stains that mark the way. They are tears of sorrow and loss, but also tears of joy. Many of you have shared those tears with us. Bill was amazing, because whatever the reason for my tears, he held me and loved me. Thank you, Mr. Bill.

On the Glory Road, I experience rainstorms of tears, both sorrow and joy. His gifts of love delivered through the hands of others bring tears of joy. In the moments when I miss Bill, God catches those tears too.

Thank you for praying for us. #Godisfaithful #TheGloryRoad

Day #55 June 13

Anchor Verse: Jeremiah 33:3
Call to Me, and I will answer you, and show you great and mighty things, which you do not know. (NKJV)

Calling on the name of the Lord is not a fruitless effort. Your voice does not bounce off the ceiling of your home but your prayers go straight to the heart of God.

God not only hears you but He listens and answers. Great are You, Lord!

This verse in Jeremiah says that not only if I call on Him that He will answer me but also show me great and mighty things, which I do not know.

I love to learn new things from others and from my heavenly Father. Life-long learning is an important quest as we travel this earth.

My grandfather who lived to be 93 was like that, always learning and when my grandpa spoke and shared his wisdom I listened.

If I was so willing to learn from my grandfather, far greater are the blessings and the call to learn from my heavenly Father.

God does not want to hide wisdom and knowledge from you. He wants us to "grow up" and mature in Him, in wisdom and knowledge and understanding.

Our heavenly Father needs us to impact the world and we need to be able to hear His voice and walk in His way to do that effectively.

On the journey to Bill's healing, we both learned so much. We learned how to listen and enjoy the beauty of silence not only with each other but sitting alone in the Lord's Presence. You could feel God's tangible presence in our home, you still can.

Now as I navigate this Glory Road, the Lord is teaching me new skills. One of those is to embrace silence and be okay with the silence. Since Bill died, I haven't turned on the television because God said He wanted to speak to me in the silence. It's more difficult to hear the Lord's voice when it's noisy. And as we all know, our lives are filled with lots of noise.

Thank you for answering the call of the Lord to pray and not to faint or give up. #Godisfaithful #TheGloryRoad

Day #56 June 14

Anchor Verse: Job 26:14
How faint the whisper we hear of Him!
Who then can understand the thunder of His power? (NIV)

God has an outside voice (thunder) and an inside voice (a whisper).

In my own experience, sometimes God "shouts" but often our heavenly Father speaks in whispers so it's necessary that we listen closely to hear Him calling us.

This morning it's sunny with a beautiful blue sky and white fluffy clouds, but that has not been the case the last couple of days. For a few days as I went to bed at night, I could hear the low rumbling of thunder. It was like the low growl of a dog warning you not to come any closer or he would "reach out" and defend his turf or his master.

Yesterday morning, the low rumble was still echoing at 4 a.m. and continued for several hours. It was a stormy day indicative of the battle that was happening in the heavens and on the earth.

Often the most powerful conversations between two people take place at a low decibel level. We whisper to each other when we don't want others to hear what is said. Conversations that take place with a "loud" voice are heard by anyone within the sound of your voice. If you've ever been caught in someone's outburst, it's like being caught in an unexpected rain shower.

How often do we miss God's whisper especially when we are seeking an answer or direction? We are waiting for the thunder of His voice when God is present in the whisper of the wind.

On this road to Bill's healing, we have heard God whisper in unusual places – places you might think are devoid of His presence – like ICU units, waiting rooms, even your own home during a coronavirus quarantine. It was God's whisper that gave us hope at each challenging turn.

As I see new terrain on this Glory Road, my ears are tuned to hear His voice. I need to hear His voice, even the smallest whisper, so that I can walk on the path He has prepared for me.

My heart's desire is to not only hear the whisper of His voice but as I kneel in awe and wonder, seek to understand the thunder of His power.

Thank you for listening to His promptings and blessing others as He leads you. #Godisfaithful #TheGloryRoad

Day #57 June 15

Anchor Verse: Nehemiah 2:2
Therefore the king said to me [Nehemiah], "Why is your face sad, since you are not sick? This is nothing but sorrow of heart." (NKJV)

Our face reflects the condition of our heart – plain and simple. There are some things that we can't hide no matter how good you are about "putting your mask on."

You might be thinking, how is every emotion a blessing?

How can you really appreciate the greatest heights of joy unless you have experienced the piercing of your heart by sorrow or the beauty of a majestic sunrise unless you have endured the darkness of a sleepless night?

Earlier in Nehemiah 1, Nehemiah received the news that the Jewish remnant that had survived the exile was back in the province but the walls of Jerusalem were broken down and its gates burned with fire.

In Nehemiah 1:4, it says that Nehemiah sat down and wept and for some days he mourned, fasted, and prayed before the God of heaven.

Nehemiah was a cupbearer to the king, King Artaxerxes. When you were in service to the king, you were supposed to be "happy" in his presence, anything less than that could have severe consequences.

The king noticed Nehemiah, and in Nehemiah 2:2 he says, "Why is your face sad, since you are not sick? This is nothing but sorrow of heart." The king was a wise man. God's hand was upon him to grant Nehemiah favor. He could have as easily said, "I don't like your sad face. Guards, take him out and kill him." Yes, kings did stuff like that in those days.

On our journey to Bill's healing, we were blessed by God's favor as we pursued Bill's "rebuilding" efforts. Not only God's favor, but favor through the hands of man, through your prayers and encouraging words, and amazing care through the medical community and support partners.

As I take the next steps on this Glory Road, I know there are times when my sorrow of the heart is reflected on my face. Thank you to each one of you who has passed on the words He has spoken to you to bring new life, hope, and love into my heart as I pursue my rebuilding efforts.

Thank you for your love and your prayers. #Godisfaithful #TheGloryRoad

Day #58 June 16

Anchor Verse: Isaiah 58:12b
You will be called Repairer of the Breach, Restorer of Streets with Dwellings. (AMP)

Did you know that God's destiny for you is to be a Repairer and a Restorer?

God sees potential in us that we often cannot see in ourselves. He knows the depth of the "bench" on your basketball team. We scratch the surface and God knows what is buried in the gold mine.

Too often we live "shallow" lives. Instead of doing a 5K run, we are satisfied with walking to the refrigerator. Our world is often contained within the walls of our own homes, not only during this pandemic season, when God wants to open the windows of heaven to pour out His blessings upon you.

God-sized dreams get me excited!

Many years ago, seems like a lifetime ago now, a person spoke into my life and challenged me to reach beyond the "status quo" where I was living. The Holy Spirit urged me to press in and see what God had in mind. It turned into a holy adventure that landed me on the other side of the state going to law school – learning how to "think" like a lawyer and learning a whole new "language."

That adventure taught me that with God ALL things are possible. If God is in it, then no man can stop it. No illness. No financial challenge. No personality. No conflict. No nothing, can stand in God's way when He wants to accomplish something in your life.

On this journey to Bill's healing, we saw God, the greatest Repairer and Restorer at work in Bill's life. The Lord showed me in the beginning how God was restoring Bill "one brick" at a time. As God "recreated" Bill, He made sure it was of the most excellent quality. That is why Bill was able to pour so much into our lives as God filled him up with His love, wisdom, mercy, and grace.

This Glory Road is a path that leads to restoration of communities and repairing of cities, and that starts in my own life and those in my sphere of influence. Remember, ALL that we do is for God's honor and glory, not our own. Every word we speak, every deed done in love comes from the overflow of God's love flowing in us and through us.

Thank you for praying without ceasing. #Godisfaithful #TheGloryRoad

Day #59 June 17

Anchor Verse: Psalm 143:5

I remember the glorious miracles of days gone by, and I often think of all the wonders of old. (TPT)

Remembering the glorious miracles… we need to do that more often. You and I need to hold those stones, those thoughts of remembrance of what God has done in our lives as we stand in the middle of our battles.

Great is Your faithfulness, O Lord! We are not forgotten. We are not alone. God is still on His throne and we are the apple of His eye. We are sons and daughters of the Most High God. We are highly favored. We are blessed. We are loved. He delights in us and desires more for us.

When I was growing up, I often remember my grandparents talking about "the olden days." They would share memories and experiences from their lives. It was how I learned about our family history but also core values and how they overcame life challenges.

This morning as I write this I am reflecting on our journey to Bill's healing. As a friend of ours is currently in the same hospital where we started Bill's journey and she has pneumonia, immediately my mind raced not to her diagnosis but of God's work in Bill to defeat pneumonia, not once, but three times on his journey to healing.

Each one of us was impacted by Bill's life, Bill's transformation through the hand of God – none of us are the same after that encounter.

Yes, Bill is in heaven doing God's work, and that he touches earth often on his journey. Greater still is the blessing, the impression that has been left on our hearts because of the loving hand of our heavenly Father as we saw Him work in Bill's life.

As I enter a new day on the Glory Road, I am so grateful for the memories of the miracles God has done in our lives, in my life. And because of that strong foundation of those mighty miracles, I can face today with joy in my heart, even if tears may fall as I remember God's faithfulness.

Thank you for your persistent prayers. #Godisfaithful #TheGloryRoad

Day #60 June 18

Anchor Verse: Acts 4:20
It's impossible for us to stop speaking about all the things we've seen and heard! (TPT)

When something good happens in our lives, especially the miraculous, we can't stop talking about it! No matter where we go, all our thoughts, our words, our prayers are filled with thanksgiving and gratitude.

Doesn't matter if you are at the grocery store, the car wash, or the church pew, God gets all the glory as others hear our story.

In Acts 4, Peter and John, after Pentecost, have been sharing "their story" – the good news of Jesus with the people in Jerusalem. They were teaching the people about the resurrection of Jesus. They were seized and put in jail the next day.

At their "trial", Peter and John are questioned by the rulers, elders, and teachers of the law, "By what power or what name do you do this?" Peter boldly shares with them the foundation of their hope, Jesus.

In Acts 4:13, it says, "When they saw the courage of Peter and John and realized that they were unschooled, ordinary men, they were astonished and they took note that these men had been with Jesus."

As I read today's verse, I was immediately taken back in time to our journey to Bill's healing. So many times we were blessed to receive miracles from the hands and heart of God. And when that happened, we couldn't stop talking about it. You can't keep that kind of good news to yourself.

On the Glory Road, the Lord gives me opportunities to stand with others and fight for them and for their lives. The miracles that happened in Bill's life are a precursor to the amazing miracles that God has planned for "us" on this road that lies ahead.

Last night, our power was knocked out for several hours. When I woke up during the power outage and it was pitch black, I found a message on my phone that said a friend who was in ICU was having difficulty breathing, so to please pray. I spend some time awake in the darkness praying for the miracle she needed. I was brought back to those nights when I "fought" for Bill's life through my prayers. This morning's report is that she's better.

Thank you for praying without ceasing. #Godisfaithful #TheGloryRoad

Day #61 June 19

Anchor Verse: Job 1:20
...and he [Job] fell to the ground and worshiped [God]. (AMP)

Grief is an interesting "animal." We all "do it" differently. As unique as our personalities and our approach to life, so is our approach to grief.

Job was a man who loved the Lord and God blessed him greatly with children, possessions, and favor in the community. And then one day, Satan presents himself before the Lord, after he has been roaming the earth.

God gives Satan permission to touch anything in Job's life except he cannot lay a finger on Job.

In the next verses we read how one calamity after another occurs. His oxen, donkeys, and camels are stolen, fire from heaven burned his sheep and all his servants are killed. And then Job received news that all his children were in the house when the roof collapsed and they were killed. What a disaster!

What does Job do? He gets up, tears his robe, shaves his head, and worships the Lord. We are familiar with a strong reaction to grief that includes weeping and shock, but when Job chooses to worship the Lord, he has our attention. Job maintains his integrity and his love for the Lord amid these great losses. He knew God was a good, good Father.

On the journey to Bill's healing, we experienced joy and sorrow. Together, Bill and I mourned, yet celebrated, my mom's entrance to heaven in February (2020). We know where our hope comes from, and that is the presence of the Lord. Hallelujah, what a Savior! Hallelujah, what a Lord!

As I step onto the Glory Road this morning, I am commemorating two months ago today that God took Bill "home." Yes, Bill is home in heaven with the Lord carrying out the plans and purposes God has for him. This morning my heart is filled with praise as I worship the Lord in the spirit of holiness. As I survey the world around me, I am filled with hope because I know that God is bigger than our circumstances.

Today, I honor my husband and his courageous approach to life. He lived each day camped in a place of hope, filled with God's love for me and for you. I can do no less than honor my Lord and Savior, Jesus, my heavenly Father who gives me life, and the Holy Spirit who directs my steps.

Thank you for your prayers and remembering my forever love, Mr. Bill with me. #Godisfaithful #TheGloryRoad

Day #62 June 20

Anchor Verse: Romans 12:10
Be devoted to one another in love. Honor one another above yourselves. (NIV)

How do we live in harmony in this world? By loving and honoring each other. When we realize that life is not always about "us" – that the world doesn't revolve around "me", our perspective changes and God has blessings to release.

What does it mean to "honor" another person? Merriam-Webster's dictionary defines "honor" in this way, "to regard or treat (someone) with admiration and respect: to regard or treat with honor."

In our lives, we quickly discover that how we treat others is usually how they treat us. It's like a mirror, how we act and conduct ourselves is returned. Like the Golden Rule, "Do unto others as you would have them do unto you."

That's a nice definition but what does it really mean in a practical way? How do I show honor to others?

Some suggestions are to treat others with respect, be patient, listen to them, empathize with their situation, forgive, overlook mistakes, and point out their achievements rather than criticizing areas where they may not be as strong.

On our journey to Bill's healing, we encountered people from all walks of life – not only those who cared for Bill in the medical community but those going through their own trials and the blessings that came from those surrounding us. People are as unique as snowflakes but one thing is the same, the desire to be treated with honor and respect. Bill and I received honor and respect and we gladly returned that favor to others.

As I encounter another turn on the Glory Road, I have the blessing, and yes, the honor and privilege, to sow seeds of honor and respect into the lives of others. To guard my lips and my heart so that my words bring life and refreshing to friends, family, business associates, and whomever God brings into my sphere of influence.

Thank you for standing with us. #Godisfaithful #TheGloryRoad

Day #63 June 21

Anchor Verse: Deuteronomy 10:21

He alone is your God, the only one who is worthy of your praise, the one who has done these mighty miracles that you have seen with your own eyes. (NLT)

He is the God of miracles.

Join me in praising the Lord this morning because He alone is worthy of our praise. Do you have any idea what a blessed people we are?

We are loved by the Creator of the universe! The one who placed each star in the night sky and painted the beautiful birds, and gave them each a unique song to sing – He made you unlike anyone else on this planet.

There are miracles in our lives, both big ones and small ones. The fact that our heart beats without our prompting and that each breath we take is at the Lord's command is something to celebrate.

Every day we encounter circumstances that remind us of God's grace, the many ways that He keeps us from harm and danger. I am beyond grateful for the guardian angels that keep watch over me, day and night. Thank you, Lord, Your heart's desire is to protect Your children.

On the journey to Bill's healing, we were the recipients of countless miracles. The fact that Bill made it out of the hospital after his "initial" round of challenges in 2018 is a testimony to the "mighty miracles that you have seen with your own eyes." Thank you, Lord, for Your faithfulness. I will spend the rest of this life and all of eternity thanking the Lord for the gift of life that He gave Mr. Bill.

As I continue on this Glory Road, I am aware of the mighty miracles God is orchestrating in my life. Many times even in one day, I turn my head toward heaven and say, "Thank you!" It's so important to fill my life with praise even as I am aware of the great loss of my dear husband. But God left me here for a reason, I must be willing to step into those places He calls me.

Thank you for being a part of our miracle story. It is through the prayers of God's people that miracles happen. God loves to hear your prayers as you pray for others and their health and the miracles they need.

Thank you for persevering. #Godisfaithful #TheGloryRoad

Day #64 June 22

Anchor Verse: Romans 12:16

Live happily together in a spirit of harmony, and be as mindful of another's worth as you are your own. (TPT)

Honoring one another and walking in unity is the most powerful way to live as a people, as the family of God, as citizens of the United States or whatever your home country.

Romans 12 says we should live "happily" in a spirit of harmony. Do you live "happily" or to you complain, criticize, and grumble as you begin and end your day?

We are the children of God. Our heavenly Father loves us with an everlasting love. His mercies are new every morning and great is His faithfulness!

The truth is we would be singing songs of praise, day and night, if we understood who God is and who He has called us to be.

There would be no division. There would be no separation or labels, because we are one in Christ.

I am struck by the second part of this verse: "Be as mindful of another's worth as you are your own."

Maybe it's not that we value ourselves too much but rather that we don't see ourselves as God sees us. We cannot love others if we have not received the gift of God's love at work in us.

Have we left God out of our present circumstances? He is the same yesterday, today, and forever. He is the God of miracles. God parted the Red Sea and delivered the children of Israel from the Egyptian army that was pursuing them. That is who our God is today on June 22, 2020.

He is the same God who protected and provided for us on our journey to Bill's healing. My God was with me as I sat in ICU units where people were dying around us, and like Psalm 91, "It did not come near me."

On this Glory Road, I am done with tiptoeing around the minefields of grief, the pits of fear that others have left behind. I will declare the goodness of the Lord in the land of the living. I will NOT be moved, I will NOT be shaken.

Thank you for praying without ceasing. #Godisfaithful #TheGloryRoad

Day #65 June 23

Anchor Verse: 2 Samuel 23:8
In one encounter… (NIV)

Your life can change in an instant. In one encounter with the man or woman of your dreams, or one encounter with a mentor who changed the direction of your academic life or career, or one encounter with the Lord Jesus Christ. Or in our case, one encounter with a health challenge.

Sometimes our lives become so "full" that we forget how important one moment, one word of encouragement, one hug, one kiss can be.

There are solitary moments we encounter on this path that have been life-changing for many. The isolation moments when "stay home, stay healthy" was the battle cry or those same moments when a loved one is isolated in a hospital bed without his family nearby.

I am reminded about how important it is to have God with us on this journey – the one who promised to never leave us or forsake us. (Deuteronomy 31:6) And in that verse, it begins this way, "Be strong and courageous, do not be afraid." Those same words are the words of our heavenly Father this morning to be strong and courageous and don't let fear gain a foothold in our lives.

The path of least resistance is the path that is the "easiest" to follow. It is often the path where the crowd is going, the path where you sort of get "dragged along" if you are not willing to stand up for what is right and good and holy.

On the journey to Bill's healing, we were blessed with many sacred moments. But one of the most powerful was Bill's "one encounter" with God when God said, "It's not your time to die. I have work for you to do." In one encounter, the hope of glory was downloaded into Bill and often renewed in the Lord's presence. The peace that passes all understanding filled Bill's heart and mind and we got to see the fruit of that "one encounter." Bill's life was forever changed and so was your life and mine.

As I survey new territory on the Glory Road, I am reminded that there will be "suddenly" moments when the Lord appears to me even as He did to Saul on the Damascus road. It won't be a "new" conversion experience but rather a new revelation of who God is and who He is calling me to be.

Thank you for holding up my arms. #Godisfaithful #TheGloryRoad

Day #66 June 24

Anchor Verse: 1 Corinthians 5:17
Pray without ceasing. (NKJV)

I may not know your name but I was with you during the night. God kept me awake so you wouldn't be alone. Whether you are a young mom or dad with a baby who was crying and couldn't sleep, or a great-great-grandma alone in her home that only echoes from the last time someone came to visit her. You might be in "trouble" with your parents or the "law." In fact, things might be so bad you were thinking about committing suicide last night or having an abortion to "solve" the problem.

Maybe you've been unemployed for months and you feel you've let your family down. The devil has been whispering in your ear about how "worthless" you are and that you are a "disappointment" to your family.

You may not speak English. You may not even live on my continent or even know the name of Jesus, but it was your heavenly Father that kept me awake so you weren't alone in your pain, your anger, your frustration, or your fear.

You might be a first responder – law enforcement, firefighter, or medical personnel who vigilantly works to keep us safe or respond to emergencies while we sleep. Maybe you are a member of the military on patrol to keep my freedom intact, and stand against the enemy.

In your hospital room, you are battling a disease, an illness all alone because of a "label" placed on you as you fight for your life, surrounded by strangers instead of the ones who know you and love you.

Sleep was illusive. God was silent. But in the silence I could only sense one thing. Pray and stay for those who have no one. Pray for the one who is afraid to ask for prayer. Pray for those who have lost their dreams.

On the journey to Bill's healing, there were critical nights when I was at his side praying that God would save his life. I reached out across time zones and asked you to pray with me. Tonight God had me on this vigil alone. Tonight, one person leaning in to listen, trusting that by only standing in God's presence lifting my hands in prayer that it was enough to shift the atmosphere and allow the Lord's favor to rush in.

As I follow God's leading down the Glory Road, I will meet new experiences head on. God will call me outside my "comfort zone" and wait for me there.

Thank you for praying without ceasing. #Godisfaithful #TheGloryRoad

Day #67 June 25

Anchor Verse: Acts 7:48
However, the Most High does not live in houses [temples, sanctuaries] made by human hands. (NIV)

If you can put God in a box, your God is way too small. Praise the Lord that He breaks out of the box we try and put Him in. As Jesus "broke out" of the tomb early that Sunday morning with resurrection power, it is that same power that is still at work in us.

The anointing of the Holy Spirit that came at Pentecost brought new life to the infant church which is the fresh anointing we need in this world.

God's love for us goes beyond reminding us that the Most High does not live in houses made by human hands, He wants a personal relationship with you, even better than the relationship you have with your BFF (best friend forever.) Jesus is your BFF. He will never leave you or forsake you.

On this journey to Bill's healing, God quickly reminded us that He would not, could not be put in a box. God didn't reside only within the walls of the church we attended. He was Lord in big and small hospitals, ICU units, therapy sessions, and ambulance rides. The Good Shepherd was with us as we navigated life at home "alone" after having a whole hospital filled with a medical team that extended across many disciplines. Hallelujah that God is the God of the universe where there are no walls.

As I find my way on this Glory Road, God is expanding my understanding of Him once again. Not only who God is, but who I am as I seek His presence, as I am tucked in with Him. My heavenly Father wants to take me to new heights – places I never dreamed of going, not because I am so "good" or have talent or potential, but because God needs me to help Him reach the world with His love and through the power of our testimony.

The morning Bill died and God tore the veil between heaven and earth and led Bill into His presence, the veil was torn for me too. Not that it's my turn to enter heaven, that's reserved for a different time and place. But rather that my understanding, my hopes and dreams are not limited by the walls, the confines of this world – but crafted by the God who created the universe who has plans and a place for me in His service, and for you too.

Thank you for praying and speaking words of encouragement into my life. Bill and I have been so blessed to have you as part of our support team. Great will be your reward in heaven. #Godisfaithful #TheGloryRoad

Day #68 June 26

Anchor Verse: Hebrews 12:27
By this He (God) means that He will sift out everything without solid foundations so that only unshakable things will be left. (TLB)

As a child, I remember that my grandma had a drawer in the kitchen where she kept flour and a little device called a "sifter." She would put the flour from its original package into the sifter and it would take out any lumps and make it nice and fluffy. It was fun to create a flour dust cloud, as I would make the sifter go as fast as I could.

Spiritual sifting is like that – designed to get the lumps and bumps out of our lives. The things that are holding us back, God will often "sift" us to "shift" us. When God is doing some sifting in our lives, I don't think I would sign up for the accelerated course. Dust clouds that come from God's sifting may seem to be more than we can bear at times. But God the "Master Baker/Master Creator" knows how much His creation can be shaken.

God is shaking whatever can be shaken because He wants to test how firmly we are anchored in Christ. Everything in the world is being tested to see how firmly attached it is to God.

It's a bit of an oxymoron – we need to be firm and unshakable, yet still willing to "move" at the Lord's command. That's what surrendering to the Lord means. Our faith is secure and cannot be moved, but as we are His hands and feet to offer light and hope to a world lost in darkness, we bend and go where God sends us.

On the journey to Bill's healing, we quickly learned that God was shaking everything that could be shaken, not to break us, but to make us more like Him that we might be used by God. Bill's body was shaken, our lives were shaken, but our hope was secure in God. We knew beyond a shadow of a doubt that God would never leave us or forsake us.

This morning as I wait for dawn and the light of a new day, I know that the world I face on this Glory Road is being shaken. What can be shaken is being shaken, and not everything will remain. God is clearing out the "junk" and the "lumps" so that He can achieve His purpose through us on earth.

Thank you for your faithfulness not only in prayer but in speaking hope and life over me and over each other. We are His hands and feet and operate under His authority. #Godisfaithful #TheGloryRoad

Day #69 June 27

Anchor Verse: 2 Timothy 2:13

Even when we are too weak to have any faith left, he remains faithful to us and will help us, for he cannot disown us who are part of himself, and he will always carry out his promises to us. (TLB)

Great is Your Faithfulness, O Lord! The words of the familiar hymn "Great is Thy Faithfulness" were not penned after a traumatic event but by Thomas Chisholm, a prolific poet, born in 1866. Chisholm became a teacher at 16, and later went on to be a minister until his health failed, and he became an insurance agent.

It was when he shared this poem with William Runyan, a musician associated with Moody Bible Institute that these powerful words were brought to life. Through the years, God's faithfulness through this song has inspired many who were struggling.

Why share this story? Because God is faithful every hour of every day of our lives. Not only in traumatic circumstances – health issues, pandemics, or war, but in our everyday ordinary lives, God is only a breath away. "There is no shadow of turning in Him."

This verse in 2 Timothy reminds us that even when you might be weak, worn out, and discouraged, it doesn't change God's faithfulness. In fact, I think He pours more of His love, His grace, and His mercy into us when we have come to the end of our own resources.

Jesus reminded His disciples that all they needed was faith the size of a mustard seed… that's very small. If you want to know how small, go to the refrigerator and take out that jar of pickles, and look for those little small yellow seeds floating around in the top, only one mustard seed is all the faith you need "to move a mountain" with God's help.

On the journey to Bill's healing, the promises of God are what kept us encouraged as we fought for Bill's life. I am so grateful for the Bible verses that I memorized as a child. His word I have hid in my heart. (Psalm 119:11) Speaking scripture out loud encourages you and truth always overcomes a lie.

In this transition period of my life, as I walk on the Glory Road, the truths in the Bible light my path. The Bible contains God's promises and reminds me of God's faithfulness throughout past generations. God's faithfulness is available to me, day or night, for as long as I live.

Thank you for your faithful prayers. #Godisfaithful #TheGloryRoad

Day #70 June 28

Anchor Verse: Daniel 2:14
Daniel spoke to him with wisdom and tact. (NIV)

If someone were to describe the way that you speak to others, would they say you speak with "wisdom and tact?"

Wisdom is defined as "the quality of having experience, knowledge, and good judgment." Tact, on the other hand, is defined as "a keen sense of what to do or say in order to maintain good relations with others or avoid offense."

The book of Daniel in the Old Testament tells the story of four young Jewish men who are taken captive and are in exile in Babylon. They were outstanding young men – "young men without any physical defect, handsome, showing aptitude for every kind of learning, well informed, quick to understand, and qualified to serve in the king's palace." (Daniel 1:4)

King Nebuchadnezzar has a bad dream one night and he called all the "magicians, enchanters, sorcerers and astrologers" in his kingdom to interpret the dream, they could not. So the king decides to put them all to death (often kings responded like this when they didn't like the answer they were given). The four men from Judah were included in the roundup.

Daniel spoke to him with "wisdom and tact." His life is on the line with his companions including all the magicians, enchanters, sorcerers, and astrologers of Babylon. What if Daniel had responded differently? Would the book of Daniel have ended the same way?

On the journey to Bill's healing, we faced situations where wisdom and tact were required. As Bill's advocate, often it was my responsibility to navigate challenging situations. What a blessing when the Lord directs the words coming out of your mouth.

In this new season on the Glory Road, I am even more aware of the need for wisdom and tact to guard my mouth. I hear my dear husband's wise words, "Listen more than you speak." Not only do you learn more, but we keep ourselves out of trouble. There is a time to speak and a time to be silent.

Thank you for your faithful prayers. Ten weeks ago, God took Bill "home" – a blessing for him, but my heart is missing him a lot today. #Godisfaithful #TheGloryRoad

Day #71 June 29

Anchor Verse: Psalm 73:24
You will keep on guiding me all my life with your wisdom and counsel, and afterwards receive me into the glories of heaven! (TLB)

"A map and a nap" – my cousin shared this phrase with me this weekend. We were talking about navigating this coronavirus season and the challenges there are to overcome. Often we don't know where we are going from day to day, and I think we could agree that this season drains the energy out of you.

What does the Bible say about "a map and a nap?"

"You will keep on guiding me all my life with your wisdom and counsel, and afterwards receive me into the glories of heaven!" (Psalm 73:24)

God knows the path that we take. He knows the way even when it feels like we are in a dense fog and can't see more than a few footsteps ahead of us.

The Lord leads us with "wisdom and counsel." What a great reminder that God not only will give us wisdom as we spend time in the scripture and pray, asking Him for guidance, but He will surround us with good people.

We were not meant to go through life alone. I'm not talking about marital status here but rather that we live in "community." With the advent of advanced technology we can seek counsel from those who live down the street, across the United States, or around the world.

On our journey to Bill's healing, we were often in need of "a map and a nap." Whether we were blessed to be at home or in an ICU unit, the Lord was ready, willing, and able to guide us to a place of safety – where He was. Bill has already moved to the second half of that verse, "and afterwards receive me into the glories of heaven." Yes, Bill is seeing the glories of heaven – an experience greater than our tongues can tell.

As I find my way down the Glory Road, I am so grateful that God is providing "a map and a nap." Oftentimes these days, the Lord "wakes me up" to have a chat with me. Sometimes He will send a message, a next step in a dream, but He likes the "one on one" approach. "Speak, Lord, Your servant is listening." Thank you, Lord, that you have a plan, a purpose, and a path for me.

Thank you for walking with me. #Godisfaithful #TheGloryRoad

Day #72 June 30

Anchor Verse: Habakkuk 1:5
The Lord replied: "Look, and be amazed! You will be astounded at what I am about to do! For I am going to do something in your own lifetime that you will have to see to believe. (TLB)

We are living in unprecedented times. Our great-great grandparents might have stories to tell but the circumstances they encountered did not affect the world on a global level as we are seeing today.

Yet, the final chapter of the story has not been written. Chaos, confusion, anger, and lawlessness seem to pervade the headlines. Many may not look forward to the morning, or the evening news, as they used to do.

It was part of my father's routine to read the newspaper before going to work. Now in his retirement, he can choose to scan the headlines on his iPad. Sometimes the news is too much to digest with your breakfast.

More than ever, I am so grateful for the gift of prayer. Not only to receive the prayers of others but to pray for those who having challenges.

Prayer is direct communication with God, our Creator, our heavenly Father, and the One who holds the whole world in His hands. Our heavenly Father loves us so much that He is invested in every detail of our lives.

Many times in the Bible it seemed to be over and then suddenly the Lord moved and the children of Israel were saved from certain death at the Red Sea, Noah and his family were saved as the whole world was destroyed, people were miraculously healed after years of suffering, and more.

On our journey to Bill's healing, we, too, experienced God arriving in those 11th hour moments. We trusted God with our past, present, future. His faithfulness has been known throughout ALL generations. His faithfulness shone brightly in our lives, and still shines in mine and through Bill's legacy.

This Glory Road that I'm walking is not for the faint of heart. I can't hold Bill's hand in the flesh, but the precious memories of Bill's unflinching determination to win the battle spur me on. God hasn't written the final chapter in the book of our lives. We must persevere through this fire, like Shadrach, Meshach, and Abednego, and we will see victory.

Thank you for not giving up. #Godisfaithful #TheGloryRoad

July 2020

No weapon formed
against you will prosper.
~ Isaiah 54:17

Day #73 July 1

Anchor Verse: 2 Corinthians 1:20
For as many as are the promises of God, in Christ they are [all answered] "Yes." So through Him we say our "Amen" to the glory of God. (AMP)

The Lord sees you where you are this morning. He knows your struggles, your thoughts, your doubts, and yes, that mustard seed of faith that is firmly rooted in your heart.

When the Bible says that He will "never" leave you or forsake you – your heavenly Father means never. He is our solid rock; all other ground is sinking sand.

This verse in 2 Corinthians 1:20 is a powerful verse. It contains a promise and an action step for us. "For as many as are the promises of God, in Christ they are [all answered] "Yes."

"For as many as are the promises of God" – and my friends, God's promises are many and they are powerful and they are true. They will never change. They are as true for you as they were for your ancestors and will be for generations yet to come.

All of those promises are fulfilled, answered in Jesus Christ. Nothing was left undone after Jesus' death on the cross and His resurrection from the dead. Thank you, Lord, for the fulfillment of all Your promises in Jesus. That's why we can walk in hope every day.

On this journey to Bill's healing, we have seen the many promises of God fulfilled in Jesus. Bill and I stood on those promises, you stood with us, and we saw God's hand move and do amazing miracles. Now I have an opportunity to add my "amen" to the glory of God for God's work in Bill's life. It is a story of transformation, of love, hope, and yes, of victory.

As I open my eyes to the dawning of a new day on the Glory Road, I trust the Lord to bring something beautiful out of my life. Some days my offering is a handful of ashes, the remnants of my time in the fire. Other mornings it is an offering of praise that first erupts from deep in the pit of my soul. Then there are moments when the altar is watered by my tears, not only of sorrow but of gratitude, for choosing me to be Bill's wife and walk this unprecedented, uncharted path with God.

Thank you so much for carrying us with your prayers. Yesterday as I was putting together a picture memory book, I could see God's hand every step of the way. #Godisfaithful #TheGloryRoad

Day #74 July 2

Anchor Verse: Galatians 2:20

It is no longer I who live, but Christ lives in me. The life I now live in the body I live by faith [by adhering to, relying on, and completely trusting] in the Son of God, who loved me and gave Himself up for me. (AMP)

"It is no longer I who live, but Christ lives in me." What a powerful truth for those who have invited Jesus into their hearts and lives.

Because of that decision, we no longer need to live in fear. We no longer face an uncertain future. We no longer live "under" our circumstances, we live above them.

The life we now live, we live by faith. Not faith in ourselves and what we can do, but faith in the Son of God, who did what? Who loved me (and still loves me every day) and who gave Himself up for me, who went to the cross and died a horrific death that the price was paid for my sins, so I can live in fellowship with God for eternity. All of that might sound like a lot of theology, let's bring it to a more personal level.

2020 has been a year that has changed our lives, not only as individuals, but as a nation. In fact, the whole world has been touched by this pandemic and its overflow.

On the journey to Bill's healing, Bill chose to embrace each day with hope. No matter how difficult the circumstances or how much pain he was experiencing, or the uncertainty of the future, Bill chose to be present in the moment and encourage others. It was beautiful to watch and to be a recipient of God's love at work through Bill.

Every day, no matter if Bill had a good night or rough night, he got up, got dressed, had breakfast, took his meds, and was ready to embrace what God had for him that day. There was not even one day that Bill stayed in bed, not one.

On this Glory Road, the Lord continues to show me the "better" way, how I can live surrendered to Him in the midst of chaos in my own life and in the world around me. He is a God of order and not chaos. Now that Christ lives in me, my propensity is to long for that order, not the chaos that surrounds me. I find that when I am in constant fellowship with Him.

Thank you for choosing the path of life. #Godisfaithful #TheGloryRoad

Day #75 July 3

Anchor Verse: Lamentations 3:25-26
The Lord is good to those who wait for Him, To the soul who seeks Him. It is good that one should hope and wait quietly for the salvation of the Lord. (NKJV)

God's timing is ALWAYS perfect. Yes, always. I know you are shaking your head and saying, "But you don't understand." God has the view from the perspective of heaven – He sees all of time and the whole universe and our view is comparable to the head of a pin… very small, too small.

"The Lord is good to those who wait for Him." As I read this slowly this morning, I was reminded once again about the power and privilege of "waiting" for God to move, for God's perfect timing.

Often God asks us to wait to see the answer to our prayers, for the miracle we need, for the healing that seems afar off, for the prodigal child to come home, or for our bank account to be blessed.

There is a new hunger for the Lord in the waiting – our souls need to be fed the truth, the bread of life. God has a limitless supply, like the manna that was provided to the children of Israel on their way to the Promised Land through the wilderness.

On this journey to Bill's healing, time and time again the Lord made us aware of God's perfect timing. God always had the right people in the right place at the right time. The best doctors, nurses, therapists, etc. were on duty when Bill needed their expertise. And then there were often times of "waiting" until connections could be made before a next step was put in action. For example, when Bill came home from the hospital in June 2018 and there was a month's delay before home health nurses and therapists were brought on board. In that month, the Lord gave me strength and wisdom beyond my own, and in Bill's dreams, Jesus "helped" Bill with his walking skills. It was pretty amazing.

As I turn the corner on this Glory Road as we head into July, I am blessed by the realization that in the "waiting" God continues to reveal himself to me. It is why I have hope for the future, hope for today. Nothing is impossible for God, so nothing is too hard for me.

Thank you for passing along your blessings. #Godisfaithful #TheGloryRoad

Day #76 July 4

Anchor Verse: Matthew 10:8
Freely you have received, freely give. (NKJV)

Sharing – it's a concept that many of us were taught at an early age, learning how to share our toys with brothers and sisters, or friends. I can still hear the phrase ringing in my ears, "Sharing time is a happy time."

There is a blessing that comes as we share what is good with others. Joy is multiplied. Not only when we share good news about an accomplishment or when we receive a financial blessing and we are able to help others, but when we share our faith and our freedom, it has a great impact.

Today is Independence Day in America, the Fourth of July, when we celebrate our nation's freedom, our birthday. Our celebrations this year will look much different than years past but the truth still remains, freedom is a powerful gift, a privilege that we should not and cannot take for granted.

The greatest freedom we have is not experienced only in the physical realm but in the spiritual realm. The freedom we have in Christ to be all that God created us to be is the greatest gift of all.

In the Passion translation of Matthew 10:8 it says, "Freely you have received the power of the kingdom, so freely release it to others." The power of the kingdom is to be shared in the lives of others.

On our journey to Bill's healing, we were blessed with the opportunity to let the light and love of Jesus shine through us. Wherever Bill was, Jesus was there too. We were blessed to fill some dark places with Christ's love. We could be encouragers even as we were being encouraged by our heavenly Father and by you.

As I continue on the Glory Road, I am reminded of the cost of freedom, not only physically but spiritually. They are both privileges that I must steward wisely. To further protect our nation's freedom, I pray for this country and its citizens. May God's grace fall upon us. Spiritually, I am grateful for the freedom I have in Christ, to choose to walk in obedience to God and receive His best for me.

Thank you for celebrating the gift of freedom with me including Bill's freedom from sickness, and the blessings he is experiencing in heaven. #Godisfaithful #TheGloryRoad

Day #77 July 5

Anchor Verse: Acts 12:5

So Peter was kept in prison, but fervent and persistent prayer for him was being made to God by the church. (AMP)

Prayer has changed the course of history on more than one occasion. There is something beyond explanation that happens when God's people pray. What once seemed impossible turns to the possible. Great revivals have sprung up out of prayer meetings. The course of a battle has changed and victory has arisen out of the jaws of defeat.

We are reminded to pray without ceasing. People are healed, delivered, and set free when God moves and heals because people prayed. In Acts 12:5, Peter is locked up in prison, but meanwhile across the city, there are many who are praying for him. The Passion translation says, "The church went into a season of intense intercession, asking God to free him." (TPT)

God heard their cries, and sent an angel to free Peter. His chains fell off and the angel guided him right out of the prison and to the home where the church was praying for him. This was God's supernatural intervention; (it's not a suggestion for a jailbreak, just to be clear.)

On the journey to Bill's healing, so many people prayed for Bill. Across the world, we had people praying around the clock. God moved in a mighty way. The medical world could not explain what happened, when what seemed like the end of the road, turned into an open door for God to continue Bill's path to healing.

As I continue on the Glory Road, my life is shaped by the power of prayer. It is a blessing to stand with so many of you and pray, and bring your requests for healing before the Lord, and watch Him answer. As you have prayed for God's provision and healing in my own life, God has heard your prayers and answers them.

Your prayers matter. They do not fall useless to the floor. Instead they ascend to heaven and it moves the hand of God. We can't dictate the outcome, but we sure can ask, seek, and knock, as the Bible tells us to do.

The Bible tells us to "boldly" enter the throne room of grace. We are called to "pray and not to faint", in Luke 18:1. Our mandate is clear, the time spent on our knees is priceless, and God's response is miraculous.

Thank you for your prayers on our behalf, they moved the hand of God. #Godisfaithful #TheGloryRoad

Day #78 July 6

Anchor Verse: 1 Corinthians 12:22
If one part suffers, every part suffers with it; if one part is honored, every part rejoices with it. (NIV)

In Psalm 139 it says, "I thank you, God, for making me so mysteriously complex! Everything you do is marvelously breathtaking. It simply amazes me to think about it! How thoroughly you know me, Lord!" (TPT)

It is that mysterious complexity that makes us so unique. God's handiwork is displayed in the creation of our bodies. It is beyond human understanding.

The human body will never be fully understood, but what we do know is that our bodies when God created them were intricately woven together.

1 Corinthians 12 talks about not only the human body but the body of Christ and how we each have a part and we all need each other.

It is our uniqueness that should be applauded, because even as a hand is different than a foot, or the eye different than my heart, each one is essential to the working of the whole. This goes beyond our own personal bodies. When one person in our family suffers, we all are impacted by it.

On our journey to Bill's healing, I hurt when he hurt and I rejoiced when he rejoiced. There is something about that bond between husband and wife and the two being "one flesh" that accentuates that point. It's also true with a parent and child and even good friends.

We were created to be in community with each other. Our lives and our choices impact each other. That's why unity is so important. Not that we are identical to each other, but united in spirit and purpose.

Some are gifted as artists or plumbers, others as doctors or teachers, and yet others as mechanics and computer programmers, etc. As we embrace the gifts and qualities in others, we begin to get a glimpse of the complexity of God's handiwork in us.

On this Glory Road, I am grateful for the wide spectrum of God's people that surround me as I learn to appreciate the complexity of my own body and brain. In this new season of my life, I'm learning more about sleeping, eating, and exercise, as a new rhythm for my days is taking shape.

Thank you for the beauty that you bring to the garden of my life.
#Godisfaithful #TheGloryRoad

Day #79 July 7

Anchor Verse: Matthew 26:40
Later, He [Jesus] came back to His three disciples and found them all sound asleep. He awakened Peter and said to him, "Do you lack the strength to stay awake with me for even just an hour?" (TPT)

Sometimes staying awake can be difficult. When your body is tired, it's tired. No matter how hard you try and stay awake, mind over matter, it doesn't work.

In Matthew 26, we find Jesus and three of His disciples in the Garden of Gethsemane. They have finished eating dinner, what is often referred to as the "Last Supper" and Jesus invites Peter, James, and John to come with Him when He goes there to pray. It's evening. Before Jesus goes a little further to be alone, He leaves the disciples there to watch and pray with Him. "Then he said to them, "My soul is overwhelmed with sorrow to the point of death. Stay here and keep watch with me."

The disciples heard Jesus say how important this was to Him, but instead of staying awake, all three of them fall asleep.

Jesus returns and finds them sleeping. He wakes them up and asks again if they will watch and pray with Him. This happens three times. And each time they fell asleep. When Jesus returns, He wakes the disciples and tells them that the betrayer is at hand.

"Will you watch and pray with me for one hour?" Jesus is asking you this same question. Yes, our lives are busy. We have the time, but are we willing to spend it in prayer? That really is the question.

On this journey to Bill's healing, we learned the importance of prayer on a whole new level. I have been a prayer warrior for years, but God decided to put me in "advanced training." When you are called upon day or night, to pray for the needs of those you love, and for others, friends or strangers that need God's help, Bill and I learned God was calling us to serve in a new way.

Prayer on the Glory Road has taken on a new dimension. During Bill's journey to healing, we were often up several times during the night so my prayers ascended to heaven. In this new season, the Lord is waking me up and keeping me up to pray, sometimes for hours during the night. I am honored to be part of God's advanced prayer team – I need to figure out how to fit some sleep in there somewhere.

Thank you for your faithfulness. #Godisfaithful #TheGloryRoad

Day #80 July 8

Anchor Verse: Job 13:15
Though He slay me, yet will I trust Him. Even so, I will defend my own ways before Him. (NKJV)

How much do you trust God? Does all your hope rest with Him?

Faith in God means you are willing to "put all your eggs in one basket." If God doesn't save you, nobody else can or will. I call it "all-in" or "sold-out" faith in God. If God doesn't save us, we're toast.

God already has a rescue plan in place, His name is Jesus. Jesus came on the scene long before the latest pandemic came into play or any other battle.

He is not surprised by what you are facing, feeling, or struggling with. In fact, God is waiting with open arms to receive you. There is no condemnation in Christ… none. Jesus led with love throughout the years of His ministry on earth and it is the love that comes from God that changes lives.

On our journey to Bill's healing, the Holy Spirit showed me how to pray bold prayers. To stand at heaven's gates and boldly approach the throne of grace, and then falling on my knees before my heavenly Father and crying out to the Lord for Bill's healing – that God would spare Bill's life.

Calling out the devil for the lies he was speaking, and the seeds of doubt he was trying to plant in the beautiful garden of healing that God had already ordained for Bill.

One night at a critical juncture in the road, I remember crying out to the devil, "You can't have him. Bill belongs to God." The Lord heard the cries of my heart and Bill moved into his healing once again.

I entrusted God with Bill's life and with mine – our hopes and dreams were placed in God's hands, and it was by His grace that we would move forward.

On this Glory Road, I continue to meet obstacles, giants in my path, distractions from the enemy, lies that he seeks to plant in my mind, but I am not moved by what I see. My hope rests in Him, the one who calls me by name because I belong to God, I'm His daughter. You are His child, too.

Lord, thank you for Your grace, mercy, and peace. We trust you, Lord.

Thank you for covering me with a blanket of love, hope, and peace.
#Godisfaithful #TheGloryRoad

Day #81 July 9

Anchor Verse: Isaiah 41:9
I drew you to myself from the ends of the earth and called you from its farthest corner. I say to you: "You are my servant; I have chosen you. I have not rejected you!" (TPT)

Called by God. He knows your name. He knows where you live. God knows the plans He has for you, and those plans include serving Him.

To be chosen is a powerful place to be. When our future spouse chooses us, the person they want to spend their life with, it's a priceless moment. When you are chosen for a promotion at work, or picked for a team when you are a child, those are the moments you remember.

The most important choice that will ever be made is when God chooses you when He calls you by name because you belong to Him.

In verse 10 it says, "So do not fear, for I am with you; do not be dismayed, for I am your God. I will strengthen you and help you; I will uphold you with my righteous right hand."

On our journey to Bill's healing, we faced many places in the road when fear tried to capture us, lay a trap for us, and suck us in. But because of our faith in God's goodness and grace, we chose to be strengthened by the Lord as He upheld us, carried us by His righteous, powerful, strong right hand.

Now as I walk alone on this Glory Road, I ask the Lord for the same courage to face what lies ahead. Many places are still veiled in the dusk, they are in places I can't see, and that's okay. I am called to stay in the present and not run ahead of the Lord. His grace is sufficient for this day, and this day is all that I need.

The truth is that God has chosen me to be His servant and where my heavenly Father leads me, He will provide for me.

Thank you for your prevailing prayers. #Godisfaithful #TheGloryRoad

Day #82 July 10

Anchor Verse: Job 42:10

And the Lord restored Job's losses when he prayed for his friends. Indeed the Lord gave Job twice as much as he had before. (NKJV)

The happily ever after part of the story… isn't that what we all are looking for?

In a great movie, in a good novel, in a real-life situation, we can empathize with those going through the hardships but there comes a time when we can't wait for the happy ending. We need the hero to rescue the damsel in distress, for the orphans to find new parents, for the destitute family to find a home and an income to sustain them.

We are wired for the happy ending. The book of Job delivers that happy ending. The God who loves Job so much comes through for him in the end. After all the chapters we read where the devil strips away Job's fortune, his family, and even his health, and Job's friends turn against him, God remains faithful. The devil only has a short leash. Evil can only run so far before God yanks on the chain and says, "Enough!"

God is not unaware of your suffering, your challenges, your fears, your frustrations, and even your seeming abandonment. There are times when God wants you all alone.

What did Job have to do before the Lord restored his losses? Job had to pray for his friends. After Job's encounter with the Lord earlier in chapter 42, and God brings Job to a new level of understanding about God and His ways, God asks Job to "stand in the gap" to intercede for his friends who have been "trash talking" about him and to him.

On our journey to Bill's healing, we walked through valleys of suffering, places of uncertainty, made choices that weren't always clear to those around us, but we followed in God's footsteps. We followed Him. The Lord always provided everything we needed – we never lacked for anything.

As I take new steps on the Glory Road, I am reminded that God is good, just, and holy. His plans prevail through the calm and the storm. God is not surprised by our circumstances or the mud puddles on our path, the tornadoes and hurricanes, or the calm waters where He restores our souls. God's ending to our story is the best grand finale possible.

Thank you for your encouraging words. #Godisfaithful #TheGloryRoad

Day #83 July 11

Anchor Verse: Psalm 3:2-3

Lord, I have so many enemies, so many who are against me. Listen to how they whisper their slander against me, saying: "Look! He's hopeless! Even God can't save him from this!" Pause in his presence. But in the depths of my heart I truly know that you, Yahweh, have become my Shield; You take me and surround me with yourself. Your glory covers me continually. You lift high my head when I bow low in shame." (TPT)

King David knew what it was like to have many enemies surrounding him. Not only strangers and foreigners but also from those close to him, his own son, and even Saul, his father-in-law.

Greater than the enemies that surrounded him was the God who stood for him. Yahweh was the one who would never leave David or forsake him. "But in the depths of my heart I truly know" – what a powerful truth.

"Your glory covers me continually." How beautiful is that. It is the glory of the Lord where we find our power. It is in the glory of the Lord that we find our strength. It is the glory of the Lord that shines so brightly that our enemies are overcome and fall at the feet of the One who saves us.

We are facing "enemies" of many shapes and sizes. Satan comes to steal, kill, and destroy, but Jesus said, I have come that you might have life abundantly. This morning our eyes do not rest on the battlefield where it seems that troops are being "slaughtered" but instead our eyes are raised to the heavens where our help comes from – it comes in the name of the Lord, the Maker of heaven and earth.

On our journey to Bill's healing, we found God's word to be true. Not only the truths found in the Bible but the spoken word that came to us in dreams and visions in the night. Bill knew that his God was greater than his circumstances or anything that was "named" by man. We both watched God rise above the natural and raise us up to a supernatural place where ALL things are possible with God – all things!

As I walk this Glory Road, I encounter enemies – new ones and some familiar companions as I fought for Bill's life. I choose to silence the voices in the world that cry out to us that "it's hopeless" and instead "in the depths of my heart I truly know that you, Yahweh, have become my Shield; You take me and surround me with yourself."

Thank you for speaking words of life. #Godisfaithful #TheGloryRoad

Day #84 July 12

Anchor Verse: Proverbs 15:1
A soft and gentle and thoughtful answer turns away wrath, But harsh and painful and careless words stir up anger. (AMP)

Words are powerful. Words have brought men and women to great levels of success and also their own words have destroyed them.

In this day of technological advancement, our words are spread more quickly than when a letter was sent by Pony Express.

It takes time to write a letter by hand and it also gives us time to think about what we want to say rather than quickly "shooting off" a text message or posting a reactionary Facebook comment.

Taking a moment to think before we respond always brings life rather than a misguided "bullet" – a word spoken hastily – which wounds not for a moment but for a lifetime.

The proverbs written by King Solomon include great words of wisdom to live by and to operate under every moment of every day.

Listen again to these words from Proverbs 15 – "A soft, gentle and thoughtful answer turns away wrath" – seems like a good word for our culture. What we often see play out on the television are not words that are "soft, gentle and thoughtful" – they ignite a fire rather than pouring a bucket of water to quench roaring flames.

Test your words. What is the mission of your words? Do your words put out the fire of anger or do they pour gas on the fire?

On our journey to Bill's healing, we learned the power of our words – not only the words spoken to others but the words we spoke to ourselves. Words can bring life or death, they are that powerful. It was a blessing to speak good words in those five hospitals in two states on our journey to Bill's healing.

As I walk this Glory Road, I must be aware of the words that I release – the words that others hear from my mouth and those silent conversations I have with myself. As an author and editor, words are where I live. Every day God has granted me the honor and blessing to use my words and help others to use their words to see His honor and glory be magnified in their lives.

Thank you for your faithfulness. #Godisfaithful #TheGloryRoad

Day #85 July 13

Anchor Verse: Psalm 4:1

God, you are my righteousness, my champion defender. Answer me when I cry for help! Whenever I was in distress, you enlarged me. I'm being squeezed again—I need your kindness right away! Grant me your grace, hear my prayer, and set me free! (TPT)

Feeling squeezed this morning? Like you are an orange and orange juice is on the breakfast menu?

Right now, it seems that everything that could be shaken is being shaken. It is a great test to see how firmly our roots are planted in Him. Our pastor put it this way, "The devil shakes us to break us, but the Lord is shaking us to wake us!" Are you awake yet?

When you are in the midst of a crisis, what is the first thing you do? Look for help. As a believer, there is only one place to run and that is to God. With "one word" everything we need is available at His command. Lord God Almighty, Maker of heaven and earth is on our side.

It's like when you hit "fast-forward" on a movie and everything goes into hyper-speed. That's how fast God can move.

Sometimes God resolves the problem instantaneously. Other times, there is a process that involves waiting as He continues to build our faith in Him. We learn to trust God as we never have before. And then, as I have come to realize, it's not really about us at all. God is using our lives as a "stage" to illustrate a lesson for others, to show them what God can do through people who are completely surrendered to Him.

On our journey to Bill's healing, yes, God taught us many lessons. The God of Abraham, Isaac, and Jacob was, and still is, the God of Bill and Barb. We had Red Sea moments – where there was a roaring river in front of us and our own version of an Egyptian army behind us. Like Esther, who was new to life as a "queen" and living in a foreign kingdom, God brought us to those hospitals "for such a time as this."

As I find my way through uncharted territory on the Glory Road, God is releasing His glory in different ways. Sometimes I am in the audience and God allows me to watch the lesson unfold on the stage, and then other times, I am the lead actor. There are some lessons that can only be learned in the "refining fire."

Thank you for holding up my arms. #Godisfaithful #TheGloryRoad

Day #86 July 14

Anchor Verse: Psalm 119:116

Lord, sustain me as you promised, that I may live! Do not let my hope be crushed. (NLT)

Crushing sounds like a painful process because it is.

Crushing is not only reserved for the natural world, it's a concept that we discover in our own lives. "Crushing", although not a desired exercise, it's how God can bring about even greater growth and glory in us.

When I think about this journey that Bill and I walked over the last two years, and now this new stretch of the road, crushing seems like a good word to describe it.

What was crushed? God allowed us to go through the refining fire, the "crusher", and the storms of adversity so that we might be more like Him. That we would get rid of the "junk" in our lives – like the things that are stuffed in your closets and storage units. The "stuff" that you don't think you can live without, yet you never look at, use it, or likely think about it, until someone says, "It's time to get rid of it."

We must go through the crushing before the true gift – the greater blessing can pour forth out of us. Another illustration that came to mind is of a walnut tucked inside its shell. The only route to get at that delicious "meat" of the walnut is to crush its shell. In the breaking, comes the blessing.

On the path to Bill's healing, there was a lot of crushing. From the minute I called the ambulance on January 10, 2018, our expectation, our preconceived view of what a "normal" life looked like went out the window. But in the "crushing" God brought something beautiful we never could have experienced in the ordinary. Our love for each other and our love for God crescendoed to new heights. (Crescendo is a musical term that means to get louder.) Finding joy in the midst of pain and laughter as the winds of the storm howled around us. Some of my greatest memories with Bill were created since we entered the hurricane of our lives from 2018-2020.

Now as I continue on this Glory Road, there is more crushing involved. I am learning to live life as a widow with the warm memories of a life well-lived with Bill to keep me company. But God is not content to let me rest on the memories of the past. He knows that there is "sweet wine" in me, and so the crushing continues to bring "new wine" out of me.

Thank you for your encouraging words. #Godisfaithful #TheGloryRoad

Day #87 July 15

Anchor Verse: Psalm 16:5

Lord, I have chosen you alone as my inheritance. You are my prize, my pleasure, and my portion. I leave my destiny and its timing in your hands. (TPT)

"My prize, my pleasure and my portion" – does that describe your relationship with the Lord? God is not a "side dish" or a "spare tire" – He is all we need, and if He is all we have, we lack absolutely nothing.

Life lived with God is a roller coaster ride and a carnival all rolled into one. It is never boring. Bill used to tell me that God had a very loud laugh. In Bill's encounters with the Lord, God said that Bill made Him laugh. And Bill confirmed that the Lord does laugh very loud. Listen for the Lord's laughter.

Are you willing to put your destiny and its timing in God's hands? God sees a bigger picture, a bigger plan that is far greater than anything we could ever imagine. We see the caterpillar, and God sees the future beautiful butterfly.

On the journey to Bill's healing, Bill and I chose to trust in God and God alone. In the natural realm, often I know our choices didn't make sense, because God was orchestrating them from the supernatural realm. We asked the Lord for spiritual eyes to see because often our physical eyes become dimmed by time or our human perspective. What glorious things the Lord showed us as we submitted our lives, our hopes and dreams to Him. We received way more than we could have ever expected.

As I navigate the Glory Road, I find that my destiny and its timing are on a different time clock than my previous experience. Not only God's timing but also His plans and purposes for me look different from a bicycle built for one rather than the bicycle built for two that Bill and I traveled.

My trust in the Lord grows daily especially when it seems like fog has drifted across the road and the way ahead is obscured.

God's promises spoken out loud are the headlights, the fog lights that cut through the mist ahead of me. Even if I can only see the next step, it's enough. Even when I can't see the next step, I know God will make a way.

Thank you for traveling with me. #Godisfaithful #TheGloryRoad

Day #88 July 16

Anchor Verse: Psalm 17:6
You will answer me, God; I know you always will, like you always do as you listen with love to my every prayer. (TPT)

When you pray to God, do you pray with confidence believing that not only does God hear your prayer, but that He will answer you? God wants to remind you this morning that He loves you so much He "hangs" on your every word.

For those of you who have been in love in your lifetime, you understand what I mean. When you fall in love with someone, it seems that every word they speak "brings life" to you. You treasure their words and you repeat their words. You might even write them down.

God loves to hear our words and also to listen to hear His words in return. Our heavenly Father wants the blessings He has stored up for us to fall upon us and encourage us and bring us hope even on our darkest days.

In Psalm 17:6, it says in the Passion translation, "You will answer me, God; I know you always will, like you always do as you listen with love to my every prayer."

Look at how many times King David, the author of the psalm uses the word "always." "I know you always will, like you always do as you listen."

"Always" means that every single time, every occasion, good times, bad times, times when I feel like it, times when I don't – there are no exceptions to this rule, and my friend, "always" is a word we can seldom use authentically in this world.

On our journey to Bill's healing, we stepped into that level of confidence. We could pray prayers of faith for the seemingly impossible and know that God was listening with love to our every prayer. If God promised it, God will deliver.

The Glory Road is a place where God's faithfulness lights the way. On this new section of the road, sometimes I don't know how to pray, God knows that too, but in His kindness, love, and faithfulness, He guides my feet to the place where His glory may be seen in me.

Thank you for every prayer you prayed. #Godisfaithful #TheGloryRoad

Day #89 July 17

Anchor Verse: Proverbs 23:7

For as he [a man] thinks in his heart so is he. (NKJV)

Do you know how powerful your thoughts are? You might, but I'm not sure that you really do.

What we think determines whether we succeed or fail. I'm not talking about your career or the sum total of your life, but what we do every day. Henry Ford, who created the Model T in 1908, believed that our thoughts determined the outcome.

Those words are still true. It's about our attitude and our skillset.

Your thoughts are fed by what you value in your heart. A well that is muddy will produce water that is not fit to drink while a clear, mountain brook refreshes not only your body but your soul.

Our actions, whether positive or negative, telegraph to others the kind of person we are. What we do and how we do it is reflected in every action. Do you go about your day filled with joy looking at the positive things of life or do you always see the negative in everything? Living with a negative outlook must be exhausting!

On our journey to Bill's healing, I was impressed by Bill's attitude and his outlook. I know there were moments that were very difficult when the news rocked our world. But Bill would take a moment and run with the situation to the Lord, and emerge from the throne room of grace determined to face that mountain and beat that challenge.

Now as I begin each day on this new road, the Glory Road, I have the opportunity to choose my attitude. Bill used to call it his "altitude" not his attitude. I can choose what I focus on. I choose to walk in faith knowing that God has a future and hope for me. (Jeremiah 29:11)

God, our heavenly Father, knows whether your heart is rebellious or tucked in with Him. "Thy word have I hid in my heart that I might not sin against thee." As we fill our hearts with God's word, God's promises, we have all we need to face the battles that will come our way in this life.

Thank you for sowing love into my life. #Godisfaithful #TheGloryRoad

Day #90 July 18

Anchor Verse: 2 Chronicles 20:17

You will not need to fight in this battle. Position yourselves, stand still and see the salvation of the Lord, who is with you, O Judah and Jerusalem!' Do not fear or be dismayed; tomorrow go out against them, for the Lord is with you. (NJKV)

There are battles raging all around us. It might look to you like Goliath did to the Israelite army when the giant came out to taunt them each day. Until the Lord brought the young man David into the picture. David faced the giant. One stone with the Lord's power behind it took the giant down!

King Jehoshaphat could see that they were outmanned in this battle, they didn't stand a chance. So instead of running in fear, the king ran to the Lord and stood up in the presence of his people, and spoke to the Lord of His promises and reminded God what He had done in the past.

"We have no power to face this vast army that is attacking us. We do not know what to do, but our eyes are on you." (2 Chronicles 20:12)

The Lord told the Israelites that they needed to FACE their enemy, the problem in the road ahead of them, but that God would fight for them. God didn't need their help. They were to stand still and let God do it. The king bowed down with his face to the ground and worshiped the Lord and all the people did the same.

On our journey to Bill's healing, many times we faced an enemy that was bigger than us. We ran to the Lord and asked Him for help because in our own flesh we didn't have the resources, but we knew that He did. And God in His faithfulness fought for us and the enemy was taken down.

This morning as I start a new day on the Glory Road, I am reminded that there are enemies that I face, both those seen and unseen. Some of them seem like giants and others like armies that have greater resources than I do. But this is what I know, that God who called me by name is fighting for me. The Lord says, "Stand still and see the victory that will be won for you today!"

Thank you, Lord, that our battles are Your battles. We surrender them to You, and praise and worship You for the battle that has already been won.

Thank you for your faithful prayers. #Godisfaithful #TheGloryRoad

Day #91 July 19

Anchor Verse: Psalm 25:20

Will you protect me from their [my enemies] power against me? Let it never be said that I trusted you and you didn't come to my rescue. (TPT)

You may be facing "vicious enemies" this morning. In this pandemic season, they come in different shapes and forms, both in the physical world and the spiritual world.

The good news is the Lord is fighting for you and He always wins. Greater is He that is in you than he that is in the world. (1 John 4:4)

"Let it never be said that I trusted you and you didn't come to my rescue." David boldly speaks to the Lord not only about his great need for protection but also that he is totally counting on God to come to his rescue. God's reputation is on the line. Everyone knows that David trusted in the Lord, so if God fails to rescue him, it's not David who will get the bad rep, it's God.

God has so far exceeded my expectations time and time again, that I can't imagine telling my heavenly Father that I was disappointed in His provision or protection.

On our journey to Bill's healing, many times I can remember the "vicious enemies" that pursued us on many levels. Yet, as we were tucked under His wing, resting in the shadow of the Almighty, we found refuge and strength to face every battle. Often, the Lord said, "Stay here in the cleft of the rock. I will go out and fight that battle for you." Our victory was assured when God dispatched His angel armies.

Now as I travel this Glory Road, the enemies may look a little different but they can be just as vicious in this ever-changing world environment. His promises are still unshakable, and so am I, when I walk with God.

David's bodyguards were God's perfection and faithfulness. God was his hope and he trusted in God as his only protection. Some trust in chariots and horses, but we trust in the name of the Lord our God.

Today marks three months since God took Bill home to heaven. In some respects, I say it's "only" been three months, and on the other hand, it seems like yesterday. I am so grateful that there is no distance in the spirit. Bill is still close by although I can't touch him or be held in his arms of love.

Thank you for your faithful prayers. #Godisfaithful #TheGloryRoad

Day #92 July 20

Anchor Verse: Psalm 116:12-13

What will I give to the Lord [in return] for all His benefits toward me? [How can I repay Him for His precious blessings?] I will lift up the cup of salvation and call on the name of the Lord. (AMP)

How often do we stop and reflect on the goodness of the Lord? Do you stop to count your blessings daily or only on a special occasion or holiday like Thanksgiving?

"But this I call to mind, therefore I have hope. It is because of the Lord's lovingkindnesses that we are not consumed, because His [tender] compassions never fail. They are new every morning; great and beyond measure is Your faithfulness." (Lamentations 3:21-23 AMP)

Have you ever thought about how you could repay God for the many blessings you have received from His loving hands?

It can be challenging to purchase a gift for a friend or family member who seemingly has everything, so what can you give God who created the whole world and everything in it? The psalmist realized it wasn't something that he could give to the Lord, but an action, to take the cup of salvation.

Elisabeth Elliot in her book, *Suffering is never for Nothing* describes life, this path that includes pain, sorrow, suffering, and grief, as a cup from God's own hand. She trusts God so much that and knows that He wants the best for her, so she will receive it all in His name, and I would add, for His glory.

On the journey to Bill's healing, God flooded us with so many blessings, alongside a healthy dose of challenges. But His grace, mercy and peace far outweighed the "momentary troubles" that we experienced. We trusted God with our very lives and He was not found lacking in any way.

As I follow this Glory Road, I am finding a new batch of blessings as I drink from His cup of salvation. Yes, there are days when the cup is bitter, the grief still rushes in like a flood, but greater still are His blessings. I find peace in the middle of this pandemic storm, and turn my face toward heaven as I navigate new paths of His righteousness and trust Him with my every step.

Thank you for being a blessing to us. #Godisfaithful #TheGloryRoad

Day #93 July 21

Anchor Verse: Psalm 30:11-12
You have turned my mourning into dancing for me; You have taken off my sackcloth and clothed me with joy, that my soul may sing praise to You and not be silent. O Lord my God, I will give thanks to You forever. (AMP)

Mourning and dancing, sackcloth and being clothed with joy – they are the exact opposites of each other.

When you are in a season of mourning, dancing is the furthest thing from your mind. What is the appropriate attire for a widow in mourning? Joy isn't the first thing that comes to my mind.

God is the God of opposites. He turns our world upside down. Jesus' life is a great example of that. The Son of God was born in a stable and laid in a manger at His birth. Jesus has come from the splendor of glory yet was willing to be brought to our level that we might have life forevermore with Him.

On this journey to Bill's healing, we learned that life was not about what our eyes could see but what we saw with our spiritual eyes, God's glory at work in us. How else can you have laughter in the midst of the storm and peace that passes all understanding when your boat is filling with water?

In this season of Bill's illness and his entrance to heaven, the Lord has given me permission to fully feel the weight of it – both the joy and the sorrow, so there was nothing left untouched in my body or soul.

It reminds me of a habit that Bill had of not emptying a glass of water, there was always a little left in the bottom. God's call to us is to drink all of it. The blessings of life are often found in the bottom of the glass. Your heavenly Father wants you to enjoy every sip of the river of life, the fountain of blessings He has for you.

As I open the curtains this morning to a new day on the Glory Road, I sing praises to the Lord's name. God is taking off my sackcloth, like a parent removes the clothes off a young child and replaces them with fresh garments. The Lord is taking off my mourning clothes that are saturated with dust and tears. Before He puts on that garment of praise, the mantle of joy, God holds me in His arms of love and reminds me how much He loves me and that it's going to be okay. God's got this!

Thank you for your faithfulness. #Godisfaithful #TheGloryRoad

Day #94 July 22

Anchor Verse: Psalm 31:7
In mercy you have seen my troubles and you have cared for me; even during this crisis in my soul I will be radiant with joy, filled with praise for your love and mercy. (TPT)

I am so grateful for God's mercy. What is mercy anyway? Mercy is defined as "compassion or forgiveness shown toward someone whom it is within one's power to punish or harm."

Because of God's mercy, David, the author of this psalm, is able to declare, "I will be radiant with joy!" Radiant with joy in our trials – it's not always the stance that we take when we are going through the fire. We may be crawled up in a ball in the corner or we'd like to pull the blankets over our head and stay in bed all day, but God in His faithfulness says, "Come walk with Me. Come talk with Me. Together we will make it through this deep valley."

One of the greatest weapons that we have as a believer is that we can praise the Lord in the midst of the storm. We praise the Lord for His love and mercy because we know that without those attributes of God we would surely perish.

On our journey to Bill's healing, we couldn't have made it without God's mercy. When you think you have been pushed to the end of your resources, God picks you up and you soar with Him into the heavenlies. You soar on wings like the eagle and you run and are not weary, you walk and will not faint.

I am so blessed by Bill's example of pressing in to the Lord in his most difficult trials and not only asking the Lord for strength, but allowing God to fill him up. God can offer the "world" but we must be willing to humble ourselves and admit we can't do it alone and graciously accept His gifts.

As I find my way on the Glory Road, that same God is faithful to me. In the NIV version it says, "You saw my affliction and knew the anguish of my soul." There have been times when my soul was overcome by anguish. My faith never diminished, in fact, it was being tested and tried, but in my humanity, the pain was real. Sometimes it still is. There are afflictions that come into our lives that bring us closer to the Lord. They are described as "light and momentary" – and in the larger scope of eternity, yes, they are.

Thank you for praying me through. #Godisfaithful #TheGloryRoad

Day #95 July 23

Anchor Verse: Psalm 34:15
The eyes of the Lord are toward the righteous [those with moral courage and spiritual integrity] And His ears are open to their cry. (AMP)

The Amplified version defines those who are righteous as "those with moral courage and spiritual integrity."

Moral courage is defined as "the courage to take action for moral reasons despite the risk of adverse consequences. Courage is required to take action when one has doubts or fears about the consequences." (Wikipedia)

Spiritual integrity is rising above the world's standard of integrity of morally doing the right thing to using God's Word as our compass. It is a standard far higher than the world's – it helps us bring the holiness and justice of God to earth through our beliefs and actions.

These are the people of God who God watches, for they will change the world in which they live. God can trust them, as He trusted Job. When we choose to walk in moral courage and spiritual integrity, God is attentive to our cry. His ears are "open."

God's reward for choosing to go higher with Him is that we have His ear – day or night, every season for any reason. There is no question that He will turn aside. There is no emotion that is forbidden. There is no grief too deep or no joy too great for God to understand.

On our journey to Bill's healing, we were taken from a place of brokenness to a place of wholeness in God's presence. We didn't have all the answers, we never did, but we had the Lord, and His power, and His presence, 24/7, whether we were at home or in the hospital. His love never changed.

Now as I walk this unfamiliar path on the Glory Road, I am so grateful that I have a history of trusting the Lord, and my heavenly Father knows that He can trust me, even when the way is difficult and the storm is swirling around me. I choose to walk in moral courage and spiritual integrity as I navigate this new season of my life. My friend, I pray that you will join me there. It is not a popular path, but it is God's way.

Thank you for your persistent prayers. #Godisfaithful #TheGloryRoad

Day #96 July 24

Anchor Verse: Psalm 35:1-2

O Lord, oppose those who oppose me.
Fight those who fight against me. Put on your armor, and take up your shield.
Prepare for battle, and come to my aid. (NLT)

Our lives are lived on a battlefield every day. It is not only in history books that we read about great wars of the past like the Revolutionary War, Civil War, World War I, and World War II to name a few.

We face a different kind of battle – a war against an illness and the fallout which is affecting the whole world. But even greater is the battle against good and evil that is at the core of every skirmish we face.

Battles are not new to our time and generation. King David was a warrior, a man who fought battles for the Lord and often led his people into war, victoriously. As a young man, David faced the giant Goliath and with the Lord's help, defeated him with one small stone.

However, there were times in his life when David cried out to the Lord, as we see here in Psalm 35, and asked the Lord to fight for him. David was battle weary. Not only from those who were obviously his enemies, but people that should have been on his side, were speaking against him.

Being a leader isn't always easy. I was listening to a speaker the other day and he was talking about the cost of leadership. When the symbol of Christianity is a cross, know that you have not chosen an easy path, when Jesus says, "Take up your cross and follow me."

On our journey to Bill's healing, we faced battle after battle; often the events came at us rapid fire, with barely enough time to catch your breath. Yet, the Lord was always there to defend us and protect us by His love and grace, while dispatching the angel armies to fight for us.

As I encounter new skirmishes on the Glory Road, I call upon the Lord to fight for me. In our life together, Bill was always my defender. When we were apartment managers, I was known as the diplomat and Bill was the warrior. It remained that way until the day Bill went to heaven, although God did some cross-training in our skillsets.

Thank you for standing with us in the battles we have faced. Now as I face life without Bill, I am not alone because I know that God has a great cloud of witnesses that surround me. #Godisfaithful #TheGloryRoad

Day #97 July 25

Anchor Verse: Psalm 37:39

But the Lord will be the Savior of all who love him. Even in their time of trouble God will live in them as strength. (TPT)

The Bible is filled with the promises of God, here are a few. "The joy of the Lord is my strength." (Nehemiah 8:10) "When I am weak, then I am strong." (2 Corinthians 12:10) "He gives strength to the weary and increases the power of the weak." (Isaiah 40:29)

It's God in you that gives you strength – it's not because of how good you are but how good God is.

In this Covid season, the world has been turned upside down. The places we thought were solid and unshakable have fallen in pieces around us. At various times on this journey, we have found ourselves sheltered in place in our homes. The good news – as Christians, we have had the opportunity to be tucked in with the Lord in a greater way.

On the journey to Bill's healing, the Lord was there at every turn and even on the straightaways where we "gained speed" during his accelerated healing. But Bill's strength did not come from his own Herculean effort; it came when Bill submitted himself to the Lord and asked the Lord to be his strength. When the supernatural meets our natural efforts, miraculous things happen.

I can remember watching Bill walk with his walker up this really steep hill in our apartment complex with his physical therapist at his side, and me walking behind them, and being filled with awe and wonder at God's hand at work right in front of my eyes. There was a holy confidence in Bill because God had taken Bill by the hand and was leading him on this appointed path of righteousness for His name's sake.

Do you have that kind of trust in God? Or are you teetering on the edge of unbelief and despair? The Lord is your guardrail this morning. The Holy Spirit is hovering close by to lift you up if you fall.

On this Glory Road, I have encountered mole hills that morphed into mountains, and mountains that at the Lord's word, were moved into the heart of the sea and destroyed. Daily, it is a walk of faith, but with every step God is found faithful. My prayer is that I would be found faithful.

Thank you for standing strong with me. #Godisfaithful #TheGloryRoad

Day #98 July 26

Anchor Verse: Acts 27:25
So keep up your courage, men, for I believe God and have complete confidence in Him that it will turn out exactly as I have been told. (AMP)

Are you an encourager by nature or do you see the cup as half-empty?

The Bible is filled with the truth. It is packed with God's promises and with testimonies of God's healing miracles, and so many times when situations seemed impossible, God made a way.

This passage from Acts 27 tells us the story of Paul on a ship encountering a horrific storm as he is being transported to stand trial before Caesar. After being tossed around by the storm for many days, Paul tells the crew they should have taken his advice and not set sail. Not the best way to make friends. Paul goes on to share some good news. An angel of the Lord had appeared to him the previous night and told Paul that he and the whole crew would survive the storm.

Paul ends with verse 25, "So keep up your courage, men, for I believe God and have complete confidence in Him that it will turn out exactly as I have been told."

The enemy can only cause so much mayhem before God says, "Enough!" Then the Lord makes all things right according to His plan.

On Bill's healing journey we encountered storms – some big and some bigger. But through it all, we could hear the voice of God reminding us that He would never leave us or forsake us. God had a plan and purpose for our lives and nothing could short circuit that plan. Trusting the Lord brings holy confidence.

As I find my way on this Glory Road, I need to remember that God's promises are for me too. God's promises are not for one and not another, He loves all His children the same. As we are going through this hot weather spell, I am reminded of how Bill and I navigated the heat and of God's faithfulness. Tucked in with the Lord, I am blessed by His Power, His Presence, and His Peace.

The other day someone encouraged me with this truth. God is holding me (and you) in His hand and the enemy cannot snatch us out of God's hand. Isn't that beautiful?

Thank you for your faithful prayers. #Godisfaithful #TheGloryRoad

Day #99 July 27

Anchor Verse: Romans 5:3-4

Not only so, but we also glory in our sufferings, because we know that suffering produces perseverance; perseverance, character; and character, hope. (NIV)

There are words and situations we like to avoid or even talk about. That would include the words: pain, suffering, patience, perseverance, etc. You know the ones I mean – you might have your own personal list. They are realities that come with living in this world, a world that is tainted by sin, a place where pain and suffering are part of life.

Jesus endured pain and suffering during His time here on earth. The apostle Paul writes a lot about his pain and suffering in the New Testament. Out of our most dire situations, the Lord can bring something beautiful.

On our journey to Bill's healing, God taught us about this ripple effect from Romans 5. I watched Bill go through these phases: suffering producing perseverance, perseverance (patience) producing character, and character, hope. It was the hope that we can only find in Jesus, a hope that never fades, it is ours both now and for eternity. What a blessing to be married to a man that submitted to the Master's hand and trusted God through the most difficult parts of his journey.

As I follow Jesus on this Glory Road, the Lord is teaching me new lessons on this path. There are lessons that can only be learned in the "doing" of them. It's like learning how to ride a bike. You can watch YouTube videos or watch someone else, but the only way that YOU can master it, is by getting on that bicycle and doing it. I'm learning how to "ride a bike" again.

Have you been able to see beyond your pain and suffering to the place where God is making something beautiful out of the challenges of your life?

My encouragement is found in God and His assurance in the Bible. "I lift up my eyes to the mountains, where does my help come from? My help comes from the Lord, Maker of heaven and earth." (Psalm 121:1-2 NIV)

Thank you for your encouragement. #Godisfaithful #TheGloryRoad

Day #100 July 28

Anchor Verse: 1 Corinthians 13:7
It's not important who does the planting, or who does the watering. What's important is that God makes the seed grow. (NLT)

What a great reminder that we work together as a team and it doesn't matter who gets the credit. All we do and say should bring honor and glory to the Lord. It is for His honor and glory that we live, move, and have our being.

There are grandmothers and grandfathers whose sole purpose in their retirement is to pray and tarry in the Lord's presence. I can see God nodding His head in approval as they humbly come into His presence, not asking for themselves but for those who need a healing touch or provision or those wandering in the darkness that they would find the light.

This morning I am so grateful for those who have prayed for me over my lifetime which has allowed God to move and do such incredible things for me, in me, and through me. To be a vessel of honor for God is the highest calling, the highest privilege I can imagine.

I am not the best gardener in the world when it comes to "real" plants… honestly, I have a black thumb. God has honed my skills to be a "spiritual gardener" instead where my true joy lies.

On our journey to Bill's healing, we had a vast team to help Bill that was led by the Great Physician. We never tried to attribute a particular success to a particular person or procedure, but we knew that God was working "all things together for Bill's good." Thank you, Lord.

Now as I find my way on this Glory Road, so much of this path is through territory I have never seen before. It is foreign land to me, but I know that even here, the Lord is with me, He is guiding my path for good and for His glory. So grateful to be a part of God's team with you.

Thank you for praying. It's been 100 days since Bill went to heaven. When I am weak, He is strong. #Godisfaithful #TheGloryRoad

Day #101 July 29

Anchor Verse: Psalm 50:15
Call on me in the day of trouble; I will deliver you, and you will honor me. (NIV)

The Lord tells us to call on Him in the day of trouble. We don't need to beg God to listen to us or expect He will turn a deaf ear when we call but rather we have an invitation to come. And more than an invitation, we have His promise that He will rescue or deliver us.

That fills me with hope in the challenges we face, we are NEVER alone in our battles. When the world around us is so chaotic and that chaos leaks into our spirits, God is reminding us that He is the solid rock, unshakable and unmovable. Our heavenly Father is for us and not against us.

There is a second part to this "rescue" operation; it is the duty or responsibility that we have in response to this gift. The Passion translation puts it this way, "Honor me by trusting in me in your day of trouble." We are to honor and glorify the Lord in thought, word, and deed.

On the journey to Bill's healing, we had the opportunity to put our trust in God, to remember His faithfulness on the path behind us and know that because His promises are forever true that we could trust Him on the path ahead. Every day we gave thanks to the Lord for His work in Bill's life, not only when God rescued Bill in health situations. As we honored God, He drew us closer to Him.

On the Glory Road, I am blessed with the opportunity to trust God, and yes, cry out to Him to rescue me in times of trouble. The God of Abraham, Isaac, and Jacob is the same God who knows me, provides for me, and has great plans for me and I praise His holy name.

Obedience brings life, not only for me, but for others. Your obedience to the Lord is a sweet aroma that rises to His throne room of grace. In His presence, we find the fullness of His joy. In God's presence, we find the peace that passes all understanding as it guards our hearts and minds.

Thank you for your love and prayers. #Godisfaithful #TheGloryRoad

Day #102 July 30

Anchor Verse: Psalm 51:15

O Lord, open my lips, that my mouth may declare Your praise. (AMP)

What the heart is full of comes out of our mouth. If your heart is full of joy and thanksgiving, you will speak encouraging words and life to yourself and others. If your heart is filled with negativity and darkness, you will suck the air out of the room when you speak.

Psalm 51 is a psalm of confession and repentance by King David after he committed adultery with Bathsheba. Nathan the prophet brings it to David's attention and the ramifications of his sin from a spiritual perspective. King David runs to the Lord and declares in verse 4, "against You, You only have I sinned and done what is evil in Your sight." "Create in me a clean heart, O God and renew a right spirit within me." (Isaiah 51:10)

David doesn't try and justify his actions. He admits and confesses that they are wrong and that he wants to be restored to a right relationship with God.

Only after David has mended the fence, so to speak, can he once again declare God's praise.

Praising the Lord comes from a heart that is tuned into the Lord and His word. Otherwise, it is only lip service, the words are hollow and filled with dust, not life.

On our journey to Bill's healing, we recognized that it was through our praise that God could move on our behalf. Instead of focusing on what had been taken away by an illness, we choose to be tucked in with the Lord and asked to see things from His perspective. That is how we could speak joy, live in joy, and sing praises to His name in the middle of the storm.

The Glory Road is filled with opportunities to navigate the potholes and swampland and to find joy in the journey, even when life in this Covid season would seek to steal our joy and silence our voices of praise.

When my heart is overwhelmed, as it has been in recent days, I run to the Lord and empty my heart before Him, and ask that He would restore my peace and fill me with joy. When we abide with the Lord and are firmly rooted, like a tree that bends, but doesn't break, when the winds of adversity come, then we will not break.

Thank you for your prayers that lift me up to higher ground. #Godisfaithful #TheGloryRoad

Day #103 July 31

Anchor Verse: Psalm 55:23
But I will [boldly and unwaveringly] trust in You. (AMP)

Who do you trust? How do they earn your trust? The definition of trust according to the Merriam Webster's dictionary is the assured reliance on the character, ability, strength, or truth of someone or something.

To earn someone's trust is one of the highest compliments another person can give you. Trust is a "gift" that is not quickly distributed to others. It's not "free" for all.

When it comes to trust, God's character doesn't allow Him to be one way and then another. When God makes a promise, He carries it out. When God says, I will never leave you or forsake you, He means it.

Psalm 55:23 in the Amplified version is so powerful, "But I will [boldly and unwaveringly]trust in You!"

Boldly and unwaveringly means there is no reservation when it comes to trusting God. In my mind's eye, I see a warrior advancing on the battlefield knowing beyond a shadow of a doubt that he will be victorious. There is no other position. Failure and defeat are not even an option.

On our journey to Bill's healing, God proved over and over again that He could be trusted. Boldly and unwaveringly, with our hands in God's hand, we faced adversity, the refining fire, difficult medical diagnosis, and even "lions" in the lion's den like Daniel. And every time, God was there. Always we could trust Him with that day and with all of our tomorrows.

Now as I find my way on the Glory Road, one of my greatest "weapons" is my trust in God. Trusting God means that I don't have to worry about what is happening in the world around me, because everything that happens is filtered through His fingers of love. Even when difficulties arise, I run to my heavenly Father, and together we face life boldly and unwaveringly. My help comes in the name of the Lord, Maker of heaven and earth. (Psalm 121:2) The name of the Lord is a strong tower and I run to Him and I am safe. (Proverbs 18:10) I cannot imagine life without God.

Thank you for boldly walking beside us. #Godisfaithful #TheGloryRoad

August 2020

I can do all things through Christ.
~ Philippians 4:13

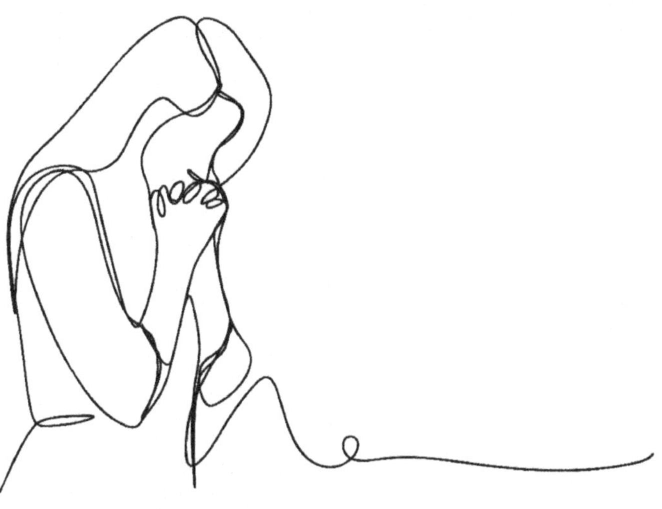

Day #104 August 1

Anchor Verse: Psalm 59:17
You are my strength, I sing praise to you; you, God, are my fortress, my God on whom I can rely. (NIV)

It's a brand new month filled with new mercies and new opportunities to see the goodness of the Lord in the land of the living.

This morning declare with me that God is your strength. I will sing praise to You, God, for You are my fortress. He is my God on whom I can rely.

God is our strength, our fortress, the one on whom we can rely. In a time when the world is still in chaos, it is such a blessing to know that God is unshakable, unmovable, and unstoppable.

Is God your strength this morning? Do you know that He is a fortress where you can run and be safe and protected from the storms of life?

On this journey to Bill's healing, it was only in the presence of God that we found our strength. When the world was filled with uncertainty, together at home or even in the hospital, we would run to the Lord and find refuge in God. In our home, the peace that passes all understanding could be found in His presence. Thank you, Lord.

As we enter a new month, the eighth month of 2020, as I walk the Glory Road, my hand is firmly placed in the hand of God. My trust is in God and God alone. Every day I believe that God will intervene on my behalf, and yours, and that soon this upside-down world will be turned right side up.

August is Bill's birthday month. He would have been 77 this year. So I am celebrating his life and his legacy including releasing a book with Mr. Bill's words of wisdom and words of hope later this month on his birthday.

Lord, thank you that You are our strength, our refuge, the one we can rely on. We sing praises to Your name this morning because You are so good to us. May we keep our eyes fixed on You, Lord, and You alone.

Thank you for being a prayer warrior. #Godisfaithful #TheGloryRoad

Day #105 August 2

Anchor Verse: *Deuteronomy 8:7*
For the LORD your God is bringing you into a good land – a land with brooks, streams, and deep springs gushing out into the valleys and hills. (NIV)

The first half of 2020 has felt like a dry desert where many have grown weak and weary in the battle. As we have been at home and isolated, we have learned some valuable lessons.

We need each other. We need human contact and interaction because God created us to enhance each other's lives. Anyone else feeling like you've been on a forced march across the Sahara desert?

The great news about our heavenly Father is that He never leaves us alone. The God who created you is also the God who sustains you. You are not like a wind-up toy that is set in motion to walk out your path until you run out of energy. God knows your every breath, your every heartbeat, and He delights to hear your laughter.

Reading this passage in Deuteronomy 8:7, I felt the refreshing of the Lord pouring over me. "For the LORD your God is bringing you into a good land – a land with brooks, streams, and deep springs gushing out into the valleys and hills." This is God's promise to us. We WILL come out of this dry season of our souls and the Way Maker will lead us into a good land – a land with brooks, streams, and deep springs "gushing" out into the valleys and hills. No water shortage in that land.

This outpouring is not only for the land, but for our body, mind, and spirit. May we find that rest and refreshing this day.

On our journey to Bill's healing, we went through some desert places. There were days in the eyes of man where there wasn't much progress, but God had a different perspective. The seed that had been buried (Bill) was not dead instead new life was sprouting up within him. What a blessing to watch God, the Master Gardener, at work.

As we enter August, I am entering a new season on the Glory Road. God is doing a new thing in me. As I submit to His pruning, as He cuts those branches that need to be removed so that greater life will come from me, I choose to trust Him in the process. Jesus bought my life back for me. I have eternal life with Him, starting right now.

Thank you for your faithful prayers. #Godisfaithful #TheGloryRoad

Day #106 August 3

Anchor Verse: Habakkuk 1:5
The Lord replied: "Look, and be amazed! You will be astounded at what I am about to do! For I am going to do something in your own lifetime that you will have to see to believe." (TLB)

We are living in a time in which we are seeing events that seemed impossible. Who would have thought on New Year's Day that we would be facing a world-wide pandemic that would have us isolated at home for months? Our world has been turned upside down. We are facing not only an "enemy" that has attacked us with physical symptoms but emotionally, mentally, economically, and even spiritually we have been at "war" for months.

Be of good cheer! The Lord is with us. Even when we see a landscape littered with casualties, God sees opportunity to provide new hope to many.

John 14:8 says, "Philip said, "Lord, show us the Father, and we will be satisfied." We long to have stability in times of instability. We are creatures of habit and when the structure of our lives is rickety like an old stepladder, we start to worry.

"Look, and be amazed! You will be astounded at what I am about to do! For I am going to do something in your own lifetime that you will have to see to believe." (Habakkuk 1:5)

On our journey to Bill's healing, there were places that from a human perspective looked scary at first glance, and then the Lord said, "Come with me, and let's look at this from a heavenly perspective." His thoughts are so much greater than our thoughts, and His ways than our ways. We can trust Him with today and tomorrow.

In these early days of August, 2020, I stand on the crest of a hill. I see a winding road and my destination is cloaked in clouds. There are places that are dry and flat, and others, that are bumpy and look challenging.

With my staff in hand, I take the next step and I put my trust in God, who is faithful. His promises are true. My heavenly Father loves me so much that I know that what lies ahead of me is filled with His blessings even in the challenging places.

Thank you for your encouragement. #Godisfaithful #TheGloryRoad

Day #107 August 4

Anchor Verse: Psalm 66:16
Come and hear, all who fear God [and worship Him with awe-inspired reverence and obedience], and I will tell what He has done for me. (NIV)

Telling our stories about what the Lord has done in our lives is more important than ever before in our lifetime because we need to be encouraged. In a world where we are isolated as never before, we need to be connected through the power of God.

We will not find our comfort from statistics and headlines that speak of the latest horrific things that have happened or storms that are on the horizon. We find our hope in the name of the Lord.

As I scroll through my Facebook newsfeed and see the many needs, I am grateful to find a balance through the "fun" things that people are finding to do like walks and playtime with their puppies, and creative ways to stay connected.

Focusing on the positive brings life and hope, while focusing on the negative tears us down even more. Research has found that focusing on the positive actually helps to boost our immune systems. Let's focus on the positive.

On our journey to Bill's healing, we were blessed with so many opportunities to share what God did in our lives, and those opportunities continue. The legacy of the "Miracle Man" continues, not only daily on Facebook, but a new book will be released in a few weeks, highlighting Bill's path through Bill's words and conversations with God.

Walking on the Glory Road, opportunities to tell the story of Bill's journey of faith continue to unfold. It's also an opportunity for me to share God's faithfulness in this new season of my life. The transition from wife to widow, full-time caregiver to living life alone in a pandemic world, and listening to God's voice in the silence have been a few opportunities to see God's mighty, loving hand at work in my life.

Thank you for your persistent prayers. #Godisfaithful #TheGloryRoad

Day #108 August 5

Anchor Verse: 3 John 2

Dear friend, I am praying that all is well with you and that your body is as healthy as I know your soul is. (TPT)

Our perspective determines our reality. It's not only the "facts" of our lives that define the path we take but how we respond to them.

In our early years, we don't let a bump or bruise or skinned knee slow us down. One expression is "rub some dirt on it" and we keep on going.

Maybe we need to adopt that kind of attitude. There are some health issues that cannot be fixed with some mud or a Band-Aid, it's far more serious. But what we can "fix" is our attitude about the trials we face, especially our expectations, our outlook on life. Will we live in fear or walk in faith?

"Dear friend, I am praying that all is well with you and that your body is as healthy as I know your soul is." (3 John 2)

Do you have a "healthy soul" this morning? That is the foundation of an overcoming life.

On our journey to Bill's healing, the condition of our soul was strengthened on the solid rock of Jesus, where God continued to restore and rebuild Bill's physical health. As Bill pressed into the Lord, and grew in intimacy with his heavenly Father, God renewed Bill's strength. And the conversations Bill had with God were amazing. I learned a lot about soul health and body health on our journey.

Now as I enter new territory on the Glory Road, in the middle of this pandemic season, my first responsibility, my first fighting position is to make sure that my soul is in good health and that comes from reading the Bible and listening to the Lord speak to me.

What a blessing to feel and watch and know that as my soul prospers so will my body's good health. Reading Psalm 91 and being reminded that God's angels surround me to protect me and lead me and guide me. I don't need to fear. I need to be wise, but not fearful.

Thank you for tending to your own soul's health so God can use you. #Godisfaithful #TheGloryRoad

Day #109 August 6

Anchor Verse: Psalm 70:5
But I am in deep trouble. Rush to my aid, for only you can help and save me. O Lord, don't delay. (TLB)

Are you in trouble this morning – deep trouble?

There is only one effective place to run and this to the Lord. David knew that. "Only you can help and save me."

I find it interesting that David, the author of this psalm, uses both "help" and "save" in this passage. I think it speaks to the level of help that we need.

The picture that came to mind is someone wandering through a wooded area that has lost their sense of direction and is crying out for help. When they get reoriented or with a small amount of help, they can find their way back to safety without injury.

However, if they have gotten stuck in "quicksand" or fallen and are hurt, they need someone to "save" them – they are beyond helping themselves. Without the "complete" help of another, they could perish. In either case, David says, "O Lord, don't delay." It's like a heavenly 911 call.

On our journey to Bill's healing, there were many times when we were in deep trouble. Even now as I think about it, my heart beats faster, and my pulse rate increases. But God was always so faithful. In those times when I needed to call 911 for immediate help, my first cry was a "heavenly" 911 call at the same time I was reaching for my phone. Don't be afraid to ask for help in your time of need, God hears the cries of your heart.

The Glory Road is not always "glorious" as in care-free or without trouble. However, it is ALWAYS filled with God's glory. Some of you who have been with me on this journey since the beginning (January 10, 2018) know that there were critical times when we needed God desperately and He heard our cries and your prayers.

Every day I receive direction and protection from the Lord. He is near to the broken-hearted and saves those who are crushed in spirit. (Psalm 34:18) My soul finds rest in God alone. (Psalm 62:1) Surely goodness and mercy will follow me ALL the days of my life and I will dwell in the house of the Lord forever. (Psalm 23:6)

Thank you for speaking hope into my life. #Godisfaithful #TheGloryRoad

Day #110 August 7

Anchor Verse: Psalm 73:28
But as for me, it is good for me to draw near to God; I have made the Lord GOD my refuge and placed my trust in Him, That I may tell of all Your works. (AMP)

But as for me…

There are times in our lives when we need to make a decision about what is best for us as God gives us revelation. It may not line up with what other people think, but God is whom we need to please.

"But as for me, it is good for me to draw near to God." Yes, it is! God is my shelter in the storm. He is my refuge and strength, an ever-present help in time of trouble. In James 4:8 it says, "Draw near to the Lord and He will draw near to you."

God who created the whole universe wants to have a close relationship with you. That is a far greater honor than a relationship with any person on earth. There is no greater treasure.

The psalmist goes on to say, "I have made the Lord God my refuge and placed my trust in Him." In this pandemic season that has spanned a significant part of 2020, many have been seeking refuge from the virus and the other turbulence that has pursued us. It has been a relentless battle.

This passage from Psalm 73 tells us that the psalmist has made the Lord God his refuge AND placed his trust in God. It's the double blessing. Not only do you find safety and refuge, but God is trustworthy. He will never let you down. God loves to talk with you but He doesn't share your innermost thoughts with others. Your heavenly Father is with you day and night, in the good times and the challenges.

On our journey to Bill's healing, we learned how to better draw near to God, both individually and as a couple. God was our safe place as we ran to Him for shelter in the storm or needed someone to rejoice with when we celebrated a victory. Bill and me and God – we were an unbeatable trio.

As I continue on the Glory Road, God is still my refuge, the place I run and know that I am safe. And trusting God, it's the best position to take; it's the only smart thing to do.

Thank you for trusting the Lord and crying out to Him on our behalf. #Godisfaithful #TheGloryRoad

Day #111 August 8

Anchor Verse: Psalm 74:13
It was you who split open the sea by your power. (NIV)

Lord God Almighty, Maker of heaven and earth – He is my heavenly Father.

How often do you think about how powerful God is? Not only did He create the world in six days and rested on the seventh day but His mighty power is evident every day of our lives.

Often we read of the miracle of the parting of the Red Sea and how the children of Israel walked through on dry ground, but take a minute and think about it.

Gallons and gallons of water rose up out of its place of rest to form unimaginable high walls of water that hundreds of thousands of men, women and children walked through on dry ground. He is the same God who is with you in your pain and suffering. He watched over you last night, whether you were sleeping or awake. If you were calculating your next business move or crying out to Him in intercessory prayer because of a friend or loved one's needs.

On the journey to Bill's healing, the God of power met us at many turns. If we needed a door opened that seemed to be closed, nailed shut, God made a way where there seemed to be no way. God is so faithful.

As I walk on the Glory Road, I am fascinated by new sights and sounds. Sometimes when I hear strange noises in the bushes or like on a camping trip, the wild animals calling out to each other in the dark, and I am afraid of what I can't see, I am reminded that I serve a God of power. He is my shield and defender. Nothing is too hard for Him, nothing! The problems in my life are never too much to handle – never!

What about you? Do know God as a God of power? Do you understand that because of His love for you, He will fight for you? God sent His only son Jesus to lay down His life for you, to pay the price for your sins so you might have eternal life and live forever in heaven with Him.

When life seems too overwhelming, your pain level too high, your financial distress too great, remember His love for you is even greater than His power. God will contend against those who contend against you. God always wins.

Thank you for sharing your strength. #Godisfaithful #TheGloryRoad

Day #112 August 9

Anchor Verse: Psalm 78:32
Even when they saw God's marvels (miracles), they refused to believe God could care for them. (TPT)

"I need to see it with my own eyes before I will believe."

How many times have you said this or heard someone else say it? We often think of Doubting Thomas, one of Jesus' disciples when we hear this phrase. Thomas wasn't there when Jesus first appeared to the disciples after His resurrection. John 20:25 says, "So the other disciples told him, "We have seen the Lord!" But he said to them, "Unless I see the nail marks in his hands and put my finger where the nails were, and put my hand into his side, I will not believe."

One week later, Jesus appeared to the disciples again and Thomas was there. In verse 27 it says, "Then he (Jesus) said to Thomas, "Put your finger here; see my hands. Reach out your hand and put it into my side. Stop doubting and believe."

Thomas believed in that moment. Jesus continued and said that blessed are those who have not seen and yet have believed.

Faith is trusting God even when you cannot see. When you don't have all the answers or you are going through a difficult time, yet you trust God that His best for you will come to pass.

On our journey to Bill's healing, we saw God's marvels and miracles, Bill and I both believed that God would care for us. And caring for us didn't always mean that we would see the outcome we hoped for or expected. Our help and hope came in the name of the Lord, Maker of heaven and earth. God could always be trusted. I still believe that today.

Walking on the Glory Road in this new season of my life in the midst of this pandemic, God often appears in unexpected ways or unexpected places. My hand is securely in His hand, my ears are tuned to His voice, and my eyes are set on the hills where my help comes from. He does not slumber or sleep, God's eyes are always on you and me, my friend.

Thank you for being His hands and feet. #Godisfaithful #TheGloryRoad

Day #113 August 10

Anchor Verse: Luke 7:13
When the Lord saw her (the grieving mother), his heart broke for her. With great tenderness he said to her, "Please don't cry." (TPT)

The tears may be fresh on your pillow and your eyes are red. You're looking for some eye drops so you look like "you have your act together."

There are seasons in our life where tears communicate what words cannot. We often hear the expression that "a picture is worth a thousand words." An artist can capture on canvas not only the facts surrounding a situation but capture the emotions behind it.

In Luke 7, Jesus, His disciples, and a large crowd are entering the town of Nain when they meet a funeral procession. The only son of a widow woman has died, and his mother and a large crowd from the town are going to bury him. Verse 13 says, "When the Lord saw the grieving mother, his heart broke for her. With great tenderness he said to her, "Please don't cry."

Jesus' heart broke for her, a woman who was a stranger, yet her circumstances moved His heart with compassion. With great tenderness, Jesus tells her not to cry.

Then Jesus takes action, His words were not the end of His empathy. Jesus approaches the funeral bier, touches the man, and says, "Young man, I say to you, get up!" In the next verse it says, "The dead man sat up and began to talk, and Jesus gave him back to his mother."

He turned the most devastating moment in this mother's life into a day of rejoicing. My heart was touched by Jesus' actions, "His heart broke for her." But greater still when He took action to relieve her pain.

On our journey to Bill's healing, there were times when my tears flowed freely. I remember a moment when Bill said, "You're lucky that you can cry. I was taught that crying was a sign of weakness." My tears accelerated as he shared that truth with me. Even Jesus wept when His friend, Lazarus, died.

As I find my way on this new path, the Glory Road, there have been sections of the road that have been watered by my tears. They are not all tears of sorrow and grief; they are mixed with tears of joy and gratitude. The day that Bill died, the Lord told me to let the tears flow and not hold them back. God catches our tears, they are a language He understands.

Thank you for your persistent prayers. #Godisfaithful #TheGloryRoad

Day #114 August 11

Anchor Verse: Psalm 84:5

Happy (Blessed) are those who are strong in the Lord, who want above all else to follow your steps. (TLB)

Our walk with the Lord is the ultimate adventure, the ultimate pilgrimage as we seek to follow in His steps.

Through the Bible and its instruction, the Lord sheds light on our pathway and asked us to follow Him, walking in obedience to His commands. It is the path to life – to hope and to healing.

When we wander off into the swampland or the wilderness or that side road that looked so enticing, we find ourselves stuck in a thicket of trouble. We find our strength in the Lord. That's great news!

It's easy to find yourself drained of energy when you get sucked into the chaos of the world. Instead we are called to rise above it and follow in Jesus' steps, which is where our strength comes from.

The Message translation paints a beautiful picture of this path, "And how blessed all those in whom you live, whose lives become roads you travel; They wind through lonesome valleys, come upon brooks, discover cool springs and pools brimming with rain! God-traveled, these roads curve up the mountain, and at the last turn – Zion! God in full view!"(Psalm 84:5-7)

On our journey to Bill's healing, we found our strength in the Lord even as we traveled dusty roads and desert places. What a blessing to find those cool springs and pools brimming with rain from the Lord's favor and His grace, mercy, and peace. God's love offered a steady stream of hope into our hearts every day of our journey.

Now as I continue on my pilgrimage on the Glory Road, my eyes are open looking for Jesus' footsteps, the places where I can plant my feet securely without faltering. There is such joy in His presence and refreshing at those pools of living water. I can't imagine life without Jesus at my side. I carry the memories of my beloved husband in my heart and my mind, and they spur me onward as I hear Bill often say, "That's my girl."

Thank you for praying without ceasing. #Godisfaithful #TheGloryRoad

Day #115 August 12

Anchor Verse: Psalm 35:4-5
Humiliate those who seek my harm. Defeat them all! Frustrate their plans to defeat me and drive them back. Disgrace them all as they have devised their plans to disgrace me. Blow them away like dust in the wind, with the Angel of Almighty God driving them back! (TPT)

If you are feeling discouraged this morning, like the whole world is against you and they are winning the battle, you need to read this powerful passage from Psalm 35:1-10 in the Passion translation.

As believers, we know that we are in the middle of a spiritual battle as we live in this world. It's not only what our eyes can "see" in the physical realm but it's the powers of good and evil at work behind the scenes that cause so much chaos and destruction in this world.

David, who wrote this psalm, is crying out to the Lord to fight for him. In verse 1, it says, "O Lord, fight for me! Harass the hecklers, accuse my accusers. Fight those who fight against me." David knows that the Lord can bring victory over his enemies, those who are relentlessly pursuing him.

Do you ask the Lord to fight for you or do you try and fight your battles alone until you are exhausted and laying on a heap on the floor?

On our journey to Bill's healing, we knew that our hope was in God alone. God was not only the Great Physician who was in charge of Bill's care, Jehovah Rapha, Bill's healer, but Jehovah Gibbor, the Lord Strong and Mighty, Mighty in Battle, was fighting for Bill's life. God had plans for Bill and nothing was going to stop the Lord from helping Bill to fulfill that mission.

As I follow the Glory Road, I encounter new situations, new people, new circumstances, some I know how to deal with and others are new to me. In Psalm 35, David asked the Lord for help, I also ask the Lord to contend for me. "Frustrate their plans to defeat me. Blow them away like dust in the wind, with the Angel of Almighty God driving them back."

Your fears will run at the sound of His voice and His peace will fill your mind and your home. We are victorious in Jesus' name.

Thank you for being part of the army of prayer warriors that have covered us on our journey. #Godisfaithful #TheGloryRoad

Day #116 August 13

Anchor Verse: Ephesians 2:10

For we are God's masterpiece. He has created us anew in Christ Jesus, so we can do the good things he planned for us long ago (in advance). (NLT)

You are God's masterpiece. Did you know that? Maybe the better question is: do you believe it?

In this world filled with chaos, pain, suffering and deception, we need to look away from the landscape that seeks to "suck us in" to the vortex of despair and turn our eyes to heaven where our hope comes from this morning.

Hope is one breath away. Victory is yours with one word, "Jesus."

It's not what we have done that will save us from anxiety, fear, and destruction but it's because of God's mercy and Jesus' sacrifice that we, as a people, will be restored.

We must come to God individually but it is our collective obedience, our collective prayers and petitions prayed in agreement that will move the hand of God.

On our journey to Bill's healing, we saw God move in our lives and Bill's body become God's masterpiece. Bill was made "new" in Christ Jesus and he was able to do the "good things" that God had planned for him in advance, before he was ever born. What a blessing and a joy to walk the path of righteousness that God has planned for us. Not because we are good and holy, but because Jesus is.

This morning as I open my eyes to begin a new day on the Glory Road, I find my hope and confidence in the Lord. Having spent time in God's Word, my soul is feasting on the bread of life and my spirit has been renewed through my prayer time with Him, and with others.

I praise the Lord that He sees me as His masterpiece and I ask the Lord to open my eyes to see myself that way too. That I would not use the world's measuring stick to gauge my progress or worth, but instead I would celebrate that I am a child of the King of kings and the Lord of lords. The Lord is my shepherd. I lack nothing today or any day of my life.

Thank you for being such a gift to me. #Godisfaithful #TheGloryRoad

Day #117 August 14

Anchor Verse: Psalm 89:1

I will sing of the mercies of the LORD forever; with my mouth will I make known Your faithfulness to all generations. (NKJV)

I will sing of the mercies of the Lord forever. There is something powerful about singing.

From the time we are little children, we learn to sing. It may be "new" songs that a child creates from their own imagination or familiar songs like "Jesus Loves Me." Our spirit is lifted when joyful songs come from our heart.

Music sets the tone for an environment. The right song can lift you up or bring you down. The choice is always yours and mine.

The life we live now and the battles we overcome are not only for us. As we tell stories from generations past about what our ancestors did and the hardships they overcame, and how their faith grew through the trials, we have the honor and privilege, and yes, the responsibility, to tell of God's faithfulness.

It's one of the blessings of books. They continue to tell our story long after we are gone from this world. Take a moment and think about your favorite book. Sometimes it is written by a contemporary author but often it is an author that has long passed from this world.

On the journey to Bill's healing, we were so blessed to tell our story of God's faithfulness wherever we went. We sang of the mercies of the Lord. Bill would tell you that he couldn't sing "well." One of his favorite lines was: "The Bible says to make a joyful noise, but my singing is pure agony." Your singing voice might be like that too but God didn't say that your voice needed to be beautiful – you need to be faithful.

April 19, 2020, minutes after Bill went to his heavenly home God put my feet on the Glory Road, a place where I would continue to tell our story and where my story in this new season would be woven into a new tapestry. Always the golden thread of God's faithfulness is present. Always I will sing of the mercies of the Lord and declare His faithfulness. I know that His love will extend to all generations and gladly I will write our story and pass it along to testify of God's goodness.

Thank you for praising God with me. #Godisfaithful #TheGloryRoad

Day #118 August 15

Anchor Verse: Romans 15:4
For whatever was written in earlier times was written for our instruction, so that through endurance and the encouragement of the Scriptures we might have hope and overflow with confidence in His promises. (TPT)

God had you on His mind long before you were even born. Your heavenly Father knew the plans and purposes He had for your life – the amazing surprises and even the challenging crossroads that would test your faith.

Romans 15:4 reminds us that "whatever was written in earlier times was written for our instruction." That's why it is so important to study the Bible and learn from it. As I have shared previously, Pastor Dave often says, "Knowledge is what we learn from our own mistakes, Wisdom is what we learn from the mistakes of others." I will take "wisdom" any day!

Look at the second half of the verse, "so that through <u>endurance</u> and the <u>encouragement</u> of the Scriptures we might have <u>HOPE</u> and <u>overflow</u> with <u>CONFIDENCE</u> in His promises."

Life is not always going to be easy. We will have to endure some hard things and difficult circumstances. As we read the Bible, we see that those who have lived before us had to endure hardship, but we also see God's faithfulness in their lives. Not only faithfulness but they were encouraged as they went.

His purpose is so that we might have hope and "overflow" with confidence in His promises. That's God's promises are true and they are for me and for you.

On our journey to Bill's healing, we leaned on God's promises to support us through the storms of our lives. We had hope every day that God would see us through and we could rejoice in the God of our salvation. Not only were we encouraged by God's Word, but we could encourage others – like you.

As I take new steps on this Glory Road, God is reminding me that His promises weren't only for "us" as a couple. But now as a widow, a woman who seeks to walk in obedience to the Lord, His promises will help me endure all things and overflow with hope and confidence.

Thank you for praying without ceasing. #Godisfaithful #TheGloryRoad

Day #119 August 16

Anchor Verse: Daniel 10:18-19
Again the one who looked like a man touched me and gave me strength. "Do not be afraid, you who are highly esteemed," he said. "Peace! Be strong now; be strong." When he spoke to me, I was strengthened and said, "Speak, my lord, since you have given me strength." (NIV)

Are you lacking in strength? Are you overwhelmed by the world and your circumstances? You are not alone.

Reading the Bible we find stories of those who experienced great trials and hardships. In Daniel, chapter 10, we move past Daniel in the lion's den and the fiery furnace episode with Shadrach, Meshach, and Abednego, and we enter the portion where Daniel is shown visions of the future.

The magnitude of what Daniel saw weakened him. He was overcome by anxiety and sapped of his strength. It sounds like life today.

"Again the one who looked like a man (Gabriel) touched me and gave me strength. "Do not be afraid, you who are highly esteemed," he said. "Peace! Be strong now; be strong." When he spoke to me, I was strengthened and said, "Speak, my lord, since you have given me strength."

The Amplified version identifies the "one who looked like a man" as Gabriel, and it says in verse 18, he touched Daniel and gave him strength. Gabriel also reminded Daniel about how God saw him. Daniel was highly esteemed, greatly beloved, treasured by God, highly valued – God also sees you like this. Now, you can receive the rest of the gift. "Peace. Be strong now: be strong."

On the journey to Bill's healing, we encountered places where we were stripped of our strength – physically, emotionally, and mentally. But when we turned to the Lord, He "touched" us and restored our strength immediately. The joy of the Lord is our strength. We couldn't have survived the journey without God's word and His help.

As I walk forward on the Glory Road, many times my strength was sapped. Mourning for Bill, dealing with the pandemic, and being isolated in so many ways, rebuilding my own physical strength, and learning to navigate life without the one I love at my side. God has NEVER forsaken me. He hears my heart cry, day or night, and my heavenly Father rushes to comfort me.

Thank you for your faithful prayers. #Godisfaithful #TheGloryRoad

Day #120 August 17

Anchor Verse: Psalm 100:2
Serve the Lord with gladness and delight; Come before His presence with joyful singing. (AMP)

Good morning. How's your attitude?

More and more I realize how important our perspective is, our attitude about circumstances and people, what happens to us and the promises we are still waiting to have fulfilled.

Sometimes we get weary in the waiting and then we may not be serving the Lord with "gladness and delight." Our attitude might need a slight adjustment.

His mercies are new every morning and great is God's faithfulness. Repeating God's promises from the Bible can bring us great joy.

When I think about Psalm 100, it reminds me of Sunday morning going to church and entering the Lord's presence with other believers. There is a sweet fellowship in the family of God like no other place on earth.

"Come before His presence with joyful singing!" But that's not only for Sunday mornings – it is God's invitation every moment of every day.

Not only singing, but "joyful" singing! I was talking with someone yesterday about how important praise music is to set the atmosphere in your home or workplace. It really does help.

On our journey to Bill's healing, we weren't always able to gather with church family, but we could always enter the Lord's presence wherever we were – because God is everywhere. Bill was a good example of showing others how to approach life with gladness and delight. It wasn't often that the weight of the world dragged him down. And the joyful singing… it was joyful in his heart, but not always to your ears. (Bill was the first one to admit that fact.)

As I find my way on the Glory Road, there are days I wake up with a song in my heart or if it's been a rough night, then I must "choose" to ask the Lord to fill me with gladness and delight. Our heavenly Father is always ready, willing, and able to infuse us with heavenly joy.

Thank you for your persistent prayers. #Godisfaithful #TheGloryRoad

Day #121 August 18

Anchor Verse: Psalm 102:18
Let this be recorded for future generations, so that a people not yet born will praise the LORD. *(NLT)*

We often speak of our ancestors, those who lived in previous generations, but how often do we focus on generations that haven't been born yet?

Often we tend to be occupied so much by the present that we really don't consider either our past relatives or future great-great-great-great grandchildren.

Our challenge from the psalmist is to record what God is doing in our lives so that future generations, those not yet born will praise the Lord. Are you game?

Revelation 12:11 says, "They triumphed over him by the blood of the Lamb and by the word of their testimony; they did not love their lives so much as to shrink from death." (NIV)

"The word of their testimony" – that is our challenge. We don't need to wait for generations yet to come – we need to share our testimonies now.

At the beginning of our journey to Bill's healing, the Lord directed me to write down what was happening in our lives and how God intervened in so many ways, so many times. As God gave me a fresh word every day to encourage me, I was to share that "daily devotion" with you. That's how the first devotional book, "Our Walk of Faith: The Journey to Bill's Healing" was born.

Now as I walk this new path, the Glory Road, I will have my own story to record and tell of God's faithfulness. In some ways the road will be similar, as I do not have a "trip itinerary" – I don't know the next stop or next assignment. Heaven is my ultimate goal but not for a while, and Google Maps or Siri isn't going to be able to guide me there. That's God's territory, and I am grateful to put that mission in His capable hands.

Look for "one" opportunity to share a blessing. It will improve your day and encourage others – like a rock thrown in the water creates ripples.

Thank you for sharing your testimonies. #Godisfaithful #TheGloryRoad

Day #122 August 19

Anchor Verse: 1 Corinthians 2:4-5

The message I preached and how I preached it was not an attempt to sway you with persuasive arguments but to prove to you the almighty power of God's Holy Spirit. For God intended that your faith not be established on man's wisdom but by trusting in his almighty power. (TPT)

In our lives, there are a lot of "fast talkers" and "slick speeches" hoping to persuade you to buy their product or purchase their services. In years gone by, we often looked at the used car salesman in that light.

It's not only about what we see in the "world" and how we speak and what we share. In the kingdom of God, our commission, our mission is to share the gospel, the good news of Jesus Christ to everyone who has breath. God wants everyone to know of His love for them and how will they know unless we tell them?

This letter to the church at Corinth, written by the apostle Paul, talks about this very topic. It's not about glitzy speech or who has the most facts to back up their argument.

Paul says God intended your faith to be established not on man's wisdom but by trusting in God's almighty power. We are fallible in our humanity. We will always fall short at some time, in some place, with some person – even when our heart is set on getting it right.

On our journey to Bill's healing, we shared our story with many. It was part of God's purpose and plan for this time, this place. You had a bird's eye view of what it looked like to trust in God's almighty power not in man's wisdom. Our trust was rooted firmly in the Lord because we knew on earth we stood on shaky ground, but in heaven's realm, we were on God's solid foundation.

As I take new steps on the Glory Road, God has given me a second chance to trust in His almighty power and not rely on my own wisdom. Second chances are such a gift of God's amazing grace. It's also an opportunity to share that grace with others, and offer to them what we have been given by our heavenly Father. Be lavish as you share His grace with others.

Thank you for pouring some of that strength into me through your prayers. #Godisfaithful #TheGloryRoad

Day #123 August 20

Anchor Verse: Psalm 106:8
Even so You [the Lord] saved them – to defend the honor of Your name and demonstrate Your power to all the world. (TLB)

In the face of God's mighty miracles, often the people rejoiced and then soon forgot what God had done for them. They were bent on going their own way and doing their "own thing."

As a society and individuals, we are guilty of that today.

Throughout this psalm, we are shown what an amazing heavenly Father we have that loves us so much. In verse eight it says, "Even so You [the Lord] saved them – to defend the honor of Your name and demonstrate Your power to all the world."

God looks beyond our failures and He remembers the promises He has made to us. God's love will always shine above the chaos and confusion of the world. He will never stoop to the level of those who drag His name through the mud, or in their blindness, doubt His existence.

The cross at Calvary, the empty cross, continues to stand as a testimony to God's faithfulness to ALL generations, even ours. He will NEVER leave you or forsake you. God will always defend the honor of His name and demonstrate His power to all the world… always!

On our journey to Bill's healing, we were shown the honor and glory of God. He was always there – in the hospital, home, church, or driving on the streets of our city. As we passed through the fires of adversity and the flood of overwhelm, our heavenly Father was always there holding our hands and speaking life and hope to us. His whispers often greeted us in the night hours.

Now as I walk alone on this Glory Road, the cadence is different, yet the same. God's word is a lamp to my feet and a light to my path. The light that shines brightly from the testimony of God's faithfulness in the past spurs me onward to my own victory. I am blessed that my husband's legacy burns brightly in my heart and often his whispers of encouragement, and always Bill's love envelops me.

Thank you for choosing to walk with God in this season, to walk with me. #Godisfaithful #TheGloryRoad

Day #124 August 21

Anchor Verse: Psalm 107:29
He [God] hushed the storm to a gentle whisper, So that the waves of the sea were still. (AMP)

There are times in our lives where it is the contrast that gets our attention.

For example, if someone is "yelling" and you respond in a whisper or quiet voice. In order to hear what you are saying, their decibel level must decrease.

Our world feels like it's in the midst of a continuous storm – hurricane-force winds and tsunami-level waves. The rhetoric of the day inflames like gas poured on a fire rather than the gentle lullaby of a mother singing her baby to sleep.

As believers, we have a choice. We can keep our eyes focused on the Lord and listen to the words of life we find in the Bible. We can choose to make good choices about what we speak and where we spend our time and energy and how that makes our own homes an "oasis" in the desert of life. Individually, we have to make the choice ourselves. God will not make that choice for us.

In Psalm 107:29, we have a beautiful picture of God reaching out to us from heaven and meeting our needs here on earth. "He hushed the storm to a gentle whisper, So that the waves of the sea were still."

As I read this verse, I feel a calmness settle over my spirit. We know what a storm looks like and feels like because we have weathered many of them. However, we have all experienced the calm and stood on the seashore and watched the still waves that brought peace to our souls.

On our journey to Bill's healing, we saw God turn some roaring storms to a "gentle whisper" – by His word. God spoke and nature responded. The winds and the waves still know the sound of His voice – so do you. The change in our circumstances wasn't always instantaneous but the presence of the Lord reminded us that His love would never fail. His peace was available.

The Glory Road has its own storms and places where the waves are still. The Lord is teaching me more about the "weather" and not only in the natural. There will be times in our walk with God when life is stormy and we think we are about to be blown off course or meet our demise. Yet God knows how much we can take, and He will always make a way.

Thank you for praying without ceasing. #Godisfaithful #TheGloryRoad

Day #125 August 22

Anchor Verse: Psalm 112:7
He does not fear bad news, nor live in dread of what may happen. For he is settled in his mind that Jehovah will take care of him. (TLB)

Do you trust God? A little bit or are you willing to hand everything over to Him?

The definition of trust is the "firm belief in the character, strength, or truth of someone or something."

The truth is that God is the only one we can trust completely. And when we trust God this verse in Psalm 112:7 is true. "He does not fear bad news, nor live in dread of what may happen. For he is settled in his mind that Jehovah will take care of him."

For me, the meaning of this verse is even more profound in this pandemic season. For months now, the ongoing saga of our lives lived differently has been dragging on. If it were an "enjoyable" ride, for many of us that would be much easier, but the truth is that life is difficult for a lot of folks. Yet, in the face of discouragement and disappointment, God is there.

Why? Because we have God's promise that He will take care of us. And God doesn't lie – ever!

On our journey to Bill's healing, far before the coronavirus appeared on the scene, Bill and I chose to put our trust in God. We chose not to fear bad news or live in dread of what might happen because when you do that, it steals today's peace and tomorrow's joy.

Your heavenly Father WILL take care of you. Your circumstances may not look like what you expected but life can be dull and boring, if everything is scripted out exactly. Surprises can be good!

Now as I walk on this Glory Road, my stance has not changed. The scenery is different and making decisions alone and navigating new places without Bill as my steady rudder can be challenging at times, but I rely on God's faithfulness. He will NEVER leave me or forsake me. If God hasn't left me in the last two years of this journey, or through the events of 2020, my heavenly Father surely is not going to leave me now.

Thank you for your faithful prayers. #Godisfaithful #TheGloryRoad

Day #126 August 23

Anchor Verse: Proverbs 4:23
Above all else, guard your heart, for everything you do flows from it. (NIV)

"Above all else" – there are multiple things that compete for our attention. From the minute you wake up, and maybe even in your dreams, your mind is at work, processing, thinking, planning… maybe some resting too.

The author of the book of Proverbs reminds us that the most important thing "above all else" is to guard your heart. Not only your physical heart, which is very important about what we eat and managing our stress levels etc., but also the spiritual center of our being.

Our values, our decisions, our actions, our morality all flow from our "heart" and how we choose to live.

If our heart is a "muddy clogged-up stream" nothing good is going to flow from it. In fact, nothing will be able to flow out of it, it's stuck.

Instead the Lord is asking us to tend to our hearts. We are to feast on the Word of God. Read the truth found on its pages. Then we are to rely on God's promises and use them as "planks" to build a solid road through the dangerous waters of life.

We are invited to drink from "springs of living water" to refresh our souls. Psalm 23:3-4 reminds us, "He makes me lie down in green pastures, He leads me beside quiet waters, He restores my soul."

On our journey to Bill's healing, Bill faced challenges with his "physical" heart but we knew that when we tended to our spiritual hearts that our relationship with each other and the Lord would bear much fruit. The fruit of the spirit were seen in our lives: love, joy, peace, patience, kindness, goodness, faithfulness, gentleness, and self-control. (Galatians 5:22)

As I walk the Glory Road, I am learning that my heart needs extra care. Not only do I need to tend to the physical aspects of it, and feed it spiritually, but remember that it is a wounded heart, a grieving heart. And what that means is that I need to be patient with myself as I heal and extend grace to myself and others, because many have wounded hearts in this season.

Jesus is near to the brokenhearted and saves those who are crushed in spirit.

Thank you for your persistent prayers. #Godisfaithful #TheGloryRoad

Day #127 August 24

Anchor Verse: Psalm 118:15
Songs of joy at the news of our rescue are sung in the homes of the godly. The strong arm of the Lord has done glorious things! (TLB)

What we focus on determines our perspective. If we focus on what's wrong, or what's negative, we will see life through that lens. If we look for what's right in the world and the goodness of the Lord, our perspective and our lives are filled with God's light.

Even as I write this, and peek out the window, the darkness of the pre-dawn hours remind me that the earth is still at rest. God has not "turned on the lights" in our neighborhood for this new day. God is here with me. His gentleness and His peace surround me as quiet instrumental music soothes my soul. Time spent in the Word of God, as it fills me with His truth and His promises set my feet on a secure path this morning. As I sit and listen for His voice, in the silence, I can feel our hearts beating together, I know that I am safe in the hollow of His hands and I can be at peace.

For a moment, I recount the joys of this weekend – time spent with family and friends – mostly virtually – but nonetheless seeing their faces and sharing laughter, praying prayers, and telling of the good things the Lord has done for us, still echo through my heart this morning.

On our journey to Bill's healing, what a joy to share with you the many times we were able to sing "songs of joy" as God rescued Bill. The strong arm of the Lord is still fighting our battles and winning victories.

I see God's hand at work like people recovering from an illness, learning to walk again after a long time in bed, babies born, a promotion at work, moving into a new home, celebrating a 5-year-old's birthday, or playing golf with friends. These are the miracles of God. Join me in celebration.

As I begin a new week on the Glory Road, ahead of me on Friday, I see Bill's birthday, the first one without him here on earth. Instead of being overwhelmed by the loss, I will sing songs of joy for what the Lord is doing in my life. I look forward to the birthday surprise on Friday and the amazing way God has chosen to honor Bill's legacy.

Yes, I mourn Bill's loss. We all are mourning something or someone, but the Lord is challenging us to not be overcome by despair. Choose joy.

Thank you for celebrating our joy. #Godisfaithful #TheGloryRoad

Day #128 August 25

Anchor Verse: Psalm 119:11
Your word I have hidden in my heart, that I might not sin against You. (NJKV)

The Bible is the Word of God written down and passed along to generation after generation. The most widely distributed book and translated into many languages, the power of the Word of God never diminishes; it grows stronger.

Many of us were blessed to start reading the Bible or having it read to us at a young age. As we matured and grew up, we were able to read it on our own. As adults, the Lord continues to give us revelation and understanding through the Bible, the living, breathing Word of God.

It never grows stale, like day-old bread. In fact, there is new life each day. Fresh bread every morning! That brings back memories from my grandmother's kitchen – what a lovely aroma.

This verse reminds us that we need to "hide" God's word in our hearts. It's a treasure that needs to be kept in a safe place. What is hidden in our hearts is what fuels us in our trials and our challenges. The provisions we have stored are what will sustain us.

On our journey to Bill's healing, I was so blessed to be able to speak words of life over Bill while he was fighting for his life in ICU units. It was God's Word that was hidden in my heart that flowed out of me like a river of living water. Not only was Bill's soul refreshed, but so were my soul and my faith.

As I see new scenery on the Glory Road, one thing remains the same, the Word of God that is hidden in my heart. God's Word still encourages me and challenges me. I find new revelation about who God is and who I am in Christ. The old is gone, behold, the new has come.

God's Word also acts as a guardrail for us. In the last part of the verse it reminds us why we hide God's Word in our heart, so that we won't sin against God. If Bible memorization is new to you, start with something simple, like Psalm 23. There is power in the Word of God. Tap into that power.

Thank you for your walk of obedience.. #Godisfaithful #TheGloryRoad

Day #129 August 26

Anchor Verse: 1 Corinthians 8:1
Knowledge [alone] makes [people self-righteously] arrogant, but love [that unselfishly seeks the best for others] builds up and encourages others to grow [in wisdom]. (AMP)

"Knowledge puffs up" – that's what it says in the New International Version.

The visual image that comes to mind is a cartoon character filled with hot air… and we all know what's about to happen – a big burst.

There are times in our lives when we gather knowledge and information and we can get a little "big for our britches" is an old-fashioned term I remember.

Oftentimes this happens in academia, like college or an advanced degree, when we are being fed lots of great information and we begin to swell up.

I speak from personal experience when I think back to my college days. After you get out of high school and you are now at a university learning all this great stuff, you think you're pretty smart. But as the Bible reminds us, "pride comes before the fall." We often called it the "ivory tower" syndrome that separated us from life in the "real" world. Once you leave the doors of academia, you discover that maybe you're not quite as smart, at least in a practical sense, as you thought you were.

On our journey to Bill's healing, Bill's path was lined with opportunities to let the light and love of Jesus shine in and through him. Bill's kindness and courage even in the midst of difficult, often life-threatening situations, was a picture of God's grace and love and mercy in action. My friends, we learned quickly, it's not about "you" rather it's all about God at work in you. We are a blank canvas for Him to illustrate His love for others to see.

Now as I navigate the Glory Road, I am blessed with opportunities to love others as I have been loved, to speak words of life into those who are weary, and to comfort those who mourn as I have been comforted by Jesus. In humility, I thank God for the gift of His love and the opportunity to liberally share that love with others.

Thank you for your encouraging words. Thank you for your faithful prayers. #Godisfaithful #TheGloryRoad

Day #130 August 27

Anchor Verse: 1 Corinthians 9:24
Do you not know that in a race all the runners run, but only one gets the prize? Run in such a way as to get the prize. (NIV)

Run to win! That's the way the New Living Translation spells it out.

I'm not an athlete, but we each have a race to run, it's called life. My husband wasn't an athlete either, but what I do remember about Bill was that anything that he started to do, he gave it his best effort, all his energy. During a time of health or a time of sickness, the spirit within him, the God of hope within him, gave Bill the courage, drive, and bravery necessary to run the race to win.

In the Spokane area, we host a huge event called Bloomsday, a timed 12K road race that has been an annual event since 1977. What started out as a race with 1200 runners has blossomed into an event with over 50,000 participants who run, jog, walk, push children in strollers, even wheelchair participants take on Doomsday Hill.

Each person who participates prepares themselves for the race, whether that means actually training for such a long run or only signing up, but they have to make a commitment before the day of the race. When they show up, their plan is to finish, not stop part way through and raise a white flag in surrender. It's the same way in our walk of faith. We run to finish the race and win the prize. Jesus is at our side to encourage us and cheer us on.

On our path to Bill's healing, there were countless opportunities to trust the Lord with Bill's healing and Bill putting forth his best efforts to finish the race and collect the prize. We trusted the medical professionals that God brought into our lives, but ultimately our trust was in God and God alone.

As I pass new landmarks on the Glory Road, I continue to run my race to win the prize. God is calling me to give my best efforts in everything I do – leave nothing on the table, but do it all for the glory of God. What an honor and privilege to be part of the Lord's army, to be His hands and feet in service to others in need.

One of the races God called me to run was to write a book in Bill's honor and have it completed by Bill's birthday, tomorrow, August 28, 2020. God was very specific about the content and how to make it happen, I needed to follow His lead.

Thank you for running this race with me. #Godisfaithful #TheGloryRoad

Day #131 August 28

Anchor Verse: 1 Corinthians 12:31
But now let me show you a way of life that is best of all. (NLT)

Have you ever noticed that some of the greatest treasures of life are tucked in places that often get overlooked? There are treasures that are hiding in plain sight on your desk or kitchen counter or junk drawer.

This "jewel" is tucked in at the end of 1 Corinthians 12 as we launch into the Love Chapter, 1 Corinthians 13.

Paul says in spite of all this wonderful discussion we had about spiritual gifts, we need to talk about love, "but now let me show you a way of life that is best of all."

Love is on my mind. It is the day my dear husband was born, 77 years ago. Today I am celebrating his birthday without him. I have mixed emotions. There is the gaping hole of loss because I loved him so much, and also an opportunity to honor Bill, his life, and legacy.

On our journey to Bill's healing, we learned a lot about love. True love, unselfish love is far deeper than a romantic gesture or romance novel. Our love had God in the middle of it and it was the most beautiful love story I have ever lived. Love is what sustained us through the white rapids of life. Love allowed us to smile in the face of death and find joy where others only saw sorrow.

The Glory Road is paved with our love. The legacy of our love and God's love for me move my feet forward every day to the future and hope God has for me. In the early days of this new path, God whispered to me that He had plans for Bill's first birthday in heaven.

This day a book is born to honor Bill's legacy using Bill's words to describe his journey and liberally laced with the Word of God to point others to the hope that is only found in Jesus.

"Musings of the Miracle Man: Words of Wisdom Words of Hope" is my love gift to Bill and our love gift to you.

Please join me and Bill as the footprints we leave behind are footprints of God's love.

Thank you for sowing love into our lives. #Godisfaithful #TheGloryRoad

Day #132 August 29

Anchor Verse: Psalm 126:3

The LORD has done great things for us, and we are filled with joy. (NIV)

Good morning! The Lord has done great things for us, and we are filled with joy. Are you filled with joy? You should be.

Psalm 126 is calling its readers to remember what the Lord has done for them. In verse 1, it says that the Lord returned the fortunes of Zion and we were like those who dreamed. They were so happy that their mouths were filled with laughter and their tongues with songs of joy.

Not only did the people of Israel know of the great things that God did for them, but "All the nations saw it and joined in, saying, 'The Lord has done great miracles for them!'" (Psalm 126:2 TPT) The great things, the miracles God does for us are not for us to hoard but rather to share.

On our journey to Bill's healing, we were blessed with the opportunity to share what the Lord did for us, the mighty miracles He did in Bill's life. We were also blessed to share that joy with you along with the weight of our journey. At pivotal points, the Lord turned our mourning into dancing, and took away our mourning clothes and clothed us with joy.

Now as I find my new footing on the Glory Road, it is an honor and privilege to choose joy and to speak of the good things the Lord is doing in my life. Isn't it often about our perspective, not only the facts? One thing I remember from our journey was in the early days after Bill's brain bleed and surgery, Bill later shared with me that he was "blind" for about 6 weeks, all he could see were shadows. He could hear my voice and would turn toward me and that was how he marked his days.

We had no idea because Bill couldn't communicate with us. But this is the most profound part, Bill said he wasn't sure about the quality of life we would have, but he was alive and we had each other and that was enough. It still makes me cry as I type this.

We whine and moan about such trivial things in comparison to this, yet Bill found joy, he had hope and appreciated the gift of life even in those circumstances. Lord, forgive us for the things we complain about that really don't matter much in the whole scheme of things.

Thank you for choosing joy in every circumstance. #Godisfaithful #TheGloryRoad

Day #133 August 30

Anchor Verse: Ruth 4:15

May he restore your youth and take care of you in your old age; for he is the son of your daughter-in-law who loves you so much, and who has been kinder to you than seven sons! (TLB)

The blessing that comes at the end of the story, at the end of a long trial, or a deep valley – it's always worth the wait.

Many of you are familiar with the book of Ruth in the Bible. The book starts out with a famine in the land. So a man with his wife and two sons moves to Moab to find food so they would not starve. While they were there, the husband dies and the two sons marry Moabite women. Ten years later, her two sons die. Sounds like Naomi had quite the tragic life.

Word came that the Lord had provided food in the land of Judah once again, so Naomi and her daughters-in-law prepared to go back to Naomi's hometown of Bethlehem. Naomi urged the two women, Orpah and Ruth to stay in Moab and prayed that the Lord would bless them with a new husband. Orpah decided to stay, but Ruth wanted to go.

The rest of the story is that as the women return, Boaz, becomes Ruth's kinsmen redeemer, and ultimately, her husband. And God blesses them with a child, Obed, who becomes the father of David, of the lineage of Jesus.

Naomi blamed God for the misfortune that came upon her, yet, the Lord knew the end of the story. The end of the story in Ruth 4 is that Naomi now holds her grandson in her arms. This was God's hope, God's promise to her. This child would renew her life and sustain her in her old age. As grandparents, you understand this joy.

On our path to Bill's healing, there were places in the road where life was pretty rough. There was a lot that was taken away, stripped away often within minutes, without time to prepare for a big change. God in His faithfulness restored abundantly more than we could ever have imagined. What we received was far greater than what we lost.

My steps on this new Glory Road are ordered by the Lord. I know that the Lord is restoring my youthful spirit and providing for me in my old age (although I'm not that old yet). He is the God of miracles and the restorer of those who diligently seek Him. He will never leave me or forsake me.

Thank you for your faithful prayers. #Godisfaithful #TheGloryRoad

Day #134 August 31

Anchor Verse: Psalm 130:6

I long for you more than any watchman would long for the morning light. I will watch and wait for you, O God, throughout the night. (TPT)

Waiting for the morning light… it can be the longest stretch of darkness known to mankind. Whether you are night watchman, in the military on guard duty, a mother with a young child, a caretaker for a loved one who is ill, or a student pulling an all-nighter to get an assignment completed, those last hours before dawn are the most grueling hours of the day.

For those of you who suffer from insomnia, the night can be an endless abyss of attempted efforts to relax and go to sleep, while millions of things are swirling around in your head and heart.

During our journey to Bill's healing, many were the nights that our toughest battles were fought. When the enemy would attempt to sneak in during the cover of the night to steal, kill, and destroy only to be met by a legion of warring angels that were there to protect Bill from this unsuccessful attempt.

I have seen the Lord move in mighty ways often before dawn and the peace that passes all understanding that guards our hearts and minds would come rushing in like a mighty wind and smooth the troubled waters.

On this new path, the Glory Road, there are still nights that I struggle with sleeping. There are places I don't have life figured out yet. And as I come to this last day of Bill's birthday month, I will confess that I type this with tears pouring down my face. Don't get me wrong, it has been a beautiful month of celebrating Bill's life and our love, and launching a book to honor his legacy. As great the joy, so great is the depth of the loss of the man I loved so much.

However, I will dry my tears and drink a cup of tea, and regroup, and continue on the path that God has for me. I know that healing comes in time, like daylight always follows the night. There will be other losses, but also other victories. The Lord and I will face them together and we will be victorious in Jesus' name.

My heart longs for God, He is my only refuge in this life; the only unshakable rock on which to build my house. Bill knew that too and that is where our home, our lives, our love was anchored.

Thank you for loving without counting the cost. #Godisfaithful #TheGloryRoad

September 2020

Pray without ceasing.
~ 1 Thessalonians 5:17

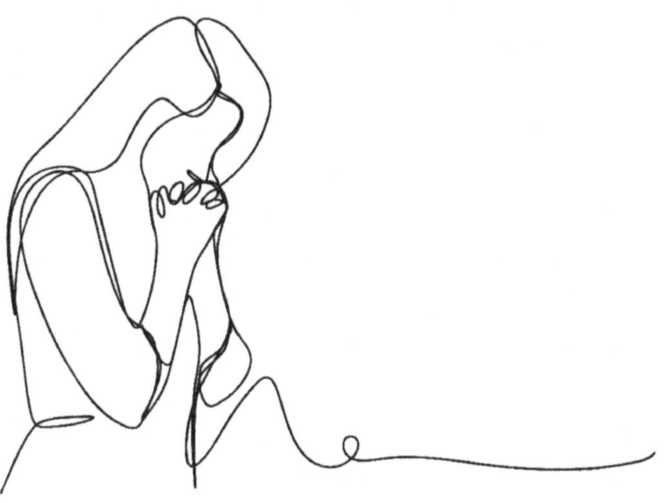

Day #135 September 1

Anchor Verse: Psalm 136:26
Give thanks to the God of heaven, For His lovingkindness (graciousness, mercy, compassion) endures forever. (AMP)

When was the last time you thanked the Lord for something He gave you? Maybe your heart that beats by His command, not left up to us to manage or the oxygen in the air we breathe that gives us life?

We often come to the Lord in "prayer" but really it's a laundry list of our needs rather than a time to thank our heavenly Father for what He is doing in us and what He wants to do in our lives.

It is the first day of a new month, the month of September. September represents a change of seasons in our life. The first day of autumn, or fall, happens this month as we walk into a time of shedding, letting go of the vibrant beauty of spring and summer in exchange for the beauty of the fall leaves as they say good bye for the season. It's a time to rejoice! It's a time to give thanks for the gift of life, the gift of love.

Grace is often referred to as "unmerited favor" from God when He sent Jesus to pay for our sins that we might be in a right relationship with Him. It is God's grace and mercy that get us through the day.

His mercy is that He forgives us when we fail and choose to go the wrong way. As we ask God to forgive us, He is faithful and just to forgive us our sins and cleanse us from ALL unrighteousness. (1 John 1:9)

On our journey to Bill's healing, we were given many opportunities to give thanks to the Lord, to "choose" to give thanks even in the midst of difficult circumstances. We didn't deny the problems existed but we refused to let them have power over us.

As I awake to a new day on the Glory Road, a new month of possibilities and miracles, my heart is filled with joy and thanksgiving. I give my heavenly Father an offering of praise. I will rise up from the pile of ashes of the past and march forward into all that the Lord has for me in this new season. Dying to self, I find new life in Christ. May His grace, mercy, and compassion be the fruit that is evident in my life every day.

Thank you for your persevering prayers. #Godisfaithful #TheGloryRoad

Day #136 September 2

Anchor Verse: Psalm 139:23
Search me, God, and know my heart; test me and know my anxious thoughts. (NIV)

When was the last time you invited God to search your heart and know your anxious thoughts?

The Message translation frames it in the context of a legal proceeding. Investigate my life, cross-examine and test me, and get a clear picture what I'm about.

Since the "trial" has been going on for months, many of us tend to burrow in deeper and hide rather than bring our problems to the surface. We are like caterpillars in a cocoon. It can be lonely.

God is there with you. Whether you are in the spaciousness of the great outdoors or tucked into a small bed of affliction or illness, your heavenly Father is a companion who will never leave you or forsake you. Another thing I have found is that He is available for comfort and conversation around the clock. Thank you, Lord.

On our journey to Bill's healing, we both had times when we went to the Lord and talked with Him. I was honored and privileged that Bill shared some of his interactions with the Lord with me. In "Musings of the Miracle Man" – short snippets of some of those conversations are included.

The Glory Road has been filled with many moments and places of self-reflection, and also God-guided reflection. The Lord has been a good, good Father on this path to come alongside of me, not only to comfort me through the Holy Spirit but draw me into His arms to extend His love when I was missing Bill's arms of love around me. I continue to learn many new lessons. Thank you for the opportunity to share them with you.

Prayer is one of the ways that we learn more about God and how God grooms us for the next steps in our lives. Prayer is not only about talking but also about listening… sometimes "more" listening is actually our best choice.

Are you willing to be the answer to someone's prayer? Are you willing to be interrupted by God to do His work through you? May your answers be "yes" and "amen."

Thank you for being the answer to the prayers we prayed. #Godisfaithful #TheGloryRoad

Day #137 September 3

Anchor Verse: Psalm 142:1-2
God, I'm crying out to you!
I lift up my voice boldly to beg for your mercy. I spill out my heart to you and tell you all my troubles. (TPT)

Is this your story this morning? You have been begging for God's mercy. You have been spilling out your heart and telling God all your troubles. God wants you to know that He has heard your cries. Victory is near!

This psalm was written by David as he was hiding in a cave from his enemies. He was fearful for his life. Not only were these men pursuing him but they wanted to kill him. When you are overcome by troubles, they can drive you to the edge of the ledge.

Do what David did. Run to the Lord and pour out your heart to Him. Quiet your heart before Him like a newborn child who finally finds comfort in its mother's arms and falls asleep.

"So I cried out to you, Lord, my only hiding place. You're all I have, my only hope in this life, my last chance for help." (Psalm 142:5) This is David's declaration against the forces of the enemy that have come against him. You are my only hiding place. You're all I have. You are my only hope. You are my last chance for help. These phrases are not empty sentences or spoken with fear, but rather with power.

On our journey to Bill's healing, we were blessed to see God's hand move in so many ways. For days, weeks, and even months, my dear husband was confined to a bed in a hospital and many of those days sedated and intubated, YET God was there in that "cave" with him. Bill and God had conversations that we will never be privy to, but you know they talked. I'm certain Mr. Bill had many questions for his heavenly Father and on many occasions not only was Bill comforted by also "schooled" on his path to healing.

The Glory Road is filled with new experiences for me, places I have never been either with Bill or alone. Every cave-like place where I have been placed or stumbled into or went for protection from an "enemy" moving against me, God was there, is there, and forever will be at my side. He knows the way out of the cave, and in the meantime, His presence brings me comfort and joy, and freedom in Christ and through the Holy Spirit.

Thank you for your faithful prayers. #Godisfaithful #TheGloryRoad

Day #138 September 4

Anchor Verse: Psalm 143:1
Lord, hear my prayer, listen to my cry for mercy; in your faithfulness and righteousness come to my relief. (NIV)

The Lord invites you to cry out to Him in your distress. Instead of turning to social media, the world, your favorite comfort, or even your family, your heavenly Father wants to hear your prayer, to listen to your cry for mercy.

Because the truth is … God is the only one who can solve our problems. He is the only one who can heal our heart wounds, quiet our fears, turn our anxiety into peace, and turn our mourning into dancing.

Our God is an awesome God! He is Jehovah Jireh – our Provider. He is Jehovah Nissi – our Banner. He is Jehovah Rapha – our Healer. He is Jehovah Shalom – our Peace.

You may feel like you are at the bottom of a pit looking up to where the rest of the world is living, and your power and purpose have been stripped away. First of all, that's a lie from the enemy. The Lord is with you, the God of Jacob is with you and He will deliver you. He promised. The one who is fighting for you is Jehovah Gibbor – the Lord Mighty in Battle! This morning the words God is speaking to you come from Exodus 14:14, "The Lord will fight for you, you need only be still."

Sometimes where we find relief is in the arms of Jesus, to be tucked under the shadow of His wings like we read in Psalm 91. Resting is our best posture as we let "the Lord Mighty in Battle" fight for us. When God fights for us, He fights to win. God always wins… and so do we.

On our journey to Bill's healing, we put our faith in God, not in the hands of man alone. Yes, God used the medical community to aid Bill on his path to healing, but ultimately God, Bill's healer, had the final word about the who, how, when, and where it all happened.

As I find my way on this Glory Road, I am grateful for the many facets of my heavenly Father. There are days when I need His peace and other days when I need the Lord Mighty in Battle to pound on the enemy. The Lord my Healer is still in charge of healing my grieving heart, and preparing me for the next challenge. God in His faithfulness is never missing. The resurrection power of Jesus Christ abides in me… and as His child, it's in you too.

Thank you for your abiding prayers. #Godisfaithful #TheGloryRoad

Day #139 September 5

Anchor Verse: Psalm 147:4
He determines the number of the stars and calls them each by name. (NIV)

God decided how many stars to create AND God not only gave each one of them a name, but He calls them by name.

Take a moment to think about that… mankind hasn't even been able to number all the stars in the sky yet God has given each one of them a name.

God doesn't look at the world and sees billions of people, He sees you. Your heavenly Father sees you sitting there with your coffee cup in hand reading this on your phone as you wake up and decide how to face the day. Or maybe your eyes are puffy and red this morning because it was a rough night. Your baby wasn't feeling well or you aren't feeling good because it was too hot in the house.

Each of these situations, but more importantly, your life, your circumstances, your relationship with God is on God's heart this morning. He has a breakthrough planned for you. Just like a cake takes a certain amount of time to bake to be "perfect" – God has perfect timing for us.

Luke 2:6-7 says, "Are not five sparrows sold for two pennies? Yet not one of them is forgotten by God. Indeed, the very hairs of your head are all numbered. Don't be afraid; you are worth more than many sparrows."

Did you get that? A sparrow which essentially is sold for 2/5th of a penny is not forgotten by God. We walk past pennies all the time, yet God does not forget one sparrow that is worth 2/5th of one penny. Then it tells us that God has numbered the hairs on your head. So don't be afraid or worry or be anxious because you are worth more than many sparrows – you are priceless!

On our journey to Bill's healing, we learned a lot about God's specific care and how He delighted in the details. It was the "little things" God delighted in doing for Bill that brought him great joy. Yes, God knew Bill by name.

Now on this Glory Road, I am developing a new fascination with the details of my life. As I listen to my heavenly Father's voice, He reminds me of how much He loves me. That I am not forgotten and even when I don't always know the way, my heavenly Father does. I trusted God with Bill's life; I surely will trust Him with mine.

Thank you for your love and care. #Godisfaithful #TheGloryRoad

Day #140 September 6

Anchor Verse: Psalm 147:11

The Lord favors those who fear and worship Him [with awe-inspired reverence and obedience], those who wait for His mercy and lovingkindness [unfailing love]. (AMP)

The Lord's favor – it's something we all seek. There is nothing else on earth that compares to what God can do for you. To be loved by God and have His blessings flow into your life creates a life of satisfaction like none other.

To be clear, God's favor doesn't mean that everything is always "perfect" – not even. What we do know is that the Lord never leaves us or forsakes us as He makes us into something more beautiful – all for His glory.

Verse 11 says that we worship Him with "awe-inspired reverence and obedience" – that's powerful. Obedience is the greatest offering we can give to our heavenly Father. Not delayed obedience but "instant" obedience – doing what He asks right away, not when we feel like it.

What is the blessing that comes from our reverence, respect, and obedience of God? His unfailing love – mercy and lovingkindness are our reward.

I can't imagine living in this world without God's love and mercy. We face enough challenges trying to maneuver around the hurdles that life puts in front of us. But to do it with God by our side speaking words of life, hope, love, and comfort would be an ominous task.

On our journey to Bill's healing, we were blessed by the favor of God many, many times. However, there was something we needed to do. Our call to action was to worship God, to trust Him in the difficult places, when we stood in front of what looked like a "dead end" and open our hands and hearts to receive God's unfailing love.

Now as I pursue a new path on the Glory Road, I choose the path I take. When my eyes open to the morning light is my mouth filled with praise and anticipation of the day that lies ahead of me? Always, God can work through those who praise Him. We praise you, Lord.

Thank you for your faithful prayers. #Godisfaithful #TheGloryRoad

Day #141 September 7

Anchor Verse: Proverbs 1:5
The wise will hear and increase their learning, and the person of understanding will acquire wise counsel and the skill [to steer his course wisely and lead others to the truth]. (AMP)

There are always lessons to be learned as long as we are alive. Our education doesn't end when we graduate from high school, college, or graduate school. You may not sit in a classroom the same way you did as a young child (although that has changed in this Covid season) but God has something for you to learn every day.

Growing up in the Depression years, Grandpa learned to be creative about finding a job. Learning by example and watching others is a great way to pick up a skill… probably not brain surgery, but there are many other skills that we learn from each other. He lived into his 90s and Grandpa stayed "young" because life was always there to be explored, and then the knowledge shared.

As I read Proverbs 1 this morning, I was struck by the first part of the verse, "The wise will hear and increase their learning." Two things: 1. The wise listen for information that will improve their lives. Their minds are not closed, they understand that to become wiser a river of knowledge needs to flow into your head. You can't be like a stagnant pond – it starts to stink really quickly.

And the second note, the wise "will increase their learning." It's been a while since I was in a formal classroom. I graduated from Gonzaga Law School in 1991, before some of you were even born. I learned a lot about learning while I was there for three years, lessons that I still apply.

On our journey to Bill's healing, early on God made it clear that this journey wasn't only about us. Our path wasn't only about Bill's healing or teaching me about loving Bill and caring for him, it was about you. In God's kingdom, we are in this battle together. We get to help each other through the rough places; we aren't "stuck" with taking the test by ourselves.

As God put me on this new path called the Glory Road, quickly I realized there was so much that I didn't know. There were areas I had experience and wisdom but 2020 was a whole new chapter in my life and I needed the help of others, I needed God's help. Thanks be to God who gives us the victory through Christ our Lord.

Thank you for teaching me so much. #Godisfaithful #TheGloryRoad

Day #142 September 8

Anchor Verse: Proverbs 22:6
Start children off on the way they should go, and even when they are old they will not turn from it. (NIV)

For many children, it is the first day of school (2020). Many of them will be learning from home with their parents as their "teachers" guided by teachers from their schools.

It's a big transition for many… a transition that needs our prayers.

For a moment, please stop reading this and ask the Lord for His blessing, His protection, His wisdom, His grace to be multiplied to our students, our teachers, our parents whether learning will be taking place at school in the classroom, online, or at home. Thank you.

I like how the New International Version starts this familiar verse, "Start children off on the way they should go."

Like the first day of school complete with a photo-op on the front steps, we are sending our children off on the way they should go, not only to school, but on the path of life God has for them.

Whether you still have children at home or yours are grown up, or God has placed you in a position to influence children, I pray that we would get them off on the "right foot", the "right path" because this sets the course for their lives. The end result: when they are old they won't depart from the path God has for them.

On our journey to Bill's healing, we were so blessed to be reminded of the course God had for us. That God's plans for us were not defined by an illness or our circumstances. God's love wrapped us in a warm blanket of hope on a cold winter's day and His peace calmed the roaring fires in our lives. We knew that our blessings came from His hands not by our works. We were God's children who were loved and blessed.

Now as I find my way on this Glory Road, I am so grateful for the path that I was set on from my childhood. The blessing of being raised in a Christian home established deep roots of faith. God has blessed me with an amazing church family that blesses me through their prayers and words of encouragement – you are part of that extended family blessing me.

Thank you for choosing the path of life. #Godisfaithful #TheGloryRoad

Day #143 September 9

Anchor Verse: Isaiah 6:1
In the year that King Uzziah died, I saw the Lord sitting on a throne, high and lifted up, and the train of His robe filled the temple. (NKJV)

It's all about perspective and where we are looking. Two people standing in exactly the same place can see things differently. Ask a police officer as he interviews two eyewitnesses at an accident scene.

We often have heard the expression of "cup half full" and "cup half empty"… looking at things from a positive perspective or a negative one.

When the world changed in March with the pandemic, we were thrust into a place where the landscape of our lives was altered. Like entering a house of mirrors at the carnival, what had been normal was distorted and all of us had our "leashes shortened" in some way.

What we thought would be temporary has now lasted through the summer season into the fall. But one thing that can keep hope alive is our perspective – keeping our eyes on the Lord.

In Isaiah 6:1, it starts off by saying, "In the year King Uzziah died." Many of us when we refer back to 2020 will use similar words. You may refer to it as the year a close family member died – a mother, father, husband or brother, celebrity, neighbor, or friend.

I was listening to a message last night on this verse and the speaker said that Uzziah means strength. It was the year that strength died. It may feel like your strength died this year… but God is still on His throne and His strength will never fail.

On our journey to Bill's healing, we faced many obstacles but what sustained us was keeping our eyes on Jesus. Looking above our natural circumstances and into the Lord's face, and running to His throne room of grace in the heavenlies and declaring our dependence on God and that He alone was our source of strength. God is high and lifted up!

Now as I face my own health challenge on the Glory Road, my eyes are fixed on heaven where my hope comes from – it comes in the name of the Lord, Maker of heaven and earth. The battles I face in this world may bruise me and knock me around, but they will not break me. My hope lies in heaven.

Thank you for your faithfulness. #Godisfaithful #TheGloryRoad

Day #144 September 10

Anchor Verse: 2 Corinthians 3:12
So then, with this amazing hope living in us, we step out in freedom and boldness to speak the truth. (TPT)

Living life as a believer in Jesus Christ is not for the faint of heart. It is not boring. It is not calm. It is a lifelong adventure spent watching God do the impossible in our lives and the lives of others.

Writing to the church in Corinth, the apostle Paul says in 2 Corinthians 3:12, "So then, with this amazing hope living in us, we step out in freedom and boldness to speak the truth."

There are two parts to this verse. The first part reminds us of the source of our strength to perform the second part, "with this amazing hope living in us."

For a moment, picture in your mind a person filled with hope. How do they look? What do they say that conveys that hope? A person's countenance seems to be transformed when they have "amazing hope" living inside of them. That amazing hope is Jesus Christ.

The second part draws a picture of our action: "We step out in freedom and boldness to speak the truth." Not only do we "step out" in that freedom and boldness, but then we "speak" the truth.

My spirit is stirring within me. We are living in a world often defined by chaos and confusion. As I read this verse, I find order, a plan and purpose to what God has for me to do.

On our journey to Bill's healing, there were many times we stepped out in faith without knowing where we were going. But always our actions were fueled by the amazing hope living inside of us. Hallelujah for the gift of Jesus! Walking into dark places, the light within us pushed back the darkness as we spoke the truth of Jesus' love.

As I find my way on this Glory Road, the amazing hope within me is paired with God's amazing grace. They are quite the combination. The offspring of that union is that I step out in freedom to pray bold prayers and declare the truth of Jesus that makes the darkness flee. All power and authority belongs to Him and flows through me as I stand boldly on His promises.

Thank you for praying without ceasing. #Godisfaithful #TheGloryRoad

Day #145 September 11

Anchor Verse: 2 Corinthians 4:18
So we fix our eyes not on what is seen, but on what is unseen, since what is seen is temporary, but what is unseen is eternal. (NIV)

The gift of our eyesight is often not appreciated until it is compromised. For those of you who wear glasses or contacts, you understand what I mean. At some point, when what's far away is difficult to read or we need to "extend" our arms to read the fine print, suddenly what was "okay" now is not.

Whether you have friends with macular degeneration or cataracts, or other eye ailments, you can see evidence of their trouble. Often I ask God to move on their behalf.

In addition to the biological working of our eyes, we also have a choice about what we focus on. What we choose to "fix" our eyes on. Because what holds our gaze is our choice, we are not forced to look at the bad and ignore the good. Where are your eyes focused?

We can choose to focus on the Lord and the things of His kingdom. Will we focus on the eternal, or the light and momentary troubles of this day which are part of the earth that will one day pass away? The unseen is eternal and will last forever.

On our journey to Bill's healing, every day we had the opportunity to decide where we would "fix" our eyes. We acknowledged our circumstances but that's not where we set up camp. We kept our eyes on Jesus and the hope that comes from heaven, both now, and for eternity.

As I head into the next mile on the Glory Road, I have the choice about where I will fix my eyes – today's problems or tomorrow's victories. In America, September 11 is often a day we remember because of the horrific events that happened on 9/11/01.

This day I will remember those who lost their lives and those who sacrificed their lives that others might live. Then I will turn my eyes toward heaven and thank God for His eternal perspective, the future and hope that await me.

Thank you for your faithful prayers. Your faithfulness in prayer has moved the hand of God in my life. #Godisfaithful #TheGloryRoad

Day #146 September 12

Anchor Verse: 2 Corinthians 5:20
We are ambassadors of the Anointed One who carry the message of Christ to the world, as though God were tenderly pleading with them directly through our lips. So we tenderly plead with you on Christ's behalf, "Turn back to God and be reconciled to him." (TPT)

You are an ambassador. Did you know that? What is an ambassador? An ambassador is an authorized representative or messenger. Sounds pretty official, doesn't it?

As a believer, you have been chosen by God to carry the message of Christ to the world. We carry that message not only by the words we speak but by how we live our lives. Is your life a reflection of Jesus?

This passage from 2 Corinthians 5:20 says as an ambassador for Christ, it is as though God is tenderly pleading with others we meet directly through our lips. Your words bring life. Your words bring the greatest gift another person could ever receive – the gift of Jesus.

In a world of chaos, we offer an invitation to turn back to God and to stop running from here to there to find solutions. Your heavenly Father knows exactly what you need far better than you do. His love is the greatest gift you can ever receive and His faithfulness extended to a thousand generations of those who love Him.

On our journey to Bill's healing, we quickly understood that we were "Ambassadors of the Anointed One to carry the message of Christ to the world." The Lord chose Bill to be His when in Bill's flesh it would appear he was at his weakest, often at death's door. God used Bill's life as a canvas to paint a picture of what God's love and faithfulness looks like. God often uses our weakness to accent His strength.

Quite rapidly on this new path, the Glory Road, God said He had plans for me. With this cancer diagnosis, I, too, have an opportunity to be an ambassador for Christ, not only through my words but through my life. In what might be viewed as a "bad thing", God will be glorified.

Thank you for your encouraging words. #Godisfaithful #TheGloryRoad

Day #147 September 13

Anchor Verse: Proverbs 16:20

God blesses those who obey him; happy the man who puts his trust in the Lord. (TLB)

Obedience brings life. From the time we are small children, our parents teach us the benefit of following their instructions. Although in your mind right now you may be picturing a little two-year-old child who is confident that they know better. I'm not saying whether that little one is you or your own child.

But listening or not listening, obeying or not obeying, is not a struggle left only to children. It is something that we all get to choose every moment of every day. Will I do the "right" thing or the "wrong" thing?

Sometimes people need to look at the bigger picture to help them make that correct decision and choose to walk on the path of righteousness in step with God.

The Book of Proverbs is filled with wisdom statements that can help guide our lives. In Proverbs 16:20 it says, "God blesses those who obey him; happy the man who puts his trust in the Lord."

Obedience has a reward. God blesses those who obey Him. The blessings of the Lord are far greater than your greatest Christmas memory. The blessings of the Lord are far greater than any gift you could give or receive from another here on earth.

On the journey to Bill's healing, we experienced the blessings of the Lord as we chose obedience. Blessings came from the Lord's hands and often through your hands.

Even in the midst of great life challenges, even health challenges or pandemic conditions or fires raging out of control, we can still choose to obey God and trust Him. God's peace that passes all understanding guarded our hearts and minds as we walked in step with Him.

This new terrain on the Glory Road is often unfamiliar to me. But one thing I have learned is that trusting God even when I can't see the path ahead is the best choice. My heavenly Father has never failed me, and He never will. God delights in His children and a tsunami of blessings flow from His heart into our lives. There is joy in serving Jesus.

Thank you for your persistent prayers. #Godisfaithful #TheGloryRoad

Day #148 September 14

Anchor Verse: Proverbs 20:27
The human spirit is [A person's words are] the lamp of the Lord that sheds light on one's inmost being. (NIV)

A lamp sheds light so you can see where you are walking. In modern times, we have become so used to street lights and smartphones with a flashlight app that it seems we always have light to guide our way.

But that's not always true. There will be times in your life where you find yourself in a dark place, a place where it seems that the light had been extinguished. The moment a diagnosis is spoken over you or an ambulance ride results in an unexpected hospital stay, or a phone call tells you of a loved one's accident or even death – suddenly all the air is sucked out of the room.

There is only one place to run and that's to your heavenly Father who will never leave you or forsake you – never! You will find His arms open wide where you are cushioned from the blows of life and His love overcomes every fear. For a moment, you can rest there before you face the unknown. And then by faith, you take the first step knowing that He will direct your path.

Proverbs 20:27 reminds us how our words are also indicative of what's in our hearts – the light within us. Think about the words you speak. Are they positive or negative? Are you speaking life to yourself and others or do your words tear down and destroy?

What words have you spoken out loud this morning? What are the words you have spoken silently to yourself this morning? Are they words of life – joy, anticipation, encouragement, excitement?

On our journey to Bill's healing, we quickly learned the power of our words. Not only our words, but the words spoken by others – the people who worked with Bill each day but also the prayers that you prayed. Bill and I focused on the positive words and asked the Lord to take away the sting of anything that wasn't good and wasn't from Him.

Now as I face my own health challenge on this Glory Road, I am more aware than ever of the words I speak, the words others speak to me, over me, or about me. I listen to what God says about me, "I am loved", "I am His beloved", "I am healed and whole in Jesus' name", and "I am victorious in Jesus' name!"

Thank you for speaking words of life. #Godisfaithful #TheGloryRoad

Day #149 September 15

Anchor Verse: Proverbs 23:18
Your future is bright and filled with a living hope that will never fade away. (TPT)

Proverbs is not only filled with words of wisdom but words of hope. It's not like a fortune cookie filled with words created by man. They are from God's heart, words to encourage, and set you free.

The Lord's promises are high and lifted up this morning. They rise above our circumstances. They ring louder than the noise of the battle. The light of the glory of God shines forth over the landscape of our lives.

Proverbs 23:18 says, "Your future is bright and filled with a living hope that will never fade away." Yes, it is! Your future is bright and filled with a "living hope" – it will never fade or run out. Your living hope tank is always filled when the Lord is with you.

If you are a believer, and Jesus is your first love, then keeping your eyes focused on Him will keep your head above the water, it will keep your feet from falling, and your legs from becoming too weary.

On our journey to Bill's healing, our love for each other was rekindled each day but our love for the Lord grew by leaps and bounds. His promises were true for us, they still are. We could rest in them, lean on His promises, declare His promises, and believe in a bright future. God's living hope fueled our path even in the most treacherous terrain and circumstances.

Now on the Glory Road, the Lord continues to show me every day the bright future He has for me. My life, my hope, my dreams are not cut short or diminished because of a health diagnosis – it's merely a bump in the road, another place that the glory of the Lord will shine brightly.

I am excited to see what God is going to do in me and through me. Last week, a friend and I went on a prayer walk while another friend was having surgery. Seven laps around the hospital in prayer and praise, like Joshua did around Jericho, brought forth amazing miracles not only in the person's life having the surgery but in our hearts, and even those we encountered on our path.

Thank you for your faithful prayers. Today is my next chemo treatment – another dose of the "blood of Jesus" to heal me. Thank you, Lord, that You are my healer. #Godisfaithful #TheGloryRoad

Day #150 September 16

Anchor Verse: John 9:1-3
As he was walking along, he saw a man blind from birth. "Master," his disciples asked him, "why was this man born blind? Was it a result of his own sins or those of his parents?" "Neither," Jesus answered. "But to demonstrate the power of God." (TLB)

We are a people who want solutions. We want answers. We want to tie cause and effect together.

Jesus' disciples weren't "super saints." Fisherman and tax collectors, men who were used to living in practicality not philosophy. They saw a man who was born blind. Was it because of his sin or his parents? Jesus essentially said, "Wrong answer." In the Passion translation it says, "Neither. It happened to him so that you could watch him experience God's miracle."

His disciples were "schooled" daily. What lesson is God teaching you?

On our journey to Bill's healing, Bill and I often found ourselves in God's classroom. Many days were spent watching Bill experience God's miracle – again and again. They were also preceded and followed by some tough stretches of road. Some days the next healing miracle seemed far away. In those moments, God fueled our faith by reminding us of the miracles of the past that we might trust Him for His promises for the future.

Each day on the Glory Road, I watch and pray for God's next move – because I know when it's coming. The Lord is here with us in the chaos and confusion. He is mindful of the natural disasters – hurricanes, fires, smoke, unrest, unimaginable losses. We have not read the last chapter of this story – more will soon be revealed.

A few days after this cancer diagnosis, at naptime, very clearly these words were spoken in my spirit, but instead of His miracle, His power being demonstrated, my heavenly Father switched it up and said, "So that My glory might be seen in you. This is your story. My glory will be seen in you."

As many have commented and you have seen, God's glory is written all over my story. In fact, some of you have commented how I "glow with God's glory" – it's true. I am being transformed from a caterpillar to a butterfly. It's my turn now to experience that transformation, like Bill did.

Thank you for your persistent prayers. This morning the day after chemo, I have no nausea. God hears and answers. #Godisfaithful #TheGloryRoad

Day #151 September 17

Anchor Verse: Proverbs 28:1
The wicked flee when no one is chasing them! But the godly are bold as lions! (NLT)

Our thoughts and our beliefs guide our actions. It's not always the "truth" that guides us, especially when the enemy of our soul is speaking crazy things into our heads and we choose to believe the lies over the truth of God.

When we are anchored in the Lord, we can stand as bold as a lion. A lion is known as the king of the jungle here on earth. A male lion is typically about 4 foot tall at the shoulders, about 6 feet long, and can weigh between 420 and 600 pounds. They are fearless predators focused on their target.

Proverbs 28:1 says the "godly" or other translations say the "righteous" or "those who do what is right" are as bold, brave, or confident as a lion.

In contrast to that, the first part of the verse says, "the wicked flee when no one is chasing them." The Passion translation says, "Guilty criminals experience paranoia even though no one threatens them." God created us with the knowledge of right and wrong and when our spirit is tuned to Him, we, the godly, the righteous, those who do what is right stand boldly on His promises and walk in God's way to bring His kingdom to earth.

The wicked, the guilty those who have walked away from God, or even run away, are taunted day and night by the enemy and can find no peace. They run even when no one is pursuing them, because they can't get away from their own thoughts.

On our journey to Bill's healing, we learned how to stand as bold as a lion as we faced adversity but also to roar with praise as we stood in victory. What a blessing to know Jesus and to walk with Him over any terrain you face.

The Glory Road is where the Lord's glory can be reflected in my life. It is a place where I stand in faith, not fear. The enemy may throw things at me – unexpected circumstances, health issues, grief, etc. but none of them have a hold on me when my hope and faith are planted in Jesus. I will stand as bold as a lion and roar the truth to the enemy, "I am victorious in Jesus' name. Take a hike, devil. You have no place here. I am standing on holy ground."

Thank you for your faithful prayers. #Godisfaithful #TheGloryRoad

Day #152 September 18

Anchor Verse: Proverbs 31:25

Strength and dignity are her clothing and her position is strong and secure; And she smiles at the future [knowing that she and her family are prepared]. (AMP)

The Proverbs 31 woman is a role model and example to follow. At times it may look like that bar is raised high, but doesn't God ask us to walk with a standard of excellence like He does?

Proverbs 31 describes the qualities of a woman who watches out for her household, but these are qualities we all should strive for – men, women, and children. This will be the legacy we pass along to the generations that follow.

"Strength and dignity are her clothing" – a woman who has the strength to not only conquer her daily duties but emotional strength to navigate the rapids of life. That strength comes from the Lord; our well is not deep enough to navigate life alone.

Dignity is defined as the state or quality of being worthy of honor or respect. This is a value that is important to me, and as believers, it should be to all of us. Why? It reflects Jesus who lives in us. Throughout Jesus' time here on earth, we see that wherever He went Jesus treated people with honor and respect. From women to lepers, the sick, the poor, the tax collectors, Jesus even attempted to honor the religious leaders as they spoke ill against Him. This is an example we, too, should follow.

On our journey to Bill's healing, we learned a lot about strength and dignity. I admired Bill's strength as he faced unimaginable challenges. There was also the lesson of the three-cord rope – God, Bill, and me – that was the strength needed for our journey. Our strength comes from God alone. I fought hard to protect Bill's dignity in situations especially in a medical environment where saving your life can trump all else. Strength and dignity were among Bill's attributes and honoring them when he could not, was important to me.

The Glory Road in 2020 has offered many opportunities to navigate this new path with strength and dignity. There are times when my own strength has taken a hit, but the joy of the Lord is my strength and His strength has no boundaries. As I prepare for the future, like you, we face the unknown, but God knows the Jeremiah 29:11 plans He has for us – hope and a future, to prosper us and not harm us.

Thank you for holding up my arms. #Godisfaithful #TheGloryRoad

Day #153 September 19

Anchor Verse: Ecclesiastes 3:3b
A time to destroy; A time to rebuild. (TLB)

"There is a time for everything"… these are the words of the wisest man who ever lived, King Solomon. We often talk about not having enough time – others complain about having too much time on their hands. The truth is that God makes everything beautiful in His time.

Ultimately, there is order to the chaos in God's design. We run around like Chicken Little declaring that the sky is falling when the reality is that our course is likely the one that is out of alignment. God is still on His throne and the earth will rotate around the sun another day.

We are living in an environment where there are "enemies" that need to be destroyed so that we can rebuild our lives.

On our journey to Bill's healing, we faced many "enemies" – illnesses or body parts that weren't functioning as they should. They had to go. Get rid of what was unhealthy and restore Bill's health. God gave me a picture to help guide our journey. God showed me that He was recreating Bill, the old damaged body was being "destroyed", and God was rebuilding Bill one brick at a time. Each brick was "sound" and of good quality. Only when it was perfect would God move on to the next brick. This new building would last.

Demolition can often happen quickly with a wrecking ball or a bomb blast or a natural disaster, but the building up part can take more time. A strong foundation is crucial as we rebuild our lives. We don't want our "new" life to fall apart a few miles down the road because it was built in haste.

As I find myself on the Glory Road, five months down the road from when God took Bill home, I, too, am in the destruction and rebuilding stage. This cancer diagnosis is an enemy that is being destroyed and evicted from my body, and in its place, God is designing a new creation. This new "woman" will go on to love God and serve Him in new ways.

Sometimes the demolition process is painful. The tumor demolition crew does its best work at night, like the highway construction crews. God knows the exact pace for this reconstruction project.

Thank you for your companionship. #Godisfaithful #TheGloryRoad

Day #154 September 20

Anchor Verse: Ecclesiastes 5:20
God keeps such people so busy enjoying life that they take no time to brood over the past. (NLT)

Where are your eyes focused? Do you live life looking in the rear view mirror or is your focus on today and the promise of tomorrow?

Often our unhappiness is not based on our circumstances but because we choose to dwell in the land of days gone by. My husband often talked about his "altitude" rather than his "attitude." Choosing to take the high road and not be overcome by the muck and mud of life.

Our perspective makes so much difference. Why waste your energy on things you can't change? Let's use our limited resources – in every area of our lives for the most good rather than waste them needlessly.

If you happen to fall into the pit of despair and have one of those self-pity days, likely you will find that your energy has been sapped. There is nothing energizing about brooding over the past, our mistakes or someone else's – so let's move on.

"God keeps such people so busy enjoying life that they take no time to brood over the past." (Ecclesiastes 5:20)

Yesterday included good times with a friend. Simple pleasures. Joy and laughter. Good food. Good fun. Counting our blessings and thanking God for the gift of life. Try it. It will change your perspective.

On our journey to Bill's healing, perspective was essential. There were some terrifying turns, crash sites where life seemed to explode, but they were far outweighed by the joy we found in God's presence as we treasured the gift of our love and God's love for us. Laughter and joy are great antidotes to life's unexpected trials.

The Glory Road has had its share of unexpected side trips. My joy in the Lord, my hope, my purpose, and my pleasure are found in the presence of my loving heavenly Father. When enjoying life is your lifestyle, then you don't have to waste any energy making that choice every day.

Thank you for being a part of our life. #Godisfaithful #TheGloryRoad

Day #155 September 21

Anchor Verse: 2 Corinthians 13:11
Finally, brothers and sisters, rejoice! Strive for full restoration, encourage one another, be of one mind, live in peace. And the God of love and peace will be with you. (NIV)

Conversations are filled with facts, opinions, and advice.

Something to remember as we read this passage is that the apostle Paul is writing a letter to the church at Corinth. Some of you might remember the art of letter writing; it's what we used to do before emails, text messages, or video calls.

One thing about a letter is that you don't have the back story, the question behind the answer. Often the last words of a letter are filled with final thoughts or an epiphany. Words we need to pay attention to for a moment.

Paul is giving those in Corinth some last words of advice that we might find helpful to heed. We are to rejoice, strive for full restoration, encourage one another, be of one mind (unity), and live in peace – all with God's help.

On our journey to Bill's healing, we encountered many different people and situations – not all of them pleasant. We discovered that there was a lot we could do as individuals to shift the atmosphere.

Our response guided our path. Our attitude and choices could fan a fire or extinguish a flame. Wise choices brought peace and harmony.

The Glory Road is filled with many lessons. How I navigate life is shaped by my choices. There are some circumstances beyond my control – I have to walk through the fire or over the mountain, but one thing that never changes is that I can choose to walk with God through those places.

Choosing His highest and best is my goal – rejoicing, encouraging, walking in unity, sharing His love.

Thank you for your persistent prayers. I'm praying to make greater progress on this battle to my healing. #Godisfaithful #TheGloryRoad

Day #156 September 22

Anchor Verse: Proverbs 11:11
Through the blessing of the upright a city is exalted, but by the mouth of the wicked it is destroyed. (NIV)

Blessing comes from the heart of God. It's the truth we stand on, the place as believers we live our lives from, and the power of God through His blessing that propels us forward.

Blessings are not only reserved for times of ease and prosperity, but blessings come in our darkest nights, our deepest pain, our greatest loneliness, and yes, even on that hill you are trying to conquer.

God is for you and not against you. In Romans 8:31, it says, "What then shall we say to these things? If God is for us, who can be against us?" (NKJV)

The truth is that with God on our side we are overcomers, we are more than conquerors. The trial, the temptation, the failure, the hopelessness, the heartache, the pain you face is NOTHING compared to God's love, God's provision, God's mighty power.

Our heavenly Father moved heaven and earth to make a way for us to be reunited with Him because He loved us so much. Jesus is the way back to fellowship with the Lord. Jesus leads us on our path to victory.

This morning I was on a prayer call with people from around the world, our word of encouragement from the Lord and the prayers that surrounded it were this, "You are not on your hill alone." The hill you are facing, there are many who surround you in prayer, even some by their presence, but most of all, God is with you, cheering you on saying, "Take the hill!"

On our journey to Bill's healing, we learned about the power of God's blessing, not only in words but in action. God worked through people but God also supernaturally did what was not possible with man. That's why Bill became known as the "Miracle Man."

As I find my way on the Glory Road, my steps are ordered by the Lord. There are some days when the beauty of green pastures surrounds me, but often these days, it is hill country that greets me in the morning and ends my day. God has a new hill for me to conquer, not only for me, but for you too. We will climb this hill together – not only climb it, but CONQUER it!

Thank you for running this race with me. #Godisfaithful #TheGloryRoad

Day #157 September 23

Anchor Verse: Matthew 5:7
God blesses those who are merciful, for they will be shown mercy. (NLT)

Jesus took his disciples, his students up on a mountainside away from the crowds to teach them. There were important lessons that they needed to learn as they would be teaching others after Jesus was gone. Jesus is calling us to "ascend the hill" with Him to learn the lessons we need to learn.

Matthew 5 is thick with powerful lessons to be learned. Each verse is a lesson unto itself. This first section of the chapter is called the "Beatitudes." Many of them are familiar to us.

This morning verse seven caught my attention. "Blessed are the merciful for they will be shown mercy." What does mercy mean or to be merciful? Mercy is when we offer compassion, kindness, or grace to someone who deserves to be treated harshly or even punished. It is a perfect picture of the grace and mercy that God offers us.

From the beginning of time after Adam and Eve sinned, we have followed in their footsteps. Our human nature would lead us down the path of poor choices and bad decisions but because of God's mercy and grace we have a better way to live.

As we choose to make Jesus the Lord of our lives after we have accepted Him as our Savior, we are set on a new path. Our heart's desire is to be more like Jesus and follow in His steps. Then the attributes we read about here in Matthew 5 are seen in our lives.

On our journey to Bill's healing, we found that compassion and kindness paved the way to a brighter day, a better outcome. Kind and compassionate hands tended to Bill's needs, but it is our spirits that raise people up and encourage them on their journey.

The Glory Road is often surrounded by battlefields that are not of my choosing. But one thing I do have control over and that is how I respond to life, to others, and to their actions. There are battles I refuse to take up, offenses I will gladly lay down as God in His mercy shows me His heart of compassion.

Thank you for your faithful prayers. As I prepare for my next chemo session next week, let's rally the troops and pray for the miracle God has with my name on it. #Godisfaithful #TheGloryRoad

Day #158 September 24

Anchor Verse: Galatians 3:28

And we no longer see each other in our former state – Jew or non-Jew, rich or poor, male or female – because we're all one through our union with Jesus Christ with no distinction between us. (TPT)

The last few days I have been praying for a friend who has vision issues – whose eyesight is being stolen by macular degeneration. Often in my prayers for others God shifts my perspective to pray not only for the "obvious" physical/mental/emotional challenges they are facing, the request that is spoken, but to pray for the work God is doing in the spiritual realm.

My prayer for those with vision issues shifts for God to open their spiritual eyes to see. When our perspective changes to look at a situation or our circumstances from God's point of view, something changes.

Bill, my dear husband, was often known to say, "Look at it from a third person's perspective." When the person he was speaking with considered that, they often talked themselves right into the solution.

Often we are "blind" to the very thing that is holding us back – whether that is an offense that is lodged in our heart, a lie that we are believing about ourselves or someone else, an inaccurate description of the situation or being deceived by the enemy of our souls [the thief] who, as we know, comes to steal, kill, and destroy.

On our journey to Bill's healing, God often changed our perspective. I am beyond grateful for the many times God opened my spiritual eyes so I could see beyond what Bill looked like in the flesh. It was that change of perspective that filled me with hope when often others were discouraged. And as you know, Bill earned the title of "Miracle Man" because of God's handiwork in his life – the many healing miracles.

Now as I walk the Glory Road, there are many battles that line the way. We live in a world right now where there is much division on top of the personal battles each one of us is facing. Life is complicated, but God is not. His perspective hasn't changed. Jesus is the answer, the antidote, the solution, the truth to any question, problem, illness, or lie that we face. He is our hope. He is our peace.

Thank you for your powerful prayers. #Godisfaithful #TheGloryRoad

Day #159 September 25

Anchor Verse: Song of Solomon 8:7
Many waters cannot quench the flame of love, neither can the floods drown it. If a man tried to buy it with everything he owned, he couldn't do it. (TLB)

Love – the love between a husband and a wife is one of God's greatest gifts.

Will there be hard times? Oh, yes! Will your love help you navigate them? Without a doubt.

My heart is filled with joy as I recount the amazing gift God gave me in the person of my husband, Bill. God gave us over 26 years together to love, to live, to grow, to experience treacherous places but also to know the joy that comes in the morning, the victory on the mountaintop. I rejoice this morning that I am a blessed woman – a woman who is still so grateful for the forever love I have and always will have for Bill.

This verse from Song of Solomon 8:7 is God's way of showing us how valuable love rooted in marriage is to Him and to us.

In the Message translation it says, "Hang my locket around your neck, wear my ring on your finger. Love is invincible facing danger and death. Passion laughs at the terrors of hell. The fire of love stops at nothing – it sweeps everything before it. Flood waters can't drown love, torrents of rain can't put it out. Love can't be bought, love can't be sold – it's not to be found in the marketplace." (MSG)

"Love is invincible facing danger and death" – yes, this is a portion of our story.

On Bill's journey to healing, we faced danger and death. Bill's life hung in the balance more than once and our love intertwined with God's love for us carried us through. Our love grew stronger during those weeks and months as together we fought a common enemy. Love refined in the fires of adversity becomes stronger and purer. It didn't even seem like a sacrifice to love Bill like that through the circumstances we faced.

The Glory Road has been illuminated by our love. The fire of the love Bill and I shared gives me confidence as I encounter new challenges and face new mountains. A forever love doesn't die when your spouse is no longer at your side, this powerful love still courses through your body with every heartbeat. There are times that I still rely on Bill's wisdom.

Thank you for rejoicing with me. #Godisfaithful #TheGloryRoad

Day #160 September 26

Anchor Verse: Galatians 5:13b
Through love serve and seek the best for one another. (AMP)

Love is one of the most powerful weapons we have as we partner with God to influence the world. In 1 Corinthians 13, the whole chapter is dedicated to love and describing for us the attributes of love as God sees it.

"Love is patient, love is kind. It does not envy, it does not boast, it is not proud. It always protects, always trusts, always hopes, always perseveres. Love never fails."

Defining love in the abstract is not enough. It's not enough to have a "heart change" but rather the Lord is calling us to walk it out. To let the world see that we are not Christians in name only but rather that we are people who "walk our talk."

Several years ago the Lord impressed upon me the difference between "good enough" and "better" and "best." There may be areas of our lives where we are willing to settle for the standard of "good enough." It's like a student who is willing to accept a "passing" grade… only enough to squeak by while expending the least effort possible. That's not what God wants.

Others are willing to put in a little more effort. They don't want to only get in the door. With a little more effort, they will reap the rewards. But they too are living far beneath their potential.

Finally we arrive at the highest level of achievement, when the person is willing to identify the areas in their life where they are gifted and partner "with" God, not only by giving all their effort but to do it to benefit others and to give God glory. This is the place where there is the greatest joy.

On the path to Bill's healing, we had many opportunities not only to be served but to serve others through our prayers and encouraging words. Someone we met at one of the hospitals later told me, "You have no idea the impact you and Bill had on the medical community." Love in action means serving and seeking the best for others.

The Glory Road in this season is filled with so many who need an encouraging word, who need to be loved and hear words of life spoken over them. I am so grateful for opportunities to be Jesus' hands and feet.

Thank you for being a prayer warrior. #Godisfaithful #TheGloryRoad

Day #161 September 27

Anchor Verse: Galatians 6:10
So then, while we [as individual believers] have the opportunity, let us do good to all people [not only being helpful, but also doing that which promotes their spiritual well-being], and especially [be a blessing] to those of the household of faith (born-again believers). (AMP)

You are blessed to be a blessing to others. Blessings shared are blessings multiplied.

Many of us were taught that it is more blessed to give than to receive. Little children might not always agree with that premise, but as we mature and grow we learn that it really is true.

We come to the end of the book of Galatians, in the previous verses the apostle Paul is reminding the church that whatever we sow, we reap. It is the law of nature. When we plant carrots, we don't expect to harvest peas. If we plant corn, we won't expect to see zucchini.

The same thing is true in our actions. If we do what is good and right, we will receive a blessing from the Lord. On the other hand, if we violate the law and do what is wrong, we will be punished according to the law.

In verse 9, Paul encourages them not to grow weary in doing good, because in due season they will reap a harvest… if they don't give up! Some of you reading this are weary, and it seems like the end is not in sight, hope is wearing thin, but still you are hanging on – barely. Keep holding on! Now is not the time to give up, victory is near.

On our journey to Bill's healing, we had the opportunity to receive blessings from so many, not only to be helpful in the flesh, but to feed our souls. We also learned that no matter your physical state – healthy or ill, God can use you to encourage others, to lift them up in prayer. We were so blessed by our local household of faith – Spokane Dream Center and all of you who span the globe. Thank you!

As I pass through new scenery on the Glory Road, God continues to show me new things. There are new opportunities to be helpful and to contribute to the spiritual well-being of others. I am called to fight spiritual battles alongside you and also bring your needs in prayer to God's throne room.

Thank you for your faithful prayers. #Godisfaithful #TheGloryRoad

Day #162 September 28

Anchor Verse: Ephesians 1:17
I pray for you constantly, asking God, the glorious Father of our Lord Jesus Christ, to give you wisdom to see clearly and really understand who Christ is and all that he has done for you. (TLB)

Praying for each other is one of the greatest gifts.

There are times in our lives when we cannot carry the load alone. Whether illness, broken relationships, financial distress, family life, etc. we are too weak and weary, we can barely take the next step. It is then we need to be picked up and carried. Often that means friends, family, church family surround us and hold up our arms like Aaron and Hur did for Moses.

The apostle Paul as he writes this letter to the church at Ephesus is reminding them about how often he prays for them. "I pray for you constantly." Paul's prayer life modeled how to "pray without ceasing" – to be in an attitude of prayer, so when a need arises you are ready to ask God to intervene in the situation.

When Solomon takes over leadership of the Israelites, the Lord comes to him and says, "Ask for whatever you want me to give you." (1 Kings 3:1-15) Instead of asking for gold or silver, land or possessions, or anything else, King Solomon asks for wisdom to know how to lead these people.

Paul's prayer for the church is for wisdom so that they would clearly and really understand who Jesus is and what He had done for them. That is my prayer for you this morning.

On our path to Bill's healing, we were invited into a deeper place of understanding about who Jesus is and that revelation changed our lives. How else can you find such great joy and peace in places where death and life are separated by only a breath? Bill and Jesus had some amazing discussions where great wisdom was imparted to Bill.

After Bill died the Lord invited me to walk this new path, the Glory Road with Him. One road had ended, the path to Bill's healing, but the Lord had a new place of revelation reserved for me. This new path has given me many opportunities to be drawn into a greater intimacy with Jesus.

Thank you for persevering with me. Tomorrow is my next chemo session. I am expecting God to do the miraculous because He is the Lord my healer – Jehovah Rapha. #Godisfaithful #TheGloryRoad

Day #163 September 29

Anchor Verse: Ephesians 2:8

For it was only through this wonderful grace that we believed in him. Nothing we did could ever earn this salvation, for it was the gracious gift from God that brought us to Christ! (TPT)

In the world in which we live, it is often our efforts that are tied to our rewards. We climb the corporate ladder because of how hard we work, how many hours of our lives we give at the office, and how much we value our upward climb more than family, rest, or even our own personal health.

Even in this world turned upside by a virus, we still haven't quite figured out where we belong and how to get there. The path to the greatest gift isn't always paved with our efforts, it's a gift, and gifts aren't earned, they are given from a heart of love.

Gifts are often great surprises. Sometimes we may have a clue about what a special Christmas or birthday gift might be, but on the other hand, some of the greatest gifts I have ever received were more than I could have asked or imagined.

This passage in Ephesians 2 reminds us that it is because of God's grace that we have a relationship with Him. There is nothing that we could ever do that would earn our salvation. We could do "good things" every day of our life, follow all the rules, generously donate to ministries or non-profit organizations, and it still wouldn't be enough to earn a place in heaven.

On our journey to Bill's healing, we saw the hand of God move in mighty ways – miraculously. But it wasn't because we were so special or that our prayers were more holy, but Bill's life, his healing was a gift from God. We couldn't take the credit for any good thing that happened in those two years. Yes, we sought God's face, and walked in His way to the best of our ability. But at the end of the day, it was God's grace that gave us peace, joy, and great love for each other and for Him.

As I step out on the Glory Road, I am overwhelmed by the gift of God's grace for me. Today is chemo treatment #4. I go in the power of the risen Savior, Jesus, at work in me. I have been doing so well, because of God's grace, because He has chosen my life to show the world His love, His mercy, His peace. So grateful that God called me by name and I belong to Him.

Thank you for your love. #Godisfaithful #TheGloryRoad

Day #164 September 30

Anchor Verse: Isaiah 9:2

The people who walk in [spiritual] darkness will see a great Light; Those who live in the dark land, the Light will shine on them. (AMP)

Bad things happen when we try to navigate in the dark. A great example is getting out of bed in the middle of the night and stubbing your toe on the bed or another object. If we answered honestly, most, if not all of us, could identify with the pain that accompanied it.

As we walk in the darkness, our vision is compromised because there is no light to illuminate our eyes and direct our path. We were not created with sonar like bats, because God is asking us to walk in the light.

Greater than the light of the daylight hours is the Light we find in Jesus. Our spiritual vision is the key to a life filled with light. Stress and anxiety come when the darkness blots out that light. Where our eyes are focused – especially our spiritual eyes – determines our course.

When we keep our eyes on Jesus, the author and finisher of our faith, we are less likely to stub our toes on the obstacles or circumstances that we will encounter in this world. He is our Peace…yes, Peace with a capital "P".

On our journey to Bill's healing, we learned so much about where to focus our spiritual eyes. Walking in peace using our spiritual eyes netted far greater results than using our natural eyesight, which can be easily distorted and often not with 20/20 vision to guide our way. Jesus was, is, and always will be my Peace.

This Glory Road is filled with new experiences but often old experiences, memories, or even a crisis, will rear its ugly head and try to steal my joy and peace. At the moment, I turn my eyes away from the darkness the enemy is seeking to sow into my mind and heart, and boldly declare, "Jesus is my Peace. I am choosing to walk in the Light of my risen Savior. Jesus is Lord of my life. Jesus, I receive Your Peace."

In the world we will encounter places of darkness, even sections of the road where there are no street lights, places where darkness dwells, but if we turn our eyes toward heaven, our eyes are filled with the eternal flame of hope that burns brightly. Even in a dark night's sky, the God of the universe has placed stars, who He calls by name, to light up the night with hope.

You have blessed us in so many ways. #Godisfaithful #TheGloryRoad

October 2020

With God all things are possible.
~ Matthew 19:26

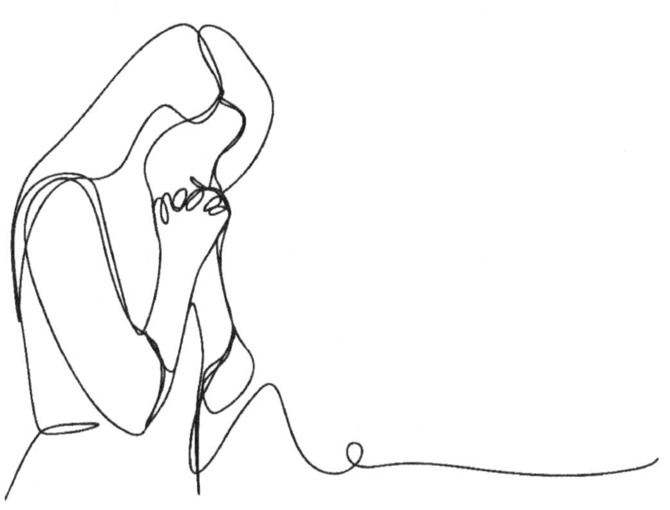

Day #165 October 1

Anchor Verse: Isaiah 12:5

Sing praises to the Lord, for He has done excellent and glorious things; Let this be known throughout the earth. (AMP)

Is your heart full of praise this morning? Did you wake up with a song on your lips or was it a grumble or a sigh?

There are so many reasons to be filled with joy and to sing praises to the Lord. You can see – your eyesight is good. You are reading the words on this page – you understand English. Your heart is beating – you have a reason to live. You can breathe – the breath of life fills your lungs.

Is your glass half-full or half-empty? Do you have a positive outlook on life or a negative one? Do you look for the positive attributes in others or is a critical judgmental spirit your default position?

Many of the problems we "see" in the world are really about how we view our circumstances. It might be triggering an issue in your own heart that hasn't been dealt with, but that's between you and God.

This morning let's focus on singing praises to the Lord and testifying of the excellent and glorious things He has done and is doing in our lives. Focusing on them even in our body is releasing endorphins that make us feel better. The God of the universe has a great reward planned for His children.

From adults to children, we like to receive gifts, to be validated for our opinion, and recognized for our wisdom or an achievement. But God wants even more for us. He wants to give us not only this lifetime but all of eternity to sing praises to His name. Heaven is our greatest reward.

On our journey to Bill's healing, we were so blessed to be able to let the overflow of God's love, mercy, and grace to us overflow into the lives of others. God's goodness was too great for us to contain in our lives, our bodies, and in our home, we wanted to share it with you.

Out of the overflow, God guides me on the Glory Road. Many of the lessons I learned from Bill and from God on that journey from January 2018 to April 2020 have forever shaped my life and my outlook. They have set me on a new course – a place where bringing honor and glory to God is my only focus, everything else pales in comparison to that goal.

Thank you for your faithful prayers. #Godisfaithful #TheGloryRoad

Day #166 October 2

Anchor Verse: Isaiah 14:24

The Lord Yahweh, Commander of Angel Armies, makes this solemn decree: "Be sure of this: Just as I have planned, so it will be. Every purpose of my heart will surely come to pass." (TPT)

God is in control. There is something refreshing in knowing that the God who created the universe is not taken by surprise. We often are shocked by the daily events in our lives – what we see on the news, what we experience in our lives. But God is not.

Jesus slept through a storm on a rough sea while his disciples, many of them seasoned fishermen, were certain they would die because of the waves and the wind that threatened their boat.

"The disciples went and woke him, saying, "Master, Master, we're going to drown!" He got up and rebuked the wind and the raging waters; the storm subsided, and all was calm. "Where is your faith?" he asked his disciples. (Luke 8:24-25)

Is Jesus asking us the same thing? We are living in a world that has many chaotic things happening. They overlap each other and seem to be multiplied and magnified at times. Yet, we are called to walk in His peace through the stormy seas because we trust the one that is in our boat.

It might seem that Jesus is asleep, that God is immune to your cries of distress, yet, He is our ever-present help in time of trouble. (Psalm 46:1)

On our journey to Bill's healing, the Lord Yahweh, Commander of Angel Armies was in charge of Bill's path. There was not one place in the road where God threw up His hands in despair and said, "I didn't see this coming." No, instead God carefully laid out a plan that would be for our good and for His glory. And would remind those who surrounded us that God's love knows no boundaries and His power and might prevail over any storm. He is a good, good Father.

Now as I seek direction on the Glory Road, I am blessed to have the same navigator in charge of my path, my destination. God has a plan and a purpose for this stretch of the road. Watch with me and see what God's going to do. I am certain it will be abundantly more than all that I could ask or imagine. He has a future and hope for me – and for you.

Thank you for your persistent prayers. #Godisfaithful #TheGloryRoad

Day #167 October 3

Anchor Verse: Psalm 4:1
O God, you have declared me perfect in your eyes; you have always cared for me in my distress; now hear me as I call again. Have mercy on me. Hear my prayer. (TLB)

Prayer is one of the greatest gifts that God has given us. Yes, we find comfort in formal prayers, prayers that have stood the test of time. Jesus modeled what prayer should look like when He taught His own disciples the Lord's Prayer, as we call it. (Matthew 6:9-13)

There are times that our strength, our courage, our resources will come to an end… and yet, the need is still great. And then God steps in to fill the gap.

David as he wrote this psalm was crying out to the Lord. "You have always cared for me in my distress; now hear me as I call again. Have mercy on me. Hear my prayer. " He declares God's faithfulness and asks for mercy, that the Lord would hear his prayer.

Have you been there? I have – many times. Last night I had the opportunity to come alongside someone who couldn't carry their burden alone, they needed help – help that only God could provide. They needed a supernatural solution manifested here on earth.

Prayer can do that. Many of you sacrificed sleep through the night hours for Bill when we were on his journey to healing. I know what a difference it made in our lives, so I was honored to do the same for my friend. I laid the burden at the feet of Jesus, then grabbed some sleep, and then woke up for an update and prayed some more, until the tide turned and relief came.

Only God could love us so much that our tears, our prayers, our cries of mercy move Him to action. He has a tender father's heart. God is not only moved by your burden, but is willing to listen to your prayers and petitions and cries for another.

As I find my way on the Glory Road, God is showing me new things and reviewing lessons from days gone by. Prayer has always been a blessing to me, not only for me and those close to me, but to lead others on a prayer journey for a specific purpose or season.

Prayer changes things. Prayer changes us. Prayer moves mountains. Prayers prayed in unity can transform a family, a church, a nation – a world.

Thank you for your faithfulness in prayer. #Godisfaithful #TheGloryRoad

Day #168 October 4

Anchor Verse: Ephesians 6: 16
In every battle, take faith as your wrap-around shield, for it is able to extinguish the blazing arrows coming at you from the Evil One! (TPT)

"Above all" pick up the shield of faith to extinguish the flaming arrows of the enemy. In verse 11, Paul tells his readers to put on the full armor of God as they take their stand against the enemy.

As important as each piece is, it is the shield of faith that deflects the flaming arrows that are aimed at us.

That is why our faith is so important. When seeds of fear are being so liberally sown, we need to pray for a crop failure. We must choose "not" to water those seeds but instead stand in faith, move in faith, take action in faith, and the Lord will help us in our battle.

Have you ever pictured yourself in your armor as you fight the spiritual battles in your life? As I "pray on" each piece, I picture it. (I used to do this for Bill, morning and night.) But when it came to the shield of faith, my shield was not something small in my left hand as I wielded the sword of the spirit in my right hand, my shield covered me from the top of my head to the soles of my feet. Our shield of faith must cover us from the enemy's attack. Note that the Passion translation describes it as a "wrap-around shield."

Our faith in God should not have any holes in it. There should be no doubt. Many times I have said and declared, "Either I believe in God or I don't. There is no middle ground."

On our journey to Bill's healing, our shield of faith was always present. It's how we navigated difficult places and even the straightaways where Bill made great progress. Our shield of faith must always be present, never put it in the closet or the corner.

The Glory Road is filled with opportunities to raise my shield of faith high. What a comfort to know that our faith in God is secure, there is no room for doubt, there is nothing missing. When we stand behind our shield of faith, fully equipped with the armor of God, and our ears tuned to the voice of the Holy Spirit, we can walk in victory in Jesus' name. The God of Angel Armies will direct our steps as we fight our battles, ultimately we "win!"

Thank you for the many times you have tipped your shield of faith over me. #Godisfaithful #TheGloryRoad

Day #169 October 5

Anchor Verse: Philippians 1:3-4
My prayers for you are full of praise to God as I give him thanks for you with great joy! I'm so grateful for our union. (TPT)

Prayers filled with praise and thanksgiving – full of joy! When was the last time you prayed prayers like that? I hope it hasn't been too long.

Our prayers are not a laundry list, a shopping list of our needs or the needs of others, but like the psalmist says, we should, "Enter into his gates with thanksgiving, and into his courts with praise: be thankful unto him, and bless his name." (Psalm 100:4-5)

Praise the Lord that you have the breath of life in your lungs! Praise God for the gift of a new day! Praise the Lord for the blessings that come from His hands and His heart full of love! Praise the Lord!

In this verse, the apostle Paul is writing to the church at Philippi. After Paul's opening greeting in his letter, he jumps in and tells them that his prayers are full of praise and great joy.

When you think about the people in your life, those who are near, those you haven't seen for a while, whether due to our present circumstances or that life has but some distance between you, may your prayers be filled with praise and joy.

On our journey to Bill's healing, there were times that my prayers for you were watered with tears of joy and gratitude. Even this morning as I write this, my eyes and my heart are full. When we walk through deep valleys, not only is our heavenly Father with us every moment, but often He strategically places people in our path. They are there to encourage and help carry our load, to pray and to stay – day or night. They are a gift from God. You have been that to us, and I pray that others have been that for you.

Now as I round another curve on the Glory Road, I am surrounded by a great cloud of witnesses, both from heaven and earth. This part of the journey is different without Bill by my side. Often the path I walk is alone, day or night, yet your prayers sustain me and I count it all joy, not only for the path but for the people God has brought alongside of me.

Thank you for staying and praying. #Godisfaithful #TheGloryRoad

Day #170 October 6

Anchor Verse: Philippians 2:2
So I'm asking you, my friends, that you be joined together in perfect unity – with one heart, one passion, and united in one love. Walk together with one harmonious purpose and you will fill my heart with unbounded joy. (TPT)

"Make my joy complete." Completion – it indicates that there is a process – maybe many layers like an onion. Often with a process there are other people involved and their actions and reactions… which can spell complications.

In the first verse of this chapter, Paul is setting the stage for this verse. "If you have any encouragement from being united in Christ, any comfort from his love, if any common sharing in the Spirit, if any tenderness and compassion"… then make my joy complete.

This passage seems so relevant for the times in which we live. Unity is what we need. God created us to be people of order, not of chaos. Maybe that's why we are struggling so much in this season of disorder… it goes against our grain.

The Passion translation describes perfect unity as "one heart, one passion, and united in one love. Walk together with one harmonious purpose."

It reminds me of a team of horses. For the team to make their way successfully down the road, they must work together – step for step. One horse can't decide that he wants to go to the left if his partner is going straight ahead… united in mind, united in purpose, united in their destination.

On our journey to Bill's healing, we quickly learned that it was about the team coming together with one purpose – restore Bill's health. God, the Great Physician, headed up that team and the rest of us here on earth joined in with our resources to create this beautiful healing symphony. Sure, there were times it got a little messy but then you go back to the "big picture" – why are we doing this? Once you get refocused, progress can resume.

The Glory Road so far has been a daily exploration of new paths as I walk out the plans God has for me. Even though I don't ultimately know my destination here on earth, I have the Bible and the Holy Spirit to guide me knowing that my heavenly Father's plans for me are good. (Jeremiah 29:11)

Thank you for your persistent prayers. #Godisfaithful #TheGloryRoad

Day #171 October 7

Anchor Verse: 1 Corinthians 12:4
There are different kinds of spiritual gifts, but the same Spirit is the source of them all. (NLT)

You have unique gifts and talents… yes, you!

When God created you, He uniquely designed you, not only your physical attributes like your height and eye color, but the gifts you carry within you – your talents.

Let's look at a few of them as mentioned here in 1 Corinthians 12. To some are given a message of wisdom or a message of knowledge. To others God has given wisdom, gifts of healing, or prophecy.

Not only is it important to discover your gifts, but your gifts need to be activated so that we all benefit.

Gifts that are not used and activated are similar to having a whole kitchen and refrigerator full of food yet the person is starving to death because they haven't prepared any of the food to eat and actually eaten it.

The power is in the doing and in serving others. Often we have no idea how important our gift is in God's hands until we step out in faith, take the risk, be brave, and offer it in service to others.

"God's various expressions of power are in action everywhere; but God himself is behind it all. Each person is given something to do that shows who God is: Everyone gets in on it, everyone benefits. All kinds of things are handed out by the Spirit, and to all kinds of people!" (1 Corinthians 12: 6-7 MSG)

On our journey to Bill's healing, we learned so much about gifts and people putting their gifts in action. What may seem small and insignificant to you is powerful to the person who receives it. We thank God for the many ways you poured into our lives, especially through prayer.

The Glory Road is exposing new gifts and talents in me and others. Well-used gifts create a strong foundation but God often wants to dig deeper into the gold mine of His children's gifts and talents and expose what has been buried. There is great hidden treasure in you to share with the world.

Thank you for walking with me. #Godisfaithful #TheGloryRoad

Day #172 October 8

Anchor Verse: Philippians 4:5

Let your gentle spirit [your graciousness, unselfishness, mercy, tolerance, and patience] be known to all people. The Lord is near. (AMP)

Who you are matters. How you act matters. What you say. How you treat people. How you walk down the street matters, as the spirit within you impacts the atmosphere around you.

Some describe it as "atmosphere shifting." You know exactly what I mean, even if you don't call it by that name.

When a person enters the room, their spirit enters with them – either in a positive way or a negative way. You may already have a mental image of a person or two that immediately comes to mind.

In this passage, Philippians 4:5, Paul is reminding us that we need to let our gentle spirit be known to ALL people. What does a gentle spirit include? Graciousness, unselfishness, mercy, tolerance, and patience.

Are those qualities part of your daily repertoire?

As we look across the landscape of our nation, our world, often we see the opposite happening on our streets, in our homes, on social media, through news outlets, even in our own hearts.

The change begins in us. The change begins in my heart and mind, and then it is lived out through my actions.

On our journey to Bill's healing, we learned a lot about having a gentle spirit. Kindness and patience and being gracious go a long way in this world, especially in a hospital setting where often there is a lot of chaos and crisis. We are called to be a reflection of Jesus in the darkest of places that His light might be seen in us.

The Glory Road is filled with opportunities each day to be His hands and feet. I am encouraged, even challenged, to be the kind of person that brings the light and love of Jesus to the world. Treat others as you want to be treated. Speak words of life, not words of criticism or words that tear down. Think a moment before you speak or text someone. May our actions be filled with mercy, patience, and grace. Living unselfishly… life isn't all about you. Putting others first has a great reward in the Kingdom of God.

Thank you for being His hands and feet to a world that needs to know His love. #Godisfaithful #TheGloryRoad

Day #173 October 9

Anchor Verse: Isaiah 33:2

O Lord, be gracious [merciful] to us; we have waited [expectantly] for You. Be the arm of Your servants every morning [that is, their strength and their defense], Our salvation also in the time of trouble. (TPT)

In times of trouble, where do you run?

Our greatest source of wisdom, power, and deliverance is our heavenly Father, Lord God Almighty, Maker of heaven and earth. Not social media, not a Google search, or even the collective wisdom of friends and family.

Here in Isaiah 33, Isaiah starts out the verse asking God to be gracious to them, to be merciful. Isaiah knew that he must appeal to God's grace because the Israelites were far from perfect. It was not their merits that would win God over and earn them help in the Lord's eyes.

They had waited with expectation for the Lord to deliver them from their troubles. With hope they had gone through difficult places and tough times because they believed unflinchingly that God was coming to rescue them.

Every morning do you ask the Lord to be your strength and your defense? I do. We can't make it on our own to fight all the battles we encounter on a daily basis; it is beyond our mortal strength. The enemy is very creative when he tries to trip us up. We often call it the "wiles and strategies" of the enemy that come against us but nothing is too hard for God. He knows every trick in the enemy's toolbox and God has a counterattack to neutralize him.

On our journey to Bill's healing, God was the first stop in our battle plan. The very first morning, January 10, 2018, when Bill was having such a hard time breathing, simultaneously I cried out to the Lord and called 911. I knew that supernatural help and healing is what Bill needed. The Lord created us and the Lord is our best defense against anything that threatens our health and welfare. He is Jehovah Rapha, the Lord our Healer.

Now as I follow this new path on the Glory Road, I find myself crying out to the Lord, day and night, not only for myself but for many of you. The needs are great. Our lives are filled with challenges, but none of them are too difficult for God. Often with tears, the Lord hears my prayers for you, what breaks His heart breaks mine too.

Thank you for your persevering prayers. #Godisfaithful #TheGloryRoad

Day #174 October 10

Anchor Verse: Psalm 41:3
The Lord nurses them when they are sick and restores them to health. (NLT)

He restores them to health… those words are like a cool glass of water on a hot day, a refreshing word for our souls.

I don't know about you but my prayer list is filled with those who are sick and need to be healed. Every day it seems that more people, friends, family, or even strangers, are finding themselves in distress.

Whether you are the patient or the caregiver, the road to healing is a challenging process. We all need an extra measure of grace and mercy wrapped up in the healing power of God's love.

In the Bible we read of times when healing happened immediately, but often there is a progressive healing, step by step a person returns to health.

This verse, Psalm 41:3, reminds us that the Lord himself is with us while we are sick and it is His hand that restores us to health.

Have you had this experience or maybe a loved one?

On our journey to Bill's healing, we were so blessed to see God's hand at work in Bill's life, day after day, moment by moment. I can remember times when during the night, the Lord would appear to Bill in a dream or vision and be Bill's "physical therapist." In the night hours, Bill and Jesus would be walking on the shores of Galilee, walking on the sand was definitely helping to strengthen his legs. And as they walked, they talked, and Bill was encouraged and strengthened in the Lord – physically, emotionally, mentally, and spiritually.

The Glory Road has been a place of healing for me. I am still healing in so many areas. In nine days, October 19, will mark six months since Bill went to heaven. In some ways, it seems like yesterday, and in other ways, so much longer. But now as I face my own need for physical healing, I have Bill's journey – his attitude, perspective, and experiences to drawn upon. God never creates the exact same path for any of us, but what we do know is that His love and compassion always lead the way.

For me, there have been times in the night as I walk this path to my healing when the Lord came and blessed me with the gift of His peace, the kind of peace that puts you into a deep healing sleep. And for that I am so grateful.

Thank you for your faithfulness in prayer. #Godisfaithful #TheGloryRoad

Day #175 October 11

Anchor Verse: Colossians 3:13
Make allowance for each other's faults, and forgive anyone who offends you. Remember, the Lord forgave you, so you must forgive others. (NLT)

No one is perfect. Each day we have the opportunity to overlook the faults of others, as we graciously appreciate it when others overlook our faults.

Colossians 3:13 says, "Make allowance for each other's faults, and forgive anyone who offends you. Remember, the Lord forgave you, so you must forgive others." That's pretty clear.

What does it mean to forgive someone? Merriam Webster's dictionary defines "forgive" as, "to cease to feel resentment against (an offender)."

I have heard some say, "But you don't know what he did to me or what she did to me or what my parents did to me, etc."

Many things have been done that are horrific. Not only actions by individuals, but groups of people, organizations, governments, etc. But the Bible doesn't include any exceptions in this verse or any circumstances where we should not forgive. It says "forgive anyone."

When it talks about forgiveness it says, "Drop the issue, let it go." It's the only way that our heart and mind are released to be filled with love, and then love that person. It is only as we forgive others that God can forgive us. We can only walk in right relationship with Him, with nothing between us as we forgive others.

On our journey to Bill's healing, we learned about forgiving others and keeping a clean slate. There are lots of bumps in the road when you are on a healing journey, being quick to forgive, and forget the offense, is the only way to live in peace and to live in the fullness of His joy.

The Glory Road is also filled with many opportunities to forgive and to be forgiven. My relationship with God is so important that I don't want anything to deprive me of the joy I experience in His presence. Forgive others as I have forgiven you. Drop the issue and let it go. Forgive and put the memories and the record of it in the fire of His love, and it will no longer have a hold on you.

Thank you for your willingness to forgive and to be forgiven. #Godisfaithful #TheGloryRoad

Day #176 October 12

Anchor Verse: Isaiah 40:11
He will care for you as a shepherd tends his flock, gathering the weak lambs and taking them in his arms. He carries them close to his heart and gently leads those that have young. (TPT)

Psalm 23, a familiar passage to most of us, speaks of the Lord as a shepherd. "The Lord is my Shepherd, I lack nothing." (Psalm 23:1 NIV) Throughout the Bible the Lord is referred to as a shepherd who tends to His sheep (that would be you and me.)

Throughout the Bible, we read of shepherds. In fact, shepherds were the first guests to welcome baby Jesus. Many of the Jews were shepherds so this was something they could identify with easily. The caring manner of shepherds for their sheep is often the focus of many passages including this one.

In verse 10, it shows us the contrast to the comfort of the shepherd we find in verse 11, "See, the Sovereign Lord comes with power, and he rules with a mighty arm." (NIV)

Our heavenly Father loves us and comforts us like a shepherd, but He is also the Sovereign Lord, Maker of heaven and earth, our Protector, a Mighty Warrior who fights for us.

There are days in our lives when we need to be comforted, and other times when we need God's mighty power to move on our behalf.

On the journey to Bill's healing, I can remember the days when God would gather Bill up in His arms and carry him. For those of you who have read "Musings of the Miracle Man", you will find passages when the way was difficult, but Bill found encouragement and hope in God. He was the Good Shepherd and led us to green pastures, and at times had us lie down beside still waters to give us rest.

Day by day, my path on the Glory Road is filled with new adventures, new obstacles, and new opportunities for the Lord to lead me and guide me. I am so grateful for God's shepherd heart that carries me when I am weak and weary, and leads me from that place to a new place of strength. Without the valleys, we wouldn't appreciate the view from the mountaintop of victory.

Thank you for helping to carry my load. #Godisfaithful #TheGloryRoad

Day #177 October 13

Anchor Verse: Isaiah 41:6-7
They help each other [their neighbor] and say to their companions, "Be strong!" The metalworker encourages the goldsmith, and the one who smooths with the hammer spurs on the one who strikes the anvil. (NIV)

An encouraging word can change a person's life.

That's why it is so helpful when you are surrounded by those who encourage you – those who lift up your arms when you are weary. Aaron and Hur lifted Moses' arms during the battle so that the Israelites could win, we are called to do that for each other.

As I read Isaiah 41: 6-7, it is such a beautiful picture of teamwork and people encouraging each other. "They help each other and say to their companions, "Be strong!" The metalworker encourages the goldsmith, and the one who smooths with the hammer spurs on the one who strikes the anvil."

These examples that Isaiah uses are of jobs that require great physical strength and hard work. Work where literally you are sweating as you work – a lot. The point of this passage is not really the professions or working skills that are named but rather the message of encouragement, "Be strong!"

On our journey to Bill's healing, Bill and I were so grateful for the people who surrounded us on our journey – not only the medical team, but our family and church family, and our internet family who all became a prayer symphony that ascended to heaven on our behalf. We thank those who stood in the flesh with us during critical health moments.

Now as I find my way on the Glory Road, God has brought people to encourage me and walk alongside of me. I have a strong foundation of prayer warriors, including all of you. My family and our Sunday evening Zoom calls to encourage me and get my weekly dose of laughter. My church family who faithfully stands and believes for the miracle God has for me. The faithful sisters in Christ who go with me to doctor appointments and chemo sessions: Cherelle, Kelly and Mary. My new friend, Martha, who pops in with food to feed by belly laced with love that feeds my soul. My friend, Andrea, who is my prayer walk sister, as we daily encourage each other.

Thank you for your words of encouragement and your many prayers. My next chemo session is today. #Godisfaithful #TheGloryRoad

Day #178 October 14

Anchor Verse: Isaiah 44:8

Do not tremble; do not be afraid. Did I not proclaim my purposes for you long ago? You are my witnesses – is there any other God? No! There is no other Rock – not one! (NLT)

"Do not tremble. Do not be afraid." These seem like words written for us in 2020. What a great reminder that God is in control of both heaven and earth.

When it feels like the wheels are coming off your "car" or "bicycle" or "chariot" or your "sidecar", remember that God has you safe in His victorious right hand. (Isaiah 41:10)

Isaiah 44:8 also reminds us that God doesn't make His plans for our lives just before we take the next step, Lord God Almighty proclaimed His purpose for our lives long ago. The Bible says before we were born God wrote a book about our lives – your life and my life. (Psalm 139:16) And they are Jeremiah 29:11 plans, plans to prosper you and not harm you, to give you hope and a future.

We are called be God's witnesses – to testify of His goodness, grace, and blessings. There is no god like Him. "There is no other Rock – not one!"

On our journey to Bill's healing, we were so blessed to find our shelter under the shadow of His wings. We didn't need to tremble or be afraid. There were days that even through eyes that leaked with tears that our hope was grounded in Him – the immovable, unshakable, unstoppable Rock of Ages. I can't imagine walking through this life, this world without Him.

"You are my witnesses" – this is a message I often hear ringing in my ears as I walk this new path called the Glory Road. When I first stepped on this road after Bill died, God spoke into my spirit and told me its name. That the Glory Road would be a place where others would see how I grieved the loss of my dear husband but also how I would navigate walking into the future. I was called to be a witness of His faithfulness. And now with the added dimension of healing from cancer, God is showing all of us what His glory – His healing released in us looks like.

All for His glory – is a message God planted in my heart when we began the journey to Bill's healing, almost three years ago now. It's a prayer I often pray that God would use every circumstance for my good and for His glory.

Thank you for being a light in my life. #Godisfaithful #TheGloryRoad

Day #179 October 15

Anchor Verse: 1 Thessalonians 3:7
So we have been greatly encouraged in the midst of our troubles and suffering, dear brothers and sisters, because you have remained strong in your faith. (NLT)

We are here to encourage each other. That's why God delights in family and community in so many ways.

When you are a "Lone Ranger", it's hard to continually encourage yourself. Everyone will have potholes in their lives and mountains that seem immovable. But it is through the testimonies, the stories, the encouraging words of others that we overcome the world.

Take a moment and stop and think about someone you either know personally, or a person in the media, or a book written about a person who has overcome adversity, and recall how that has encouraged you.

The Bible is filled with stories of those who are overcomers. Joseph's story is often referred to as the "pit to the palace." Moses was living on the back side of the desert when God called him into service to deliver the children of Israel from captivity.

Have you been that encouragement to someone else because you have stayed strong in your faith?

On our journey to Bill's healing, we encountered troubles and suffering. It's the way of life in this world, but we did not face it alone. The Lord was always there to encourage us and remind us of those who had walked through the fire of adversity before us and came out not even smelling like smoke.

Now on the Glory Road, there are stretches of sunny days and places where I encounter storms and torrential rain. There are new experiences – things I am not familiar with that I must lean into the Lord and garner hope from others who have walked this path before me. There is always hope in the name of Jesus… always.

Thank you for your unceasing prayers. This morning I hit some new side effects on this cancer treatment journey. Thanks for standing with me. Nothing is too hard for God. #Godisfaithful #TheGloryRoad

Day #180 October 16

Anchor Verse: Isaiah 48:10
Indeed, I have refined you, but not as silver; I have tested and chosen you in the furnace of affliction. (AMP)

The furnace of affliction is an appropriate phrase to describe the year 2020.

Has it been easy? No. Will we look back on this time and be grateful for so much? I believe so. In fact, when we look at it from a heavenly perspective, there is so much to be thankful for already.

Isaiah 48:10 says, "Indeed, I have refined you, but not as silver; I have tested and chosen you in the furnace of affliction."

The Lord reminds us here that being refined has a purpose. The refining fire, the furnace of affliction, is not meant to destroy you but instead to get rid of the impurities so that your potential is even more evident.

Gold and silver are put through the fire to improve their purity. The more pure the substance, the greater its worth. The same is true for you and me.

On our journey to Bill's healing, there were many places where Bill entered the furnace of affliction. In fact, the first five days of his journey is a good example – from pneumonia and his heart in afib, heart attack that night, then influenza A, followed the next morning by a brain bleed – wow! And Bill survived, because they were not for his destruction but that the glory of God would shine more brightly through him.

This passage also reminds us that we were "tested and chosen" in the furnace. There is a dual purpose. Tested to refine us and help us to "clean up our act" and then chosen to fulfill God's purpose for us.

Pastor Alice shared this verse with me the morning Bill died. That God has chosen Bill in the furnace of affliction. Thank you, Lord, for such a gift.

Now as I follow the Glory Road, God too has tested and chosen me in the furnace of affliction. Sometimes we think that the "rubber band" of our life has been stretched as far as it can go, and God says, "No. There's more "stretch" in you. Just trust me." Daily, I am being stretched. I trust my heavenly Father to not give me more than I can bear with His help.

Thanks for your faithful prayers. Things are looking better. #Godisfaithful #TheGloryRoad

Day #181 October 17

Anchor Verse: Isaiah 50: 7
Because the Lord God helps me, I will not be dismayed; therefore, I have set my face like flint to do his will, and I know that I will triumph. (TLB)

No one said that life would be easy. Jesus didn't make that promise, in fact, He said, "In this world you will have tribulation, but be of good cheer, I have overcome the world." Be of good cheer. Ultimately, we win!

How do we face daily living? Not every day is a hard day – there are days that are so filled with joy we don't want them to end.

The key to making it through the difficulties of our lives is found here in Isaiah 50:7. "Because the Lord God helps me, I will not be dismayed; therefore, I have set my face like flint to do his will, and I know that I will triumph."

"Because the Lord God helps me" – yes, that is the key right there. With God helping us through the trials we face, the result is that nothing is too hard for us because nothing is too hard for Him.

Sometimes we need help, okay, seriously, we always need help. If you don't think you do, meditate for a moment on what would happen if you were the one who was in control of your body functions – like your heart beating and your lungs functioning. Trying to keep your heart beating on your own, you wouldn't make it for very long. God knew that, so that's why He took care of programing our bodies and leaving a few functions for us to do "manually" – thank you, Lord.

On our journey to Bill's healing, we experienced both the adversity and the overcoming. It was by God's grace and through His strength that Bill triumphed. Many lives were touched in the process as we made sure that all the praise and honor and glory went back to God.

In this new season on the Glory Road, there are opportunities to ask the Lord to help me. Many are the days when I set my face like flint to pursue what He has for me – the path, purpose, and blessing, for myself and others. And yes, I will triumph. Every day I triumph with great joy because His grace is sufficient and His power is made perfect in my weakness.

Thank you for your encouraging words. #Godisfaithful #TheGloryRoad

Day #182 October 18

Anchor Verse: Isaiah 55:6
Seek the Lord while He may be found, Call upon Him while He is near. (NKJV)

The Lord is inviting you to come to Him. Come as you are. He sees you. He knows you. God loves you.

Isaiah 55 starts out with an invitation for those who are thirsty. In verse 1, it says, "Is anyone thirsty? Come and drink – even if you have no money! Come, take your choice of wine or milk – it's all free!" (NLT) This invitation is for you.

I don't know about you but I learned a long time ago that I can't live my life well without God's help. Not only will He supply my every need but there is such joy in living life with Him.

His joy is unspeakable, beyond our understanding. It's higher than the highest mountains. It's deeper than the deepest valleys. It's a river of blessing that never runs dry because it flows from heaven itself.

In verse 6, Isaiah reminds us that we are to "seek" the Lord while He may be found. The word "seek" means to go in search of, to try and discover, or to try and acquire and gain. It means you need to put some effort into the task.

God is calling you to make the effort to find Him. The Bible is a great source of knowledge to learn more about God and to meet Him. Then the pursuit continues as we build a relationship with Him and talk with Him through prayer as the Holy Spirit guides our path. Come together in fellowship with believers, a church family that helps you flourish and grow.

On our journey to Bill's healing, the first place we always ran was God. I knew God was always near but so often we needed wisdom about the next step to take. He was always a present help in time of trouble. God was also with us when we celebrated life with great joy and laughter.

The Glory Road is a path that is new to me but one of the greatest gifts that I carry with me is my relationship with God. With Him by my side, I know that I have the best navigator I could ever hope for. The Lord reminds me I am guided by the "Holy Spirit GPS system" – it's better than anything you can buy online or in the store. He will make my path straight.

Thank you for your prayers of faith. #Godisfaithful #TheGloryRoad

Day #183 October 19

Anchor Verse: 2 Thessalonians 2:16-17
Now may the Lord Jesus Christ and our Father God, who loved us and in his wonderful grace gave us eternal comfort and a beautiful hope that cannot fail, encourage your hearts and inspire you with strength to always do and speak what is good and beautiful in his eyes. (TPT)

A beautiful hope that cannot fail… wow… somebody that is reading this needs to know that God has given you "a beautiful hope that cannot fail."

In this world, there are no lifetime guarantees that a product will not fail. Many products are designed with a limited life so that you have to replace them. But our heavenly Father we loves us so much has given us eternal comfort and this beautiful hope that cannot fail.

What does this mean for us as we live our lives? Paul as he writes to the church, goes on to say that this knowledge will "encourage your heart and inspire you with strength to always do and speak what is beautiful in His eyes."

It changes our behavior. When we have that secure foundation because of God's grace, we are encouraged and inspired and we can "sow" that encouragement and inspiration into the lives of others.

Isn't that what life is about in God's Kingdom? We share what we have been given. Jesus told us to "love another as I have loved you." (John 13:34) Jesus' love transforms lives.

On our journey to Bill's healing, we held on to God's promises like the one we find here. Because of God's grace, our eternal comfort and that beautiful hope that cannot fail, we were not only encouraged ourselves but we could encourage others. God is such a good, good Father.

The Glory Road spans new hills and valleys, but every stretch of road is filled with opportunities to share His love, hope, and comfort. What God is doing inside of us is reflected on the "outside" of us. When your countenance reflects hope and joy, others are drawn to Jesus. May you and I reflect the fruit of the spirit in our lives today (love, joy, peace, patience, kindness, goodness, gentleness, faithfulness and self-control.)

Thank you for your words of encouragement. Six months ago Bill passed from earth to glory. I appreciate your prayers as I remember my forever love. #Godisfaithful #TheGloryRoad

Day #184 October 20

Anchor Verse: 2 Corinthians 13:11
Finally, beloved friends, be cheerful! Repair whatever is broken among you, as your hearts are being knit together in perfect unity. Live continually in peace, and God, the source of love and peace, will mingle with you. (TPT)

Unity and peace… it's something we all desire… but are we willing to put in the work to achieve it? It's not like we can go to the grocery store and pick them up off the shelf or have Amazon Prime deliver them to our door the next day. It's not that easy.

Remember when people who were "Points of Light" were recognized for what they did to make the world a better place to live? It was a powerful time to remember how our actions really make a difference – the gift of encouragement, doing a selfless act of kindness, using your gifts and talents – neighbors helping neighbors.

What if every person instead of being a "Point of Light" was a "Place of Peace"? The Holy Spirit whispered to me, "Be a pocket of peace." A pocket? What's different about a pocket?

A pocket is a place where you place something you want to keep safe.

What if we chose to live in that peace in our own lives? What if we were "Pockets of Peace?" When a person came into our presence their anxiety, their fear, their hostility was extinguished in God's pocket of peace that resides in us. What a concept!

Looking at map of this country, millions of "Pockets of Peace" would shift the atmosphere; it would forever change our lives.

On our journey to Bill's healing, we learned to live in God's peace – that place deep inside of us where anxiety and fear are forbidden. They are extinguished like when a campfire is doused by a bucket of water. Thank you, Lord, for the gift of Your peace.

The Glory Road in this 2020 season has taught me so much about seeking God's peace – in the midst of a nation in chaos, my own grief, my own health issues, and the collective uncertainty of a world seeking healing in every area. God's peace is the only solid rock on which I can stand. It is from His peace that I navigate the winding road ahead of me.

Thank you for your love and faithfulness. #Godisfaithful #TheGloryRoad

Day #185 October 21

Anchor Verse: Isaiah 63:9
When they suffered, he suffered with them. The Angel of His Presence saved them. Out of his enduring love and compassion he redeemed them. He lifted them up, carried them in his arms, and cared for them all the days of old. (TPT)

When you suffer, Jesus suffers with you. Did you know that? It grieves the heart of your heavenly Father when your pain is so intense that you're not sure you can take the next step. Yet, He knows that it is through the refining fire that you will become more like Jesus. It is through the refining fire that you will become purer gold. It is through your trials that you will come to a place where He can use you for His kingdom here on earth.

The places in the road where we think we have it "all together" are often the places of our greatest need. Why? Because we think it's all about us and what we bring to the table. The truth is, it's always about God and His honor and glory.

In Isaiah 63:9 it goes on to say, "The Angel of His Presence saved them. Out of his enduring love and compassion he redeemed them. He lifted them up, carried them in his arms, and cared for them all the days of old."

Thank you, Lord, for redeeming us and carrying us this morning.

"He lifted them up and carried them in his arms" reminds me of watching little children at church when they fall asleep in their mom or dad's arms. The child is so relaxed and peaceful because they know they are safe. They can feel the love and strength that flows through their parent's arms.

On our journey to Bill's healing, we thanked the Lord for carrying us through the trials of our lives. It was God and God alone that saved us. His enduring love and compassion gave us hope every day. He cared for us so well over every mile of rough terrain. Thank you, Jesus.

As I navigate new territory on the Glory Road, I am aware of His presence. On difficult days, His presence is with me. I feel His arms of love around me, and yes, His strong arms carrying me. We cannot do life alone, that is a fallacy, it's a fantasy. Without Him, I can do nothing, but with Him, all things are possible. When the impossible is accomplished, we celebrate.

Thank you for being co-laborers with me. #Godisfaithful #TheGloryRoad

Day #186 October 22

Anchor Verse: 1 Timothy 2:1-2
Most of all, I'm writing to encourage you to pray with gratitude to God. Pray for all men with all forms of prayers and requests as you intercede with intense passion. And pray for every political leader and representative, so that we would be able to live tranquil, undisturbed lives, as we worship the awe-inspiring God with pure hearts. (TPT)

"It's time to pray." How often have I heard those words? Many times. Not only has it been spoken by leaders, pastors, parents, friends, but often it is the cry of my own heart.

Prayer is one of God's greatest gifts. It is our communication link with our heavenly Father, the Creator of the universe, the one who holds the whole world in His hands. There are many answers that can only be found in Him, the solutions we need to the problems that we face.

With only two weeks until the election (2020), I reflect on the words of this passage in verse two, "And pray for every political leader and representative, so that we would be able to live tranquil, undisturbed lives, as we worship the awe-inspiring God with pure hearts."

This was the "command" that came from Paul as he wrote to Timothy way before the United States of America was even a twinkle in someone's eye. In the Passion translation it specifically says, "Every political leader and representative." Paul knew what it was like to live under Roman rule. As we read through the Bible, we see many examples of the treatment God's people received under good and bad leaders – those who followed God and His ways and those who chose another path.

On our journey to Bill's healing, although our lives were often filled with health concerns, "life" still had to be lived. That included praying often and much. We were so grateful that even when it might have seemed that we were "sidelined" there was always a place and time to pray.

The Glory Road is a place of prayer – praising the Lord for this gift and for His faithfulness in times past with the expectation of what lies ahead. We need not fear for the Lord has us safe in His loving hands. At the same time, I take my responsibility seriously to pray for our leaders at every level – not only politically, but in every area of our lives.

Thank you for your persevering prayers. #Godisfaithful #TheGloryRoad

Day #187 October 23

Anchor Verse: Jeremiah 1:9
Then the Lord reached out his hand and touched my mouth and said to me, "I have put my words in your mouth." (NIV)

Many times we have talked about the power of our words. Not only the words we speak to others but the words we speak to ourselves.

God had an assignment for Jeremiah. Jeremiah had an excuse about why he wasn't the person for the job. "I am too young." As many of us can testify, when God has a task for you, our "lame" excuses are not going to hold any water with the Lord. If God has chosen you, then He will make a way for you. It is that simple.

Jeremiah 1:9 says that the Lord reached out His hand and touched Jeremiah's mouth and said, "I have put my words in your mouth."

If God did it for Jeremiah, He can do it for us. I know God has done it in my life many times, and likely you have a similar story.

So if we have God's words in our mouths, why is it that it's not always "God's words" that come out of our mouths? You know it's true. There are comments you have made or critical words that have been spoken or words of anger – those are not God's words.

"Our words" need to be spit out and not spoken. If you swallow those "rotten" words, they likely would give you a stomach ache. The best idea is to keep your mouth "clean" and filled with only God's words.

On our journey to Bill's healing, we encountered many words spoken by others. Some were God's words and others were not. But as the recipient of words spoken, we have a choice about how we respond. A word timely spoken, a good word can be taken in. A critical word can be stopped before it takes root. We can turn it back at the door as we say, "I'm not interested. Go away."

The Glory Road is filled with a multitude of words. If we could get an aerial view of the world and all the words spoken, in color, some of them would be bright with God's love and others would be pitch black, not God's words. I ask the Lord to help me filter the words I take in, and the words I speak or write. It's important to bear His standard of light every day in every way.

Thank you for your encouraging words. #Godisfaithful #TheGloryRoad

Day #188 October 24

Anchor Verse: 1 Peter 5:8-9

Be sober [well balanced and self-disciplined], be alert and cautious at all times. That enemy of yours, the devil, prowls around like a roaring lion [fiercely hungry], seeking someone to devour. But resist him, be firm in your faith [against his attack – rooted, established, immovable], knowing that the same experiences of suffering are being experienced by your brothers and sisters throughout the world. [You do not suffer alone.] (AMP)

You do not suffer alone. Are you surprised to hear that this morning? It's one of the enemy's best strategies – to isolate us and deceive us. The enemy wants you to "reason contrary to the truth." It's like that roaring lion that he tries to imitate…note the scripture says the devil is "like" a roaring lion… in truth, he is a toothless foe.

A lion will isolate its prey and get it away from the rest of the herd. Our sanctuary is in the company of other believers. Not only are we fortified by hope but we are fueled by the encouragement and faith of others when our fuel tank might be a little low.

Peter reminds us to be alert. Be cautious… when? At all times. Because when we let our guard down, the enemy comes rushing in like a flood with doubt, fear, and discouragement. It's easy to capsize your boat of faith when you let in all that negativity.

On our journey to Bill's healing, we were so grateful for the promises of God in the Bible. It was the best weapon I used to fight for Bill's life, telling the enemy to "take a hike", because we belonged to God. As His children, we are in good company, not only with believers nearby, but around the globe we are in this battle together.

The Glory Road has given me deeper insight into the spiritual battles we face and the camaraderie of Jesus' followers all around the world. There is more we have in common than what divides us. Resisting the enemy means we stand shoulder to shoulder, back to back, hand to hand, as we resist our common foe. Focusing on what is the "same" rather than what is "different" is how we will win this battle.

Thank you for being God's warrior. #Godisfaithful #TheGloryRoad

Day #189 October 25

Anchor Verse: Romans 8:26

And in the same way –by our faith – the Holy Spirit helps us with our daily problems and in our praying. For we don't even know what we should pray for nor how to pray as we should, but the Holy Spirit prays for us with such feeling that it cannot be expressed in words. (TLB)

Are there times when you don't know what to pray or how to pray?

We could be in prayer 24 hours a day as we survey the world's problems, and that's before we start on our own list.

Our heavenly Father knew there would be times when we would feel overwhelmed. The list of needs would be great and our minds would be challenged to sort it all out. Enter the gift of the Holy Spirit to intercede on our behalf.

What does it mean to intercede? It means to intervene on behalf of another. Or as it says here in Romans 8:26 in the Living Bible translation, "the Holy Spirit helps us with our daily problems and in our praying."

The end of the verse says the Holy Spirit intervenes for us in a way that cannot be expressed in words. The Message translation says it this way, "He does our praying in and for us, making prayer out of our wordless sighs, our aching groans."

Have you been there? Wordless sighs, aching groans, streams of tears. We probably all have been, if we were honest.

Praise the Lord that He made a way to turn what seems like a dead end road to a path that leads to the throne room of grace. There our loving, heavenly Father waits for us to restore, refresh, and make us whole again.

On our journey to Bill's healing, there were times that words failed to express our needs. In His mercy, God intervened through the help of the Holy Spirit and our heart cries were turned into prayers that God heard and answered.

The Glory Road and its new challenges are a place where I often have the opportunity to run to the Lord in prayer. Yes, there are times when I can't formulate the need and surely not the solution. But I trust in my loving heavenly Father to meet my needs as the Holy Spirit intervenes on my behalf. You can trust Him. God is faithful!

Thank you for the gift of your prayers. #Godisfaithful #TheGloryRoad

Day #190 October 26

Anchor Verse: Jeremiah 10:6
There is none like You, O Lord; You are great, and great is Your mighty and powerful name. (AMP)

It's time to praise the Lord!

I know it's early in the morning and your eyes are barely open, but God has been watching over you all night. Your heavenly Father woke you up to the morning light and another day to walk with Him.

Instead of focusing on your list of things to be done, join me in a time of praise and worship singing to the King of kings and the Lord of lords. When you finish reading this, turn on your favorite praise music because it will shift the atmosphere in your home, your office, or your car – wherever you are.

In Jeremiah 10:6, in the midst of some pretty "tough" messages to God's people, this statement is tucked in, "There is none like You, O Lord; You are great, and great is Your mighty and powerful name."

When was the last time these were your words to the Lord? Acknowledging that there is none like You, O Lord. That God is great and great is Your mighty and powerful name.

There are many "names" of God that describe His characteristics and what He does. He is Jehovah Rapha – our Healer. He is Jehovah Jireh – our Provider. He is Jehovah Shalom – our Peace. These are only few of the names that we find in the Bible.

On our journey to Bill's healing, we found that when we put God in His rightful place – first place in our lives – that everything else fell into line. God is not our "last" resort; He is the first place we should run. God heard us often and much because we ran into His presence, day and night. Not only with our petitions but with our praise.

The Glory Road is a place to acknowledge God's rightful place in my heart, my life, my world. In the midst of the chaos, I know that God is still on His throne. My heavenly Father is in control of my circumstances and anything that I face – planned or a surprise. My hope is secure in Him. He will never leave me or forsake me.

Thank you for sharing your joy as you worship the King of kings and the Lord of lords. #Godisfaithful #TheGloryRoad

Day #191 October 27

Anchor Verse: Exodus 34:29

Moses didn't realize as he came back down the mountain with the tablets that his face glowed from being in the presence of God. (TLB)

"His face glowed from being in the presence of God."

My question this morning is, "Does our face glow after we have spent time in God's presence?"

How do we spend time in God's presence? By reading His Word, the Bible and then coming into His presence in prayer, not with a laundry list of our needs and wants, but to come and be with our heavenly Father and listen to His voice and then walk in His way.

When Jesus walked on this earth, people were transformed in His presence. Scripture is filled with many healing miracles during Jesus' ministry – the blind could see, the lame could walk, the dead were raised, and the lepers were cleansed. But more importantly was how their lives were forever changed, when they chose to become followers of Jesus, so they might spend eternity with Him.

On our journey to Bill's healing, we saw God do the miraculous. There were places in the road where the medical people saw a dead end – this was the end of the road, and God said, "No. This too will be for my glory." And God touched Bill and spoke new life into him – and he lived. So that Bill could testify to God's glory.

I saw the radiance of God on Bill's face like the Israelites saw on Moses' face. He reflected the glory of the Lord. Bill continued to look "younger" than his 76 years as God recreated him from the inside out.

This Glory Road for me is an opportunity to give God the glory for what He has done – in me, through me, and for me – all for His glory. 2020 has been filled with unexpected events, circumstances and tragedies in our world. One thing has not changed – God is still on His throne and He is not worried. I will choose to believe and not doubt.

We are called to be radiant like Moses so that the world can see the light of the love of Jesus in us. Individually, we can be a lighthouse of hope.

Thank you for your persevering prayers. Today is chemo day. Thank you for lifting up my arms. #Godisfaithful #TheGloryRoad

Day #192 October 28

Anchor Verse: Jeremiah 17:7
But blessed are those who trust in the Lord and have made the Lord their hope and confidence. (NLT)

Do you believe and trust and rely on the Lord? All three of them?

Maybe you believe in God but you might not trust Him all the time. Or you still tend toward "self-reliance" as in "I'm sure I can handle this situation alone, God, I don't really need You right now. Please take a seat in the corner and I'll call You when I need You."

The key is surrender. Not the "white flag" surrender to our enemy, but the knee-bending surrender of submission to our heavenly Father who loves us so much. He wants the very BEST for us but that can only happen when we are "willing" to let go of our way for His way.

Looking at this verse from Jeremiah 17:7, "But blessed are those who trust in the Lord and have made the Lord their hope and confidence," Jeremiah takes it one step further. The second part says we also make the Lord our "hope and confidence." Maybe some of us think more often of God being our "hope" but as you trust in God did you know that you can make God your "confidence?" Yes, it's true.

On our journey toward Bill's healing, we learned that our confidence in God helped Bill and me become confident that healing was possible and that the road ahead of us was filled with hope and joy, not gloom and doom. There is freedom in trusting God and making Him our hope and confidence. Those seeds of hope planted in us take root and soon blossoms of hope and joy are blooming in our lives.

This stretch of the Glory Road is teaching me new things. Especially as I take on this new "enemy" in my physical body, I have found new strength by building my faith and trust in the Lord. As my spiritual muscles grow stronger, it is reflected in every area of my life. The enemy has no hold on me when my "complete" trust is in the One who loves me best – my heavenly Father. Praise the Lord for His faithfulness!

Thank you for your love for me and others. #Godisfaithful #TheGloryRoad

Day #193 October 29

Anchor Verse: Psalm 67:1
May God be gracious to us and bless us and make his face shine on us. (NIV)

Every day God's blessing is upon us but sometimes we forget. Sometimes the "yuck", the heaviness of the world is so overpowering it leaves an "icky" film on us that seems to repel the feeling that we are blessed.

The truth is that we are always blessed. As a child of God, our blessings are so abundant we can't even begin to count them. There's an old hymn called "Count Your Blessings" that reminds us to count our blessings and "name them one by one" which would take the rest of our lives.

We live in a world that has a lot of noise, a lot of action, a lot of grief, fear, tension, frustration, and division BUT in opposition to that we have the light of the love of God in the midst of all that darkness.

You see as believers in Christ we have His light in us… a flame, a spark that never dies. Our light shines more brightly on some days than others. There might be some clouds or fog around us, but that's why each day we need to spend time with our heavenly Father and reading His Word, the Bible, so that our "vessel" – body, mind, and spirit are cleaned. God is counting on us to be a lighthouse for those who are lost at sea.

Our lives are like a city set on a hill that cannot be hidden. You might be trying to hide from life, but you can't. What you do, what you say, how you live is seen by all who come in contact with you.

On our journey to Bill's healing, we soon discovered what it meant to have the light of Jesus living in us. It's something you can't hide. It radiates from you – you can't help it. Bill, even with his health challenges, was a light everywhere he went – not only in the flesh but also in the spirit.

This Glory Road is an opportunity for me not only to experience the blessings and favor of the Lord but to let His light be seen in me. The Lord has called me to be transparent through Bill's healing journey and now mine. I ask the Lord for His help and the help of others.

Asking for help is a sign of strength, not a sign of weakness. It is an opportunity for others to serve using their God-given gifts and to love as God loves them.

Thank you for each act of kindness. #Godisfaithful #TheGloryRoad

Day #194 October 30

Anchor Verse: 2 Timothy 4:5

But you should keep a clear mind in every situation. Don't be afraid of suffering for the Lord. Work at telling others the Good News, and fully carry out the ministry God has given you. (NLT)

Paul in his letter to Timothy gives him an idea about what to expect on the road ahead. It could be called a survival guide for 2020.

The Message translation puts it this way: "You're going to find that there will be times when people will have no stomach for solid teaching, but will fill up on spiritual junk food – catchy opinions that tickle their fancy. They'll turn their backs on truth and chase mirages. But you – keep your eye on what you're doing; accept the hard times along with the good; keep the Message alive; do a thorough job as God's servant."

We have almost reached November 2020… only two months before this year comes to an end. It has been a trying year in many respects – for everyone. Anyone who has lived on planet Earth this year has been touched in some way by unusual circumstances and events – directly or indirectly.

Paul is telling young Timothy that no matter what you see others doing or saying, that Timothy is to keep his eye on what he has been called to do – the work of the Lord. Accept the hard times along with the good times. Keep the Message alive. And as an ambassador of Christ, we are called to carry out the job God has ordained for us.

Are you in? Are you willing to pay the price? Are you ready to stand up to opposition for the sake of the Good News of Jesus?

On our journey to Bill's healing, God had a path for us. It wasn't always a path that others understood, even today some may not understand. But it's okay. Because when God has a mission, a ministry for you, we are called to be faithful to His voice and walk in His way. Stand strong. Trust God. Take hold of His hand and never let go.

This path on the Glory Road has been filled with a mix of unusual experiences. I have been stretched to let my light shine, while at times, the Lord has had me tucked in with Him away from the roaring crowd. I have learned how to dig deeper and pray but also how to sit in silence and listen for my heavenly Father's voice. I play to an audience of one – Lord God Almighty, Maker of heaven and earth, who is my heavenly Father.

Thank you for your faithfulness in prayer. #Godisfaithful #TheGloryRoad

Day #195 October 31

Anchor Verse: Titus 3:2

And remind them to never tear down anyone with their words or quarrel, but instead be considerate, humble, and courteous to everyone. (TPT)

We often need reminders to be on time, to do the "right thing", and to rest.

Titus 3 is filled with great wisdom about how to live well together. Since this is the weekend before Election Day 2020, it seems appropriate to revisit the wisdom found in this letter to Titus from the apostle Paul.

The Passion translation says, "And remind them to never tear down anyone with their words or quarrel, but instead be considerate, humble, and courteous to everyone."

Paul uses strong words… "never" "anyone" and "everyone"… those are words that speak loudly. Note it doesn't say that you can exclude those you disagree with or don't like or don't look like you… it says "never" tear down "anyone" with your words. The New International version says "to slander no one" – Paul was very serious about the message he was trying to convey.

This is God's heart this morning. "Love one another as I have loved you." (John 15:12; John 13:34) This is what Jesus said, "I am giving you a new commandment." We must "go beyond" loving only the lovable, the cute and cuddly. As followers of Jesus, we are called to be considerate, humble, and courteous to "everyone."

What would the world look like if we walked that path every day? It would be a lot different than what we see today.

On our journey to Bill's healing, we encountered difficult places – places of negativity and darkness but with the love of Jesus inside of us God turned those places around. Don't be overwhelmed. Keep your eyes focused on Jesus and speak life to each other. Good things will happen!

The Glory Road in 2020 is littered with debris but also monuments to the goodness of God and altars to give praise to His holy name. Speaking truth and life and hope to others brings joy to our own lives. As an author and editor, I'm a "word girl" and I know that words must be carefully chosen.

Thank you for your uplifting words. #Godisfaithful #TheGloryRoad

November 2020

Rejoice in the Lord always.
~ Philippians 4:4

Day #196 November 1

Anchor Verse: Jeremiah 24:7

Then I will give them a heart to know Me, that I am the Lord; and they shall be My people, and I will be their God, for they shall return to Me with their whole heart. (NKJV)

God has given us a heart to know Him… that He is Lord. We have everything we need to walk in relationship with God. He has planted the seed in our hearts. Now all we have to do is follow Him.

It's like having a toolbox full of tools. You may be fully equipped but you need to "use" the tools or your need will still be unmet, the problem stills needs to be fixed.

Here in Jeremiah 24:7 God says, "And they shall be My people and I will be their God." We are His people. God loves us, cares for us, and provides for us. Psalm 91:1 says, "He who dwells in the shelter of the Most High will rest in the shadow of the Almighty."

Where are you resting? Are you tucked in with the Lord, your heavenly Father, or do you find yourself in the midst of the chaotic storms of this world?

On our journey to Bill's healing, we had our hearts placed firmly in God's hands. There were many times they needed to be protected from the storms of life. Our heavenly Father was faithful to keep us close to His heart so we could hear His voice and walk in His way. Thank you, Lord.

The Glory Road wanders through the hills and the valleys, sunny days and storm-filled nights, but always my heart knows His voice and rushes into His warm embrace. I couldn't do life without God. I wouldn't even want to try!

God's people will return to Him with their "whole" heart. It's an important detail. All of my heart – not a little bit or even 99%, but all of my heart will bow to the King of kings and the Lord of lords.

It's like the difference between the chicken who "participates" as she contributes "eggs" for breakfast as compared to the pig who is "totally committed" as his contribution is the bacon.

Thank you for your commitment to God. #Godisfaithful #TheGloryRoad

Day #197 November 2

Anchor Verse: Titus 3:4-5

But when the goodness and kindness of God our Savior and His love for mankind appeared [in human form as the Man, Jesus Christ], He saved us, not because of any works of righteousness that we have done, but because of His own compassion and mercy… (AMP)

Goodness, kindness, compassion, and mercy – these are characteristics of God, these should be our characteristics too.

When you are in the middle of a battle – at home, at work, at church, at school, wherever you are, these civilities can fall by the wayside. We often focus on the negativity and destruction of the conflict rather than the opportunity to build a bridge.

Most of the conflicts in our lives are just "conflicts" that will arise, be resolved, and we will move on changed by the experience. They are not like video games and "battles to the death" with only one person is left standing. We are not living life in the Roman Colosseum – thank you, Lord.

Our enemy who prowls around "like" a roaring lion, knows this scenario very well. In nature, an adversary stalks its prey, so the enemy of our souls is "licking his chops" as he watches us in our turmoil and conflicts. It looks like there will be many casualties of war BUT that's not the end of the story.

The Lion of the tribe of Judah is also on the prowl. He is vigilant. He is mighty. He is loving. He has a plan, and that is, that not even one soul should perish. Jesus ultimately wins!

On our journey to Bill's healing, we encountered conflict. It wasn't always pretty but where we chose to stand was in the light of the love of Jesus. We were called to love others from that place of love and acceptance even when we didn't always agree with them. Ambassadors of Christ bring the light, love, and hope of Jesus to a dark and troubled world, let your light shine.

The Glory Road in 2020 has been a new experience for me and for you. It has offered opportunities to gain the Lord's perspective on life and love. Not only to view life differently, but to live life differently. This isn't only about living life with a virus at loose in the world that has altered our behavior but about how to live with hope for today and for the future, when many sources proclaim negativity and despair.

Thank you for your love. #Godisfaithful #TheGloryRoad

Day #198 November 3

Anchor Verse: Jeremiah 31:13

The young women will dance for joy, and the men – old and young – will join in the celebration. I will turn their mourning into joy. I will comfort them and exchange their sorrow for rejoicing. (NLT)

"Waiting is the hardest work of hope." ~ Lewis Smedes

Waiting – we are all waiting for something or someone or our circumstances to change. It's like patience, a trait we all need but walking through the places where we acquire it, is often difficult.

In Jeremiah 31, the Lord tells Jeremiah that His people that have been scattered "all over creation" (so to speak) will be brought home, out of captivity. Once again joy will return to them and their land.

As a nation, we are looking for joy and rejoicing to return to our land, our homes, and our lives. It's been a difficult year in so many ways; we don't need to recount them. Instead we need to look forward with hope to the greater things that are yet to come.

Most of us are motivated by the reward, not always so much the process. If you are wanting to lose a little extra weight (Covid pounds), it's not the changing of your eating habits or the exercise that brings you "joy", it's the end result of meeting your goal and feeling better in the process.

"The young women will dance for joy, and the men – old and young – will join in the celebration. I will turn their mourning into joy. I will comfort them and exchange their sorrow for rejoicing."(Jeremiah 31:13)

On our journey to Bill's healing, we had moments when we "danced for joy" and God did the miraculous in our lives. Celebrating God's goodness and declaring the great things He had done was a blessing for us and others. Make sure that you share your joy with others – it's multiplied.

Praying my way through 2020 on the Glory Road is a daily, hourly, and sometimes minute by minute adventure. What a blessing to live in His Presence and to find comfort in God's arms of love. I look forward to the days of restoration in my own life but especially in our nation and in the lives of those I know and love.

Thank you for celebrating God's goodness. #Godisfaithful #TheGloryRoad

Day #199 November 4

Anchor Verse: Lamentations 3:24
"The Lord is my portion and my inheritance," says my soul; "Therefore I have hope in Him and wait expectantly for Him." (AMP)

Having hope in the Lord is not like a light switch that we turn on and off as we enter or leave a room. Hope in the Lord needs to burn brightly day and night – it's like an emergency beacon that must never fail – a lighthouse for the lost.

God's love never fails and our trust in God must never fail. There will be circumstances that put it to the test, moments when the teeter-totter of life is uncertain as to which way it will fall. But through it all, our faith, our hope is in the Lord, Maker of heaven and earth.

This verse from Lamentations 3:24 reminds us, "The Lord is my portion and my inheritance," says my soul; "Therefore I have hope in Him and wait expectantly for Him."

Why does my soul have hope and wait expectantly for the Lord? Because the Lord is my portion and my inheritance.

My hope is not found in the things of this world. My hope rests in the hands of God, the One who loves me unconditionally in every season.

As we wait in uncertainty, and for some, anxiety, about the outcome of the election in this country, God is inviting us to look beyond the headlines. God is still on His throne in heaven, that hasn't changed in the last 24 hours. You are still safe in His powerful, victorious right hand.

On our journey to Bill's healing, we encountered "white rapids" – places where life and death decisions had to be made almost instantaneously. In those moments, God gave us (me) clarity as I called on His name. I knew I could trust Him with Bill's life and his future.

Today, I still choose to trust God as we face the roaring waters of the Red Sea or the agitated waters after an earthquake with tsunami warnings. His peace comes to me like the still waters where He leads me to comfort my soul. The Glory Road is not always a place of peace in the world, it can be messy, yet, my hope is in the Lord and I wait for Him even in the chaos that surrounds me.

Thank you for your faithfulness. #Godisfaithful #TheGloryRoad

Day #200 November 5

Anchor Verse: Psalm 5:3
At each and every sunrise you will hear my voice as I prepare my sacrifice of prayer to you. Every morning I lay out the pieces of my life on the altar and wait for your fire to fall upon my heart. (TPT)

Early in the morning I will seek Your face, O Lord. Whether you are a "morning" person or not, morning comes to all of us, it signals the beginning of a brand new day.

I'm one of those "morning people", and not only that, I'm the instantly awake kind of morning person. For Bill, there was a little more of a process to waking up. But that's okay, God made us all differently.

When I get up, the first place I go is to spend time with God, to read His word, and pray, and ask Him what He wants to share with me. And what He speaks to me, I share with you. It's His gift to both of us.

What a beautiful picture written in words we find in the Passion translation for Psalm 5:3. "At each and every sunrise you will hear my voice as I prepare my sacrifice of prayer to you. Every morning I lay out the pieces of my life on the altar and wait for your fire to fall upon my heart."

"At each and every sunrise" David writes, you will hear my voice. Did you ever consider that your prayers were a sacrifice of praise and thanksgiving to the Lord?

Every day after spending time with the Lord, I am renewed, refreshed, rededicated to living my life for His name's honor and glory, not my own.

On our journey to Bill's healing, my morning time with the Lord was even more sacred. Whether that was at home in my office or on a cot or recliner in Bill's hospital room, God was there. The fire of His love touched my heart and I watched it fall upon Bill. God and Bill had their own conversations, and yes, you could see that Bill had been in the presence of the Lord.

For 200 days, I have walked on the Glory Road with the Lord to guide me and Bill's spirit very much alive in my heart. Day or night, the Lord calls me to himself, to spend time with Him, to wait expectantly. Not only to answer my prayers, but to continue this transformation into the woman of God He created me to be.

Thank you for your prayers. #Godisfaithful #TheGloryRoad

Day #201 November 6

Anchor Verse: Hebrews 3:6
But Christ, God's faithful Son, is in complete charge of God's house. And we Christians are God's house – he lives in us! – if we keep up our courage firm to the end, and our joy and our trust in the Lord. (TLB)

A house – we all have experience with a house. Whether we are living in one right now, have in the past, or have a friend or family member who lives in a house.

If you have ever watched a house being built, you understand the intricacy of its design and the solid foundation upon which it is built. (Well, a solid foundation is the plan anyway.)

This verse in Hebrews 3 reminds us that Christ is in complete charge of God's house. And as a believer, YOU are God's house, WE are God's house. He lives in us.

We also have a part to play. We must keep up our courage, hold fast our confidence, and hold firmly to "our bold confidence and victorious hope."(TPT)

This election week (2020) there has been a lot of discussion, interaction… even fear and anxiety about who will live in the most prominent house in the land – the White House. And we still wait for that outcome.

As believers, citizens of the Kingdom of God, we have a higher calling, a forever home in heaven, not of this world. The house that Christ occupies is within us, it is from that place that we let our light shine that others might see His love reflected in us.

On our journey to Bill's healing, we found ourselves in different locations "houses" (hospitals) but our greatest joy was that Christ lived in us, and we were always at home with Him. Count it all joy. His promises are true and faithful.

The Glory Road has turned a corner on this journey and I'm walking on a new street with new scenery, a new neighborhood. It's a place I've never been before but since Jesus is with me, I will not fear. Instead with my hand in His hand, we walk this path to my healing and to the fulfillment of His plans for me. Blessed be the name of the Lord.

Thank you for your encouragement. #Godisfaithful #TheGloryRoad

Day #202 November 7

Anchor Verse: Job 23:11

I have stayed in God's paths, following his steps. I have not turned aside. (TLB)

Are you good at following someone or do you like to be the one in the lead? There is an extra measure of grace that is needed to follow the leader.

When it comes to following God, there may be a similar conflict. Our human nature can come up against God's commands and the path He has chosen for us to walk. What will we choose? To follow God, no matter the cost? Or will we take the lead and run ahead, often to our peril?

If you recall the story of Job, he had a beautiful family, many possessions, status in the community and then along came Satan, to have a chat with God about Job. God allowed Satan to test Job, because God trusted Job. All Job's children died in one day, his herds were taken from him – Job lost it all. And then Job's flesh was affected by illness. Job's suffering was very personal.

Job 23:10 says, "But he knows the way that I take; when he has tested me, I will come forth as gold." (NIV) I would add a hearty amen to that statement. Even in the midst of his suffering, Job trusted God, that even in this testing and refining, he could come forth as gold – purer and more valuable in God's eyes.

Verse 11 goes on to say, "I have stayed in God's paths, following his steps. I have not turned aside." (TLB) Can that be said of us when we have gone through seasons of testing – that we have not turned aside but stayed on God's paths?

On our journey to Bill's healing, we became well acquainted with the refining fire. Bill was such an amazing fighter when it came to the trials he faced and the strength that was evident that came straight from the heart of God. Grit and grace would be the two words that I would use to describe God's gifts to Bill on his journey. Thank you, Lord.

The Glory Road may be covering new territory yet in many ways the path is the same, because it is God's path. I am following His steps. For many seasons and places in my life, I was in a leadership position, but through Bill's journey and now, mine too, Jesus is leading the way – through the deep waters and even through the refining fire. Being a follower of Jesus Christ actually means we must "follow" His footsteps.

Thank you for joining me on this journey. #Godisfaithful #TheGloryRoad

Day #203 November 8

Anchor Verse: Hebrews 4:14
...Let us hold firmly to the faith we profess. (NIV)

Storms, be they physical, emotional, mental, spiritual, financial will come and go, but God is with us forever.

2020 has been a year unlike any other (that is a gross understatement.) We have seen some of the greatest acts of kindness and witnessed some of the greatest tragedies and travesties. These have been the best of times and the worst of times as we have witnessed mankind's treatment of each other.

As believers in Christ, Christ-followers, do we look any differently to the world, to those around us?

Jesus when He walked this earth encountered all kinds of people, even those who were considered to be in the "unpopular" crowd of the day. There were many mouths that dropped wide open when Jesus approached the most unlikely people, including the mouths of his disciples.

As Christians, we are called to be "different." We are called to hold on to hope even on the darkest night. To love others, even when it's difficult and our love is not returned to us. Receiving love isn't the point of loving like Jesus did; it's in the giving that we receive the blessing of God himself.

In times of uncertainty, it is our faith that sustains us. Holding on to God's hand when we can't see the way ahead of us and listening for His still small voice to guide us across the minefield that lies across the road.

On our journey to Bill's healing, it was our faith in God that sustained us. It was the anchor in the storm, our lifeline to heaven itself that never failed. Even when life would take an unexpected turn, God never did. Our heavenly Father was always steady and faithful, and that allowed us to be unshakable and unstoppable.

The Glory Road has been a place to cling to my faith as never before in my life. I have experienced storms, and storms on top of storms, but this year gets the grand prize for opportunities to trust God. It's not what I get "out of it" that matters, that spurs me onward, but my faith in God is like a light that never grows dim, strength that never diminishes, and hope that cannot be quenched by the fires of adversity. Our God is an awesome God!

Thank you for your faithfulness 24/7. #Godisfaithful #TheGloryRoad

Day #204 November 9

Anchor Verse: Hebrews 6:11
Our great desire is that you will keep on loving others as long as life lasts, in order to make certain that what you hope for will come true. (NLT)

The Bible talks a lot about loving others, do you ever wonder why? Throughout the Bible we learn that God is love and He loved us first before we ever loved Him. It says while we were still "sinners" – lost in the darkness God wanted to have a relationship with us. God is your heavenly Father and He longs to walk and talk with you. He delights in your victories and your heavenly Father mourns when you mourn.

Jesus on the night He was betrayed shared this with His disciples in John 13: 34-35, "A new command I give you: Love one another. As I have loved you, so you must love one another. By this everyone will know that you are my disciples, if you love one another."

One of the ways that we show God how much we love Him is to love each other. In Hebrews 6:10, we are reminded that "He will not forget your work and the love you have shown him as you have helped his people and continue to help them."

There are many ways that we can help others. In 2020, we have learned how to help others in different ways than we have previously – more creatively. But the bottom line is still the same, we need to love each other because we need each other. There are many things that try and divide us but God knows that it is when we are "united" that we are the strongest.

On our journey to Bill's healing, your prayers, encouraging words, and tangible gifts blessed us more than you can understand. There is something about going through trials with others by your side that lightens the load. May you know that blessing today.

The Glory Road is a place where God gives me opportunities to love others and let my light shine for Him and for His glory. I didn't expect the road after Bill's death would include a cancer diagnosis so others could see my hope is in God, my heavenly Father. But God did!

Thank you for doing good things for others. This week is chemo week. Thanks for praying. #Godisfaithful #TheGloryRoad

Day #205 November 10

Anchor Verse: Mark 8:4

His disciples answered, "But where in this remote place can anyone get enough bread to feed them?" (NIV)

The search for "enough" – we are engaged in it every day. Whether it's enough money, enough food, enough energy, enough health, enough love… just enough.

You might be hungry and sit down for a meal, you eat, yet you are not satisfied. It isn't enough. The quantity isn't the issue, and not even the quality of the food, but it's that our hunger is for something greater than bread.

This passage in Mark 8 is familiar to many. Jesus starts out with these words, "I have compassion for these people; they have already been with me three days and have nothing to eat. If I send them home hungry, they will collapse on the way, because some of them have come a long distance." (Mark 8:2-3)

Jesus says, "What do you have?" They had seven loaves and a few small fish. The crowd sat down. Jesus gave thanks, and broke the bread, and gave it to His disciples to distribute and it was enough. More than enough, there were seven basketfuls of broken bread left over.

Now what we believe and what is true when we add Jesus into the equation are two different things. With God on our side, we always have "enough" and truthfully, "more than enough." His grace is sufficient and His power is made perfect in our weakness.

On our journey to Bill's healing, we learned about the all-sufficiency of God. It wasn't the resources we had in our bank account, in our home, in our medical team, in ourselves that mattered. It was the "enoughness" we had in God, in the resurrection power of Jesus Christ that made the difference – every day.

The Glory Road is an opportunity for me to recognize daily that I have "enough" in Jesus. I have enough time. I have enough strength. I have enough talent. I have enough financially. I am enough. Because God is enough. I lack nothing as David says in Psalm 23:1.

Thank you for your faithful prayers. My 7th chemo session is today. Declaring that God is enough! #Godisfaithful #TheGloryRoad

Day #206 November 11

Anchor Verse: Jeremiah 50:34
Yet their Redeemer is strong; the Lord Almighty is his name. He will vigorously defend their cause so that he may bring rest to their land, but unrest to those who live in Babylon. (NIV)

Today we celebrate Veteran's Day in America. We remember our military members' sacrifice and the sacrifice of their families, as some made the ultimate sacrifice, and laid down their lives in defense of this nation and its pursuit of freedom.

The even greater sacrifice, the greater gift God has prepared for us was the gift of Jesus. It cost Jesus His life so that we might be able to have eternal life in heaven with Him.

Jeremiah 50:34 reminds us of how vigorous His defense is of us. The New Living translation says, "But the one who redeems them is strong. His name is the Lord of Heaven's Armies." (NLT)

Our Redeemer is STRONG! The second part of verse 34 says, "He will vigorously defend their cause so that he may bring rest to their land, but unrest to those who live in Babylon."

This morning I was reminded to be intentional about pursuing God. That 99% obedience isn't good enough, it falls short, and truthfully, it's disobedience. God wants ALL of you – every part, every area of your life. Are you willing to let go of following your will and your way for God's will and God's way?

On our journey to Bill's healing, we were blessed to see the actions of the Lord of Angel Armies as He directed the angels to fight for us and make a way where there seemed to be no way. Instead of a dead end, a brick wall, it would turn into an open door. Yes, the Lord fought for us.

The Glory Road is filled with opportunities to surrender to the Lord and keep my eyes focused on Him, to look beyond the immediate mountains in front of me, to the blessings and glory that lie ahead of me. It is in submitting to God's will and God's way that I not only find peace and joy, but I am most effective for His kingdom. How can I reflect His glory if I am covered in the mud of my own mistakes or missteps when I choose "my way" over "God's way?" Not my will, but Thine be done, O Lord.

Thank you for your service to this country. #Godisfaithful #TheGloryRoad

Day #207 November 12

Anchor Verse: Matthew 18:20
For where two or three gather in my name, there am I with them. (NIV)

There are words in the Bible we read, but do we really stop to think about what they mean? This passage in Matthew 18:20 is one of those places.

Jesus is talking with His disciples, instructing them as they would be those who would carry on after Jesus. Jesus was "schooling" them.

Let's look at Matthew 18:18-20: ""Truly I tell you, whatever you bind on earth will be bound in heaven, and whatever you loose on earth will be loosed in heaven. Again, truly I tell you that if two of you on earth agree about anything they ask for, it will be done for them by my Father in heaven. For where two or three gather in my name, there am I with them."

As I read these verses, I sense that Jesus was trying to give His disciples a "clue" about the power and authority we have as we walk in partnership with Jesus. We are connected to heaven and Jesus' resurrection power as we come together in His name.

This is not power and authority to do the things that serve us, but to work in partnership with God to bring His kingdom to earth.

Prayer is one of my favorite activities. Being a prayer warrior is one of the highest callings that God has on my life. What an honor and privilege to be in relationship with God, and with others, so that I can be a bridge between heaven and earth.

Individually, God hears our prayers and answers, but when two or three come together in Jesus' name, He is with us. There is magnified power as we approach the throne room of grace to find mercy and help in our time of need.

On our journey to Bill's healing, we were so blessed by the many times, that you and so many others came together as two or three or more, to lift us up to our heavenly Father, Jehovah Rapha, to touch and heal Bill.

My path on the Glory Road contains not only stretches of the road where it's me and Jesus, but where I have the joy and privilege of walking with at least one or more others. It is those moments of togetherness when my strength increases, my blessings are multiplied, and laughter and joy mark the path like beautiful rose petals.

Thank you for walking this path with me. #Godisfaithful #TheGloryRoad

Day #208 November 13

Anchor Verse: Psalm 40:8
I take joy in doing your will, my God, for your instructions are written on my heart. (NLT)

What brings you joy? Did something instantly come to mind or did you need to think about it for a moment?

Joy is defined as a feeling of great pleasure and happiness.

As your brain scans through your memories, it will encounter moments of joy that even now bring a smile to your face. In fact, you may be preparing for some events that will bring you great joy.

I'm curious whether any of you associated "joy" with doing the will of God?

In Psalm 40, that's what the psalmist says, "I take joy in doing your will, my God, for your instructions are written on my heart."

There is a joy like none other when we are walking in the will of God, when we are walking in harmony with Him. When the Lord directs our path, there are treasures forevermore. The Christian life is not boring – far from it. God delights to bring joy and happiness to His children; He is a good, good Father.

On our journey to Bill's healing, there were many moments of joy, we lived in a spirit of joy. That may sound strange to some of you knowing what we went through, but when God is on your side you can find joy anywhere.

The Glory Road is a new place to discover both the joy in doing God's will but also pay attention to God's instructions that are written on my heart. We don't have to go looking for an instruction manual on Amazon or our local bookstore, God has written His instructions for "right living" on our heart. We need to pay attention and spend time with the Lord as He reveals His will and His way for us.

You are invited to pay attention to what brings you joy. Ask the Lord to show you His path, His instructions that are written on your heart. Walking hand in hand with the Lord will bring you joy like none other.

Thank you for sharing your joy. #Godisfaithful #TheGloryRoad

Day #209 November 14

Anchor Verse: Hebrews 10:36
For you have need of patient endurance [to bear up under difficult circumstances without compromising], so that when you have carried out the will of God, you may receive and enjoy to the full what is promised. (AMP)

Some weeks are long… and some weeks are longer, even though each of them has seven days. The burdens and joys of our lives ebb and flow and each day is not like a cookie cutter cookie – exactly the same.

There may be days when life is "easy" and other days when the burdens are great. But the good news is that God is faithful every day.

In Hebrews 10:36, we are reminded of the need to persevere as we experience difficulties in our lives, "For you have need of patient endurance [to bear up under difficult circumstances without compromising], so that when you have carried out the will of God, you may receive and enjoy to the full what is promised."

As we hold on and do not compromise, and complete the will of God in our lives, we will receive and enjoy "to the full" what God promised.

The Message translation says, "But we're not quitters who lose out. Oh, no! We'll stay with it and survive, trusting all the way." That's right! You are not a quitter and neither am I.

On our journey to Bill's healing, we learned the power of perseverance. Bill and I had walked through some deep waters previously, so we knew that God was trustworthy, but this stretch of the road called for blind faith. We enjoyed the gift of God's presence and the peace that abides there.

The Glory Road is a new path, yet God's mercy and grace are the same. His love for me is evidenced as He walks with me and talks with me. Joy is found in the most unusual places. I can't imagine life without my heavenly Father guiding me through the hills and valleys I encounter. I look forward to receiving my inheritance after I have completed my course.

Thank you for your encouraging words. #Godisfaithful #TheGloryRoad

Day #210 November 15

Anchor Verse: John 8:32
And you will know the truth, and the truth will set you free. (NLT)

When a person testifies in a courtroom they take this oath, "Do you swear to tell the truth, the whole truth, and nothing but the truth, so help you God?" (It's possible that in some places, the last part of this oath has been removed in the present day.)

"The truth, the whole truth, and nothing but the truth" – that sure seems like the way we should live our lives each day. It should be the standard about what comes out of our mouth, and honestly, what we take into our hearts and our minds and dwell upon.

Jesus said in John 8:32, "And you will know the truth, and the truth will set you free." There is freedom in knowing the truth and walking in it.

Walking in the web of tangled lies and deception, we lose our way. We are drawn off the path of life and end up in the ditch or caught on a merry-go-round of lies and someone else has the controls.

Truth or a lie – which will we believe? When the question is posed that way, quickly we respond, "Of course, I would choose the truth." But too often the reality is we choose to believe the lie or speak the lie.

On our journey to Bill's healing, we were presented with lots of information, from so many sources – not only medical teams but across the spectrum of life. There was only one plumb line – that was God and His Word. That is where we weighed the facts and determined the path to take. God's path was always the path to life.

The Glory Road in this season is filled with truth and lies. It seems that in 2020 there have been countless opportunities for all of us to sort out the truth from the lies. The only way to do that is for me to have a close relationship with God – to listen to the truth that comes from His Word, from His heart. Taking time to listen to God is critical on this new path.

Thank you for your persevering prayers. #Godisfaithful #TheGloryRoad

Day #211 November 16

Anchor Verse: Hebrews 11:29

Faith opened the way for the Hebrews to cross the Red Sea as if on dry land, but when the Egyptians tried to cross they were swallowed up and drowned! (TPT)

Our faith in what God can do makes the difference between what is possible and what is impossible.

We walk by faith every day because we don't know what's ahead of us. There are some who script out their days, weeks, months, and even years of their life. My life has never been that organized.

Yes, there were moments when I was in college and law school where I knew that my education would take a specific number of years to finish, if all went according to plan. But as to the individual days of my life – I couldn't predict the details.

When you let God have control of your life, you put your time, your schedule, and your priorities in His hands.

Hebrews 11 is known as the "Hall of Faith" as we look at many from the Bible who did extraordinary things as God directed their path. This verse in Hebrews 11:29 recounts the miracle of the Red Sea. "Faith opened the way for the Hebrews to cross the Red Sea as if on dry land, but when the Egyptians tried to cross they were swallowed up and drowned!"

Egyptian soldiers were in hot pursuit and before them was the Red Sea at flood stage – either way looked like certain death. And then God moved. Moses held up his rod out over the water, and the priests moved forward. As their feet got wet, God held back the waters and they walked on dry ground. But the Egyptian army perished in the waters.

On our journey to Bill's healing, we had some Red Sea moments with his health. We were caught between impassable waters and the "enemy" approaching from behind. But in that moment, we cried out to the Lord, and He heard our prayer. As we stepped out in faith and moved "forward" into Bill's healing, God parted our version of the Red Sea.

The Glory Road is now a place for me to step out in faith. It is a place where I encounter new situations and challenges. Every day I ask the Lord to direct my steps. When I am faced with a mountain, the Lord hears my cry and makes a way where there seems to be no way.

Thank you for holding up my arms. #Godisfaithful #TheGloryRoad

Day #212 November 17

Anchor Verse: Hebrews 12:7
Endure hardship as discipline; God is treating you as his children. For what children are not disciplined by their father? (NIV)

Hardship, suffering, hard times, trials and training – all of these are "gifts" from God that help us to become more like Him. Did she really say that hardship and suffering are a gift?

For many of us, 2020 has been filled with "gifts" that looked like this. Many times there wasn't even beautiful wrapping paper on the gift or a nice gift bag, but the "gift" of suffering, trials, or calamity was thrust into our hands.

What might seem like persecution or loss to us, if we could see from God's perspective, we might have a different perspective.

Hebrews 12:7 says, "Endure hardship as discipline; God is treating you as his children. For what children are not disciplined by their father?"

Discipline – another topic we might rather skip. But it is through discipline, either administered by another, or self-discipline, that changes our lives. It calls us to a different standard, a higher place.

On our journey to Bill's healing, we learned about discipline on two planes: the natural and the spiritual. Bill learned the disciplines involved in healing from a medical perspective, what he needed to do to work in partnership with his team. On a spiritual level, God called him to "rise up" and "sit" with God and see life from a different perspective. Now, Bill has 20/20 vision.

As I find my way down the Glory Road, there are places where the Lord disciplines me as His daughter. Places where the Lord wants to have me rise to a higher place with Him to carry out His will in His way. It's not always easy, but it's always worth it. Letting go of what so easily entangles me in the world and exchanging it for His robe of righteousness as I walk the path where He is honored and glorified in me.

Thank you for your persevering prayers. #Godisfaithful #TheGloryRoad

Day #213 November 18

Anchor Verse: Hebrews 13:2
Do not neglect to extend hospitality to strangers [especially among the family of believers – being friendly, cordial, and gracious, sharing the comforts of your home and doing your part generously], for by this some have entertained angels without knowing it. (AMP)

Entertaining angels…God is a God of surprises.

Often we encounter people in our lives who we do not know. That might be in the grocery store, a restaurant, on vacation, or even a Zoom call. But in that encounter, heaven touches earth. They may not have wings like an angel but they are definitely messengers from God to encourage, to speak truth, to give direction in our lives.

They are often God's way of either keeping us on track or getting us on a "new" track.

Remember the story of Abraham and Sarah from Genesis 18. Abraham is sitting in the entrance of his tent in the heat of the day when he looks up and sees three men coming. He doesn't recognize them but that doesn't stop him from rushing out into the heat to greet them and offer them food and drink.

Abraham even offers them a place to rest under the tree and to have their feet washed. The food is prepared and while they were eating, one of them tells Abraham that he would return in about a year and Sarah would give birth to a son. Sarah and Abraham were old. Sarah was past her childbearing years, but that didn't stop God's plans for her. Sarah did indeed become pregnant and give birth to a son, Isaac. God changed the course of their lives with this visit from angels.

On our journey to Bill's healing, there were many times God sent "angels" to Bill to intersect his path. We don't have an Abraham and Sarah story, but I know there were many heavenly encounters – often clothed in human flesh. Many of you were like angels to us.

The Glory Road is filled with new experiences, new people, and new lessons to be learned. This verse from Hebrews 13:2 reminds us, "Do not neglect to extend hospitality to strangers [especially among the family of believers—being friendly, cordial, and gracious, sharing the comforts of your home and doing your part generously], for by this some have entertained angels without knowing it."

Thank you for your faithful prayers. #Godisfaithful #TheGloryRoad

Day #214 November 19

Anchor Verse: James 1:22
Do not merely listen to the word, and so deceive yourselves. Do what it says. (NIV)

Listening is not enough when it comes to the Word of God. We must couple our new knowledge with action. Otherwise, we are no better off than those who have never read God's words of truth.

We are living in a time in history where so much information is available at our fingertips. It's almost like we think about a topic, and everything and more than what we want to know, is right there on our phone or computer screen.

Head knowledge is not enough, it needs to make the short distance to our hearts. "For what profit is it to a man if he gains the whole world, and loses his own soul?" (Matthew 16:26 (NIV)

Following Jesus will transform your life. Doing what Jesus did. Thinking like Jesus did not only internally, but following that with how He treated others. The Son of God left the glory of heaven and came to earth, not to be served but to serve others. And we are called to do likewise.

On our journey to Bill's healing, many parts of our lives were turned upside down, and not only physically. God invited us to look at life differently, at others, our own priorities, and how we were choosing to live life. Bill's health journey also radically transformed our relationship with God and each other.

The Glory Road offers me the opportunity not only to listen to what God has to say about how to live my life but to do it. It's an opportunity to "practice what I preach" or model what the Bible says about how a Christian should live their life. "Love another as I have loved you." Jesus showed me that there is no greater joy than serving others, laying down my will for His will, to submit to the Lord and watch what He can do with a life surrendered to Him. There is great joy on the Glory Road even in a season of difficulty in the world around us.

Thank you for choosing to live out the spirit of the gospel. #Godisfaithful #TheGloryRoad

Day #215 November 20

Anchor Verse: Isaiah 54:2
Increase is coming, so enlarge your tent and add extensions to your dwelling. Hold nothing back! Make the tent ropes longer and the pegs stronger. (TPT)

There are four seasons: Winter, Spring, Summer, and Fall. Each of them has a different purpose – a purpose that was designed by God when He created the world. Most of us probably have a "favorite" season – but in God's eyes, each one is His favorite.

In our lives, there are seasons like this too. There are times of joy and times of sorrow. There are times of plenty and times of scarcity. There are times to stay and times to go.

Isaiah 54:2 talks about a time to grow. "Increase is coming, so enlarge your tent and add extensions to your dwelling. Hold nothing back! Make the tent ropes longer and the pegs stronger."

This morning as I was sitting with the Lord, this verse struck me. If we look at the world around us, with great chaos in many areas and illness on the rise once again, it doesn't really look like "good soil" for growth.

However in God's kingdom, often the opposite holds true. In the spiritual realm, God sees things differently.

It reminds me of farmers, and even gardeners, who plant bulbs, seeds, or crops before the winter storms come, and then in the spring, new growth appears. "Increase is coming" – those are the words of the Lord to us this morning. Blessed be the name of the Lord.

On our journey to Bill's healing, we saw God work in unusual ways. What might have seemed to be a "barren time" in our lives to many, instead the Lord was bringing us a rich harvest. We experienced so much joy in the midst of adversity. In the natural, resources might have been scarce, but God multiplied them and we always had more than enough.

The Glory Road is also filled with seemingly opposites. Where it seems there should be sorrow, there is joy. Where the world predicts one outcome, God produces the opposite. Out of sickness is coming greater strength and resiliency. Only God…

Thank you for standing on the wall and being the watchman in the night. It was seven months ago yesterday that God called Bill home. The Lord is my refuge and strength. #Godisfaithful #TheGloryRoad

Day #216 November 21

Anchor Verse: James 3:13
If you are wise, live a life of steady goodness so that only good deeds will pour forth. And if you don't brag about them, then you will be truly wise! (TLB)

During the course of my lifetime, I have often heard the phrase, "Wisdom comes with age." As we live life, we learn a lot from our experiences. It's not always from what we do right where we find the lessons, but in our mistakes and missteps we learn lessons never to be forgotten.

Our pastor often reminds us, "Knowledge comes from making our own mistakes. Wisdom comes from learning from the mistakes of others."

In Job 12:12, it says, "Is not wisdom found among the aged? Does not long life bring understanding?" (NIV)

This may be true, but this passage in James 3:13 broadens the audience of those who are wise. It is not only for the aged or those who have lived a long life. "If you are wise, live a life of steady goodness so that only good deeds will pour forth. And if you don't brag about them, then you will be truly wise!"

Living a life of steady goodness is something that is always admired and valued. But in this season, the light, love, and encouragement that springs out of these actions is even more important.

On our journey to Bill's healing, we learned so much about the shadow our life casts. God's light in you, walking in obedience with God, and doing good deeds shines brightly in a world filled with darkness. A simple "thank you" can pierce the night with God's love. Our actions impact the world around us – one way or the other.

As I follow this new course called the Glory Road, I am learning so much about wisdom. Bill used to say that the "Ancient One" had great wisdom. Wisdom comes from following the Lord and walking in step with Him. Living a life of steady goodness makes a difference. Even if only one person was impacted by a loving, kind gesture, it's worth it. It's about how you live not only how you talk.

Thank you for your encouragement. Thank you for living lives filled with good deeds not only "good talk." #Godisfaithful #TheGloryRoad

Day #217 November 22

Anchor Verse: James 4:4
Therefore, anyone who chooses to be a friend of the world becomes an enemy of God. (NIV)

There are two sides to every battle. There is right and wrong. There is day and night. There is friend and enemy. The world is filled with opposites.

God is very clear that He draws the line between His way and the way of the world. They are polar opposites. You cannot have your feet planted on both sides of the fence.

Matthew 6:24 says, "No one can serve two masters; for either he will hate the one and love the other, or he will be devoted to the one and despise the other. You cannot serve God and mammon [money, possessions, fame, status, or whatever is valued more than the Lord]."

In the Old Testament, the same decision was placed before God's people time and time again. What they decided to do determined their course. Either they were blessed by the Lord or they were not. In fact, on some occasions the punishment was pretty heavy for their disobedience.

This passage in James 4:4 tells us, "Anyone who chooses to be a friend of the world becomes an enemy of God." Those are pretty strong words. But we know that the apostle Paul was never one to pull punches, he spoke the hard truth.

On our journey to Bill's healing, the Lord was gracious to us because we walked in obedience to Him. We chose to be God's friend, and not align ourselves with the world. It was His hand that sustained Bill. God will fight for you when you choose to live a life that honors the Lord.

The Glory Road traveling through 2020, a place where the world seems to be fighting battles on many levels, is a place to declare my allegiance to the Lord. It is by His love, grace, and mercy that my feet walk on solid ground.

This is the question before us, individually, as families, as the church, and as a nation. We must determine whether we will walk on the path that leads to life for all eternity with the Lord or settle for the momentary pleasures of the world. The choice is yours.

Thank you for your friendship. #Godisfaithful #TheGloryRoad

Day #218 November 23

Anchor Verse: James 5:11

Indeed we count them blessed who endure (persevere). You have heard of the perseverance of Job and seen the end intended by the Lord – that the Lord is very compassionate and merciful. (NKJV)

Life is not easy. It is, in fact, a bag of "mixed blessings." There are good times and hard times. There is joy and there is sorrow. But there is one constant that remains – God's love for us.

If you are going through a time of suffering right now in your own life or someone you love, know that "the Lord is close to the brokenhearted and saves those who are crushed in spirit." (Psalm 34:18)

The Passion translation says, "We honor them as our heroes because they remained faithful even while enduring great sufferings."

Heroes – those who go above and beyond the call of duty, those who endure suffering without complaining, who serve others without counting the cost, who love God so much that they rest on His faithfulness, and who know that one day, their story will be like Job's story.

In the Old Testament, we read about Job who went through tremendous loss and then his friends weren't exactly the best encouragers in the world, but ultimately, God said, "Enough is enough." Everything Job lost was restored, and even more.

On our journey to Bill's healing, we learned the depths of God's compassion and mercy. Yes, Bill suffered, probably more than I know, but God was faithful and only allowed it for so long before relief came. I am so grateful for God's love. His mercies are new every morning and great is His faithfulness. (Lamentations 3:23)

The Glory Road is a place where God's love, compassion, and mercy fill every step. There have been many places along the way where God said, "It's not going to be as bad as you think it's going to be." And God in His mercy stepped in and was a shield about me. It wasn't necessarily "painless" but it wasn't as bad as I thought it was going to be.

Tomorrow is my last chemo treatment (11.24). I thank God every day for His mercy and grace on this section of the road. As to what lies ahead, God knows that too, and He will reveal it.

Thank you for your persistent prayers. #Godisfaithful #TheGloryRoad

Day #219 November 24

Anchor Verse: Psalm 96:11-12

Let the skies sing for joy! Let the earth join in the chorus. Let oceans thunder and fields echo this ecstatic praise until every swaying tree of every forest joins in, lifting up their songs of joyous praise to him! (TPT)

It is Thanksgiving week. It's time to turn our hearts away from the distractions of the world and lift our praises toward heaven. The Lord has done great things for us; the Lord has done great things!

Praise fills the Bible, not only from God's people, but that all heaven and earth sing praises to the King of kings and the Lord of lords.

The psalms written by King David are filled with songs of praise and thanksgiving. If you need an "attitude adjustment" or your "hope" tank needs to be filled, head over to the book of Psalms and be filled up.

Psalm 96:11-12 says, "Let the skies sing for joy! Let the earth join in the chorus. Let oceans thunder and fields echo this ecstatic praise until every swaying tree of every forest joins in, lifting up their songs of joyous praise to him!"

Those words paint a picture – a picture of all of creation praising their Creator. The chorus of praise is magnified as they do it together.

On our journey to Bill's healing, we learned about praising the Lord. Your heart can choose to praise the Lord even in the midst of difficulties. One of the greatest joys I can recall was when Bill was feeling well enough at the rehab hospital that I could take him outside. Fresh air, sunshine, seeing the trees, hearing the wind, these are the sounds of life, the signs of God's love for us. Never take them for granted.

The Glory Road is a place where God has called me to look at things differently. No one else but our heavenly Father can turn mourning into dancing and exchange your clothes of mourning for a garment of praise.

Today was supposed to be my last chemo treatment. Yesterday, the doctor said, "No more." God said seven chemo treatments were enough. We have "changed lanes" and are pursuing a different path to the finish line. God's loving hand is all over this new dance. I praise Him this morning for His love for me and that the best is yet to come. Join me in a dance of praise with those swaying trees in every forest. We love you, Lord.

Thank you for your faithful prayers. #Godisfaithful #TheGloryRoad

Day #220 November 25

Anchor Verse: 1 Peter 2:5a
Come and be his "living stones" who are continually being assembled into a sanctuary for God. (TPT)

Jesus Christ is the cornerstone of the Christian faith. In Isaiah 28:16 it says, "See, I lay a stone in Zion, a chosen and precious cornerstone, and the one who trusts in him will never be put to shame." To those of us who believe, the stone is precious, to those who are unbelievers, it is "A stone that causes people to stumble and a rock that makes them fall." (Isaiah 8:14)

It goes back to obedience again. If we follow the path Jesus set out for us, it is the path of life. For those who choose not to follow Jesus, it is a path of darkness.

In 1 Peter 2:5a, it tells us that those of us who have chosen to follow Jesus are His "living stones" and we are being assembled into a sanctuary for God.

We are "living stones" because our lives reflect the hope that comes in Jesus' name.

You have heard the expression that you're the only Jesus that some may ever see. It's a high calling, a big responsibility we have as Christians to let our light shine so that Jesus is seen in us.

Instead of revenge, we turn the other cheek. When we are wronged, we forgive. We love when others hate. We give, not to receive, but out of the abundance of what God has done for us.

On our journey to Bill's healing, we were called to be "living stones" in some unusual places. In the midst of chaos and confusion, Bill and I were called to reflect God's peace. Where people were hurting, we were called to bring His love, in both word and deed.

The Glory Road is a place where I see "living stones" – people who are doing good to reflect the light and love of Jesus in a world that is stressed out and sees more darkness than light. We have the choice to be more like Jesus or like the world where each man's personal survival is his only goal. When I choose to live in faith instead of fear, I am choosing to trust Jesus who walked His own path of suffering. Make me more like You, Lord.

Thank you for your faithfulness. #Godisfaithful #TheGloryRoad

Day #221 November 26

Anchor Verse: Psalm 147:1
Praise the Lord! For it is good to sing praises to our God; For it is pleasant, and praise is beautiful. (NKJV)

Bless the Lord, O my soul, and all that is within me, praise His holy name!

It's Thanksgiving Day (2020) in America and it's time to praise the Lord. Pandemic or no pandemic, God's goodness is not limited by what is happening around us. Good times or bad times, in joy or in sorrow, God doesn't change. His love for you is as great today as it was yesterday, or as it will be tomorrow.

Our response should be a heart filled with praise and thanksgiving. Many songs have been written that remind us that "the Lord inhabits our praise."

There is something about getting together with the family of God, or your own family or friends, and singing praises to the Lord that shifts the whole atmosphere around us. It chases away the darkness and the light grows brighter. It's like turning on a flashlight or lighting a candle and instantly the shadows that surrounded you that made everything look scary are gone. Just like that! Because darkness is the absence of light, where there is light, darkness cannot abide.

On our journey to Bill's healing, we discovered that praising the Lord, filling our hearts, minds, and mouths with praise and thanksgiving, turned the dark places into places of hope. It's not only words of praise and thanksgiving, but words that honor each other and lift each other up that bring the light of God's love.

The Glory Road has been filled with songs of praise and thanksgiving. Yes, there have been times when those songs were watered with my tears, but through it all, God's faithfulness reigns. I can't imagine life without God in the middle of it. His faithfulness endures to ALL generations.

Thank you for your faithful prayers. I'll be missing Bill a lot today but he is always with me in spirit. Yesterday I was thinking of all the Thanksgiving dinners my mom cooked and time with aunts, uncles, and cousins.

Thank you, Lord, for precious memories and new ones to be made.
#Godisfaithful #TheGloryRoad

Day #222 November 27

Anchor Verse: 1 Peter 4:11
Do you have the gift of speaking? Then speak as though God himself were speaking through you. Do you have the gift of helping others? Do it with all the strength and energy that God supplies. Then everything you do will bring glory to God through Jesus Christ. All glory and power to him forever and ever! Amen. (NLT)

For as long as we live, we are like a gold mine, with more God-given gifts and talents to be discovered. Thank you for sharing your gifts with us.

This verse in 1 Peter 4 is a continuation of the previous verse where Peter speaks to the followers of Jesus and reminds them that they should "use whatever gift you have received to serve others." They are faithful stewards of God's grace in its various forms.

In verse 11, Peter speaks specifically to two gifts: speaking and helping others (serving). If you are called to speak (preach) "speak as though God himself were speaking through you." Through the Holy Spirit, God is speaking through you, if you choose to be God's mouthpiece, and not for your own edification or ego. Like clay in the potter's hand, we can choose to let God use us to our full potential if we yield ourselves and our gifts to Him.

Peter also speaks about helping others and serving, to do it with ALL the strength and energy that God supplies. How are you feeling the day after Thanksgiving? Did you serve in God's strength or your own?

On our journey to Bill's healing, we learned about using our gifts and encouraging those who served us. It is a blessed experience when we allow others to serve us as we also serve others. "Thank you" goes a long way when serving is your life.

I think of those serving on the frontline, especially those in healthcare. Thank you so much for your service and putting your life and your energy into serving those who are sick among us. May the Lord bless you abundantly.

The Glory Road is an opportunity not only to use my gifts but to encourage others in their giftings. These last few years the tables were turned. Usually Bill and I were the ones who were always serving others, now it is my opportunity to let others serve me.

Thank you for using your gifts to help us. #Godisfaithful #TheGloryRoad

Day #223 November 28

Anchor Verse: Romans 15:5-6
May the God who gives endurance and encouragement give you the same attitude of mind toward each other that Christ Jesus had, so that with one mind and one voice you may glorify the God and Father of our Lord Jesus Christ.(NIV)

Endurance and encouragement come from the hand and the heart of God. We are closing in on the end of November, coming into the last month of 2020. Some of you may be sighing with relief… finally we're almost done with the year.

This year has been filled with unexpected surprises – some good and others not so good. This verse in Romans 15 reminds us of the power of unity.

"May the God who gives endurance and encouragement give you the same attitude of mind toward each other that Christ Jesus had, so that with one mind and one voice you may glorify the God and Father of our Lord Jesus Christ." With one mind and one voice may we glorify God!

A Christmas tradition in many communities is Handel's Messiah choral arrangement presented by a choir from the local area, including my hometown. It's so powerful for a wide range of voices, and ages, to come together to praise the Lord. Music is powerful in itself but blended hearts and voices filled with praise to the Lord, "raises" the ceiling.

On our journey to Bill's healing, we were grateful recipients of God's endurance and encouragement. And so blessed by the huge "choir"/"symphony" of people including you, who with one mind and one voice with your prayers and petitions on Bill's behalf brought honor and glory to the Lord. It was a beautiful picture of unity. Thank you.

The Glory Road on this stretch of tarmac has challenged us to encourage one another as individually we persevere and endure many circumstances. New strength comes when we are united rather than divided. When we have the attitude of Jesus, who was the greatest servant leader to walk the face of the earth, mountains are overcome and barriers knocked down.

I have found new strength in the Lord in this season as I have taken on the attitude of Christ. Even Jesus suffered in His life, I can expect nothing less. There is great glory that awaits all who persevere, now and for eternity.

Thank you for your encouraging words. #Godisfaithful #TheGloryRoad

Day #224 November 29

Anchor Verse: 2 Peter 1:3

By his divine power, God has given us everything we need for living a godly life. We have received all of this by coming to know him, the one who called us to himself by means of his marvelous glory and excellence. (NLT)

In Psalm 23:1, it says, "The Lord is my Shepherd, I lack nothing." That's a powerful statement. Too often we talk about what we don't have rather than focusing on the blessings God had given us.

When it comes to the power to live a godly life, the work has already been done. God has given us EVERYTHING we need for living a godly life.

Maybe think of it in practical terms. Your bank account is sufficient to cover all of your needs today and every day of your life. Your kitchen cupboards and pantry, and refrigerator are filled with every food need and many of your wants. Your energy level is always there to meet the challenges of the day and you sleep well all night.

When we look at the spiritual aspect of our lives, it is even greater than that. 2 Peter 1:3 says, "By his divine power, God has given us everything we need for living a godly life. We have received all of this by coming to know him, the one who called us to himself by means of his marvelous glory and excellence."

"God has given us everything we need for living a godly life!" We lack nothing. We have been given the gift of the Holy Spirit to direct our path and daily help us to walk in rhythm with God, step by step, day by day.

It's like having your kitchen fully stocked. If you don't make the effort to prepare a meal or go to the cupboard or refrigerator and get the food and eat it, you could still starve to death. There is some effort necessary on your part.

On our journey to Bill's healing, every day we made choices. Bill chose in every moment what he would do, seek the Lord and life or just "be" and have life happen to him. Godly living requires active participation on our part. We must be a "doer" of the word not only a "hearer." (James 1:22)

This new stretch of road, the Glory Road, I must choose between pursuing God's best for me or the path of complacency. God has not called us to mediocrity, but to excellence. It's what I tell my clients. I have one standard and that's God's standard: excellence.

Thank you for holding me up in prayer. #Godisfaithful #TheGloryRoad

Day #225 November 30

Anchor Verse: Ezekiel 38:1
The word of the LORD came to me. (NIV)

When God created the world, He created man and woman in His own image. God wanted to have a relationship with them. In the early chapters of Genesis, we read about how God would come and visit Adam and Eve in the cool of the day. (Genesis3:8)

Our heavenly Father's heart's desire is to walk and talk with us. When we start our day off in the Word of God, we learn more about God and His character and our call to godly living.

God wants us to learn to hear His still, small voice and to walk in His way. It's like our relationships with those we know and love, family and friends, when they call us on the phone we recognize their voice. Our voice reflects what is going on in our heart and mind. Whether it is joy, sorrow, anger, frustration, or anything else in-between, it is difficult to keep our emotions out of our voice.

In Ezekiel 38:1 it says, "The word of the Lord came to me." Ezekiel is a prophet in the Old Testament who was appointed to be a mouthpiece for God. In Ezekiel 38, he is receiving another message from the Lord to share with God's people about events yet to come.

On our journey to Bill's healing, Bill had many encounters with God. Some of them at critical intersections of his life, and often the Lord would speak to him during his dreams at night and sometimes would give him visions. I was blessed when Bill would share their conversations.

Walking the Glory Road I have learned to hear God's voice in a new way. Not only is the Bible, alive and filled with God's power, as we read and study it but when we take the time to sit and listen to God, He has more to say.

Thank you for holding up my arms on when I am weak and for celebrating my joy. Your friendship is priceless. #Godisfaithful #TheGloryRoad

December 2020

You are the light of the world.
~ Matthew 5:14

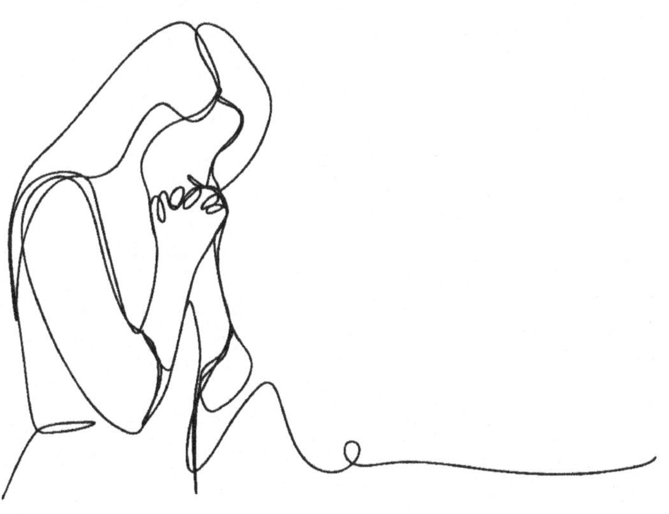

Day #226 December 1

Anchor Verse: 2 Peter 3:1

This is my second letter to you, dear friends, and in both of them I have tried to stimulate your wholesome thinking and refresh your memory. (NLT)

Writing letters has become a lost art for many in this day of technology. So when we receive a handwritten note or letter, it is something we treasure. Re-reading an email or text message doesn't have quite the impact of a letter written in a friend or loved one's handwriting.

We have the option of many forms of communication but in Peter's day, writing letters was "the" way it was done. And we can only imagine how long it might have taken to get a letter from one place to another. This was long before "Pony Express" in the U.S. or overnight Priority Mail.

And Peter's letter had a purpose, so did the ones that Paul wrote to many churches throughout the region.

In 2 Peter 3:1, Peter clearly points out the purpose of his letter. "This is my second letter to you, dear friends, and in both of them I have tried to stimulate your wholesome thinking and refresh your memory."

Do we need to be reminded to stimulate our wholesome thinking and refresh our memory?

On our journey to Bill's healing, God was often in the business of "course corrections" or in the famous words of GPS – "recalculating." When you invite Jesus to be the Lord and Savior of your life, He will point out areas that need to be polished to become more like Him. More like Jesus was the order of the day.

The Glory Road is definitely a path of learning, a path where the Lord reminds me, sometimes night and day, of His plans and purposes for me. And in the process of walking the Glory Road, God continues to remind me of what matters – to walk in obedience to the Lord's commands and to become more like Jesus every day.

Thank you for your persistent prayers. They move the hand of God. Great news yesterday about my healing – it's progressing forward – more documentation for God's miracle. #Godisfaithful #TheGloryRoad

Day #227 December 2

Anchor Verse: Colossians 1:13
For he has rescued us from the dominion of darkness and brought us into the kingdom of the Son he loves. (NIV)

You have been rescued. Did you know that? A picture comes to mind of a person shipwrecked on a deserted island with no resources, no one else there, waiting to be rescued. And days, maybe weeks pass and he sees a plane fly overhead to rescue him or a ship at sea. But finally, he is delivered from this barren place where it seemed that all hope was gone.

God knew the ending of the story, His rescue plan. There was hope – unseen hope. The man needed to have faith in the One who loved him so much. The man was not abandoned, he was only waiting to be found.

That is our story. You might feel overwhelmed by the dominion of darkness that surrounds us in this season. It looks dark to your left and to your right. In fact, you continue to look for the light to rescue you from the darkness.

The good news is that the Light has already come into the world – His name is Jesus. In this Advent season as we approach Christmas, we have the opportunity to get reacquainted with Jesus – the hope of the world.

We are no longer captives of the darkness but we are conquerors. In Romans 8:37 it says, "No, in all these things we are more than conquerors through him who loved us." And "all these things" includes whatever horrific, scary, overwhelming thing or circumstance that you or your loved one is facing.

On our journey to Bill's healing, we faced some scary places. Places where it looked like a brick wall but instead God opened a door where His truth, His love, His presence was greater than anything we faced. We chose to walk ahead with our hand in God's hand and let His love lead the way.

The Glory Road is a path where I have the honor and privilege to make those same choices every day. To the darkness that surrounds me, I will boldly declare, "Greater is He that is in me than he that is in the world." Greater is He that is in me than this cancer that has attacked my body. Greater is He that is in YOU than any weapon that has formed against you.

Thank you for your faithful prayers. #Godisfaithful #TheGloryRoad

Day #228 December 3

Anchor Verse: 1 John 2:17
And this world is fading away, along with everything that people crave. But anyone who does what pleases God will live forever. (NLT)

The world we see today as we survey the landscape is not the same world we knew five years ago, or 10, 25, 50 years ago, and definitely not 100 years ago. In some areas, it seems that we are advancing.

We are reminded in the Word of God, that in fact, the world is fading away. For eternity, it is God and God's Kingdom alone that will remain. Our mission, both now and for eternity, is to dedicate our lives to living for God and walking in obedience to His commands.

It's time to do a self-check this morning. Ask yourself, where am I storing my treasures? For where your treasure is, there your heart will be also. (Matthew 6:21) If your treasures are stored up in heaven, your faith and your focus will be on God. If your treasures are here on earth, then they will fade away. You will be left with nothing.

On our journey to Bill's healing, we learned a lot about what really mattered. Material possessions, status, finances, fame, fortune – the representation of a "successful" life in the world were not the markers of our success. Every day we lived for Jesus and let His light shine in us and through us, was a victory. May we all be lighthouses of hope.

This path on the Glory Road has been a great reminder of what it says in 1 John 2:17, "But anyone who does what pleases God will live forever." I walk to please the Lord, not to please others in my life or make the world's standard, my standard. What people crave will soon pass away, but Jesus the rock of my salvation cannot be moved.

My hope comes in the name of the Lord, Maker of heaven and earth. As I fight this physical enemy in my body, that has chosen to attack the temple of the Holy Spirit, I know that God is mightier, and ultimately, I am victorious in Jesus' name. But like any journey, there is a beginning, middle, and end. I am in the middle someplace. God knows exactly where. He knows the day of my healing. Your heavenly Father knows the day of your victory too.

Thank you for your faithful prayers. Thank you for the hope that lives in you because Jesus lives in you. #Godisfaithful #TheGloryRoad

Day #229 December 4

Anchor Verse: 1 John 3:1

See what an incredible quality of love the Father has shown to us, that we would [be permitted to] be named and called and counted the children of God! And so we are! (AMP)

The love of God the Father who calls us His children – we are named, and called, and counted as the children of God. If you were struggling with your self-worth this morning, I pray that this verse will set the record straight.

The Creator of the universe who put the spots on the leopard, the stripes on the zebra, painted the colors on each bird, and determined the size and shape of each leaf on every tree, designed you to be uniquely you. And as much as God loves the world, He loves you even more. God, the Father, sent His only son, Jesus, into the world to pay the price for our redemption that we might live with Him forever.

When we were kids in Sunday School, we sang a little song that was created from this verse. And we sang it as a "round" – where one group would start and the other would echo the song. Do people even sing like that anymore?

In the world, it seems that we have a sharp contrast between God's love and what the world calls "love"… or more accurately, how we "love" each other in the world. God's love is not a superficial love or "what's in it for me" kind of love, but God loves deeply and unconditionally.

On our journey to Bill's healing, we were blessed not only by God's love but by the love of others. Often children of God are known by their actions and the way they treat others, even more than by what they say. Bill and I had an opportunity to show that love to each other and those who cared for Bill.

The Glory Road has given me an opportunity to not only reflect God's love but to receive God's love as His daughter in a brand new way. As a 61-year-old woman, I have been blessed with good health for pretty much my entire life. So being in a position where I am fighting a significant health challenge is a new place for me. But God has shown me His love in amazing ways. Not only in the darkness of the night when I am alone, but by day, from the love of others, like you. I am so grateful to be a child of God and for all my brothers and sisters in the family of God too.

Thank you for loving others. #Godisfaithful #TheGloryRoad

Day #230 December 5

Anchor Verse: 1 John 4

We love, because He first loved us. Love is the greatest gift of all. To love and be loved is our heart's desire. Why? Because God first loved us. (AMP)

When your heart is filled with love, it can't help but overflow to others. It's like a pitcher of liquid, whatever is in it will flow out of it as you begin to pour. The question is: what is your heart filled with today?

God created us from His heart of love, and as a child, we come into the world filled up with God's love – a love gift from heaven.

As we continue to grow up and be exposed to the influences of the world, we determine what we "feed" ourselves. I'm not talking about the food you put into your mouth, but rather what you put into your heart and mind. Are you feasting on things that build you up or tear you down? Is it life-giving or does it make you angry, frustrated, and depressed?

On our journey to Bill's healing, it was important to guard what Bill was exposed to on his road to recovery. After his brain bleed and weeks of sedation, as Bill woke up into a "new" world, I was vigilant about who was around him and what was spoken in his presence. As much as possible, we aimed for "good" seed to be planted in the "soil" of Bill's heart and mind.

This path on the Glory Road is a place to love others as God has loved me. People need God's love more than ever. And how do they receive it? Through the lives of God's children – we must be carriers of the light and love of Jesus. They need a "transfusion" of God's love.

Loving others is not tied to how much money we spend on each other. God's love for us came in the form of His son, Jesus. That gift cost Him everything. The best gift we can give in return is to live our lives to honor Him and bring glory to His holy name.

During this Christmas season, I invite you to give the gift of love. That might be your time, attention, gifts, and talents to bring cheer to another person in your life. Look around you. There are many in our own neighborhoods that might need an extra measure of love, or someone in the hundreds or thousands of friends you have on social media. Often those who need a dose of God's love are "hidden in plain sight."

Thank you for loving us as God loves you. #Godisfaithful #TheGloryRoad

Day #231 December 6

Anchor Verse: Daniel 4:37
Now I, Nebuchadnezzar, praise and exalt and glorify the King of heaven, because everything he does is right and all his ways are just. And those who walk in pride he is able to humble. (NIV)

Pride and humility are at opposite ends of the spectrum.

"God opposes the proud but shows favor to the humble." (James 4:6)

King Nebuchadnezzar had built a huge statue of himself. Everyone in the land was to bow to it and worship "him." The three young Israelite men who are living in captivity there, Shadrach, Meshach, and Abednego, refused to bow to the statue because they knew that God was the only true God. And it was God alone who would receive all their worship and praise.

They are thrown into the fiery furnace and a "fourth person" appears in the fire with them and their lives are spared. King Nebuchadnezzar has a "heart change" and praises the only true God.

That lasts until the next chapter, a year later, the king is on the roof, and declares how this kingdom was built by his hand. God sends him to live with the wild animals for seven years. Upon his return, we read this revelation in verse 37. "Now I, Nebuchadnezzar, praise and exalt and glorify the King of heaven, because everything he does is right and all his ways are just. And those who walk in pride he is able to humble."

After his time in the wilderness, Nebuchadnezzar was praising, exalting, and glorifying the King of heaven. The king of Babylon knew for a fact that those who walk in pride, God is not only able to humble, but He will.

On our journey to Bill's healing, we learned very quickly that every good and perfect thing came down from the Father above. It wasn't our intelligence, connections, or expertise that helped Bill, God deserved all the glory. That's what made the difference – an attitude of gratitude, not pride.

The Glory Road is a place of humility, learning that there is nothing that I bring to the table that will change my circumstances. It is God's grace alone that keeps me each day. That is true for you. We are not so "stunning" that the world revolves around us – God is the Creator of the universe. I will give Him all the praise and honor and glory that He deserves.

Thank you for your companionship. #Godisfaithful #TheGloryRoad

Day #232 December 7

Anchor Verse: Daniel 5:23b
But you have not honored the God who gives you the breath of life and controls your destiny! (NLT)

Give honor where honor is due. This not only applies to our life here on earth but most of all to our heavenly Father.

When we think that we are so "great" that "we" accomplished "this" and "we" did "that" – we might be in big trouble.

In Daniel 5, we read the story of King Belshazzar, who was King Nebuchadnezzar's son who had now come to power in Babylon. Daniel is still working in the Kingdom's administration and is called upon to interpret some "handwriting on the wall."

Daniel calls on the name of the Lord and is given the interpretation. Note that Daniel knows it is not his own intelligence or understanding that will give the interpretation but it is a gift from God.

King Belshazzar was reminded by Daniel of his family history and the "mistake" that his father made and how pride and arrogance caused his downfall. In verse 22 it says, "But you, Belshazzar, his son, have not humbled yourself, though you knew all this."

"But you have not honored the God who gives you the breath of life and controls your destiny!" Get ready for the fall, King Belshazzar. In fact, that very night he was killed and Darius took over the kingdom.

What do we learn from this? We need to honor the Lord in ALL our ways. Each breath is a gift from God and He controls our destiny.

On our journey to Bill's healing, we recognized that Bill's life was in God's hands. It wasn't our wisdom or intelligence, or anything we possessed that could alter the direction of Bill's life, it was God and God alone, who directed our path. In humility, we trusted the Lord and followed His commands.

The Glory Road may be a "new" road but the rules are the same. Honoring the Lord who gives me the breath of life and controls my destiny is my daily goal. I can't imagine navigating life without Him. He is my guiding light, day and night.

Thank you for your persistent prayers. #Godisfaithful #TheGloryRoad

Day #233 December 8

Anchor Verse: 3 John 13-14

I have much to write you, but I do not want to do so with pen and ink. I hope to see you soon, and we will talk face to face. (NIV)

Face-to-face conversations are so insightful. It's the power of language – both what we speak with our words and our body language – the facial expressions, hand gestures, and even body movement that tell us so much.

What we see on paper, text message, or email is "flat" on the page, computer screen, or cell phone. It lacks the expression, the inflection in your voice – the joy or the sorrow. It's like getting "half" a message.

If a person is really skilled at using words, it increases the power of the message concerning what is read from the page, but it still falls short.

Have you ever been the one who misunderstood the "written" message that someone sent to you? Or on the other hand, have you been the one who was misunderstood?

In our day of "quick" communication, we quickly shoot off a response, without "thinking" and then later wish we could "delete" what we said.

Letter writing, writing with pen and ink, allows some time to make sure the message is clear, even time to do some editing, but it still falls short. John knew this when he wrote this letter. That's why in verse 14, it says, "I hope to see you soon, and we will talk face to face."

This is our theme in 2020. There are many people I can't wait to have a face to face conversation with them. It's been too long.

On our journey to Bill's healing, a written note had to suffice due to Bill's health condition. A select few saw him face to face, and those a long distance away we "Zoomed" with after he got home. It's not the same as being together in the same room, but better than nothing.

The Glory Road leads me through territory where often my communication is delivered by "pen and ink" and for that I am grateful. Those who have sent cards or emails or messages, thank you. Time taken to send a message is not only time well spent but it conveys how much we care about each other.

Thank you for sharing the hope of Jesus. #Godisfaithful #TheGloryRoad

Day #234 December 9

Anchor Verse: Luke 2:1,3
During those days, the Roman emperor, Caesar Augustus, ordered that the first census be taken throughout his empire. Everyone had to travel to his or her hometown to complete the mandatory census. (TPT)

The first census was ordered by Caesar Augustus at the time Jesus was about to be born. Interesting…and here we are in 2020, just having completed a census this year in the midst of a pandemic.

A Roman census was taken every five years. The Roman government called upon every man and woman to return to their birthplace to be counted so they could keep track of the population, for taxation purposes.

In the United States, a census is taken every 10 years. You are counted where you live (no need to go to your place of birth). And it serves two purposes: It is used to distribute federal funds to local communities, and also to determine the number of seats in the U.S. House of Representatives.

Mary and Joseph who were living in Galilee traveled to Bethlehem to be registered as they were both direct descendants of David. If you can imagine, a pregnant woman about to give birth traveling 90 miles, most likely walking, since they didn't have any other means of transportation. They couldn't fly or drive or take a bus. This was a difficult journey for Mary, and for Joseph.

On our journey to Bill's healing, often we recognized God's hand at work, as to the time, place, and the people that surrounded us. God's timing is always perfect. He will move heaven and earth to achieve His purpose for us.

The Glory Road is also a place of God's perfect timing. So many details that seem mind-boggling to us as human beings, to God they are only pieces of the puzzle of our lives. Every circumstance was created to bring out the best in us, to mine the deeply buried gold, even if that means going through the refining fire. The storms in our lives are only a weather pattern to God, a backdrop to daily living. They don't define who we are.

This year when it was "census" time, Bill was still alive and we were "counted" as living at this address in Washington State and other details about us, to serve the purpose for which the census was intended.

In this "census" year, God has another reason to count us. God counts every star and calls them by name. He loves us just as we are.

Thank you for your kindness. #Godisfaithful #TheGloryRoad

Day #235 December 10

Anchor Verse: 1 Thessalonians 5:12
Dear brothers and sisters, make sure that you show your deep appreciation for those who cherish you and diligently work as ministers among you. For they are your leaders who care for you, teach you, and stand before the Lord on your behalf. (TPT)

There is something special about our church families – the family of God – not only locally but the greater church around the world.

One of the blessings coming out of this Covid season is how the walls that once separated us in the church have been torn down – not only locally, but internationally. Online services allow you to tune into church services in places you couldn't access that rapidly in the flesh. It is one of the silver linings that has sprouted up out of our pile of troubles.

Let us give thanks to the Lord for the shepherds of our flock, pastors, teachers, and support staff who tirelessly, relentlessly, not only teach and lead you, but fight for you in prayer.

Pastors Dave and Alice Darroch at Spokane Dream Center, in Spokane Valley, WA are the senior pastors at our church. It has been such a blessing to sit under their leadership and to serve with them. They have been such a treasure in these last few years in all the storms that Bill and I faced.

My foundation of faith was conceived at First Reformed Church in Lynden, WA. The principles learned there and Bible verses memorized have been my sword and shield in the battles we have faced.

But in this season, new streams of water have come to refresh my soul through Pastor Mark Batterson and his staff at National Community Church in Washington D.C. It's good to stir up our faith with fresh water.

On our journey to Bill's healing, we learned that church family and their leadership are critical when you face life's challenges. The commitment of the family of God goes beyond Sunday church attendance; they will stand with you, night and day. What a blessing!

The Glory Road had shown me the power and necessity of strong church leaders through life's storms. When their anchor is deep in the Word of God, God will help steady their flock no matter the test. It's important to encourage those who lead us and sow into our lives.

Thank you for your faithfulness in prayer. #Godisfaithful #TheGloryRoad

Day #236 December 11

Anchor Verse: Revelation 2:9
I know how much you suffer for the Lord, and I know all about your poverty (but you have heavenly riches!) (TLB)

We have a heavenly Father who is not distant, He knows our every breath. God watches where we walk and knows both our joys and sorrows. God knows the troubles we encounter and also the amount of money in our bank account.

Revelation 2 was written to the church at Smyrna, a great trading city in Roman times founded by Alexander the Great, known for its schools of science and medicine. Jesus is telling them that He knows their works, "I know how much you suffer for the Lord, and I know all about your poverty (but you have heavenly riches!)"

Even though they are encountering afflictions and suffering because of their faith and financially they are poor, they have great treasures in heaven. This is what counts for eternity. The things of this world will pass away.

"Do not store up for yourselves treasures on earth, where moths and vermin destroy, and where thieves break in and steal. But store up for yourselves treasures in heaven, where moths and vermin do not destroy, and where thieves do not break in and steal. For where your treasure is, there your heart will be also." (Matthew 6:19-21)

This also has an application for us. Where are you storing your treasures? Are we putting all our energy and emphasis on what happens in this world or are our eyes set on eternity?

On our journey to Bill's healing, there was a shift that happened. Even though we had chosen to follow the Lord many years ago, in this new season we were called to a higher place, a new relationship with God. We received a greater revelation about what counts for eternity.

The Glory Road has ushered in a new season. What started with Bill and me and being "schooled" by the Lord, has turned into an "advanced degree" program. In this Covid season, we are all learning new things and how to thrive spiritually in a world that is bathed in chaos.

Thank you for your perseverance. #Godisfaithful #TheGloryRoad

Day #237 December 12

Anchor Verse: Psalm 3:4
But you, God, shield me on all sides; You ground my feet, you lift my head high; With all my might I shout up to God, His answers thunder from the holy mountain. (MSG)

What battle are you facing? Maybe those around you say it is hopeless, and the clouds of doubt fill the air. With God, there is always hope.

Psalm 3 was written by King David, when once again, there was a mob that had turned against him. This time it was his son, Absalom.

Here in Psalm 3:4, we learn some strategies about how to overcome the trials that will enter our lives. David declares that God is his shield. A shield protects us from the arrows of the enemy in battle. The Shield of Faith is one of the vital pieces of the armor of God. God protected David on ALL sides. You are a shield about me, O Lord. (Psalm 3:3)

Then it says, "You ground my feet, you lift my head high." When we are feeling overwhelmed, what are two things that happen? We shuffle our feet in uncertainty and our heads are bowed, we are looking at the ground in defeat. But David says about the Lord, that God helps him to ground his feet to stand steady and strong, and his head is lifted high. Because David knows that God is for him and not against him. This battle, too, belongs to the Lord.

God hears and answers, His answers "thunder"… God is using His loud voice to respond to you. It also silences those who have said your situation is hopeless. Job's friends were encouraging him to give up! God's children are not quitters. I'm not. You're not.

On our journey to Bill's healing, we encountered places that looked impossible to those around us. Sometimes we had to retreat to the mountain of the Lord, gain our strength from Him, and boldly declare our victory.

The Glory Road right now is also filled with those going many directions. Some are lost, some are deceived, and some are misguided, others are following the crowd – not a good plan. As you have heard me say, more than once, I will boldly declare God's love for me and His power to heal on every level. I know that the Lord is on my side. It's not a popularity contest, so my ears are tuned to hear His voice, not the voice of the world.

Thank you for your prevailing prayers. #Godisfaithful #TheGloryRoad

Day #238 December 13

Anchor Verse: Matthew 2:1-2
Now after Jesus was born in Bethlehem of Judea in the days of Herod the king, behold, wise men from the East came to Jerusalem, saying, "Where is He who has been born King of the Jews? For we have seen His star in the East and have come to worship Him." (NKJV)

Jesus' birth was not announced on a billboard, television, or the internet. The Son of God was born into the world which would change the world forever, yet it was less publicized than the birth of a member of the royal family.

God chose who would first receive Jesus into the world. First the angels appeared to shepherds guarding their flocks by night. It seems fitting, since in Psalm 23 we meet Jesus, the Good Shepherd who takes care of His sheep (that's you and me.) And King David, a man after God's own heart, was a shepherd boy when he was first chosen and anointed to be King of Israel.

The second group was the Magi who came from the East. They saw the Bethlehem star and came to worship Him. As they arrived in Jerusalem they said, "Where is He who has been born King of the Jews? For we have seen His star in the East and have come to worship Him."

God used a star in the night sky to announce His son's birth. It was a star so bright that these men from the East were willing to travel a long distance in pursuit of the star. What a treasure hunt – going to a place they did not know guided by a star that only appeared at night. They were willing to do whatever it took to find the star, to find Jesus.

On our journey to Bill's healing, we were guided by God's hand. It wasn't a star in the sky that we followed, but God directed our steps so we could worship Jesus, the King of kings and the Lord of lords. The gift of life for eternity was God's greatest gift to us.

The Glory Road in this Christmas season is a place where many don't know what they are seeking and others are willing to follow Jesus anywhere. I am willing to pursue that star in the East that leads me to Jesus. That star today represents the Word of God, the promises of God, and the truth of God.

Thank you for your companionship. #Godisfaithful #TheGloryRoad

Day #239 December 14

Anchor Verse: 1 Chronicles 16:31
Let the heavens be glad, and the earth rejoice! Tell all the nations, "The Lord reigns!" (NLT)

Rejoice, rejoice, and again, I say rejoice!

We are in a season of rejoicing. Christmas is coming soon and we are celebrating the birth of Jesus, the newborn King.

It is not only us, as God's children that are called to celebrate, but all the heavens and earth join with us.

As I reflect on the night Jesus was born, the sky was filled with a holy light as the angels announced Jesus' birth to the shepherds who were watching their flocks that night. We think of the night hours as being calm and quiet, with the stars shining brightly. The sheep are asleep. The shepherds are watching for anyone or anything that might come to disturb their flock, but for angels to appear and sing to Jesus, the newborn king, must have been quite a sight.

In 1 Chronicles 16:31, we read of this call to be glad and rejoice, and tell ALL the nations, "The Lord reigns!"

What a powerful mandate that is still true. Our part is to tell all the nations that the Lord reigns.

God created the heavens and the earth not only to reflect His glory but to sing praises to His name. If you take the time to quiet yourself, and sit in nature and listen to the wind, to the birds, watch the sky, whether it is filled with cloud creations, a bright sunny day, or a lightning storm, in every case, nature is speaking to us.

On our journey to Bill's healing, we had the opportunity to be removed from our regular routine and view life differently. Watching and listening were part of our daily lives and using our own words to declare, "Our God reigns!"

The Glory Road is filled with the awe and wonder of God. Not only His majesty and His glory, but His love and provision, not only for me, but for all creatures on the earth. Since I am alone a lot, the Lord and I often have conversations, and sometimes I listen for His heartbeat, for the power of His presence, and the comfort of His love.

Thank you for being faithful. #Godisfaithful #TheGloryRoad

Day #240 December 15

Anchor Verse: Isaiah 61:11
For as the earth brings forth its sprouts, And as a garden causes what is sown in it to spring up, So the Lord God will [most certainly] cause righteousness and justice and praise to spring up before all the nations [through the power of His word]. (AMP)

God is the Master Gardener. The world was created at His command and the seasons follow – all with their specific purpose and timing.

In our lives, God has His perfect timing, a season for all things. In Ecclesiastes 3, King Solomon reminds us that "to everything there is a season, and a time for every purpose under heaven."

Isaiah 61:11 is such a great reminder for us, in this year of 2020, when it seemed that chaos reigned. Instead, the truth is that God's timing has been and always will be perfect. God is never early, He is never late, but He is always right on time.

"For as the earth brings forth its sprouts, And as a garden causes what is sown in it to spring up, So the Lord God will [most certainly] cause righteousness and justice and praise to spring up before all the nations [through the power of His word]."(Isaiah 61:11)

On our journey to Bill's healing, we went through every season, not only in the natural but in our spirits. Our hope was anchored in the Lord and the power of His might. Even as we endured the winter season, the Lord and His mighty works in Bill continued to rise up and shine forth before all the nations.

The Glory Road is a place where I have seen the sunshine of His glory, the showers of His blessings, watered the fertile soil of the future with my tears, and marveled at His power as new shoots of hope spring up every day.

God is still on His throne. I will not fear. I will not fail. I will not fall. I am safe in the hollow of His hands, and so are you.

Make the Lord's grace shine upon you. You are healed and whole in Jesus' name. His arm is not too short, everything we need He will provide in His perfect timing. God makes all things beautiful in His time.

Thank you for your perseverance. #Godisfaithful #TheGloryRoad

Day #241 December 16

Anchor Verse: Luke 2:19
But Mary treasured up all these things and pondered them in her heart. (NIV)

Ponder is not often a word we use these days, but in reality, it's something we do a lot in this unusual year of 2020. To "ponder" means to think about, reflect, consider something deeply and thoroughly.

The words "treasured up" and pondered" are the words Luke used to describe what Mary did after the birth of Jesus.

There was a lot going on that night Mary gave birth to Jesus and the days that followed. Mary and Joseph were not tucked in at home when baby Jesus entered the world. Instead, as we read in the Bible, there was no room for them in the inn, so Jesus was born in a stable. This young woman chosen by God would deliver her firstborn child in less than desirable conditions in Bethlehem, the town of her birth, but not her current residence.

God will move us into position to accomplish His will in His way. The outward appearance of the place God puts us may not "appeal" to us, until we open our eyes to see the greater glory that is there. Where the presence of God is, that is where we want to be… always.

On our journey to Bill's healing, there were many moments to ponder life as I sat with Bill in hospital rooms, ICU units, places that were "undesirable" in the eyes of men, but they were birthplaces of new hope and faith. They were crucibles of fire to reveal the brilliance of God's glory.

The Glory Road is a place where I ponder a lot – often day and night. My heavenly Father has developed this "habit" of waking me up during the night for a chat, since Bill died. There were times before Bill died in our "learning" season where God would wake either one of us up for a chat or come to us in a dream or vision. God operates outside of time so our day and night are not obstacles for God's communication with us.

You might see my external circumstances – the loss of my mom, my husband, and my own cancer diagnosis against the backdrop of this Covid season and so much loss, and so many people hurting so much, but God has shown me the greater glory at work.

It is often through tears – not only tears of sorrow, but tears of joy and gratitude for God's mercy and grace in our lives, that I navigate each day.

Thank you for the power of your presence. #Godisfaithful #TheGloryRoad

Day #242 December 17

Anchor Verse: Psalm 33:20
The Lord alone is our radiant hope and we trust in him with all our hearts. His wrap-around presence will strengthen us. (TPT)

"Our radiant hope" – the picture that comes to mind when I read this is the star that appeared over Bethlehem the night that Jesus was born. It pierced the darkness of the night, and it pierced the darkness that had fallen upon the world. For so long, people had been longing for deliverance – for a savior to come – a deliverer – the Messiah.

They had written "their" story about who the Messiah would be and how He would save them from the tyranny of their day. This Messiah would have "super hero" qualities (although "super heroes" weren't in their vocabulary).

"How long, Lord, how long? We are tired. We are barely holding on to hope. Messiah, come and deliver us, we pray."

This might have been a prayer uttered by a man or woman back in the days before Jesus' birth, but honestly, it sounds like the prayers of many.

2020 has been a tough year, we all agree about that fact. Some have fared better than others but we are ready for the next chapter of this story. We, too, are asking, "How long, Lord, how long?"

Psalm 33:20 reminds us that we have all the hope we need right now, in the person of Jesus Christ. "The Lord alone is our radiant hope and we trust in him with all our hearts. His wrap-around presence will strengthen us."

On our journey to Bill's healing, we were blessed beyond measure by the Lord's radiant hope. Even this morning, I picture that radiant hope as a "light" that accompanied us day and night wherever we were. The steadfast love of the Lord never ceases. His mercies never come to an end.

The Glory Road leads me into new territory. I am so grateful for God's "wrap-around presence" that strengthens me. It helps me stand tall in the face of adversity and the unknown – because He knows the way and God is fighting for me, as He is fighting for you, because He loves you.

Thank you for standing strong with me. #Godisfaithful #TheGloryRoad

Day #243 December 18

Anchor Verse: Revelation 8:3-4
Another angel came and stood at the altar. He had a golden censer, and much incense was given to him, so that he might add it to the prayers of all the saints (God's people) on the golden altar in front of the throne. And the smoke and fragrant aroma of the incense, with the prayers of the saints (God's people), ascended before God from the angel's hand. (AMP)

The prayers of God's people are powerful; they move the hand and heart of God. This picture painted for us in Revelation 8 gives a glimpse of the power of intercessory prayer.

There are times in our lives, especially in a "dry" season or a very "stormy" season, when a lot is happening or when even the crickets are "silent" that we wonder if our prayers are being heard.

Our human, finite minds cannot understand, comprehend, or figure out the formula of how our prayers work. Why? Because prayer is supernatural, it does not "conform" to any law of nature. Prayer is a gift from God, the most amazing communication we have to the heart of our heavenly Father.

There is no communication tool on earth that can rival it. The prayers of God's people, intercessory prayers, ascend to God in heaven seated on His throne. In verse five, we see God's power as He answers the prayers of His people. What prayers are answered and those that are not is beyond my understanding. Our heavenly Father wants what is best for us.

On our journey to Bill's healing, we learned the power of intercessory prayer from the saints (God's people). So many of you prayed on Bill's behalf and interceded for us, asking God to do what seemed impossible in the eyes of man. God heard and answered, and we saw mighty miracles many times.

The Glory Road was birthed in a year of crisis, chaos, and confusion. The world itself seemed to be turned upside down when this pandemic spread like wildfire across the face of the earth. Many turned their hearts and their prayers toward God. That should be the first place we turn, to the throne room of grace, interceding not only for ourselves but for others.

Thank you for your prayers. #Godisfaithful #TheGloryRoad

Day #244 December 19

 **Anchor Verse: Jonah 2:6**
But you, O Lord my God, snatched me from the jaws of death! (NLT)

This may be your story too. Not that you were saved from drowning and swallowed by a whale and spit out three days later, but that you have had a "brush" with death.

Sometimes we know it, and many times we are not aware how God's angels protected us from certain tragedy.

The story of Jonah, a man who ran away from what God asked him to do, encountered a storm at sea, being tossed overboard into the depths of the water, swallowed by a whale, spit out on dry ground, and then finally carrying out his initial mission, is a story of disobedience followed by obedience.

It's also a story of God's mercy and grace, not only for Jonah but for the city of Nineveh. God wanted to give the 120,000 people who lived in Nineveh a second chance to turn away from the wickedness and back to the Lord. Even when Jonah ran away, God had a plan to give Jonah a "second chance."

God is still in the business of giving us "second chances" – thank you, Lord.

On our journey to Bill's healing, Bill was given the "second chance" at life many, many times. And we are so grateful for every minute, every hour, every day, every week, and every year that God extended Bill's life – all for God's glory.

The Glory Road has been a place that continues to be a place of second chances, not only for me, but for us individually and as a nation. God is not done with us yet. We may feel like we have been thrown into the depths of the sea but God has a rescue plan in mind.

Last night (12.18.20), my cousin's wife Hope was in a car accident. God spared her life. She has two broken legs, but in His grace and mercy, God will make a way. Please join me in prayer this morning for her healing and for her husband and children. God is the God of miracles.

Thank you for your faithfulness. Thank you for your prayers of love.
#Godisfaithful #TheGloryRoad

Day #245 December 20

Anchor Verse: Isaiah 50:2
Was my arm too short to deliver you? Do I lack the strength to rescue you? (NIV)

When we walk through life circumstances that we don't understand, we often logically try and figure out who is at fault, or maybe who to "blame" for what happened. In our human minds, we are always trying to figure things out. Taking a leap of faith and adding the supernatural to the equation isn't always the place we start.

In Isaiah 55:8-9, we are reminded of God's vantage point: "For my thoughts are not your thoughts, neither are your ways my ways," declares the Lord. "As the heavens are higher than the earth, so are my ways higher than your ways and my thoughts than your thoughts."

God's ways, God's timing, God's purpose often supersede anything we can conjure up in how we put the pieces of the puzzle together.

Lately, I have been drawn to the second part of that verse, "My ways higher than your ways and my thoughts than your thoughts." Not only are God's ways different than our ways, they are "higher" than our ways. Way better than anything we can imagine.

Sometimes that means we need to go through a valley to get to the mountaintop of victory. And in that journey, we ask, "Why?" when the better question is, "Why not me?"

On our journey to Bill's healing, we encountered a storybook full of "adventures" that we could only navigate with God's help. Sometimes the right question is not, "God is Your arm too short to deliver me, are You too weak?" but rather "What am I to learn here?"

God's faithfulness and grace always shone through the darkness, even if it was recognized through a veil of tears.

The Glory Road, with its new landscape, is an adventure every day. The path is narrow when the Lord has me focus mostly on my life, my lessons. And then there are days when the road is wide, as the Lord brings many other people into my view to pray for or to stand alongside them. It is a place of variety, but always filled with the recognition that God's grace is sufficient and His power is made perfect in our weakness. (2 Corinthians 12:9)

Thank you for your persevering prayers. #Godisfaithful #TheGloryRoad

Day #246 December 21

Anchor Verse: Micah 5:5
He will be our Peace. (TLB)

Peace – it's something we long for but often it's difficult to find. Whether that is peace on the outside or the inside, as a nation or as individuals, in the past, present, or future, it is a lofty goal. Jesus, the Messiah, holds that peace in His hands and He offers it to us.

In Isaiah 9:6, it says, "For to us a child is born, to us a son is given, and the government will be on his shoulders. And he will be called Wonderful Counselor, Mighty God, Everlasting Father, Prince of Peace."

Jesus is the Prince of Peace. Peace resides in Him and flows out of Him. When we are in relationship with Jesus, we, too, can have that peace that passes all understanding that guards our hearts and minds. (Philippians 4:7)

The world's peace is temporal and shaky at best. When we look at what's happening in the world right now, we see a lot of conflict, anxiety, and trouble, especially in this Covid season. Many would welcome a visit from the Prince of Peace especially as we are a few days away from Christmas.

Jesus is offering us peace that is not dependent on our external circumstances. His peace doesn't bounce around like a tennis ball; it is unshakable because its foundation is Jesus Christ, the Solid Rock.

The peace that Jesus offers takes away our fears and silences the enemy who is trash talking in our ears. When Jesus abides with us, we have that peace that stays with us, abides with us through every season.

On our journey to Bill's healing, we were guided by the Prince of Peace. In making decisions, we sought His peace. On our sleepless nights or going through rough waters, Jesus was our Peace. His peace filled us even when the world around us was in turmoil. Thank you, Jesus.

The Glory Road is also a path of peace. It is not just a place; it is a person, Jesus. He is with me day and night. Whether the sea is calm or waves of uncertainty threaten me, Jesus is there. In the moments when the demands are great and my resources may seem small, Jesus steps in to direct traffic, to speak peace and power to my soul. There is nothing that the two of us can't handle together.

Thank you for your encouraging words. #Godisfaithful #TheGloryRoad

Day #247 December 22

Anchor Verse: Micah 7:8
Do not gloat over me, my enemies! For though I fall, I will rise again. Though I sit in darkness, the Lord will be my light. (NLT)

2020 has been a tough year. Everyone has been touched by challenges, at least if you were living on planet Earth. But our lives are not defined by the challenges we face, it's how we react to them.

When we are born, we may have the skills we need scripted in our DNA but we still to learn how to walk and talk and eat and play – all of it! Learning to walk was not only about putting one foot in front of the other, but learning how to stand up again once we fell down. Because we will fall down.

As adults, we will face trials and tribulations. We may not "literally" fall down, but we will be "knocked down" – mentally, emotionally, even spiritually at times. It is then that our faith in God and our relationship with Him becomes so important.

In 2 Corinthians 12:10 it says, "That is why, for Christ's sake, I delight in weaknesses, in insults, in hardships, in persecutions, in difficulties. For when I am weak, then I am strong." (NIV)

As the apostle Paul writes to the church at Corinth, Paul reminds them that as he has faced these rough places – weaknesses, insults, hardships, persecutions and difficulties, it was in his weakness that Paul found strength in the Lord. That is our truth today.

On our journey to Bill's healing, there were times Bill's story wasn't very pretty. In fact, from the "outside" it may have looked like Bill had "fallen" and was "sitting in the darkness." But the light of the Lord was there. Sometimes it was a small ember and sometimes a roaring fire, but the light of God's love was always with us. We learned to not always listen to the chatter around us, but always tune our ears to the still, small voice of God.

The Glory Road is a place of "darkness and light." Our lives are lived in the "stadium" called Earth. The seats are filled with those who will be cheering us on and those who are betting against us – it's the story of good and evil that exists side by side in this world. My challenge, your challenge is to choose who we will listen to as we run the race of life.

Thank you for holding me up in prayer. #Godisfaithful #TheGloryRoad

Day #248 December 23

Anchor Verse: Matthew 2:10
When they saw the star, they were overjoyed. (NIV)

When the wise men saw the Bethlehem star, they were overjoyed. Matthew 2:1 says that the Magi from the East arrived in Bethlehem and asked, "Where is the one who has been born king of the Jews? We saw his star when it rose and have come to worship him."

In recent days, there has been the reappearance of the "Bethlehem Star" after its last sighting 800 years ago. For our world at the end of 2020, a difficult year, we have looked to the skies to see God's promise of hope, to once again, bring great joy to all the people.

The star led the wise men on their way to Bethlehem. I can only imagine their excitement. "On coming to the house, they saw the child with his mother Mary, and they bowed down and worshiped him. Then they opened their treasures and presented him with gifts of gold, frankincense and myrrh." (Matthew 2:11) What an amazing sight that must have been.

On Monday night, 12.21.20, I was blessed to "pursue" the Bethlehem star with a friend and her family. The rain earlier in the day had been replaced with afternoon sunshine but about sunset the clouds returned to the skies. We drove toward the west trying to catch a glimpse of the star before the clouds overtook it. Driving down the freeway, I kept my eyes on the sky, praying and asking the Lord for a glimpse of the "star." And suddenly in a break in the clouds, there it was!

My heart jumped for joy, probably similar to what the wise men felt as they pursued the star. We found a location to get a better view and were treated not only to the planets coming into alignment to form the star, but the moon and Mars. Our hearts were filled with joy and awe and wonder.

On our journey to Bill's healing, we saw the handiwork of Jesus, the risen Lord in Bill's life. We stood in awe and wonder of the works of His hand and gave Him all the glory.

The Glory Road has been filled with highs and lows, but through it all, the signs of God's faithfulness. To see the Bethlehem star brought an infusion of hope because like the wise men, we had to pursue it to find it. We are called to pursue Jesus. Our Savior is more than a bright light in the sky, Jesus is the hope we carry in our hearts.

Thank you for your faithful prayers. #Godisfaithful #TheGloryRoad

Day #249 December 24

Anchor Verse: Habakkuk 2:20

But the Lord is in His holy temple. Let all the earth hush and be silent before Him." (AMP)

Silence – some people treasure it and others cannot handle it.

Personally, I find the silence of the early morning hours to be a gift from God. It is there that I meet the Lord and feel His presence. I am not alone. I am with my best friend, the one who will never leave me or forsake me.

It is in the silence where we often find revelation, when God speaks in His still small voice rather than "yelling" at us in His outside voice because we are surrounded by so much noise.

Habakkuk 2:20b says, "Let all the earth hush and be silent before Him."

"Hush" – it's one of those words that when spoken sends the message in its sound and the word itself.

We have heard the word "hush" used one-on-one, often with an adult and child when it's important to be quiet or in large gatherings when an event is about to take place.

Being silent before the Lord is a sign of reverence. "The earth is the Lord's and everything in it; the world and all who live in it. " (Psalm 24:1) "Who may ascend the mountain of the Lord? Who may stand in his holy place? The one who has clean hands and a pure heart." (Psalm 24:3-4)

On our journey to Bill's healing, we have found God in the silence of our home or even in the midst of the beeping in hospital rooms. We learned to listen and quiet our hearts before Him, so God filled our body, mind, and spirit with His glory.

The Glory Road has been filled with places of noise and of much silence. When you live alone, as many of you know, there can be many quiet moments. Except it's more than quietness, it's the absence of sound. It is there we have an opportunity to shift our perspective from earth to heaven. Our spiritual eyes and ears are opened and we sense the presence of the Lord and His heavenly host. Alone, yet not alone… it's the blessed place where God meets us at the point of our need.

Thank you for all your love and support. #Godisfaithful #TheGloryRoad

Day #250 December 25

Anchor Verse: Luke 2: 11-12

"The Savior – yes, the Messiah, the Lord – has been born tonight in Bethlehem! How will you recognize him? You will find a baby wrapped in a blanket, lying in a manger!" (TLB)

The Messiah had come! The Messiah? The Anointed One that the prophets had foretold would deliver the Israelites from their Roman masters? The people were looking for a human king to solve their problems here on earth. God's promise was far greater – God wanted to save their lives from destruction forever!

Jesus' kingdom was spiritual, not an earthly kingdom. The fanfare in the heavens the night Jesus was born was fit for a king.

Angels gave the shepherds directions about where to find the Messiah, their Savior, in Bethlehem. They gave them "the sign" to recognize Jesus.

The shepherds must have been confused… the Messiah, the one that would save them was a "baby wrapped in a blanket, lying in a manger?" But they left their flocks in the field and went to Bethlehem to find Jesus. In verse 17, it tells us after they found Mary, Joseph, and the baby, they spread the word that had been told them about this child and everyone was amazed.

On our journey to Bill's healing, we were not greeted by angels singing about Jesus, but instead Jesus walked with us – day and night. The Savior of the world was Bill's Savior and Jesus is my Savior too. And yes, that truth has brought us great joy.

The Glory Road has brought me a new realization of the power and the place that Jesus has in my life. It is because of His grace that I can stand every day. It is because of His love that I am comforted and cared for day by day. It is because of His resurrection power that lives in me that I can overcome the obstacles and trials I face.

Because He was born, died, and rose again – because He lives… I can face not only today… but every tomorrow. Even this Christmas, my first Christmas without Bill in 28 Christmases, I can rejoice because my hope is in Jesus, and I know Bill is spending his first Christmas in heaven.

Thank you for your faithfulness. Merry Christmas to you and your family. #Godisfaithful #TheGloryRoad

Day #251 December 26

Anchor Verse: Haggai 1:5
Now this is what the Lord Almighty says: "Give careful thought to your ways." (NIV)

There are so many things in our lives that we do on auto-pilot. Maybe your morning routine is like that from bed to breakfast to work. Your routine is so ingrained you can't even see the rut.

It may be that way in your life, but what does your spiritual life look like? Has it become "routine?" Are you living in a rut and the river is jammed up and the life-giving water that flows from God's throne of grace is only a trickle? There's good news – it doesn't have to be that way anymore.

We are on the other side of Christmas and we are looking toward the last stretch of 2020 – the end of the year. Yes, I can hear many people cheering in the background. It's been a challenging year for many and we are looking for a fresh start in 2021.

But before we cross that portal into 2021, we should listen to this word from the Lord. "Give careful thought to your ways." Or in the VOICE translation it says, "Think very carefully about your choices."

We often look to others or our circumstances to explain why we aren't where we want to be in our lives. However, the truth is we are where we are because of our own choices. It's time to take a moment and ask the Lord to help us uncover the root of our problems.

On our journey to Bill's healing, there were parts of the road where we had to give thought to our ways. We had to make dietary changes, changes in our expectations about what Bill could and couldn't do, but most of all what God wanted Bill to do. We needed to start at the foot of the cross.

The Glory Road has taught me so many things. Besides learning how grieving and moving forward at the same time are an odd couple, but most of all the truth that God will supply ALL my needs according to His riches in glory. Life may not be what I expected it to be at the end of 2020 but it's not about my expectations, it's about my eyes being open to God's plans for me.

Thank you for your faithfulness in prayer. #Godisfaithful #TheGloryRoad

Day #252 December 27

Anchor Verse: 1 John 5:5
Who is the one who is victorious and overcomes the world? It is the one who believes and recognizes the fact that Jesus is the Son of God. (AMP)

We live in a battle zone – day and night. It's not always a physical battle that we can see with our eyes, but there is a spiritual battle that has been ongoing since the Garden of Eden.

Some days we are more aware of it than others. Because of God's hand of protection over us, there are days we feel like we are living in a "bubble" and life seems pretty calm. Other days, you feel the warfare with every step you take and every thought you think.

This verse in 1 John 5 reminds us that we are victorious and overcome the world as we believe in Jesus Christ, the Son of God.

Where have you placed your faith? Have you put it in the hands of the government, your business, bank account, or health? You fill in the blank.

If our faith is anchored in anything or anyone other than Jesus, we are on the losing side. But if Jesus is your anchor, you will be victorious and overcome the world.

On our journey to Bill's healing, we learned the intensity of the battles we face in this world – day and night. We also learned that God is faithful and He will always make a way for His children. We will not be spared trials and tribulations but our heavenly Father will provide help to walk through it.

The Glory Road in 2020 has highlighted our need for a Savior, our need for Jesus. As a nation, a world, as individuals, we have walked through the refining fire. There were times we were at the end of our strength and had no more to give. Then Jesus picked us up and carried us. Jesus still may be carrying you until you are strong enough to walk on your own once again.

Over the noise and chaos of the raging battle, I hear God's words, "I will NEVER leave you or forsake you." And God doesn't lie. In the quietness of the night or the brightness of the noonday sun, my hope is in the Lord.

Thank you for your persistent prayers. #Godisfaithful #TheGloryRoad

Day #253 December 28

Anchor Verse: Psalm 90:14

Let the sunrise of your love end our dark night. Break through our clouded dawn again! Only you can satisfy our hearts, filling us with songs of joy to the end of our days. (TPT)

What a beautiful picture! "Let the sunrise of your love end our dark night. Break through our clouded dawn again!"

Jesus often used parables to relate God's truth to us. David, the psalmist, because of his love for nature, and the time he spent as a shepherd in his youth often used nature to convey his message.

Last night as I was winding down for the day and mulling things over, I realized what I really needed was a "shot" of praise music. It might be better to start my day with songs of praise. Although the Lord did draw near during the night, as I invited Him in to be with me.

As we come to the end of 2020, this verse from Psalm 90 should be our prayer this morning. Heavenly Father, may the sunrise of Your love end our dark night. Break through our clouded dawn again. Only You, Lord, can satisfy our hearts. Fill us with songs of joy to the end of our days, in Jesus' name, amen.

On our journey to Bill's healing, every morning we were blessed with the sunrise of God's love that ended our dark night. There were some pretty rough nights but every morning we were greeted with God's new mercies. Great is His faithfulness.

The Glory Road has had its "dark" nights. Not only nights of grief and mourning, but through the early days of my new health challenge, there were some painful nights and nights of overwhelm facing a "new" Goliath alone. I do not face this giant called "cancer" alone. The Lord is with me just as He was with David. It only took one stone to take the giant down, and God has the stone is His hand that will defeat this disease in my body.

In the meantime, I get to spread hope and encouragement to others that are walking through their own dark night, and bring the sunshine of His love. This road is a place of victory in God's perfect timing, but not one step is wasted. Thank you, Lord, for the boot camp of Bill's healing journey to prepare me for my own boot camp to become a soldier in the Lord's army.

Thank you for your steps of obedience. #Godisfaithful #TheGloryRoad

Day #254 December 29

Anchor Verse: Lamentations 3:32
Though he brings grief, he also shows compassion because of the greatness of his unfailing love. (NLT)

As we draw near to the end of 2020 and look back over the landscape, it resembles a battlefield. There have been battles won and battles lost. There have been mountains moved and mountains we have passed over. There has been joy and there has been sorrow.

But if we could see from God's perspective, we would see the greatness of His unfailing love. As this verse in Lamentations 3 reminds us, "Though he brings grief, he also shows compassion." Thank you, Lord.

When you cried, your heavenly Father cried with you. When you rejoiced, so did He. When you didn't know which way to go, He was there speaking wisdom into your ears. We don't always "hear" Him, not for lack of His speaking, but we may be tuned to a "different" channel.

I'm not sure that any of us could honestly say that 2020 went the way we expected. There were many hopes and dreams, blueprints for business expansion, graduations, weddings, births, even travel plans that were interrupted by a world-wide pandemic, something you read about in a novel. Yet, here we are, not all of us, but those who have survived the trials and tribulations of this year. We are wiser, we are weathered, but we are still standing.

On our journey to Bill's healing, we experienced some unexpected places. Neither one of us expected that Bill would be watching from heaven today rather than sitting in his favorite chair giving his caregiver a hard time. But God knew. Even as grief has visited our home, so has God's compassion and unfailing love. I couldn't have walked with this path without God.

The Glory Road is a path of heartache and healing. It is where we all have experienced joy and sorrow mixed together into 2020's smoothie, depending on your taste preference. Yet because of God's faithfulness and His mercies that are new every morning, I have hope for today, and hope for tomorrow.

To become the men and women of God He created us to be, we must endure hardship, roadblocks and mountains to climb, to grow stronger and become more like Jesus. The military puts their recruits through boot camp ultimately to build them up, God has His own boot camp to train us.

Thank you for your persistent prayers. #Godisfaithful #TheGloryRoad

Day #255 December 30

Anchor Verse: Psalm 51:17

The fountain of your pleasure is found in the sacrifice of my shattered heart before you. You will not despise my tenderness as I humbly bow down at your feet. (TPT)

As we come to the end of the year, often we take time for reflection.

Some have tried to capture 2020 as a painting, and there might be a dark background that is the foundation color. However, there have been many points of light. The goodness and generosity of others have peppered the landscape accentuated by God's love.

What about the poor choices? What is the redemption we find there? Psalm 51 was written by King David after one of his poor choices. He committed adultery with Bathsheba and did some really bad things to cover it up. David confesses his sin so his relationship with God can be restored. "Create in me a clean heart, O Lord, and renew a right spirit in me."

In verse 17 in the Passion translation, we read these powerful words, "The fountain of your pleasure is found in the sacrifice of my shattered heart before you. You will not despise my tenderness as I humbly bow down at your feet."

Last night as I was having a conversation with a friend about life's hardships and choosing to walk with the Lord through them, she shared this verse.

"The sacrifice of my shattered heart" represents a broken heart that is seeking to be healed because it has wandered away from God's presence, does this describe your heart?

On our journey to Bill's healing, we found shelter in the presence of God. The Lord accepted the offering of our hearts – filled with our past, its hurts and mistakes, and gave us new hearts that were healed and whole.

The Glory Road is coming near the border that separates 2020 from 2021. The entrance to 2021 is just over the hill. I am filled with hope, joy, and excitement because God has gone before me. Humbly, I bow at the feet of Jesus this morning, and offer all I am to Him – my hopes and dreams, my shattered heart, but most of all my love and commitment. I trust Him to lead me on His path to glory and find those who will see His love light in me.

Thank you for your friendship. #Godisfaithful #TheGloryRoad

Day #256 December 31

Anchor Verse: Malachi 3:6

For I am the Lord, I do not change [but remain faithful to My covenant with you] (AMP)

The last day of 2020 – I can hear shouts of joy in the background and some weeping. This year has been filled with unexpected events and so many changes in our lives, both personally and collectively.

On this New Year's Eve, the focus is not on big celebrations but rather on what is "not" happening. For some, stepping into 2021 healthy and whole is the goal.

For a moment, let's consider what we have rather than what we have lost.

God is still God. That has not changed. This verse in Malachi 3:6 says, "For I am the Lord, I do not change [but remain faithful to My covenant with you]." God is faithful. God is true to His word. His promises do not shift like the sand or change directions like the wind. They are steadfast and true.

God's character is that He loves us – unconditionally. He empathizes with us in our difficulties and rejoices in our victories. Our heavenly Father's eyes are on us at all times and delights when we choose to spend time with Him.

On the journey to Bill's healing, it was a great comfort to know that the Lord didn't change. Often portions of our lives changed – whether in a positive or not so positive way, but always God was unmovable, unshakeable, and unstoppable. It's how we could face the challenges of the unknown because with God there is no "unknown."

The Glory Road has held many changes. In fact, it was "born" out of change. "The Glory Road" emerged the day after Bill died. In my grieving over the sudden loss of my husband on April 19, 2020, I didn't know what was ahead – the future was lost in the fog around me.

God let me grieve for a few days and then set my feet back on the path of life, the path of telling our story for His glory.

Thank you for walking with me on this Glory Road. There will be great adventures ahead in 2021 because that's what God promised.

Thank you for praying. #Godisfaithful #TheGloryRoad

Author's Note

There is something so powerful about starting a journey, but the ending, crossing the finish line, has its own beauty.

In the writing of this book, "God's Peace on the Glory Road", my heavenly Father asked me to take His hand and walk through the events of 2020. It was not an easy task. In fact, often my eyes filled with tears as I remembered both the valleys of testing and the mountains of triumph.

But one thing remained. God had you in mind as Bill and I walked this journey to his healing, and now my solo journey on the Glory Road. The lessons we learn in our lifetime are not only for us, but for those who walk with us and for generations yet to come.

Thank you for walking with me through this devotional. Thank you for your commitment to press in and to learn more about your heavenly Father who loves you so much. Jesus walked His own road of suffering that paved the way to our victory and the glory of heaven. I'm so grateful for the Holy Spirit, who is my comforter and daily companion, as I walk this road with God's favor and wisdom.

The next book in this devotional series will be released in December 2022. Every day as I write my daily devotion to post on Facebook, God gives me further revelation about who He is and who I am called to be. May the wisdom of heaven be yours and the joy of the Lord be your strength.

If your life has been touched by our journey, please share your story with me at barbara@barbarahollace.com.

Check out my website for future book releases: www.barbarahollace.com.

Other Books

Barbara Hollace, Contributing Author

- *Light for the Writer's Soul*: 100 Devotions by Global Christian Writers: Armour Publishers
- *Love, Animals and Miracles*: New World Library
- *Gonzaga Book of Prayer*: Gonzaga University
- *A Miracle under the Christmas Tree*: Harlequin
- *And Then What Happened*: CreateSpace
- *Love is a Verb Devotional*: Bethany House
- *A Book of Miracles*: New World Library
- *Faith, Hope and Healing*: John Wiley and Sons
- *SpokeWrite: Journal of Art and Writing (3 issues)*: Gray Dog Press
- *A Cup of Comfort for Military Families*: Adams Media
- *Mistletoe Madness*: Blooming Tree Press
- *God's Words for the Young*: Choat &Lederman
- *The Art of Brave Living*: Diane Cunningham
- *Divine Interventions*: Heartwarming Stories of Answered Prayer: Guideposts

About the Author

Barbara Hollace is a Christian woman who loves the Lord. God has called her to be a prayer warrior and a writer. Her greatest joy is to pray for others and see God's miracles happen. Through her own husband's health challenges, Barbara learned that prayer can move mountains in our lives.

Her love of writing blossomed from an early age when she started creating her own greeting cards for family and friends. In 1985, Barbara self-published her first poetry book, "From Dust to Dust." Since that time Barbara has been published in 24 books [as author or contributing author] and numerous newspaper articles. She has written 15 novels and is pursuing publication options.

Professionally, she is an author, editor, writing coach, and speaker. Owner of Hollace Writing Services, Barbara's goal is to "identify the good and magnify it!" This includes helping a person get the story in their heart on the page, editing the story, and pursuing publication options. She recently opened her own publishing company, Hollace House Publishing, and will be expanding its reach in the upcoming years.

Barbara has a Bachelor's degree in Business Administration from Western Washington University and a Juris Doctor degree from Gonzaga University School of Law. She is also the Communications Director for Spokane Dream Center church in Spokane Valley, Washington.

For more information about Barbara and her business, go to www.barbarahollace.com.

Made in the USA
Las Vegas, NV
05 January 2022